Grandparents Are for Making Memories

And Being Influential From the Nursery to College

Zelma

Zelma Lansford, Ed.D.

www.zelmalansford.com

Copyright

Cover design and graphics by Victoria Lansford

Spiral Publications

Atlanta, Georgia
United States of America

This book contains numerous examples from the author's experience that are used to demonstrate the concepts. These are an amalgamation of people and situations. The names have been changed to avoid any inappropriate attention or identification.

Second printing

ISBN: 978-0-9821833-8-0

Continue your exploration of grandparenting

by visiting the author at

www.zelmalansford.com

Dedication

To Skyler and Victoria

who make beautiful memories

To my beloved Saint Nicholas School

And to every grandparent who endeavors

to make the world better through love and devotion

Contents

Chapter *Page*

~ Part I ~

1 Grandparent Time is for Making Memories 9

2 Strong Family Bonds 31

3 Grandparents' Rules and Discipline 71

4 Influence During Childhood 104

5 Special Opportunities for Grandparents 128

~ Part II ~

6 The Instant Generation 182

7 Grandchildren's Personalities 219

8 Communicating with Grandchildren 253

~ Part III ~

9 Grandparents' Guidance for Decisions 293

10 Fears and Feelings 324

11 Making Memories that Make a Difference 367

12 The Splendid Results 404

References 430

Appendix 434

Introduction

All too often, we think of the grandparent role primarily as a source of indulgence for the grandchild or help with child care for the parents. It may be both, but it can be so much more. Grandparents can use their relationships to become highly influential and make beautiful memories that last a lifetime—for both the grandchild and for the grandparent.

My inspiration for this subject came from two sources; conversations with client, Julie Baumgardner, former CEO of *First Things First,* a non-profit dedicated to strengthening families, and my own experience as a grandparent, the role that has given me a treasure of incredible memories. The two came together, however, when Julie asked me to participate in a video series, *JulieBTV.* In the past, I had only thought of being a grandmother as a personal role, but the commitment to Julie motivated considerable thought and research. The result is this conversation that I trust will be useful to you and give you new ideas for enhancing your grandparent relationships.

Throughout my experience working in education, from early childhood through teaching graduate school, and my work in individual and organization development, there has been one common thread—*problem solving and helping people to thrive.* That's the theme of this little book. It's my purpose to give you ideas and a new perspective that will increase your influence with the grandchildren, your enjoyment in spending time with them, and ways to make your relationships thrive. First-time grandparents, may be tempted to stop reading after the first few chapters, concluding that the passages on addiction and conflict are for future years. Even though all of the content may not be applied for a while, consideration of later years can guide your direction during the early part of the child's life. If your grandchildren are older, you can skim the part about puppets and toys, but you may find ideas about enhancing activities with teenage grandchildren.

The importance of your influence can't be too strongly emphasized in "planting the seeds" at every age, but especially during childhood. These seeds can grow into inspiration that will become a guide through adolescence and young adulthood as we *begin with the end in mind.*

Incidentally, the University of Tennessee doctoral studies were sufficiently demanding that I still find it difficult to write informally. Nevertheless, this is a verbal format, just a conversation between you and me with intent to inspire your ideas for being an influential grandparent from the nursery to college and beyond.

The Grandparents' Prayer

We thank you, O Lord,
for the gifts of children and grandchildren.
As we thank you for each child, we give thanks for the parents,
and ask your blessings on their leadership and on our relationships with them.
Guide us as we attempt to use our wisdom and experience to support the development of character and foster a love of learning.
As we strive to guard against defensiveness in the face of change,
help us develop a reasonable optimism when confronted by the new.
Assist us as we appreciate and honor each child's differences.
Prompt our words, that they may be acceptable in thy sight,
and grant us insight as we endeavor to inspire their decisions.
Help us to set aside unnecessary fears,
and recognize our potential for a creative response.
Please keep us ever focused on the work you have set before us,
as we endeavor to live hopefully into the future.
All this we ask in the name of your child, our savior, Jesus Christ.
Amen.

From the prayerful inspirations of The Rev. William Harkins, Ph.D.

Chapter 1

Grandparents Are for Making Memories

We thank you, O Lord, for the gifts of children and grandchildren.

Grandparents are the gift that can make a profound difference in a child's life. Grandchildren are the gifts that bring joy to the second part of grandparents' lives. The relationship between these generations can significantly enhance both the young and the seniors.

When I began this project, it was with the metaphor of relaxing with you, the reader, at a favorite coffee shop. We're sitting on a beautiful patio overlooking a gorgeous river scene. Beside us is a bubbling fountain surrounded by pretty flowers. It's a serene, blue sky day when you tell me that your daughter's romantic relationship is becoming quite intense and your son has just married. You tell me that you anticipate becoming a grandparent within the next two years. Then, you mention that your son has given you a step-grandchild who is five and one who is twelve. You add that you have embraced them, but with challenges since they live on the other side of the continent.

You ask me to tell you about my experiences and expertise on being a grandparent. I'll share with you, not my grandparent perfection or expertise, for that I am not. Instead, I'll share what I've learned, the joys my grandson has taught me, and the enormous capacity that can be generated in continuing the bond that grandparents feel when we first nestle the grandchild in our loving arms. That bond is the foundation of a relationship that can extend far beyond childhood and make a positive difference in the child's life while bringing indescribable joy to us grandparents.

As I share what I've learned about this wonderful role, perhaps a good place to begin is with the end in mind—what we ultimately want to achieve. Regardless of their present age, let's think about what it is that we want for grandchildren when they're adults? As we consider our ultimate goals for these precious young ones, we probably use words like "happy, successful, stable, secure, of good character," and we may include a religious description. Beginning with the end, the goal, of what we want for our grandchildren was easy for me as I reflected on some of the incredible people I've come to know through my work in leadership development. I've looked at their qualities, their skills and abilities, at how they've achieved success and how they've handled adversity. From the park ranger to the chief executive of an international corporation, I've considered how they became who they are and how they've achieved such satisfying and admirable lives.

Along with my experiences of observing and working with happy, successful people of good character, I draw from my early career in teaching high school, a decade in developing and leading an elementary school, then teaching graduate students, and ultimately working in corporate America. I learned the effects of family and relationships at each age level. In contemplating this confluence of learning, I've found ideas to share for making grandparenting more effective and more rewarding for both grandparents and grandchildren.

Memories of Grandparents

In looking at how phenomenal the grandparents' influence can be, let's recall our experiences with our own grandparents. Let's think of what we remember about them. Sometimes, our most vivid memories describe something about our relationship with them. Did you see your grandparents as often as you would have liked? Was your time with them delightful, educational, indulgent, happy? When you think of the special times with your grandparents, perhaps there are also memories of cookies, treats, stories, swimming, unique activities, or whatever made relationships with them memorable. What are your most outstanding recollections?

Are there questions you wish you'd asked your grandparents or great-grandparents—something you wish you knew about their childhoods, struggles, triumphs, and their lives? What would you like to know about the times, their school experiences, and what their lives were like as children? Think about the many things you learned from them, or wish you could have learned from them? Go beyond the trips, the activities, the stories, and the family celebrations you enjoyed with your grandparents. Think about how they talked to you and how they made you feel. How did they influence the person you are today—your character, likes and dislikes, your hobbies and interests?

Perhaps you knew how much they loved you, not only because they told you, but because of the way they treated or interacted with you. If you were fortunate enough to have seen them often and have a close relationship with them, they probably made you feel very special. Think about how they communicated unconditional love to you—or the kind of expression of love that you wanted. Certainly, we recall the treats and the activities, but for some of us, our most prominent memories are about the relationships and how grandparents made us feel.

If you didn't have an ideal relationship with your grandparents, or they lived at a distance, you may share my grandmother's feelings. Unfortunately, her grandparents all died before she was born, but I remember her talking about how her friends at school would bring big cookies that their grandmothers had made and were always telling about their grandparents. She talked about deciding that if she ever became a grandmother, she would be a very good one—and she was! She made beautiful memories, just as we can, regardless of whether our experience was ideal—or not so memorable.

If you didn't know your grandparents, or perhaps you were unable to enjoy a relationship with them, what did you miss? Describe how you would have like the time with them to have been, the kinds of activities you would have enjoyed doing with grandparents, and how you would have wanted them to feel about you. In thinking about these relationships, let's consider:

> What is it that's so memorable about our own relationships with our grandparents?
> When our grandchildren are age 60, what do we want them to remember about us?
> What do we want our grandchildren to value, as we treasure memories of our grandparents?
> What kind of impact will we have made on the children's lives?
> How will they be better because of our relationship with them?

Of course, grandparents generally want to be loved, respected, and appreciated. We want our precious grandchildren to have warm, fond memories of us. We want them to remember what they learned from us and realize the importance of their relationship with us.

If I do my job well, by the time you get to the end of this little book, you'll have some new ideas about what your grandchildren will remember about their time with you and be even more aware of the influence that you can have in their lives. My intent in this conversation is to increase awareness of how much more we can enable grandchildren to remember. We'll look at how we can extend our influence to make a major difference in their success as happy, stable, citizens of good character who contribute to society. In addition, maybe we can think about how we will feel when our grandchildren are teens and adults and we can see the result of our positive influence.

Naturally, there will be some indulgences of treats and gifts in our relationships with grandchildren. Maybe that's part of the grandparent role, but our capacity can extend far beyond treats and child care. Our influence can help to shape the person that the child will become.

Becoming a Grandparent

In an ideal world, our adult children meet their prince or princess after they're mature, have a stable career, are financially secure, and are ready to make a lifetime commitment. Yes, that's how families begin in an ideal society, but our changing social norms may promote a different arrangement. Today's adults may choose a mate of the same gender, become a single parent, or they may not choose to marry before having children. Their choices, and our lack of control over their choices, often contribute to conflicts between parents and the adult children.

Young people aren't always aware that the results of their decisions may have a major impact on prospective grandparents. We've invested considerable time, money, and much of our lives in our children, we've sought the best of everything for them, from education to Christmas presents. When it comes to the choice of a mate, however, we may not always deem the timing to be right or the partner, prospective son or daughter-in-law worthy of our precious child. Although we may hope for a different relationship, or a better mate for them, we must acquiesce and recognize that this is a decision that is not ours to make. Even when we're certain that we could improve on the decision, we must realize that in the U.S. culture, we're not in charge of choosing our adult children's relationships.

We can, however, initiate diplomatic discussions. We can invite these young people to look at all sides of the issue and explore the unintended consequences. We can have conversations, attempt to guide, influence, and coach, then lament in private; but we cannot make the decisions for them. Although we can't be too aggressive with our reservations about their choices, perhaps, we can enhance their decision making or diplomatically plant some seeds of doubt with some of the carefully chosen questions in Chapter 12. Sometimes, we're thrilled with our offsprings' right decision making, but occasionally, we must simply accept and make the best of it.

After the mate has been chosen, the couple is committed and have children, however, the time for our guidance or attempted negotiation is over. Our job becomes to make the best of everything and adapt to this new member of the family, accepting him or her as is. Constant criticism or sarcastic jabs will not enhance family relationships. The beginning of a great relationship between grandparents and grandchildren begins, if possible, with bonding with our child's spouse/mate/partner. Our best course is to support, encourage, and build a strong relationship with the chosen one of our adult child, even if there are aspects that are unappealing to us. The best foundation for our grandchildren will be the parents' healthy relationship.

We adults are usually happiest when we feel in control of our own lives and are able to make the major decisions that affect our lives. Typically, however, becoming a grandparent is not a decision that we can make. Oh, we may talk about how wonderful it will be to have grandchildren, and we eventually become excited, but it's frequently an anticipated event that's an announcement from our adult children—not exactly a choice possible for us to make. Yet, in many ways, it's a life-changing decision that someone else is making for us. For the first-time grandparent, it can be daunting as we think of the enormous responsibility and expectations that might be thrust upon us. We may be excited or frustrated at the timing, but nevertheless, it's a new addition to our family, a new role, and a new experience.

I recall the Mothers Day lunch when, in the midst of my daughter and son-in-law's nice comments about what a devoted mother I'd been, my son-in-law asked how I felt about being a grandmother. I quipped something sarcastic about not being the gray-haired nana type because I was too busy traveling and doing exciting work. The perplexed look on my daughter's face led me to quickly add that I would love being a grandmother, but maybe I'd just avoid the image. Looking relieved, she said, "Good, because guess what you're getting for Christmas!" Of course, I was happy for them, but at the time, no one gave thought about what it would mean for me. Yes, regardless of how much or how little involvement we have in our grandchildren's lives, we're not usually part of the decision, but we accept it joyfully the first time we hold that adorable infant. Even though it may present challenges, unanticipated responsibilities, and even hardships, somehow, grandchildren make it all worthwhile.

Names

Although we may have our own ideas about the child's name, that privilege is usually reserved for the parents. Perhaps we can make general observations about the cyclical fashion of names or drop hints about how the child will feel about the name when a teen, but that decision must be left to the parents. Naming the child is an exciting decision, especially for first-time parents.

Names are highly personal, however, and what the first grandchild calls us should be our own decision, especially since it's one of the few that we get to make about becoming a grandparent. And, it sets a precedent for any grandchildren that follow. Today, some people prefer to have the grandchild simply address them by their first name. A more traditional approach is to be called, "Grandmother, Granny, Grandma, Grandpa, Grandaddy, Gampy, Papa," or some title that defines the role. Other people choose entirely different titles, such as Birdie, Doc, or Gigi. Although it's desirable to get the new parents' input, if possible, the name should be the grandparent's choice. It's always preferable to have the new parents' endorsement, but whatever makes you happy is what you may prefer to be called.

Excitement for the First-Time Grandparent

Remembering the incredibly expensive mobile that I bought for the heirloom crib, the cute baby clothes, the fancy blankets, and all of the accouterments that were purchased without much thought, planning, or my daughter's involvement, still brings a twinge of discomfort. I was so excited, but how thoughtless and uninformed I was. I'd been a mother, a teacher, head of a school, and I was well educated about children. I knew a great deal more about babies and little children than my daughter—or so I thought. And I made some other really ignorant assumptions. In my excitement about the new member of the family, I probably overlooked that this was my daughter and son-in-law's event and that I needed to be a cheerleader on the sidelines. For a very responsible professional, who'd studied and taught leadership, it wasn't always easy for me to move into the secondary role, but that's where I needed to be. And when I thought about it, I realized that's where I wanted to be. I wanted my wonderful grandson's parents to be his primary caregivers and that no adversity should ever impede their being the anchor of his life.

How I wish I'd had this book, this chronicle of grandparent learning, before my grandson was born. Sometimes, we become so excited about the awesome business of grandparenting that we overlook the parents' needs. Unfortunately, there are times that we become so intent on being a grandparent that we forget about our own child, this new parent. We can even neglect our most critical task and what should always be the center of our memory making—the loving. I needed a reminder that there was no requirement to limit my love, caring, and concern. There was nothing to reduce my devotion or quality of time with my grandson, but I needed boundaries to my enthusiasm for rushing in and doing more than was appropriate. As I came to realize my role and my opportunities, I recognized the necessity of being more supportive of my daughter. I also quickly realized that maybe I'd underestimated my daughter as I began to observe her dedicated and superb mothering. She didn't need my constant hovering and instructing. She was becoming a well-informed, skilled parent for every stage of my grandson's life.

Rule #1: ***Focus on the Child With Unconditional Love***

Perhaps a great way to ensure that the memories are always superb for both grandparent, parents, and grandchildren is to be aware of the focus. Up to the middle of the last century, in our culture, children and grandchildren always deferred to their elders—and some authorities believe it should still be that way. Adult focus was the Traditional Generation's approach. Children were to be seen and not heard. Then, when the Baby Boomers came along, that tradition seemed to be reversed. Today, for many of us, the emphasis is on the children. That doesn't mean that we capitulate to the little darlings. Perhaps, it's just that they're of greater focus than in some previous generations. Maybe that's because many of us have smaller families; but regardless, the focus makes grandparenting more fun and more influential.

When I first held my grandson, everything in my world changed—just like the world changed when we became parents. Our world no longer revolved just around us. Our world became that child. In the same way, my feared image of a gray-haired old lady became irrelevant when I held the tiny infant. That grandchild became my delight. Although we expect reciprocity in adult/adult relationships, the adult/grandchild relationships are very different. The focus is on the child. While there's enormous reward, it's an intrinsic reward. It's that leap you feel inside the first time you hug that little one and the little one hugs you back! That's a lifetime moment! It's a profound memory for the grandparent and one reason why the focus is always on the grandchild. I must remember the Rule #1 of grandparenting:

Focus on the child with unconditional love!
It's not about me, I'm the grown-up.
It's about the grandchildren and making memories that they, and we, will cherish.

Perhaps one reason that focusing on the child is so important is that grandparents may be the one source of total attention the child receives in this busy world. Because we're free from some responsibilities that the parents have, we can give our full attention to the grandchildren, especially if our time with them is limited by geography, schedules, or other circumstances. We can make each child feel special in positive ways that build confidence and independence. This focused attention is just one mode in which we can communicate unconditional love to the child, the love that becomes a tremendous reservoir from which he/she can gain strength, stability, perseverance, and much more.

Unconditional love is usually defined as caring about the happiness of another person without any thought of what we might get for ourselves. It's that strong emotional bond that we create when we love the child so deeply that we expect nothing in return. Oops, there must be a grandparent who's thinking, "Wait a minute. I put up with the kid's father, I raised him, I paid his tuition; now it's my turn for some respect from the younger generation!" Well, that respect will come. You will be the hero. Remember the descriptions of your grandparents and the awesome esteem you have for them. You'll get tons of respect and admiration, but sometimes, it's a matter of delayed gratification. Of greater importance, however, is that the grandchild will thrive on your unconditional love and focused attention. We may not always like everything that the children say or do, and we have our values, standards, and boundaries, but the love is unending and without conditions. We may say, "If you'll be quiet in church, we'll get a treat after lunch." We can say, "When you complete ____, we'll celebrate at Disneyland." However, we never say or imply, "If you'll be good, I'll love you." Behavior can be conditional, but genuine love is without conditions. We must always communicate our unconditional love to the grandchildren. In some unfortunate circumstances, grandparents may be the only source of such unconditional love.

The Culture of Touching

Personal space and touch are influenced by culture, with some cultures being more touch sensitive than others. Throughout our conversation, I refer to hugs and physical closeness with children. Young grandchildren may enjoy being held, sitting on our laps at story time, and being very physically close to us. As they grow older, the touching may be reduced to only "hello and good-bye" hugs, or the child may prefer no touching at all. As with everything we do for them, we must remain sensitive to their needs and preferences.

At times of highly contagious diseases, such as the Covid19 pandemic, we must put individual preferences aside and comply with the needs of society, not only to protect family members, but also to ensure that we'll be healthy and a part of their future. When that elusive virus was introduced into our world in early 2020, it made profound and sudden changes in what we consider appropriate social distance. Within only a few days, we stopped shaking hands with friends and became reluctant to hug our grandchildren for fear of giving or contracting the dreaded disease. Yet, throughout this discussion, I refer to the joys of hugging and the emotional intimacy that comes with building a loving relationship with grandchildren. Such physical closeness can only take place, however, when safe and when the children are comfortable with proper touching.

I frequently imply lots of embracing, and appropriate touching. We must be certain, however, that our touching is well received and understood by the children and that we never touch them in ways that could be perceived as inappropriate, sexual, or that might risk infection.

Our love and concern for family members demand that we always act in ways that are best for them and ensure our own health and longevity. For our discussion, we'll pretend that the world will again contain low risks of contagion. With the reality of new norms, however, we'll be prudent and touch or be as physically close only as geography and the health and safety of those we love allow.

The Legacy of Culture

As we contemplate that first grandchild, we realize that this is our opportunity to influence the future. When we think about older grandchildren, we know that this is another chance to pass on to the most important people in our lives, what really matters. We want to transfer what's important to us—our culture, the kinds of people we are, and what we want for this next generation.

Have you ever thought, "I wish I'd know that when . . . ?" There are some tasks we've undertaken, that when being young, naive, eager, and unaware of the risk, was an advantage. I've often remarked that, if I'd known then what I know now, I would never have undertaken the challenge of creating an elementary school, or perhaps, thinking that I could write a book about grandparenting. Yet, there's much more that if we could have known earlier —like how to communicate, how to manage money, how to deal with what seemed to be failure, and a larger perspective of life—that would have enabled us to be more effective. These are the knowledge and skill areas that we can nurture in our grandchildren that will give them an advantage in life.

We have a lifetime of learning to pass on to the young members of our family. When we think about all the things we've accomplished, the mistakes we've made, and all of the knowledge that we've accumulated, we feel the challenge. If we can give these young people the benefit of what we know, if they can absorb what we've learned, they'll have such an advantage. Sure, they'll make their own paths and their own mistakes, but if we can find ways to impart the learning that we've amassed, in ways that they can accept and adopt, they will have a head start on life.

Culture is often defined as "the way we do things around here" or the behaviors of groups of people governed by a set of shared values and beliefs. Sharing life experiences increases the probability of passing on those values and beliefs. As the grandchildren grow and spend time with you, they gradually learn about you. From the photographs that hang on your walls, the mementoes that you treasure, the foods that you cook, and what they watch you do, they learn about whom you are. As they're learning about you, you can help them to know who they are.

We realize that emotional stability and self-confidence can be enhanced by having a strong sense of knowing "who I am and where I came from." Perhaps it's a part of the stability that emanates from having strong family bonds. In this country of people of many origins, it's often important to know something about the previous generations and ethnicity. Even though family history sometimes becomes more important in maturity than in youth, we must provide this grounding of culture while the children are young. They may enjoy an intimate exploration of old family photographs and hearing stories about the people in the pictures—the relatives and friends with strange fashions and hair styles. They may especially enjoy seeing photos of us when we were their age, in high school, and with their parents when they were children. They benefit from hearing tales of our adventures, misadventures, and caveats of how they can avoid our mistakes.

Earlier, when we reflected on memories of our grandparents, there were probably memories of food—the way that grandmother cooked Christmas turkey and dressing, the barbecue that grandfather cooked on the grill, or the Sunday afternoon watermelon. Our holiday traditions, food, religion, patriotism, origins, and family history are endowments that we bequeath to the future. Elements of our culture are important to pass on to the younger generation as these grandchildren are our legacy. Many of us want to pass on to them the parts of our culture that we value. Even though food and small holiday rituals may seem incidental, somehow, they can become part of the anchor of that legacy so important to our special grandchildren—that legacy of knowing who I am and that I'm a part of something significant.

If religion is important to us, we can be an excellent role model of our faith. We can ask the blessing at meals, make quiet references to our beliefs in communications, and make our participation what we want our grandchildren's to be when they are adults. If we want the them to attend religious services when they are teens and adults, we can't wait until then to introduce the habit. Today's children live in an era when it has become socially acceptable to disavow belief in God. If we don't want the children to regress, then we must model our faith and begin their participation in religious activities in early childhood.

One of the funniest discussions I've heard about early indoctrination was while working in a manufacturing plant in Alabama. One of the supervisors had a big photograph of a baby in an Auburn University shirt on her desk. When complimented on the cute child, the grandmother said, "Yeah, he's like my daughter and a sweet little boy. I was gonna get him a University of Alabama shirt, when he was older, but his daddy's already got him on the Auburn road. I thought we should wait until he was old enough to choose, but his daddy made the decision for him." I laughed as I walked away, thinking that the football loyalty comments sounded more like talk of choice of religion. Later, I was reminded that, in Alabama, it's as if football *is a religion!*

Seriously, we too often use that method for teaching religion, suggesting that children should be introduced to religion when they are old enough to make their own choices. Although that might sound logical, it's rarely effective because children benefit from a religious environment throughout childhood, and especially in their teen years. The basics of our faith are learned in childhood, but becoming fully formed by our faith takes a lifetime. (Candler, 2017).

Because we've found other ways and organizations to substitute for religion, many families no longer attend religious activities. In much of our society, religion no longer has an influence in daily life. Yet, we can find research to indicate that people who regularly participate in worship, may have more productive lives. It seems that people who practice their religion and attend worship regularly may be more successful. Perhaps the anchor of regular church attendance promotes good habits and creates a source of emotional support and social capital. Although much of the research in this area does not meet every statistical test for proving cause and effect, regardless, finding a religious environment to provide what we want for the children may be a worthy pursuit.

Perhaps, when the child becomes an adult, he/she may choose a different mode of worship from ours, but if our religion is important to us, it is a gift that we can pass on to our grandchildren. If, like some of our adult children, they have found too many activities to crowd their schedules, and they no longer attend services, we can keep an open invitation to the grandchild to attend with us, ensuring that it's always a pleasant experience for the child. Too many people may remember being dragged to boring services, especially the part about having to sit still and be quiet. Today, there are places that offer "kid friendly" worship and programs to enhance the lives of young children and teens. We can find places that our grandchildren and we can be comfortable and consistent in our participation.

The same principle applies to patriotism. If your tradition is that of being a "flag waver," and one who is knowledgeable of American history, pass this on to your grandchildren through stories, parades, Independence Day celebrations, and trips to National Parks. If family members served in the military, share appropriate stories of their experiences. Since some of today's educational systems have abandoned the tenets of western education, American history may no longer be a part of the curriculum in some grandchildren's schools. At a time when young people may not have the opportunity to study civics in high school as we did, or to develop an understanding of our American history and government, it presents an opportunity for grandparents to compensate. In essence, if history, patriotism, and political beliefs are important to you, share them with your grandchildren and give them that gift in your legacy. Whether your politics are liberal or conservative, teach the children why democracy is important, the pledge to the flag, the words to "America the Beautiful," to be a future voter, and the parts of your culture that are no longer available in many schools.

When we travel, it's intriguing to see how other people live. In our own communities, or other parts of the world, we're fascinated by different customs and the uniqueness of other cultures. Learning about diverse cultures can help us to understand other people and enlighten our sharing the planet together. Whether in our own community or abroad, this knowledge of different cultures is fascinating and educational, but it can also be problematic.

In our youth, the fascination with other cultures can morph into romanticism. People who look different, act differently, and live differently, can captivate our imagination. Long-term relationships with blended cultures, however, can sometimes be complicated. Differences in attitudes toward work, family, women, and gender roles may become evident. Even the speed with which we move, how loudly we talk, and how loud we want our music can vary from one culture to another. What was once fascinating and exciting can become difficult or a disaster in long-term relationships. For these and other reasons, teaching children about their own cultures, what are the anchors in their lives, about shared values, and what will be important in their future can be a gift from grandparents. What can seem intoxicating when young may be different in maturity. Knowing our culture is part of knowing who we are and can be an anchor as we explore our diverse world. This background enables young people to relate to and participate with people from other cultures with the anchoring knowledge of their values, character, and whom they are.

Opportunities to Make a Difference

Because we've lived longer and experienced being a parent, we know how quickly the time of childhood passes. Although at the moment, the sleepless nights and the endless laundry and maintenance chores seem unending, the time when our children are young is a relatively short period in the whole of life. Yet, young parents may be having children when they are also trying to launch or nurture their careers, buy a home, and become part of a social community. This is when we more mature adults can tell stories, confess our regrets, and diplomatically help the young parents to see that the time when their children need them most is little more than a decade. While these years can seem an eternity to the young people, we know that it's a relatively short period in what we hope and pray will be a long and happy lifetime for them.

We grandparents can assist, encourage, and make their lives easier in untold ways, including offering emotional reassurance and some child care. But perhaps one of the most useful ways we can support is by helping them to focus on their priorities—family first, and then career. By helping them to spread their intentions and ambitions over a lifetime, we can inspire their realization that the time when they're needed to read the bedtime story or to listen to problems about school are, in comparison, very brief. With our tales and clever communications, the young parents will conclude that they can do volunteer work, engage in the community, and take an active role in society when their children are older and need less of their time. I often say that "we *can* have it all, we just can't *pursue* it all at the same time."

When career and other opportunities are presented, the immediate allure to young parents might overcome the importance of children. It's easy to assume that the meal preparation, household chores, and fussy kids will always be there, but the career option might not. That's when you and I look at the baby pictures, the mementoes, the guest room that was once a lively teenager's abode, and know the truth. The children don't seem urgent, but they are. It's easy to rationalize that the career move will produce a better means of providing for the children, but we can tactfully plant in the young parents the attitude of a *children first* priority. Whether or not we've been good role models as parents, we can contribute to this new generation's practice of living their priorities.

Extending the Significance

It was a sunny, breezy afternoon in early May. The weather was so nice that I opened the window beside my chair. I was alone, deep into the book I was reading, and enjoying the solitude of a beautiful Sunday, when suddenly, the voice of a child counting loudly by fives interrupted my concentration. Through the leafy pecan trees, I could see the nearby yard of the house that had been my grandparents' home many years ago. There were two boys and a girl of ages seven or eight visiting the elderly gentleman who currently lives in the old house. Before the counting stopped and two children disappeared behind the shrubbery, my thoughts returned to several decades ago when my cousins and I played hide and seek in that same yard. Then, as one child and another, came stealthily creeping around a far corner of the house, I was reminded of the summer afternoons when we played happily and carefree as we spent much time with our grandparents so long ago. My beloved grandparents bequeathed to me a legacy of happy memories that have been a positive influence in my life. Now, as I watched a new generation of children play, I realized that it's my turn to pass on the endowment.

The value of grandparents in other cultures can be seen in present-day China. With the government's encouragement of smaller families, the child may have the advantage of six adults to nurture and encourage development. With such support, it's not surprising that Chinese children develop the grit and studiousness to become virtuoso musicians and top scorers on academic tests. Although we may not be preparing academic super achiever little soldiers, nevertheless, every grandchild will thrive when given the support of several caring adults.

Often, when we think of the importance of grandparents, we think of the relationship with young children. We think about the baby sitting, the after school care, and the fun and adventures during early childhood. I recall turning to my friend as we sat on the beach watching my grandson play in the sand and asking her, "How much longer do you think this little boy will think it's cool to hang out with two old ladies?" We laughed as I resolved to make the most of every moment and create as many awesome memories as possible.

Being a very popular person with grandchildren is easy when they're young. We can bribe them with ice cream cones and extra trips to the playground. Around the age of seven or nine, however, it seems that some children begin to out-grow their grandparents. We're needed less for child care and we seem less relevant to their activities and their world. They may be less eager to be with us. Peer pressure may even instill in them the idea that they should spend time with others of their age rather than with "old people."

We grandparents know, from having been there, that adolescence is accompanied by incredible awkwardness. Not only do the children become too big and lanky to sit on our laps, they may be no longer interested in the once close emotional intimacy that we and they experienced. They lose the innocent wide-eyed demeanor that let them talk freely. They become less sure of themselves or of us. Where they once talked endlessly, they can become reticent to discuss what's happening in their lives. During the teen years, we may struggle for topics to engage them. Although there was a time when an ice cream cone was a delight and could spark endless conversation, suddenly there's a concern for weight or too much sugar. This is a time when it's so easy to lose our grandchildren. Actually, it isn't that they're disinterested in us, it's that they don't know how to express their interest in being with us. When they can feel awkward in so many situations, they're also likely to feel clumsy in their conversations and relationships with us.

Our love and concern for them certainly do not wane, nor does the contribution diminish that we can make to their lives. As they grow, we must find new activities, new adventures, new learning, and new ways to be with them. We must help them develop comfortable communication skills as we learn new topics to capture their growing interests. Just as their needs change from baby rattles to wooden puzzles and later to board games, we adapt to their growing needs. Just as topics of our early conversations change from *Good Night Moon* to Halloween costumes, our later discussions change to school, technology, and current events. As children develop, they need us with each succeeding year. We, too, must grow and adapt as our relationship grows and as we continue to be a significant force in their lives.

At some point, every grandchild will balk at an invitation to visit, or cry and want to go home. Such incidents may result in our feeling rejected and frustrated, but it's just another time to invoke Rule #1—*focus on the child and the child's needs.* Is there a fear of missing something at home, or of some conflict in the schedule that's upsetting the child? We must think about what might cause the reluctance and what we can do to overcome the hesitance. Regardless of age, we just look at what's happening in the child's life, conjure-up something enticing, and there will soon be an eager visitor at the door.

Instead of allowing grandchildren to lose interest or out-grow us, we must become more resourceful in our activities and in our relationships with them. We must be clever in our topics of conversation and ignore any signs of their rejection. Grandparents are not just for young children. They do not need us less as they grow. We just need to grow with them.

Summary

Although grandparenthood is often announced and thrust on us with the assumption that we will love the role, it's a grand opportunity, regardless of other circumstances. We can vastly improve our effectiveness and the satisfaction that we derive if we are thoughtful, informed, and intentional in our approach. By looking at this opportunity with a long-term view—aware of our ultimate goal—rather than just a visit, a burden, or baby-sitting, we can markedly extend our influence. The satisfaction that we derive from the grandchildren, and our highly influential relationships can help to shape their character and contribute to their success.

Becoming a grandparent can produce enormous joy, pleasure, stress, resentment, and a plethora of other emotions. It can create a whole new bond with our adult children, or become the basis of a new set of conflicts. Resolving our own feelings, however, we can become a source of solidarity for our families. Most of all, we can be the caring, reliable adults who are a positive influence and constant source of unconditional love and support for the grandchildren. We can make a significant difference in our grandchildren's entire lives.

A logical approach to this book would have been a chronological organization to consider the needs of each stage in childhood. Instead, I wanted to share my belief that we can "plant seeds" for the character, stability, success, and our goals for their later years while they are young. It's my intent to suggest ideas and approaches to guide our young ones toward an exciting life of learning, away from the disasters of addiction and harmful pursuits. With a desire to focus on how significant we can be throughout a grandchild's life, I've taken a different approach and opted for a topic focus, guided by the *Grandparents' Prayer,* to emphasize fostering the relationship and being a positive influence in the child's entire life.

Even though I'm providing information for the first-time grandparent that we assume won't be needed for more than a decade, by being very intentional in our "seed planting" throughout childhood, we can increase the power of our impact. For the experienced grandparent, there are new ideas and information to support grandparenting from the grandchildren's present age into young adulthood. Regardless of the starting point, the plan is to share concepts and encourage influence and memory making from the nursery to college and beyond.

Chapter 2

Strong Family Bonds

We give thanks for the parents, and ask your blessings upon their leadership and on our relationships with them.

The day that my husband and I brought our daughter home from the hospital is a very vivid and *mostly* delightful memory. There we were, just the three of us, a happy family. I fed and laid the beautiful sleeping infant in a fancy heirloom crib in the pretty new nursery. All was wonderfully peaceful, like a scene from one of the typical family TV shows of the day. That tranquility was short lived, however, when I heard my husband open the front door to a noisy crowd stampeding in to breech the serenity. Actually, it was only my in-laws and the great-grandparents. "I want to hold my first grandchild!" my father-in-law bellowed loudly as he seized the sleeping infant. After passing the bundle to each of the proud relatives for an inspection and accolades about her resemblance to the father's clan, the child was eventually returned to this startled mother. The baby finally stopped screaming two weeks later! Maybe it was only minutes later, but it seemed like forever to this new mom.

Although hospitals in California were changing the birthing procedures, where I lived, it was still very "medical" in those days. Babies were kept isolated and allowed to be with the mothers for only very short periods. The father and other family members could only see the newborn through a glass wall. Of course, these new grandparents were eager to see the baby, and I should have anticipated the visit. With better planning and more understanding from everyone, especially me, that Sunday afternoon long ago would have been vastly different, and years later, probably not such a distressing memory.

Achieving balanced, loving relationships in families is essential, but not easily attained. Unfortunately, the relationship among all of the grandparents and the parents is sometimes not optimal, usually because of misunderstandings and unrealistic expectations. Often, there's too much focus on grandparent needs, rather than sufficient focus on grandchildren and young parent needs. We may fail to recognize the importance of relationships over what may be petty perceptions. The road to accomplishing highly functional relationships is through calm and rational adult discussions, preferably before the first grandchild arrives. Although it seems unnatural, and even difficult to arrange, the best time to establish strong family relationships and realistic expectations is during the newly-wed period, or before there are any grandchildren. This is a time when the new couple is building their own rituals and setting precedents with both sets of parents. For example, this is a good time to establish holiday rituals —who will spend what hours of the holidays with which parents. This is the period to take some time to talk with everyone about their plans and how the new couple can fit into both sets of parents' routines and enjoy stress free holiday seasons. Then, when there are grandchildren, the routines will already be established and holidays will be the pleasant family times they should be, rather than filled with stress and unmet expectations.

Regardless of how we feel about our daughter or son-in-law's parents, this is the opportunity to build an amiable relationship with them. Whether or not we want to be friends or even friendly with them, we will do our child and the new couple no favors with snide remarks or creating tension with the other set of parents. They're similar to our child's spouse—we didn't choose him or her, but we're stuck with it. Now, it's best to be kind and focus on all of the positives we can find and nurture a personable relationship. Whether we like it or not, these people will also have an opportunity to influence our grandchildren. This is our chance to influence them, not compete with them, and set an example of excellence in grandparenting!

Agreements and Understandings

Everyone benefits from a calm, rational discussion and agreement on the arrangements and understanding of what's needed. Even though we grandparents may not agree that a pacifier will ruin the child's mouth or "all sugar is bad," if that is the parents' rule, then we grandparents must respect it. We might present research to the parent, or complain to our best friend that the parent is ridiculous, but the worst thing we can do is to criticize the parent in the child's presence or violate the parent's rule by giving the little one a sugary treat and telling the child to "keep it a secret." As I repeat throughout our conversation, unless the parent is incarcerated, abusive, addicted, or the grandparent has custody; the parent must remain the primary role model and decision maker.

The key to satisfactory, yet different parent and grandparent rules, is communications. Being able to discuss expectations calmly and rationally can make relationships smoother. When we can have such conversations without being self-focused, but focused on the child, we achieve better results and avoid the appearance of an attempt to control or be superior to our adult child or adult daughter or son-in-law. When the parents agree to occasional indulgences or exceptions, then the child soon learns that there are different expectations of behavior in different places—no jumping on the bed at home, but jumping on the bed at Gran's house is great fun. When the child has limited amounts of time with grandparents, the occasional treats and indulgences can be a delight and are unlikely to damage nutrition or well-being. If the grandparent has more of a childcare responsibility, however, then the rules must be increasingly similar to the parental expectations in order to maintain consistency in the child's life.

That practice of keeping the focus on the child, and abandoning our own self-focus and self-image can make such a tremendous difference in our attitudes and in the relationships we have with our adult children and their spouses. It is also an asset in our own maturity when we can abandon our expectations and focus on the grandchildren and family relationships. Although we may confide our disgust, disapproval, or frustrations to a trusted friend, those words must never be heard by a grandchild. Concomitantly, there should be an agreement among the parents and all grandparents that no one in the family will ever be criticized or talked about in an unattractive way in front of the child. Regardless of how we feel about a parent or another grandparent, the child must be spared from our disdain. Such negative circumstances cause conflict between the child's own feelings and what is heard from a trusted family member.

Calm, rational discussions that respect the parents as adults add to their confidence and build the bonds of family relations. In addition, our adult children may be more likely to accept our suggestions when they are in the form of stories or ideas, rather than criticism or instructions. At the end of Christmas Day, we want everyone to recall fondly the shared joys and love—even if we must use more tact and diplomacy than we thought possible. Around the table on Thanksgiving and other family occasions, we want the grandchildren to recall the warmth and special memories of those treasured days, even if we must forego some of our own self-image needs. That's how we'll get what we want in the long term. When they are 60, our grandchildren will remember happiness, rather than family disputes or emotional outbursts. The contemporary translation of Psalm 133:1 summarizes it best in, *Oh, how good and pleasant it is when kindred live together in unity!*

First Time Parents and First Time Grandparents

We grandparents can become very excited at the news of the first grandchild. Even though we know how short the "baby period" will be, we often become involved and contribute to preparations for the arrival. The first child can sometimes produce a whirlwind of interior decorating activity as the nursery is prepared. Everything from cute curtains to rugs, crib, and a changing table is installed. Yet, as soon as the new baby becomes ambulatory, much will need to be modified. It's interesting that nowhere else in our houses do we typically make such extensive alterations for a situation that will change in less than a year. Nonetheless, the excitement of a new family member requires much celebration, and sometimes, renovation.

The big difference between being a first-time parent and a first-time grandparent is that grandparents have a better concept of what's coming. First-time parents can't possibly relate to or comprehend the cumulative knowledge and experience that grandparents have acquired. We often describe what we've learned with the colloquial phrase, "This isn't my first rodeo!" We grandparents know what's ahead. We know how our adult children's lives and priorities will change the minute they hold the new-born. Since they don't know, but we do know, we can help with the preparation. Although contributing a new crib, stroller, and nursery furnishing is nice, the best place that we can begin is with the relationships. Whatever the family dynamics have been before, the anticipation of grandchildren requires that we move into our ancillary role of support, encouragement, and understanding.

We've mentioned how bringing a new member into the family changes the dynamics, especially when the grandparents have no part in the decision. If the circumstances of time and distance allow, the best way to ensure success for the family is to build strong relationships with everyone involved, long before the expenses, excitement, sleep deprivation, and altered dynamics stress all of the relationships.

The more we know about child development, the more we recognize the importance of the health and life style of the parents. At the first indication that a pregnancy is anticipated, it’s tempting to say to the daughter or daughter-in-law, “Okay, it's good that neither of you use tobacco, but no alcohol, no marijuana, and no pills for you, new Mom! Forget that headache or that muscle ache from your last run. You can't take any medication, except for some B vitamins because I won't have my grandchild's in utero development corrupted by your risky behavior!” Yes, that's what we might like to say; but that would be a curse and counter productive to future grandparent relations. Instead, we can talk about recent research that we've read about or the interesting new information on how baby's brain develops. We could even mention our own ignorant assumptions about prenatal health.

When I see somebody thumping a baby’s back in the “burping” motion, I want to rescue the child and scream, “You idiot! Don’t you realize that heavy jerking motion is rattling this baby’s brain?” I must control myself, however, as such an outburst would not be effective in changing the adult’s behavior, or keeping me from being arrested for kidnapping! Yes, we can make the essential information available, but alas, we must not lecture or control; however, we can be clever. We can be diplomatic, crafty, and quick-witted in how we present relevant information.

The first, most important, and obvious factor is that, even though the new parents have been “parented,” may have read books and attended classes, they’re in for a surprise. Until parents have experienced life with a newborn, they may not have a clue as to what to expect. Although it’s natural for young parents to have an idealized view of what life with that new baby will be like, reality may present a jolt. As grandparents, if we announce our role and expectations too soon, we may confuse the new parents *and* set ourselves up for conflicts. It's natural to express excitement and support, but it's wise to *ask* what is needed. We may or may not be able to supply what's requested, but by asking, we can be positive without expressing control. Instead, we communicate respect for the new parents.

Julie Baumgartner told the story of a new grandmother who "just didn't get it!" She was thinking only of herself, totally oblivious to the needs of the baby and new mother when she announced to her pregnant daughter-in-law, "I'll come stay with you when the baby is born. I'll rock the baby, I'll feed the baby, and I'll take care of my new grandchild and you can take care of the house, do the cooking, and take the night shift." That cannot have been an attractive proclamation to the expectant mother. Although the new grandmother may have had good intentions, her announcement seemed thoughtless and very controlling. Moreover, it would not have contributed to strong family relationships. Worse, this kind of interference could portend a controlling and flawed grandparent relationship. The tactless grandmother-to-be was overlooking the imperative of mother/child bonding. Although she may have had good intentions, she was only thinking about herself and was oblivious to the needs of baby and mother. She was also setting up potential conflicts if the prospective mother complained to her husband, the woman's son, leaving him to referee between the older and younger women. Yet, all of this potential conflict could have been avoided if, instead of her announcement, the grandmother had asked one simple question, "How can I help?"

To such an insensitive grandmother's proclamation, the young parents have two choices. They can either be angry and offended at the cluelessness, or they can compensate for the grandparent's lack of awareness with appropriate communication. They can use their diplomatic skills to thank the grandmother for her offer, but clarify, "This is really where we need your help. You're so good at______ and that would really help us. There'll be plenty of time for you to hold the baby and rock the baby as he gets to know his wonderful grandmother; but first, if you really want to help, it would be terrific if you could ____." Only the most clueless grandparent would object to such an invitation.

Sometimes, we can't ask, "How can I help?" because the young parents don't even know what they need. When it's necessary to suggest or make offers, it's useful to preface them with, "Of course, help isn't helpful if it's unneeded or inappropriate, but perhaps . . ." This somewhat tentative introduction gives the recipient the chance to accept or reject without any tinge of judgement on either part. Instead of issuing instructions and expertise, we can talk about what we've learned, tell stories, and confess our mistakes and omissions. Any way that the new parents can get the benefit of the information without having to admit what they don't already know, is face saving and avoids defensiveness. We remember that we don't need credit or acknowledgement of our wisdom, only to be effective.

Perhaps it's useful to emphasize the need for patience with first-time parents. A good example is Lauren, who lives on the West Coast. Lauren's parents, who reside in North Carolina, were more than excited about becoming grandparents when their oldest daughter made the thrilling announcement. They were especially delighted when they learned that the new member of the family would be the first baby boy in two generations. The new grandmother had arranged for the delivery of numerous gifts for the baby and new mother, including a very expensive stroller and crib.

About three months before the new arrival, Lauren called her parents and told them that the official due date was November 18. She suggested that they make airline reservations to visit sometime after December 1. Lauren said that she and her husband wanted some time to establish "their own family" and to be alone to get to know their son. Her parents were devastated, anticipating that they would be there for the birth and to offer help for the new family. Tempted to protest loudly, feel insulted, and just refuse to travel at all, the very sad and frustrated about-to-be-grandparents just complained about their disappointment and rejection. Fortunately, however, they conveyed their displeasure only to a wise friend who counseled them to remain supportive and simply say to their daughter, "Okay, we'll come whenever you want." Remaining displeased, but quiet about it, the grandparents made plans to travel in December.

When young Chris arrived on November 23, their son-in-law called with the good news and sent numerous pictures. Then, the next evening, Lauren called her parents and immediately said, "Can you come tomorrow? I'll pay the airline change fee! We really want both of you here as soon as possible. Oh, please, come as soon as you can get airline reservations—and plan to stay at least two weeks, or maybe through Christmas!" Lauren provided the best example I've seen recently of the importance of the need for patience with new parents. She demonstrated that new parents may believe they know what to expect—but they usually don't. Lauren's son is now three and everyone has lost count of how many times the grandparents have been invited and made the long trip to visit.

Like my in-laws, grandparents' eagerness to hold and coo over that new grandchild is natural, but sometimes, we must be understanding and practice some restraint. When contagious disease is widespread, we must honor the young parents' desires of restricted visits—even when we're sure they are being overly protective. That's when we must summon our empathy and just say, "Call when you think it's safe to have visitors.

Offer Support, Not Criticism or Control

All too often, we think, "Been here, done this! I know how it should go," and we say, "Honey, let me do this for you." Although we mean well, such a remark can sound critical or demeaning and indicate a lack of confidence or respect for the new parent's skills. Even when our intentions are innocent, sensitive adult children can interpret our attempts as judging or controlling. For that reason, it's often useful to be explicit about our offers of help. Sometimes, it's advantageous to begin our offers with, "If it would be helpful, perhaps I could . . ." or "I don't want to interfere with your plans, but if I can help with ___, let me know." Although this kind of approach may seem uncomfortably hesitant, it keeps the new parents from feeling inadequate or criticized. It helps to remember that we have a generation of knowledge and experience that these new parents have yet to acquire. Our job is to support and encourage—not to diminish their growth as a person and as a parent by sounding superior or judgmental. In addition, a healthy amount of positive feedback for their attentive parenting can go a long way toward building their confidence in this new role, as well as easing their comfort with grandparents' help.

For example, it's logical to assume that a hungry infant's innate capacity for sucking will make the mother's feeding easy, but that's not a certainty. Instead, it's much more effective for a reassuring grandmother to say, "It's so frustrating to have a hungry, screaming infant that you're trying to soothe and teach to suck. But just keep telling yourself that this is a new experience for both of you and it takes a bit of time for you two to adapt. It will soon be easier, but it's a learning process."

The daughter, who was an independent, confident professional before the first baby, may suddenly have a greater need for her mother. Perhaps there's a kind of bond created between the two because of their new, common understanding. It's often said that we never truly appreciate our parents until we have children. This sudden need for mother is not a new dependency, a rejection of the child's father, or anyone else. Rather, it's a new bond that often comes from mutual experience and understanding of the ordeal of childbirth and the days that follow.

At the same time that it's important to be supportive, we can overdo the reassuring. I still remember sitting in the kitchen of one of my young friends who was expressing anxiety about her child's failure to thrive and gain weight. As I fed the cute toddler, I listened to the mother's concerns about how the child could walk but didn't, and how she had unpleasant, fishy smelling breath. This young mother had clearly done her research as she commented that unusual breath in small children can indicate a metabolic problem. I surmised that perhaps she was just being obsessive and making too great a comparison to the older sister, but fortunately, I didn't deter the mother's worry. Instead, her persistence led to tests that confirmed anemia and kidney malfunction. The child soon received one of the mother's kidneys. Today, she's a healthy college student, but that experience proved to me the value of listening to young mothers and not being dismissive of their concerns. Although it's easy to slip into denial about a perfect grandchild's problem, it's essential that we listen to parental concerns before disregarding or jumping to conclusions.

My daughter experienced a challenging situation when she began to suspect that my grandson's premature birth might have resulted in a hearing loss. Pediatricians quickly dismissed her concerns with the hasty conclusion that, "A speech impediment is an indicator of hearing loss. Children who are as verbal and articulate as this little boy don't have a hearing loss." Again, only Mom's persistence resulted in a thorough hearing test to confirm the problem that hearing aids soon ameliorated.

It's critical to listen to the parents and help them explore solutions to their concerns. If we are to be truly supportive, we must help them seek their own solutions. The problem is no longer ours to solve. Rather, it is ours to share as we guide, help, coach, and encourage their search for solutions.

Regardless of distance, relationships, or prior conflicts, when the first grandchild arrives, we're usually excited and eager to help. It is better for long-term relationships, however, if we make offers of our willingness and availability rather than defining what we want to do. We can listen to offer support and encouragement when the parents are exhausted, frustrated, and anxious. Instead of sending messages of doubt and criticism, we can build their confidence. Our assurances can be a salve to their stress. We understand how exhausting and overwhelming parenting can be. When we can put our own emotions aside, and transcend our feelings, we can enhance their maturity and effectiveness.

As older experienced parents, we can become alarmed if the young parent seems distracted, or eager to return to career pursuits too soon after the baby arrives. Knowing the critical need for bonding with the infant, we're eager for the parent to remain with the infant as much as possible. That's when we must remember that babies keep the parent's hands very busy, but there may be little intellectual stimulation. That's when we can help with offers for child care beyond what seems essential. We can offer help for a few hours, to simply let the parent read a book or concentrate on a project. The combination of sleep deprivation, endless household chores, and little mental stimulation can be discouraging and depressing for a young parent, especially if the previous world was one of challenging career activities.

We know that every child needs the parents, grandparents, and several other caring adults who can support and nurture the child to adulthood. Grandparents and other caring adults will be an immense additional advocate, champion, and buttress. From the beginning, it's paramount for us grandparents to maintain our ancillary role, always remembering that unless the parent is abusive, addicted, or incarcerated, the parent must be be the primary caregiver, and decision maker in the child's world.

Family Relationships

Family is the foundation of our civilization and society. Much of life is invested in loving and supporting the family, leading us to recognize the critical importance of the family unit. Although we may have many other interests, activities, and different people who are important to us, maturity increases the value that we have for family. Whether it's a genetic, adopted, or marriage bond, we derive a social identity from our familial relationships. That foundation can be rock solid at times and egg shell fragile at other times. The latter are the times when grandparents can apply "What I wish I'd known when . . ." Although we can point to occasions when we did it right, we may remember things we wish we'd done differently. What we've learned can be useful if the knowledge is passed on to future generations with diplomacy and caring —both our opportunity and challenge.

From extensive research in organization development, it's evident that work environments containing a high degree of trust can produce many positive elements. For example, when people trust each other, they can think long-term, they feel comfortable in collaboration, they're innovative, adaptable, and try new things. Most of all, they're not threatened by a paralyzing fear of failure. The same social paradigm applies to families. When everyone feels valued, treats each other with respect, and uses good communication skills, the family creates a loving home that breeds trust, security, and confidence. Just as organizations are more effective when there is a work environment of trust and respect, family members flourish in an atmosphere of trust. Just as trust is the glue that holds an organization together, trust glues family members together.

Although it's unusual to find a family with bonds of love but without trust, it can occur when a family member encounters difficulty. It must be acknowledged that sometimes, we may have family members that we love, but who cannot be trusted completely. If they have demonstrated that they cannot be trusted with money or they have an addiction problem, then we trust them only as appropriate. While we don't stop loving them, we don't tempt them with an open wallet or an unlocked medicine cabinet. We trust only as far as past performance has indicated is appropriate.

When children sense any kind of scarcity, we can have the challenge of dealing with sibling rivalry. This is about developing an individual identity and learning to share with others. The typical cause is children's perception of scarcity. They become concerned that they won't be able to get what they want because of a lack of abundance, most often, of love. As the children grow beyond a total self-focus, and feel the assurances of love within the family, it allows them to avoid jealousy and resentment of others, especially siblings. We promote their loving brothers, sisters, and cousins. Because we foster strong family relations, we encourage family members to love each other and show kindness, respect, and value for each other. As grandparents, we especially emphasize these family ties because we, perhaps more than the young parents, have come to recognize the importance of family bonds. We not only talk about loving family members, we model the behavior of loving others through our respect, care, and the thoughtfulness that we demonstrate to the grandchildren. We teach them how to really love family.

One-to-one time with the grandchildren, when possible, removes some opportunities for envy and jealousy. From an early age, it's important to emphasize that we may do different things for different grandchildren because we're meeting individual needs, but we show equivalent love. We emphasize that our love is equal, and that we have no partiality to one grandchild over the other. It's useful to make the same statements and emphasis to the parents to avoid any conflicts or feelings of jealousy. For all family members to enjoy the bonds and feelings of support from family, everyone must feel that there is no scarcity of love and that everyone is valued the same way.

In our conversations, we speak with regard about other family members and encourage the grandchildren to love each other. Regardless of our disdain for a family member, unless that's an untrustworthy relative, we must not allow grandchildren to hear our criticism. Instead, we foster caring for family members. Trust and family unity can create a strong defense against the adversaries of today's world.

Families that exist without trust are often called *dysfunctional*. It's said that some of the most dreaded police calls are the ones of "domestic disturbance" because they're so emotional and unpredictable. Yes, as wonderful as families are, our families can also be unproductive and volatile. Whether the family bonds are rock solid or tinged with a history of anger, resentment, and hurt feelings; grandparent relationships hold the potential to transcend the squabbles, rivalry, and disagreements. Grandparents have the potential for improving family relationships, influencing, and helping to solve problems. Grandparents can surpass unproductive family situations. The maturity and experiences that grandparents acquire have enabled us to never take family bonds for granted, but instead, to overlook the trivial and focus on the priority of family. This ignoring makes it possible for us to see beyond the small disagreements to the strength that lies in lasting bonds of family relationships. Grandparents know that in the long-term, the people who enjoy strong family bonds often have an advantage in much of life.

Adult/Adult Relationships

Even with age, many of our relations seem the same—brother will always be brother, aunt always aunt, etc. Yet, the parent/child relationship is more complex. I remember my 96-year-old father putting his arm around me and saying, "You'll always be my little girl." Perhaps that's why a big photograph of me at age two always hung over his desk. He would often tell me how proud he was of some accomplishment but add the "my little girl" part. I didn't appreciate his "little girl" characterizations until my daughter became an adult. Then, I understood. Now, I know why people tell about their teenager, and pull the photo of the four-year-old from their wallet. We cherish each stage of their lives, but we treasure the special memories from their childhoods. Cherishing the memories can be pleasant, but we must be diplomatic about how we communicate our attitudes to adult children in order to avoid misunderstandings and sending the wrong messages.

Although it's essential to be in control of the infant's entire world because that newborn is totally dependent upon the adults, the process of raising children is a lengthy one of relinquishing control and responsibility gradually as the child gains independence with each level of maturity. At times, we can be so intent on parenting, that we neglect to recognize that our child is no longer a toddler, but capable of more independence. Worse, we attempt to continue the nurturing when the child is an adult. When we think about it, what we were actually trying to control was the child's world, to make it safe and happy. We soon realized the difficulty in controlling another human, even when a tiny infant. Nevertheless, we did our best to control the environment in order to surround the beloved child with safety and the most superior atmosphere possible.

Control vs. Independence

Perhaps we're most effective when we focus on being in control of what's happening around the child—the temperature, the food, the clothing, the child's comfort and safety. Then, as the child grows, we seek cooperation. With such a mindset, we'll never be remembered as the control freak. It certainly isn't easy, there's no date or ideal time, but at some point, our adult children need a mature and different relationship with us. Perhaps this diagram will help as we consider the necessities of an infant to the responsibilities of an adult.

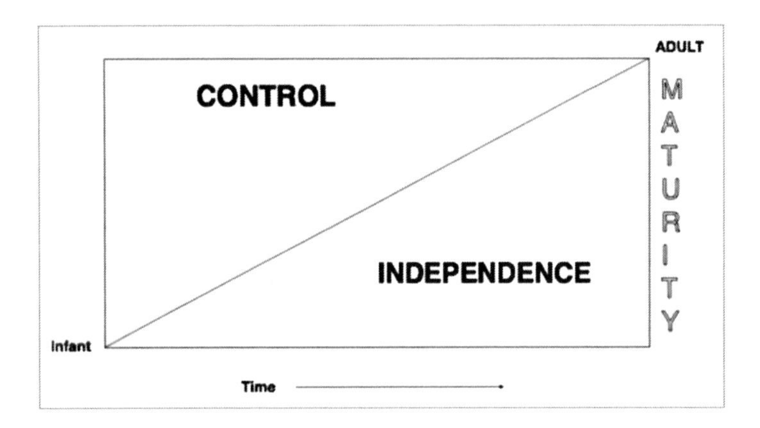

Whether or not we think they've earned it, young adults usually want to be respected as independent people, to be treated as peers and to be in control of their own world. That can be complicated if the adult child is still financially dependent, making bad life choices, or struggling in other ways. Parental interactions characterized by tact, respect, and diplomacy are really difficult under such conditions, but that's when they may be most needed. This is a critical time to coach, coax, guide, and facilitate good character and decision making skills. If we "instructed" our children at age five in where they should go and what they should do, it's tempting to continue that same practice. Yet, young adulthood is the time when thoughtful parental communication is critical if the guidance is to be accepted and effective.

Alex was an effective executive. With employees, he had learned to listen and treated them with respect. He was a superb manager—always monitoring the systems and processes to carefully keep them in control. Unfortunately, he must have used all of his available energy with the work systems because with his family, he had no patience. Instead of listening and relating to them with value, he tried to manage and control them as if they were business systems and processes. At home, he resorted to more of a "because I said so" style. Instead of using his vast training and leadership experience with his two sons, he neglected them and relegated parenting to their mother. As the boys finished college, he distanced himself even more because neither chose careers in which he had expertise. When the boys married, they saw even less of their father.

Alex goofed his parental relationship through abdication and not having enough time for his sons. When they were young, he didn't have time to listen to their irrelevant chatter. When they made unproductive decisions or demonstrated unacceptable behavior as teens, his response had been to yell and demand improvement. Unfortunately, his parenting style was one of controlling distance. When grandchildren were born, Alex began to realize his loss. Maturity had helped him recognize that, to have the kind of relationship he wanted with his grandchildren, he had to first develop a relationship of trust and respect with his sons, to really bond with both daughters-in-law and use the same skills he had learned in business leadership with his priority—his family.

The opposite of Alex's kind of distance parenting is commonly referred to as "helicopter parenting." The parent sometimes needlessly hovers over the child, neglecting the opportunity for the child to grow in independence. It's as if the parents meet their own desires to be needed at the expense of the child's capability and growth. You and I may remember talking to our parents about the courses we were choosing in high school or college, but it's unlikely that they personally accompanied us through registration. We might have asked a parent to proof-read a paper for typos, but it's improbable that any of us depended on our parents for providing research and reading assignments. Yet, today's hovering parent can be so overly supportive, especially to teens and adult children, that it reduces confidence and stifles independence.

To be fair; however, the world is different, more complex, and a less safe place. In few areas, can a parent allow the young child to play outside unattended, bike a mile to the store, or ride public transportation to downtown alone. Today, closer scrutiny in every phase of childhood is essential, but the key to growing independent, self-confident young people is in recognizing the situation. The child's capabilities and safety of the environment indicate how much independence is safe and appropriate. The parenting role is one that goes from total control of the environment to (we hope) no need for control in about two decades, as we teach children how to be in control of their own lives and their own environments.

As responsible parents, we tried to control the environment to keep the child safe. Even as we learned the difficulty of controlling a two-year-old, we learned that it was easier for us to control ourselves than to control another person. If there were any shred of belief in being controlling, it disappeared when we attempted to control the teenager. We soon learned that it was better to empower the teen than to attempt to overpower. We learned that to truly control another human being is to completely extinguish independence and self-confidence. We learned that by seeking cooperation, we could better succeed at keeping the young ones safe. By empowering them with character and good decision making, we could ensure their thriving.

As a concept, this seems logical and easy to accept. Daily practice, however, is a bit more complex. It's incredibly challenging to be responsible for the right amount of control over the environment and corresponding nurturing of independence at every stage of development. If we overdo the independence, the child can feel uncertain or even abandoned. If we overdo the control, we can cause needless rebellion and rifts in our relationships. Perhaps that's why, regardless of age, first seeking cooperation is better than trying to control everything. Getting it right isn't easy, but one way to enhance parent/adult child relations is by being very clear and intentional in our communications.

Alternative Family Structures

It's easy to think of family in traditional terms—two parents, two children, four grandparents—but that may not be typical today. There are many single-parent families where the mother or father is raising the child alone. There are parents where there is no marriage, as it is possible that up to 40% of the children under the age of 18 in this country may have been born to unwed mothers. There are also same sex families in which there are two mothers or two fathers. In many homes, there are blended families with half-siblings or step-siblings. Any of these structures can provide ideal environments for children and all of these arrangements can have challenges. Today's family structures can be warm, nurturing environments in which everyone can grow and thrive, or they can present conflicts. None is immune from difficulty.

Regardless of the parental unit or family constellation, grandparents can be a stalwart resource. As today's teens indicate that family will be of less importance to them, we grandparents may play an increasingly vital role in the future as we persuade them of the value of family.

Whether or not we like and support the family structure that our adult child has chosen, we must not allow our opinions to encroach upon our communications or our relationship with the grandchild who had no choice in whatever the arrangement. If the parent is providing a stable home environment, we cannot interfere, but we can supplement wherever appropriate. If we made mistakes in raising our children, it's probably too late for us to correct them, and it certainly can't be accomplished through the grandchildren. As repeated often in this conversation, unless the parent is engaged in illegal or immoral activity, is abusive, addicted, or incarcerated, the parent must maintain the primary caregiver and decision making role. Such was not the situation, however, with Mara.

When Mara was three, her mother and father divorced, forcing the mother to take a series of waitressing and low-paying jobs. Growing-up in day-care, and with the father soon out of her life, Mara did not experience much of what we might describe as a traditional home life. Even though Mara's mother attempted to be attentive, her work hours limited her influence in the child's life. School was boring and there was little in life to captivate her attention and support her growth as she was often left on her own. As a teen, she began vaping, tried marijuana, was cited for shop lifting, and dropped out of high school when she became pregnant. At age 20, she was convicted for prostitution and sent to a treatment center for methamphetamine addiction. That's when Mara's mother was given custody of her two-year-old granddaughter. With limited income from Social Security, and a small supplement from social services, the grandmother faced a difficult task.

If Mara follows the usual path of addicts, she will return to her maternal role for only a limited time because she will relapse, then the grandmother will resume parental duties. The child faces a stressful life of little stability and a revolving door of caregivers. Yet, this is the all too common picture of some grandparents in today's world. It is possible that between two and three million grandparents have the primary parenting role for their grandchildren, and in some instances, even great-grandchildren. Although not ideal, we grandparents can "step-up," motivated by our care, concern, and dedication.

In blended family homes there may be several grandparents or step-parents to whom the child is exposed. These additions, when facilitated well, can result in more adults to care about the children. Just because Mom or Dad fell out of love with one parent and in love with someone else, doesn't automatically change the child's feelings or relations. With different custody arrangements come different living arrangements. The child may need to adapt to one set of rules and routines during the week and a different set for weekends. The changes may occur in summers or at holidays and even with different locations and geography. Adult actions can improve a child's life, or turn it upside-down. When any kind of disruption occurs in the child's routine and circumstances, however, it can result in stress. This is when grandparents can be essential and can provide the stability that may not be available elsewhere.

All kinds of family structures can provide warm and nurturing environments, just as traditional family structures can be dysfunctional. Even though we may have anger, frustration, or strong opinions, creating conflict is not likely to enhance the grandchild's life. Unless the child's home situation is really bad, unless there is immoral or illegal activity, and unless we're prepared to take over the parental role and become the primary caregiver, we must remain in the supportive role. We must ensure that our words and actions reflect the ancillary role of grandparent and *never* express displeasure or anger in the presence of the child. In circumstances where the grandparent must move into the parenting role, one of the greatest challenges is to prevent the child's feelings of rejection from the parent. Even though the parent may have rejected the responsibility, it is essential that the child not feel the rejection that can result in emotional stress and a lifetime of psychological scars.

Changes in 21st Century Family Environments

Unlike the family structure that our parents and we may have known, today's mother is very unlike the traditional homemaker of the twentieth century. Her time is not dominated by household chores. She doesn't spend every waking moment with the child from birth until kindergarten. She may not be waiting at the door when the children arrive from school. Even when our grandchildren enjoy parents who are happily married and there are strong family bonds with no major financial or other stresses, the dynamics are different with today's typical two working parents. Under the best of circumstances, a two-career family limits the amount of time that can be devoted to the endless wants and needs of young children. Although grandparents may not be needed to provide structure and stability, we are still a marvelous resource for providing all of the little things, from making Valentines to adventures in nature.

Creating and maintaining strong family bonds is the beginning of growing healthy successful children. Grandparents can be a huge source of support for families anytime, but especially in single-parent families. It's often said that the best thing we can do for our children is to love the other parent and create a loving, nurturing, and consistent environment in which each child can grow. When divorce interrupts, however, we must cope.

When my daughter was 13 and her father left us and moved away, I was devastated, but I believed that I loved my daughter enough for two, and that I could maintain a nurturing, consistent environment. That's when I learned that children benefit from two parents. I learned how harmful the sense of rejection can be for the child when divorce occurs. Some of the rejection felt from her father was neutralized by the unconditional love from grandparents even though they strongly disapproved of her father's actions. Such circumstances make it imperative for the grandparents to be supportive. Although there may be a loud need to place blame for family problems, grandchildren must be unaware of family squabbles—otherwise, they may feel the need to be loyal, and at the same time, be conflicted by their own feelings. Whether we're needed as primary caregivers, or providers of treats and excursions; the time, love, and relationship that we provide is without measure in creating and maintaining strong family bonds.

Another of the many influences on the family that is different in the twenty-first century is that of birth order. In traditional families of the past, it was often possible to observe obvious characteristics related to birth order. For example, all of the seven original U.S. astronauts chosen in 1959 were first born. The eldest child was often formidable, dutiful, responsible, and achieving. The second child may have been regarded as less reliable, and sometimes, never quite able to excel to the level of the first-born. The third child may have seemed less aggressive, while the last born may have been regarded as the rebel who enjoyed extra attention. These characteristics of birth order may have been significantly influenced by the larger families during much of the twentieth century. The oldest child was often given considerable responsibility for younger children and other family chores. Extensive study of birth order on adult development was done by physician and psychotherapist, Alfred Adler, (1923, 1998), along with other researchers in the twentieth century.

Today, the problem with placing too much emphasis and interpretation of birth order is that the studies were conducted on a very different family dynamic from many of today's families. For example, our grandchildren are likely to experience extensive peer group settings, rather than the home environment with siblings of various ages. They may spend more hours with the primary influences of sports, day care, after school care, and other environments that place them in groups of same age children. This becomes a different environment from the classic stay-at-home mom with sibling of different ages and situations of the past. Although it may be possible to observe some of the classical traits in today's families, the different structures and environment of the twenty-first century make it a folly to over-use the Adlerian descriptions. Instead, we must focus on helping each child to grow, develop, and gain a strong sense of self-awareness, based on whom the child is and can become, rather than an assumption about a specific place in the family constellation.

It's intriguing to consider other impacts of diminishing family size. We can ask the questions, is the twenty-first century producing more hyperactivity and attention deficit disorder, or is the lack of additional sibling role models an issue? Also, is not having other children to help with child rearing, amuse, and entertain little ones, making it more difficult for working parents? There are no easy answers, and smaller families certainly contribute to the planet's problems with population explosion, but it's helpful to be aware of the many impacts on twenty-first century families.

Challenges in Family Relationships

Even though we love them and consider family to be a priority, too often, we just blurt out our feelings and thoughts, expecting family to accept and understand whatever we say, while we reserve tact and diplomacy for our public interactions. Without realizing, we may give our most polished communications and our best selves to the people who matter least, expecting family members to understand, interpret, and forgive any faux pas. Yet, considerable diplomacy is required to maintain good family relationships and positive emotions, especially between parents and adult children.

Helpful under any circumstances, being diplomatic becomes even more important when communicating with adult children who are becoming young parents. Our simple suggestions that come from "been there done that," can sound demeaning. It's too easy for us to appear critical. Being able to distinguish an offer of help from an attempt to control is a mark of adult maturity.

Grandparent diplomacy can enable our guidance to be easier for our adult children to accept and enable us to be more effective in our attempts to help rather than seeming to control. Young adults who are becoming parents may have plenty of insecurities about their new roles. We certainly don't need to add any feelings of inferiority by appearing to be controlling and critical. As mentioned earlier, our misunderstood attempts to help them may too quickly become basis for conflict. One way to avoid problems is by making intentions clear, emphasizing that we're offering help, that suggestions are only meant to assist—*influencing* rather than constantly *instructing*.

With occasional issues, it may be more realistic to grasp that some family members are incapable of behaving or responding to us the way we want. It may be that they're struggling with their own problems and battles with insecurity or fears of inadequacy. We make a leap forward in our own maturity when we can simply love and cherish family members where they are and appreciate them for whom they are. We stop regarding them only in terms of their relation to us, and instead, just value them as they are, without condition, or how we wish they would be.

Another useful technique for effective family communications and relationships can be simply "standing in the other person's shoes." A very savvy tool for negotiation is to consider the issues from the other side's perspective. By carefully analyzing and anticipating the opposite view, we can understand their perspectives and make a more informed response. When we're so focused on our own needs that we become fixated on only what we want, we overlook needs from others and opportunities for mutual satisfaction. This same technique works when dealing with with real estate agents, civic board members, and other situations of tense communications.

Developing Emotional Intelligence (EQ)

The term *Emotional Intelligence* was first used by John Mayer and Peter Salovey (1990) to describe a form of social and emotional savvy. Others have written extensively about the ability to develop an awareness and understanding of our own emotions, and then, use the knowledge to enhance our relationships with others. A high EQ contributes to maturity and independence. This knowledge of our own feelings, along with a sensitivity to the emotions of others, is an enormous advantage in being an influential grandparent. Exploration of our own feelings can lead to our overcoming insecurities that were developed in our youth and childhood. Most of all, it enables us to focus on others, rather than being distracted by our own fears and insecurities. An abundance of Emotional Intelligence can allow us to focus on the grandchildren and help them to develop their own EQ.

Throughout this discussion about grandchildren, I make numerous references to the importance of EQ, of how essential it is to developing empathy, how critical it is for us to demonstrate a strong EQ, and how we can guide and enhance its development in our precious grandchildren. To take a closer look at EQ, let's distinguish this capacity from the more familiar *Intelligence Quotient. IQ* is related to the human ability for memory, language, spatial recognition, analytical, mathematical thinking, and the ability to learn. We recognize this IQ in our grandchildren. From the first moment we meet them, we realize how intelligent and perfect they are. We never cease to be amazed at their brilliance. When, at age four, the grandson can reset a perplexing digital clock, we're convinced that he's a genius. When a granddaughter can sing the alphabet while still in diapers, we proclaim that we have a brainiac in the family. Of course, we recognize intelligence. After all, it's somewhat genetic and our grandchildren have superb genes! We recognize complex cognitive abilities, but we're only beginning to appreciate the value of EQ.

Although much research is yet to be done in this area, and experts don't seem to agree on how to measure or specifically describe EQ, the general descriptions include the ability to recognize and manage ones own feelings to develop self-awareness. That insight is then used to recognize others' feelings and better manage relationships. One aspect that's been measured and generally confirmed is that people who are regarded as having a high amount of EQ are seen as high performers in the workplace. They generally enjoy positive regard and respect by their colleagues. A major result of EQ is recognizing and developing reciprocal relationships.

It's easy to see why grandparents can be very effective at developing and enhancing this ability that can have such a positive impact on success in life. Just as we're quick to help grandchildren develop skills for hitting, kicking, and catching a ball, we can also be very influential in helping them develop other abilities that will benefit their futures. We do this naturally when the two-year-old has suddenly dissolved into tears for unknown reasons and we say, "Use your words." By helping the young child attach language to the upset feelings, we lay the foundation for developing self-awareness. Further, this development of understanding ones own feelings helps to build the beginnings of *empathy*. The capacity to understand the feelings of others, to "feel what another person is feeling," is often called *compassion*. This is another component of a stable person of good character. Because we understand the others' feelings, we care about their well-being. In adults, this compassion is a basis for philanthropy and "giving back." Perhaps compassion is empathy in action.

We continue to nurture the development of EQ when the young child becomes upset over a "no fair" situation.

With a comforting tone, we say, "Oh, I can see that you're upset. That shouldn't have happened. Tell me about how you feel." There is more about how children of different personality types respond in Chapter 7, but regardless, helping the child to associate language with feelings is very positive. Also, there's nothing quite so comforting for emotional upset as a soothing grandparent's tone, and maybe a hug, especially for toddlers at a time when it's important to help children learn to calm themselves.

When family members of children who've experienced depression or a major trauma are interviewed, they often confess that they had no idea and no indication of what was happening in the child's life. They say that the child did not talk about what was going wrong. To avoid such disasters, it's essential that we establish a solid bond with the child that includes endless open conversations about feelings. Although easier for some children and adults than others, nevertheless, it is essential to know what the child is thinking and feeling if we are to be the strong resource of support that they may need. If we want to know what's happening in the teenager's world, we must listen to endless tales and trivia throughout childhood—whether or not it's interesting and meaningful to us. It's critical to establish a bond through communications. (more in Chapter 8)

This introduction to developing EQ, talking about feelings, and our impact on others is another part of building self-knowledge. Helping our grandchildren to develop empathy, the ability to relate to others' feelings, will be a huge contribution to their growth, character, self-awareness and development of EQ.

When Family Members Lack Emotional Intelligence (EQ)

We've heard stories of families torn apart by scarcity—what seemed to be a scarcity of love and affection that turned into a legacy of greed and anger, especially over inheritances. We may have friends who grew-up in highly competitive families, who had to compete for everything from sports to the biggest piece of pizza, and we know how that needless competition can impact family bonds and trust. In the U.S., we prize competition. From competitive games and sports to competition in business, we extol the value of competing against others—Army/Navy, Ford/Toyota, *Washington Post/New York Times*. In business and organizations, striving to be better than the competition can make both better. But competition *within* the family and *inside* organizations doesn't have the same effect. This *internal* competition is often driven by a fear of scarcity—of love, position, resources, or opportunity and prevents everyone from having common goals and purpose. Instead of internal competition, families and organizations thrive on internal collaboration, cooperation, trust, and the bonds that strengthen the team against the *external* competitors. Competitive games and activities within the family may be fun until one member becomes so obsessed with winning that he/she begins to diminish another family member's status by creating a scarcity, taunting, or making demeaning remarks. Whether within a family or an organization, it's critical to recognize the real allies and the real competitors. Perhaps we might redefine how we regard winning.

We've seen public figures who sacrificed their families in pursuit of fame and power. We look at those people and wonder how they could possibly be so stupid as not to recognize the critical importance of family. Then, we look at our own families, and say, "My Cousin Joe, well, that's different. I have legitimate reasons for wanting to disregard and excommunicate him from our family." Yes, Joe may be a pain, but unless he's engaged in criminal or immoral activity, it may be better to suspend judgment in favor of family unity and just accept Joe as he is. Sometimes, by taking the first step toward kindness, or decreasing the need for Joe to protect his insecurities, we might even spark an improvement in Joe's behavior.

Another unfortunate limitation comes from a lack of growth and adaptability. Although we may believe that a family member is capable of adapting, unless that person *chooses* to grow, all of our wishing and prodding may be useless. For example, Tim seemed incapable of moving beyond his somewhat dysfunctional childhood in a family in which children were not the focus. His early life was in the midst of persistent competition with siblings, along with constant attempts to prove himself to his father. Unfortunately, he felt that he never quite measured up to his older brothers and was never successful in gaining his father's approval. Even though he earned a degree from Duke University and became professionally successful, he never grew beyond his competitive need to always win.

After Tim married, it seemed to be his chance to dominate and assume the paternal role of "king of the castle." Years of self-focus overshadowed any reason to change when he became a grandparent. Perhaps out of decades of adapting to Tim's self-focus, his wife became the family *placater,* constantly insisting that everyone defer to him. She would say, "You know his father was that way, and besides, he means well." Although his two daughters had a close relationship with their mother, they had learned to avoid Dad after the pleasantries.

Then, when grandsons came along, their grandfather's lack of EQ complicated his relationship with the young boys and their mothers. Perhaps it would have been easier for everyone if the boys hadn't been so eager for a relationship with their grandfather. From an early age, they would seek his attention and try to attract his interest. Their mothers provided Papa with books to read to the boys, and arranged activities that they thought he would enjoy. Unfortunately, the elderly man's insistence on always being the center of attention, of constantly trying to make everything about him, usually resulted in feelings of rejection for the boys. When they tried to tell Papa about something, he would hijack the conversation to make it about himself. When the girls sought their mother's help, she insisted that they were expecting too much of their father, that he loved them and their children, and that was enough. Tim's wife rationalized that being a good provider was his role and the daughters shouldn't expect more.

Finally, the daughters had to face the reality that their father was not going to change. What it meant for the boys was that they gradually lost interest in seeking time with him. Everyone had to accept that Papa was only going to talk about his interests, his hobbies, and his perspectives on the world. The sad conclusion that everyone was forced to make was that, even though they wanted so much more, the man was incapable of giving more. Tim's limited social skills and his disinterest in developing any skills severely limited his positive interactions with others, even with his family. Everyone, except Papa, recognized that it was his loss and that they were forced to accept him as he was and to love him for what he was because he would not change—no matter how much the boys and their mothers wanted it.

Although it isn't easy to explain behavior such as Tim's to young children, it's important to clarify, "Well, Papa just likes to talk about his stuff, so we'll listen politely, then we'll go play with Caleb and Aunt Suzie." While we certainly don't want to be critical, or show frustration with his behavior, it's essential to help young children avoid feelings of rejection. Even at the risk of having them join the grandmother's rationalization, it's essential that they not feel rejected.

Grandparent EQ and Rule #2

The foundation of ideal relationships with grandchildren begins with the relationship between grandparents and our adult child and spouse. For the parent who's endured a rocky road as the child became an adult, the time to clarify, develop, patch, or fix the relationship is before the grandchildren arrive. Even though it may be difficult to overcome the emotional hurdles that exist, the payoff will be in an enhanced relationship with the adult child and with the grandchildren. Whether it requires professional counseling, candid communications, or putting aside our own emotional stance, the problems won't be solved by adding a child to the dynamics.

Most of us are capable of learning and adapting, especially when we see the rewards that relationships with grandchildren provide. Even more, when we realize the opportunity that we have to love and influence grandchildren, we become eager to grow and increase our awareness. We concentrate on our chance to make an impact on the character, development, and people that our grandchildren will become.

Rarely, will a grandparent be rejecting or intentionally cruel, but sometimes it happens because the elder is tired, distracted, or simply unaware. When such occurs, the parent or another family member can diplomatically confront the mistake. When we become aware that we've made such errors, the appropriate response is to apologize for the oversight. We must assure the parent and grandchild that whatever happened was unintended and we will ensure that it doesn't happen again. Remembering that our goals are strong family bonds and happy relationships with the youngest family members, we remember Rule #2.

It isn't important to always be right,
but it's essential to be effective.

Sometimes, grandfathers can be challenged by unusual circumstances. In situations where dad is on deployment in the military, when he travels and is away a great deal, or whatever the reason, grandfathers may be particularly needed to compensate for the absent parent. If the first born is a girl and the second grandchild is a boy, the children's interests and personalities may be very different from the parents of the same gender. If the boy is not interested in the same sports, golf, fishing, or the father's favorite activities, it might be more difficult for dad to relate to the child. That's when grandfathers are a necessity. Grandfathers can remember Rule #1 and have the maturity and generosity to relate to the child, regardless of the elders' own interests. Occasionally, dads who have a very competitive personality may even tend to compete with their sons, making a father/son relationship that is problematic.

When we observe a son or son-in-law who's diminishing a young child's self-confidence with critical remarks and making everything a win/lose encounter, what we really want to do is return the guy to the manufacturer for refurbishing! But since that isn't always possible, a grandfather's opportunity is, without explanation, to supplement the role that the father is neglecting.

A misbehaving parent's actions can be diminished by a quiet but observant grandparent who supplies the child's unrecognized needs. We never let the child know our anger and disdain, but we quietly neutralize the damage by supplying what the parent isn't providing. The only hard part is in not proclaiming our feelings about the son or son-in-law who is a jerk! Instead, if the guy is absent, or beyond repair, grandfather can be more effective in supplementing the relationship than in trying to confront the child's father. The same could apply to an ineffective or preoccupied mother who needs a grandparent to compensate for what the young mom can't or isn't providing. Even though we may not have fervent feelings toward the parent, it's critical that we prevent the child's feelings of loss or rejection from the parent.

Family Conflicts

It's unfortunate that contemporary dramas and television comedies offer such negative models of family life. Watching actors blunder into conflict with stupid comments and thoughtless actions can be entertaining, but rarely offer an example of how to achieve quality family life. Instead, we need models and resources for more productive ways of handling difficulties.

Real families experience problems, but some can grow more hostile than others, and produce longer lasting effects. In the same way that it's beneficial for us to learn communication and relationship skills, conflict management skills can greatly enhance family bonds. Loving relationships in which everyone has developed a strong EQ produce better and happier environments, but additional skills are an asset for dealing with the incompatibilities that occur in families and in life.

A hermit, or maybe a monk, might be able to exist without interpersonal friction, but if we live in communities, groups, or families, we increase the likelihood of discord. Anytime we humans interact, we need skills for getting what we want without stepping on the toes of others, or preventing them from meeting their needs. Although most family members don't set out to cause conflict, it's easy to stumble into major difficulties without any clue as to how it happened. One way to avoid such unintentional family strife is by having an awareness of the levels that can escalate from a friendly conversation to open conflict with irreparable damage. (Read the model from bottom up.)

4. Conflict	Hostilities, intense negative emotions, feeling of loss, and damaged relations
3. Argument	Verbal competition, focused win/lose, escalation of emotions
2. Disagreement	Difference of views and opinions, exchange of information, learning; no threat or negative emotions
1. Discussion	Pleasant exchange, of ideas, positive emotions, no negatives

For example, I can have a pleasant *discussion* with my son-in-law about a variety of interesting subjects. He can be incredibly enlightening and energizing in conversation. Since difficulty in families often comes from a scarcity of time, love, or money, and a difference in values and priorities, as long as he accepts my different views and opinions, and I accept his as valid, we are still merely having a conversation. The key is our mutual acceptance of the validity of the other's position and our value for the relationship. No one is trying to change the other, we love, accept, respect, and learn from the other.

If we don't concur about an issue, that's not a problem if we don't make our *disagreement* personal. We can even be passionate about our different perspectives, but as long as we avoid personalizing, accusing, or putting the other on the defensive, it's not a problem, only a disagreement. We avoid such phrases as, "You're wrong! That's stupid! Why would you think that!" Our disagreement may lead to learning as we exchange ideas and consider new facts or perspectives. As we explore the subjects, I may learn from his perspective or gain new information, even if I disagree with his stance. In such interactions, our relationship is not damaged. We walk away from the disagreement with new information but the same solid family bond.

When the incompatibility of values or perspectives becomes an *argument,* we focus just on winning and avoiding any loss. If our different values or a breech of trust escalates the disagreement to a verbal win/lose competition, then I must win and try to make him a loser (which would be folly with my son-in-law who's a lawyer). The emotional level would rise as our feelings of exasperation and threat would be increased as we argued. If I become coercive and focused on my need to control or always be right, then my interactions become all about winning, convincing, or being victorious. If I needed to make my son-in-law the loser, I would become aggressive and focus on protecting my position and emotional capital.

That's when we enter the family danger zone. We've inserted negative emotions into what was previously an intellectual disagreement or a mere difference of opinion. Both of us would feel threatened, rejected, and intimidated as we attempted to convince and change the other to win the argument. If I were having the same situation with a stranger, I could walk away, be happy or angry with the outcome, and nothing more would come of the situation. But when we get into such circumstances with family members, or anyone with whom we must have a continued relationship, there is a residual anger or hurt that invades future interactions. This is not an astute negotiation because we aren't considering the other's needs, we're only protecting our position, attempting to overcome the other's position, and accomplish a win/lose. At that point, if our goals are essential to us, we could compromise—each gaining something and giving-up something—to mitigate possible damage and achieve partial gains. But compromise might not resolve much because we'd each suffer a partial loss.

The most menacing stage is that of *conflict* because emotions are hostile, the fear of loss is imminent, and the psychological damage is often irreparable. When the interactions between two or more family members become complicated by the insertion of temperamental energy, feelings are hurt and bonds can be diminished. It's the stage where the need to prevail becomes greater than the value of family, resulting in a hostile atmosphere in which relationships are damaged and repair very difficult.

One of the worst parts of such a conflict is that it can often become a major source of future conflict. We've all seen examples in families where an incident, a decision, or a problem escalated to the conflict stage, only to be followed by additional damaging conflicts in the weeks and years ahead. When I taught a university graduate course in conflict management, my favorite example of this was from World War II. Many political and world problems that presently challenge us had their roots in the end of the global war. From North Korea to the Middle East, it's easy to see that, although it was a noble intention to end conflict, the attempted resolution planted the seeds for future conflict in the unresolved prior conflict. Perhaps we rarely talk about *conflict resolution* because it seems that by the time the hostilities break out, there is too much damage to completely resolve the conflict. Instead, we focus on skills to manage the conflict.

Although it's not always productive to suppress conflict, diffusing it and using effective communications with a strong EQ can often keep the difficulties at the discussion and disagreement stage where there is less threat to damage relationships. In contrast, attempted suppression just delays the problem and can even increase the tension.

Being aware of the intent and goals of the controversy is essential in maintaining emotional harmony. If the issue is about some political hassle in a distant place, it may be best to keep it at the discussion level. Trying to assume power and convince others about the rightness of a position may not be worth the emotional jeopardy. It's also useful to be aware of the timing of an impending conflict. Why argue about the merits of Stanford over the University of Tennessee when the grandchild isn't even old enough for kindergarten? The situation may change in time. Thus, it's best to choose the most appropriate time to approach something that might become controversial or lead to arguments and bad feelings.

Expressing emotions and being passionate about an issue isn't bad, it's only when we personalize issues and begin attacking other family members that we cause harm to relationships. When we question others' values, intent, or opinions, we put them on the defensive. Then, we have to get through that wall of defensiveness to attempt to diminish the controversy. If others don't feel attacked, the target of our anger, or that we're trying to make them losers, we can exhibit our enthusiasm and passions as we pursue solutions.

The most successful, but often unused response to conflict, is *creative problem solving* because it produces an outcome less likely to result in future conflicts. Sometimes facilitated by a third party, it requires articulating and recording what it is that each side wants and does not want. Then, together both sides generate ideas for new options that would give each as much of what they want as possible, while at the same time, minimizing loss. Perhaps because of a deep-rooted need to always be right, it's often difficult to persuade us adults to try such a technique, but creative problem solving may be very successful in negotiating conflicts between children or teens. By reminding them the importance of empathy and "standing in the other person's shoes," we enhance their ability to seek a mutually positive result.

One way for us grandparents to help avoid family conflicts is to constantly focus on our ultimate goal—to be a positive influence in the grandchildren's lives. If family members are from a different culture, experience, or background, there may be many situations of dissonance, but it's essential to keep our role of being a positive influence in perspective. It isn't necessary for us to always prevail, but neither must we constantly acquiesce. Skills, diplomacy, thoughtful intent, and pleasant conversations can keep our interactions from escalating into conflicts.

Summary

We often use the term, "family" to describe any group of people having close emotional bonds, regardless of whether or not they're actually related by DNA or marriage. It's the emotional bond that lends trust and security to members of the group.

By recognizing the long-term importance of family, we increase our patience and become less judgmental of the important people in our lives. Perhaps maturity increases our value of family and gives us more tolerance of the quirks and blunders of others. When we acknowledge the importance of family bonds, we accept our loved ones where they are and as they are.

The foundation for strong family bonds and the grandparent role begins with communications and positive relations with our adult children. Although not always easily maintained, communications with young parents must be consistently adult-to-adult and without constant criticism. Building these relationships is one of the greatest, yet sometimes most overlooked opportunities in family relationships. Although we might have once tried to control where they went and what they did, when they become adults, we develop a different relationship with them. When our children become parents, we take on a new role. If the young parents are to be the primary people in our grandchildren's lives, we must respect, encourage, support, and trust them, appreciating all that they've become.

We use our conflict management skills to keep differences at the discussion and disagreement stage, avoiding harmful conflict. Avoiding the complaining, blaming, and nagging, we use the same diplomatic communication skills with them as with our best customer or closest friend.

By showing grandchildren the critical importance of family, what we value, what's important to us, and how we approach our priorities, we're laying the groundwork for helping them to grow into the happy, successful, responsible citizens that we want them to become. Grandparents can be a significant, positive influence in any child's life, creating memories and patterns that last a lifetime.

We grandparents remember that *help isn't helpful if it doesn't fit the need* and it isn't necessary to always be *right,* but we must always strive to be *effective.*

Chapter 3

Grandparents' Rules and Discipline

Guide us as we attempt to use our wisdom and experience . . .

What all grandparents have in common is *opportunity*—the chance to influence, to express unconditional love, and to help children thrive. There are countless differences, however, in the time and circumstances of our opportunities. For many grandparents, geographical distance governs the relationship as the time to be with the grandchild is very limited, maybe to just occasional holidays and a week or two in the summer. For other grandparents, there is more time when after school care or unfortunate circumstances force the grandparent to provide much of the parenting that the child receives. Regardless of the situation, grandparents have a prime opportunity to provide love and support.

Just Time for Treats, Hugs, and Indulgences

Emma, age 7, and Mia, age 5, live with their parents in Missoula, Montana, where their father is a university professor and their mother is an elementary school teacher. Their paternal grandparents reside in Atlanta and usually see the girls only at Christmas or Thanksgiving and for a couple of weeks in the summer. Before the wedding, the young couple talked with their parents about the remote likelihood that they would be able to live near either set of parents. They committed to keeping in-touch via regular video calls and visits when possible. They decided to spend alternating holidays with each set of parents—Christmas with her parents and Thanksgiving with his parents, and the reverse the following year. This ritual continued, even after their children were born. Although everyone would have liked more frequent visits, and both sets of grandparents traveled to Montana occasionally, everyone made the arrangements work. They found that technology allowed them to be closer connected than might have been possible in previous generations.

At the beginning of summer, because both parents had the advantage of flexible schedules, they began a workable routine. The young father would fly to Atlanta with the girls for a week when he would spend time with his friends and former associates at Georgia Tech while his parents indulged the girls in everything possible. They spent hours in the Children's Museum, in the children's garden at the Atlanta Botanical Gardens, having tea at the Ritz, and shopping at every toy store imaginable. Their mother would join them the second week and everyone would enjoy a relaxing week with the grandparents at their beach house in Florida. Near the end of summer vacation, the mother would visit her parents with the girls, the father would join them for the second week, and it was a repeat of the indulgences.

When asked if there were a concern about "spoiling the little girls," one of the grandfathers replied, "Look, I can tell them how much I love them during our Sunday afternoon video calls, but I only get few opportunities when I can watch them lick an ice cream cone with exuberance. The rest of the year their parents restrict such treats and focus on good nutrition." The grandmother added, "Oh, it would be preferable to spread the indulgences over the year, but when you only get two weeks in the summer and a few days at holiday time, you just have to pile it on!"

Grandparents, Steve and Janice, faced a similar situation with their only grandson living in Seattle while they reside in Tennessee. The grandparents traveled to visit their grandson occasionally, taking great pleasure in being with him and providing abundant pampering. In order to have more time with Ben, however, the grandparents offered a solution and suggested that he visit while their daughter and son-in-law enjoyed a vacation. This was such a hit for Ben, his parents, and the grandparents that it became a routine. The parents would drop-off Ben in Tennessee and continue on to New York, Europe, or the Caribbean. It became a wonderful treat for two young professionals and a grand time for Ben to be indulged by his grandparents.

Yes, *time is the governing factor for how much responsibility we have for the parenting issues.* A few hours, days, or even a week now and then doesn't upset the consistent routines that are essential for children. The amount of time we spend with the grandchildren determines our responses and the extent to which we can just be the Disney Grandad and the Fairy Godmother that grant their every wish, or whether we must provide green vegetables, consistent bath and bed times, and the stable regimen of effective parenting.

Grandparents With Child Care Responsibilities

Carlie was a ninth grader who lived with her grandparents during the week and weekends with her parents. This arrangement became necessary when Carlie finished middle school in the remote mountain area of the Sierras in which the family lived. To attend high school, Carlie would have been forced into a daily one-hour and ten-minute bus ride each way along a treacherous mountain road. After a family conference that included Carlie, everyone agreed that there were better and safer ways for Carlie to spend the almost twelve hours each week. When it came time for high school, she began living with her grandparents from Sunday evening through Friday afternoons. Since her relationship with the grandparents had always been close and warm, it was a pleasant environment for her, even though she missed her parents and younger siblings.

It was only through careful planning and discussion that everyone agreed on the rules for behavior, nutrition, study time, social activities, and other features of everyday life. It was also agreed that Carlie would make a daily phone call to her parents in the mountains just before bedtime to keep them informed and a part of her life. In a discussion that did not include Carlie, the parents and grandparents also agreed on how they would resolve problems and how they would keep each other informed. This arrangement continued satisfactorily through Carlie's first two years of high school, when her parents moved the entire family to the valley to accommodate school arrangements for Carlie and her two younger siblings.

Today, in her second year as an emergency medical technician (EMT), Carlie continues her study to become a nurse. She remembers those years when her primary caregivers were her elderly grandparents as warm, happy, and awesome. She said that she got the best of both worlds—loving parental structure and what she described as "grandparent loving specialness." She said that, even after her parents moved into town in the valley, she remains close to her grandparents and visits them frequently, still loving her time with them. Carlie described those years as having the best of both worlds with parents and grandparents.

Perhaps the reason that Carlie's arrangements worked so well was that her family unit was very strong and her extended family relationships were solid. Long before she went to live with her grandparents for school, the parents and grandparents had discussed the rules, how problems would be solved, and who the final decision makers would be. They had eliminated any possibility that Carlie would be able to manipulate anyone or play the usual behavioral tricks at which teens can be so skilled. The grandparents also understood their roles and obligations. Had they been self-focused, they might have been too concerned with being sure that Carlie always liked them. Such a distraction would have been the perfect set-up for an adolescent to be manipulative and get into trouble.

Various accommodations can work when built on strong family bonds and when there is communication ahead of and during any problems or decisions. Such arrangements can be beneficial for both child and adults.

Grandparents With a Dilemma

Emma, Mia, Carlie, and Ben are good examples of how grandparents can transcend geography and still provide the unconditional love and focused attention that's so important for grandchildren. A difficulty exists, however, when there are several grandchildren and a mix of geography. With some children living nearby and others hundreds of miles away, it becomes challenging to maintain the perceptions that we want each grandchild to have. It could be very easy for the grandchildren who live a long distance away to become resentful of the ones who are just minutes away. Even though it's a challenge, it is possible to ensure that each child feels loved and special.

Grandmother Karen demonstrated that with thoughtful communications and careful planning in scheduling and gift buying, it's quite possible to achieve a feeling of fairness and equality among the grandchildren. Presiding at a large church dinner to celebrate the grandfather's 80th birthday, she announced, "When you finish dinner, just raise your hand and my favorite grandchild will bring your dessert. And just so you'll know where to look for my favorite grandchild, would my special grandchild please stand-up." At that point, eight young people ranging in age from about 7 to 19 sprang to their feet. To greet their beaming faces, Karen added with a smile, "It's important that my favorite grandchild is aware of that special status."

Later, when complimented on her beautiful family and asked how she managed to achieve such a sense of equality and equanimity among the children and grandchildren, she admitted that it wasn't easy. She said that it's natural to rely on children who reside nearby and to more easily relate to the grandchildren that you see several times each week. Karen added that her goal, however, was to maintain a close family bond among her children, even though distance and the circumstances were different. She said the motivation was to always ensure that she planned, communicated, and acted in ways to stimulate sibling and cousin relationships, rather than create sibling resentment and distant cousins. Her goal was to maintain strong family bonds that could not be weakened by geography or time. Karen had unequal access to her grandchildren but was diligent in ensuring that they felt equally loved.

What often diminishes close family ties is that "law of scarcity," the fear that there won't be enough love and consideration for everyone. Recognition of the situation and thoughtful communications can eliminate resulting jealousy in the family, especially when geography complicates relationships. Instead of doing what was convenient or without giving thought, Karen's intent on maintaining strong family bonds extended beyond her children. She created a relationship with the parents and among the grandchildren that would not produce jealousy or resentment, but that has resulted in beautiful memories for everyone.

Like Karen's family, sometimes geography and family size determine how and when time is spent with the grandchildren. If possible, however, it is highly desirable to be with one grandchild at a time, simply because they thrive on that singular focused attention, eye contact, and attentive listening. Some will say that this kind of attention will "spoil" the children, but that may be a misperception. Of most importance is that grandchildren perceive equality, that like Karen's grandchildren, all are regarded as equal favorites. Where there is considerable disparity in ages and differences in logistics, this is not always easy. Yet, the last thing we want is for our adult grandchildren to remember us with resentment or feelings of inadequacy that they just didn't measure up sufficiently for our attention. When it comes to relationships, perhaps it's more effective to focus on individual situations, rather than trying to give everyone the *same*. Even if we cannot invest equal amounts of time and attention on each grandchild, it's imperative that they perceive no scarcity of our caring, they know we love each equally, and that the relationships are regarded as the same.

Custodial Grandparents

Malik, age 11, had a very different arrangement from Carlie or Karen's grandchildren. He lived in public housing in a crime ridden urban area with his mother who was addicted to meth. He had two older sisters, but one had left with her boy friend and the other was rarely at home. Malik's father had disappeared before he was born. Essentially, the child was alone.

Like the schools that are frequently available to children in public housing, Malik's school was always in the state's failing category. Although there was constant discussion at school board meetings, and ever present threats by the state's department of education to take control of the school, nothing seemed to change. Instead, if Malik went to school, he usually sat quietly through endless boring hours with teachers who were there, either because they couldn't get a job in a "good school," or they just needed a job with employee benefits. After Head Start, Early Start, Innovation in Instruction, and exposure to countless other expensive programs, Malik remained a mediocre, disengaged student whose attendance record bordered on truancy. Unfortunately, he was on-track to become a school drop-out, an addict, and a gang member, but his mother's unintended actions changed everything. She was jailed for selling methamphetamine. Since this was not her first encounter with the law, she pled guilty to a Class C felony and was later sentenced to five years in prison.

When his mother was first arrested, it triggered an investigation into her housing and family arrangements that led to the sister's being immediately placed in foster care. That would also have been Malik's fate except that when he learned what had happened to his mother and sister, he grabbed his only real possession, a rickety bike, and made his way to his elderly grandmother's home. He had only visited her occasionally in the past, but Malik regarded Gramama as kind, caring, and deeply religious. Although she also lived in public housing, it was a much nicer facility and in the zone for a better school.

Malik watched the tears flow down her wrinkled cheeks as he told her what had happened and she lamented the plight of her daughter. Deciding that life with one caring person would be better than all the things he'd heard about the "state's kids," Malik asked, "Gramama, can I stay with you? I'll be good. I'll go to school. I'll do everything you tell me, please..." After a long silence, the elderly woman replied, "Well, you can stay tonight, and we'll see how it works out."

That was the beginning of a whole new life for Malik. Determined that he would not follow his mother's path to addiction and crime, the grandmother requested help from social services and was given temporary, then later, full custody of Malik. First, she set strict rules about school attendance, homework, his associates, and what he did with his time. Enrolled in a different school, Malik responded to better instruction, and engaged in class activities. He developed new interests and achieved steadily improving grades for the first time in his life, but the best part was that this change continued. The consistency in meals, bedtimes, and expectations set by his loving grandmother changed Malik's world. With considerable support from the social services system through high school and community college, Malik became a diligent student. He attended church regularly with his grandmother and after college, became a Marine.

When asked what changed his life, Malik corrected the interviewer, saying, "You mean what *saved* my life? It was knowing that my Gramama loved me, that she didn't want me to be like my mother who didn't like Gramama's rules. You see, knowing how much she loved me, I had to work as hard as I could not to disappoint her. She took me in and it was my job to repay her by doing what she asked. She helped me see a life beyond gangs and failing schools. She used to say, 'Boy, you can do this. I know you can, and you know you can.' You see, Gramama taught me that I could succeed."

When asked to define the grandparent role, someone once said, "It's to provide whatever the parent is unable or unaware of the need to provide." From Emma to Malik, to Karen's brood, all existed in very different geographic, socio-economic circumstances, and had very different needs. Gramama provided full custody, Emma's grandparents provided great attention in a short period of time, and Karen dispensed appropriate attention to grandchildren who lived both far and near. Yet, the grandparents made a considerable positive difference in the children's lives. They provided whatever was needed at the time, with love, patience, and effective communications. They made many beautiful memories.

Providing the Rules and Discipline

It's easy to see that Malik's grandmother had to provide all of the structure and consistent home life. While Emma,

Mia, and Ben's grandparents had little of such responsibilities, Karen had to provide more with some grandchildren than with others. The more time the child is with the grandparents, the more we must provide stability, green veggies, and firm expectations. The more of the parental role that grandparents must provide, the more discipline and consistency must be supplied. Whether the arrangements are for legal custody, or an informal arrangement to accommodate family or school needs, the key to making it successful is acknowledging the extent to which the grandparents must provide a stable home environment. If Malik's grandmother had the resources and mistaken inclination to provide what Emma, Mia, and Ben's grandparents did, the results could have been disastrous. Conversely, if Carlie's grandparents had taken on a stern controlling persona, removing the parents from the relationship, it's doubtful that their outcome would have been so productive.

The idea of discipline may seem counterproductive to some grandparents. We think about the impossibility of keeping the grandchildren happy and loving us if we must implement rules or expect appropriate behavior. Perhaps the best way to neutralize such fears is to consider the goal of having rules and discipline. We begin by helping the child disengage from inappropriate behaviors and engage in appropriate behaviors. We make the child aware that the present behavior isn't appropriate. Then, we give cues for appropriate behavior. If we are constantly aware that what we're trying to achieve is to provide support for the parents' efforts to raise happy, healthy, law abiding citizens of good character, then our course becomes clear.

Compliance vs. Cooperation

For our great-grandparents and great-great-grandparents' generation, good discipline meant total compliance—doing what you were told, when you were told, and how you were told. Since it was not uncommon in the 1800's to have ten or more children, one can see how quick and complete compliance certainly made family life easier, if not a necessity. In the twentieth century and with smaller families, the compliance wasn't as necessary, but was often expected as a sign of attentive parenting. Whether at home or at school, the goal of good discipline in past generations was compliance—sit still and pay attention, be seen and not heard, do as you're told, clean-up your room, and do your homework!

For adults, just issuing orders and demanding compliance is much easier. It can be effective in the short-term because it's convenient and we get what we want. It may even seem logical, especially if we grew-up with an expectation of compliance. The problem is that the child doesn't learn enough in an atmosphere of compliance—except perhaps "Gran is grouchy" or "Okay, I'll do it while Gran is watching, but . . ."

In the second half of the twentieth century, by the time of the more rebellious Baby Boomers and GenX'ers, the idea of creating compliant children was rejected. Although obeying laws and observing the rules is still important, today's children live in an era of, "Think for yourself. Don't just blindly obey." Perhaps the first thing we must remember in considering discipline is that, like it or not, our grandchildren live in a very different society that does not reward compliance. Rather, contemporary society encourages creativity, individuality, and independent thinking. Today, we recognize that a compliant personality is a person who can be easily manipulated. Such a pliable and easily swayed person is a facile target for marketers, unscrupulous friends, even molesters, and people who will take unfair advantage of our precious grandchildren.

Sometimes, when grandparents are tired and the children are too rambunctious, there's a temptation to issue an order with only the explanation, "Because I said so!" Those may be easy words for the exhausted grandparent, but may be inadequate information for the child. First, such proclamations are needlessly controlling. It's easy for us adults to jump to the conclusion that immediate compliance is a matter of respect and credibility, but for the child it may be a lack of information. The child simply has inadequate understanding on which to act. Rather than becoming stern, we'll get better results when we're patient and add explanations, especially for some personality types as we'll see in Chapter 7.

Today, if grandparents issue a request or give instructions and don't get the response that was expected, maybe instead of becoming frustrated and indignant, we should change the question. Instead of asking, "Why didn't you do what you were told?" maybe we should ask ourselves why the child didn't respond. When we think about what we're saying, we may find that by clarifying, adding details, or changing the instructions, we get the desired response. In essence, compliance is convenient, but not effective in many situations of today.

When she was young, my daughter seemed to be always walking in front of me, leaving me admonishing, "Don't walk in front of Mommy." Fearful that I would fall and hurt both of us, I finally realized that all I had to say to her was, "Walk *behind* Mommy." That solved the problem. Regardless of age, we know that we get much better results when we tell the child what *to do,* rather than all of the *don'ts.* We can encourage desirable behavior and performance when we use the right communications.

When we seek children's cooperation, we put them on the path to self-discipline. We teach them by guiding their behavior with verbal, and occasional tangible rewards. Often described as "reinforcing the positive behavior," the child learns what is desirable. Sometimes, that can be as simple as giving the right verbal cues.

In our conversation, we frequently mention how much grandchildren love our attention and will try to get it, one way or another. When the behavior is not appropriate, but the child's safety is not in jeopardy, it's sometimes better to simply ignore the undesirable, and if possible, wait until the behavior stops. If the negative behavior continues, however, we must intervene, especially if safety or the ambiance of church or a restaurant is an issue.

One Place for Compliance

The child's safety is one place immediate compliance to a verbal command is appropriate and essential. When in traffic or anywhere there is immediate danger, we want the child to respond to our verbal instructions without any hesitation. Since the word STOP is often the first word many children learn to read because of the color, octagonal traffic sign, and responding action of cars in which they're riding; they understand STOP. To build on that, even toddlers can be taught how to "freeze" when grandparents say, "STOP, STOP!" That becomes code words for them and can add to their safety, as well as to our peace of mind.

By removing compliance in other situations from our relationship, "STOP, STOP!" becomes a key to safety compliance. It's like the game of "freeze tag" that some of us played as children. The technique can be taught and practiced at home as a kind of game that the child will enjoy. As a reminder, it can be practiced again when in parking lots or places that you go. Occasional reminders can produce an enormous advantage in a hazardous situation. Because this is the only circumstance in which you expect instant compliance to verbal instructions, it becomes a reassuring advantage to keeping precious ones from dashing in front of a moving car or running into danger. A loud shout of, "STOP, STOP!" can ensure safety.

Stopping What's Working

With older children and teens, we must adapt our techniques of motivating positive behavior. As we've agreed, control is rarely productive. Instead, we have a better chance of changing their behavior if we seek their cooperation and coach their critical thinking skills (more in Chapter 9). With adults, it seems that to change behavior, we must change the way people think, and sometimes, we must interrupt "what's working for them."

When James gave his granddaughter, a credit card for her high school graduation gift, he told Lori that she could use it for clothes, gas, books, or whatever spending she needed during college and that he would pay the bill each month, up to a certain amount. For the first year, the monthly totals remained under the limit. Then, the bills began increasing each month, gradually at first, then upward, significantly passing the limit. When Lori came for a Thanksgiving visit, James reminded her of their agreement. Of course, she apologized and assured him that it wouldn't happen again, and it didn't—for three months. When the totals again began to exceed the limit, James called Lori to tell her he had removed his name from the credit card. He said that she would receive the monthly statements and that he would send her a check each month for the same amount on which they had originally agreed. He diplomatically told her that any balance would be her responsibility and that it was her future credit rating to which this could be an asset or a problem. He reminded her of his love and commitment to give her spending money in college, but that he couldn't support her ignoring their agreement.

James provided logical consequences for the behavior of exceeding the limits when he stopped paying in excess of their agreement. The grandfather also instituted an effective way of changing behavior. As long as James had continued to pay, there was little motivation for the college student to curb her spending. James reminded Lori of their agreement and made it impossible for her to continue the violation. Of importance, he interrupted the misbehavior diplomatically. The clever grandfather stopped what was working for the young woman, changing her behavior without any threats, reprimands, or damage to their relationship. Thus, grandfather changed her behavior and taught the young woman a valuable lesson, both in spending and in honoring agreements.

The Goal of Misbehavior

Providing discipline for children is all too often delayed until we're forced to deal with behavior when we're angry. We criticize the behavior when we must intervene. As adults, we sometimes wait until we're really upset to confront a lack of accountability or an infraction of the rules. We somehow ignore behavior until we're "fed-up," then we explode. Yet, that's the worst possible time to teach children appropriate actions and behavior. Instead, if we think of the present behavior, not as something to which we must react, but as a learning opportunity, we make a different response.

Grandchildren love our attention, as much as we love giving it to them, but sometimes, they can be obstreperous and demonstrate behavior that cannot be rewarded with our attention. We must remember that if they can't get our attention in positive ways, they'll get it—one way or another. That may be a signal that they're bored or feel ignored. Although we certainly don't want to reward the misbehavior by then giving the child attention, we can be clever in analyzing the misbehavior and asking ourselves why is the child acting this way. If it's just attention seeking, perhaps we need to change the activity or the surroundings. Perhaps we just need to give the child a firm "no" and redirect the behavior. All too often, we concentrate on what the child is doing that's wrong. We can be more effective, however, if we simply interrupt the behavior and redirect it. Basically, we tell the child what to *stop* doing and what to *start* doing instead.

> "Oh, that might break! Let's put it on the table and move here to play with the blocks."

"No, the candy must stay here. Look, let's choose some big red apples."

When our adorable grandchildren create a public disturbance, it can result in considerable stress and frustration for us. Here we are, spending big bucks, doing our best to entertain the kid, and suddenly the perfect child turns into an embarrassing savage. There's a nano second in which we contemplate walking away muttering, "Never seen that little monster before!" but good judgement prevails and we morph into our nurturing and problem solving grandparent role.

When it becomes impossible to ignore the inappropriate behavior, recall the good grandparent memories that you have. You didn't like displeasing your grandparents, so make that work for you with your grandchildren, but don't just make it about pleasing or displeasing you. Rather, make it about appropriate behavior. We never withhold love, but we can withhold approval when the behavior isn't positive.

A typical problem with young children often involves tears, sometimes even loud wailing that we can't ignore. An infant has only one way to communicate any kind of discomfort—to cry. As the child develops language, words are substituted for tears as the child grows. Disappointments, meltdowns, and tantrums are usually less stressful for us adults when we recognize that the crying is typically caused by an upset that the child can't fully describe or fix. When we put a calming arm around the child and quietly say, "Tell me what it is that you want," or "Let's talk about why what you want isn't possible just now," we both soothe the child, disrupt the episode, and help the young child to articulate and solve the problem. Especially with younger children, it's helpful to remember that logical thinking skills may not yet be developed and that most of their decisions are made emotionally.

By observing the child's misbehavior, we can make more effective responses. First, we must consider a *cause* of the undesirable behavior. We must ask ourselves, "What does Andy need? Is he hungry, tired, or does he just need a reset—a removal from the situation and a distraction." For younger children, the answer to the first two needs often corrects the situation. If the third consideration is necessary, the easy solution is to remove the problem or remove the child from the problem. We are much more effective and likely to teach the child self-discipline by focusing on the child, rather than our own frustrations.

Second, we must eliminate the temptation to associate our own image with the child's behavior. When the grandchild has a meltdown in the middle of a restaurant, it's easy to fall into the trap of worrying about how the scene makes us look. Instead, we can diminish or interrupt the tantrum by removing the child to a quiet place, calming the child, then determining what the child needs. Is the child hungry, tired, or upset over some incident? Usually, calming and distracting is sufficient to solve the problem for younger children.

All too often, we think of disciplining children as a constant process of criticizing and correcting—behaviors, manners, grammar, and appearance—ad nauseam. Grandparent memories are more indelible and effective, however, if, instead of correcting everything, we begin by just setting a good role model. For example, if the child hears correct grammar and good language, the child will develop both. When the little one doesn't match subject and verb correctly, we need only to repeat the sentence correctly in a casual tone, and the child soon learns the language. When the child hears appropriate communications, the child will learn to express himself or herself with words, rather than with crying or aggressive behavior. If we don't want to hear a grandchild using foul language, we ensure that the child never hears us using inappropriate language.

It's very easy to ensure appropriate behavior in church or other quiet places if we just teach the child to whisper and take along some crayons, paper, and a quiet toy. Perhaps learning to whisper is what makes it work for the child—and everyone who is seated near the child. We must also remember that not everyone nearby may think our little one as cute as we do; therefore, we must be certain that the child is not a distraction to others when in public places.

If weather permits, allowing the child to remove shoes may also enhance church and quiet place behavior. The noisy slapping of the kid's sandals on hard surfaces can be jolting and distracting, but the patter of little feet can be quite pleasant. It has always seemed to me that teaching some children to walk, instead of running everywhere, is a colossal task. As I write this, I recall young Kristoff, who never walked anywhere! Even though he was usually on-task and pleasant in every other way, his boundless energy for running was disruptive and a constant challenge for every adult around him. With a choice between punishing this incredibly bright child's energy or controlling his environment, the latter proved to be the correct choice. Today, this brilliant CEO invests his still boundless energy into a successful billion dollar company. Yes, healthy, intelligent, inquisitive children are often also blessed with considerable energy. It becomes the adult challenge to direct the child's energy rather than punish or medicate it.

In an era in which gifted, energetic, curious little boys are often medicated, all of the coping tools we can give these children will be a huge asset for them. In a Ken Burns documentary (2014) on Theodore Roosevelt, biographer, Patricia O'Toole, speculated that if young Teddy had been born in the twenty-first century, his boundless energy would probably have been medicated and he'd have grown-up to be a salesman, rather than a U.S. President.

One disciplinary residual of the last century is the use of shame and ridicule. Whether a product of the Victorian era, military training, or a lack of understanding of the consequences, adults often attempted to obtain compliance by using ridicule. "Is that the best you can do? You didn't try hard enough! You're such a cry baby! That looks stupid —don't you have something better to wear?" Unfortunately, there's probably a long list of demeaning remarks that we've heard. When we think about the results of this ridicule, we realize that the thoughtless remarks only produced shame, resentment, and often worsened the situation. Although it's important to describe what isn't working or what happened that was wrong, grinding criticism into a child's self-image is certainly not effective. The result could be a lifetime of diminished performance and self-esteem.

Ridicule and shaming may come from people who've experienced such treatment. They are thoughtlessly perpetuating a familiar form of their own discontent. Although we will never intentionally ridicule or demean our adorable grandchildren, we also want to teach them to walk away from anyone who mistreats or gives them verbal abuse. We want them to know that they do not need to endure such mistreatment.

Analysis, contemplating what could be improved, and correcting mistakes are part of learning how to be or perform better. Experiencing shame and ridicule do little to aid the learning process and can do great harm to self-confidence.

Fostering Critical Thinking

The yet to develop executive brain function in teens and younger children result in their sometimes doing much of their thinking with their emotions, without extensive critical thinking. Thus, our best, most diplomatic and explicit communication skills are required. Sometimes, when the behavior is becoming a problem, it may be useful to encourage the child to pause and consider what's happening. Perhaps some of the following may be useful:

"Talk about what's happened that seems to have caused a problem."

"What can you do differently to get what you want?"

"What will produce a better outcome?"

"What do you think the consequence could be?"

"A month from now, what will you be glad that you did in this situation?"

That last question is tough because children and adolescents have so much difficulty relating to the future. With any of these thought provoking questions, we may not get the intended results with our first attempt, but it's very effective to implant the question that associates behavior with outcome.

"Is what you're doing, getting what you want?"

Perhaps dependence on the emotional part of the brain makes it tough to look ahead, keeping the focus only on what feels good *now*.

Encouraging words and considering consequences probably produce the best results with older teens, but we must not compromise our standards or be afraid to set boundaries for misbehaving grandchildren. Instead, we appeal to their strengths, reaffirm our confidence in them, and rely on our solid relationship to cajole them into appropriate behavior.

Much behavior can be guided by preparing the child for what's needed. By telling the child where you are going, what will happen there, and what the child should expect, many behavior problems can be avoided. Most children's demeanor is vastly improved by preparation. Telling the child that you're going to the grocery store and that, even though it might not seem to be fun, it will require less time if you have help in putting items into the shopping cart or pushing the cart. With communication, the child knows what will happen, what will be needed, and how it can be useful or more enjoyable. Because some children have difficulty transitioning from one activity to another or one place to another, the process can be made much easier for the child, and for everyone else, with adequate preparation and explanation for what's about to happen.

Grandparents can greatly increase a child's cooperation by providing this adequate preparation for what's next, for moving to a different situation, or changes in activities. Along with descriptions about how the new situation will affect the child, it's usually helpful to describe appropriate behavior. Just before the activity, it's useful to say something like the following:

"We're going to a new toy store where will walk around and see lots of toys, but we must keep our hands clean. Maybe you'd like to put your hands in your pockets to remember just to look before we choose which to buy."

"At the library, we'll listen to the 'story lady' read a book to us, then we'll look at lots of interesting books, and choose three to check-out and take home with us. Should we set the timer for how long we want to look at books?"

"You seem to be having great fun playing with the water toys, but we must stop soon and put on some dry clothes."

"You must be tired of riding in the car, but let's watch for a big green sign that says EXIT 3, Then, we'll be almost there. Let's look for the big 3"

> "We're going into church soon, and you'll need to be very quiet and only whisper to me. Let's practice our whisper . . ."

> "I've given you money for your project, but I will not be able to also pay for ____"

These kinds of simple explanations and preparation can often transform a stubborn problem child into a delightful and cooperative child. We adults don't like to be suddenly jerked away from something we're enjoying. Yet, we often forget that children usually have similar dislikes. As the saying goes,

> "Proper preparation can prevent poor performance."

Sometimes, no matter what we do, grandchildren are difficult, unreasonable, illogical, inconsolable, and just exhausting. They have fits, tantrums, meltdowns, and sulk when they don't get what they want—or don't know what they want. That's when we feel frustrated, unappreciated, and exhausted. Somehow, we distract the dear child and remind ourselves that this is a young brain, operating only from the emotional core, and that it will get easier as the child matures. After the child goes home, we share our exasperation with a friend who can commensurate and console us. Then, we feel better and are ready for the next exciting adventure with the adorable grandchild.

The worst thing we can do is to dump our exasperation on the parents or tell them what a rotten time we've experienced with the grandchild. Such a revelation only puts them on the defensive and makes them feel inadequate as a parent because they have an occasionally misbehaving child. The reality is that such times are bumps in the road of child growth. It would be infinitely easier for us adults if all children were born with a brain that contained a fully developed frontal cortex. If only they could always be discerning, insightful, analytical, and logical in their behavior—but that isn't reality.

Logical Consequences

By providing logical consequences to their behavior whenever possible, even in the small things, we're teaching the grandchildren appropriate behavior and how to make decisions. One of the main deficits in compliant discipline is that the children don't learn effective decision making. Perhaps they only learn about how to avoid having to comply. Instead, logical, safe, but negative consequences can be strong teaching tools.

Unlike some grandfathers who abdicate small children to the grandmother's care, Holly's grandfather nurtured a fantastic relationship with his granddaughter into adulthood. She also had an equally close relationship with her grandmother, and enjoyed much time with her grandparents including trips and all sorts of activities.

From the time Holly was a toddler, she loved to be with Papa, regardless of what he was doing. They spent almost every Saturday together. They fed ducks at the nearby pond. They spent hours at the local children's discovery museum. They had Saturday breakfast, lunch, and numerous ice cream cones together. They had grand adventures, each enjoying the other's presence and making wonderful memories. Being so bonded to her Papa, Holly rarely caused any problems. Even though it wasn't easy for this doting grandfather to be a disciplinarian, he was cognizant that it was in her best interest to nurture self-discipline. Occasionally when frustrated, however, she would have a tantrum. Papa would calmly say, "Holly, if you can't be cooperative and eat your dinner, (put your toys away, or whatever the problem might be), I can take you home now." There was no threat, only the presentation of a consequence. The mere idea of leaving Papa before the end of their day together, however, was a possible consequence quite sufficient to change the behavior.

My favorite example of logical consequences came from an interaction with my grandson when he was about ten. An avid Lego builder, he had received a large addition to his "Lego City" at Christmas. It had grown to occupy half of my living room floor and was quite complex, including a train, stations, and an elaborate track. Then, a spring trip to the Lego Store to get a few pieces of additional track convinced him that he just had to have an expensive new engine for his train set. This grandmother became quite amused and impressed with his negotiation skills and persuasive techniques in which he made commitments to pay for part of the set. Not wanting to discourage his clever negotiations and offer to pay for part of the purchase, I agreed to buy the shiny train set, but on the condition that he paid a portion of the cost. When we returned home, I wrote a contract indicating the amount that I had paid and that he would repay for his part of the set from his allowance and from yard and other chores that he would do for me and for his parents. His balance was to be paid in six weeks. He gleefully signed the contract and we posted it on the kitchen refrigerator. For the first several weeks, he complied as he built and enjoyed the new toy. Then, one day he asked what would happen if he didn't repay the loan as agreed. I referenced an ad that he'd seen on TV about the "Repo Man" showing scenes of a burly guy towing away cars. I said, "Well, if you don't do what we agreed in the contract, then I will have to become the Repo Gran." He laughed at that picture, but nothing more was said.

When I told this story to a friend, the man's quick reply was, "You wouldn't really take away that child's train, would you?" To which I retorted, "I certainly would, because this is much more than about a toy. This is my grandson's first experience with creating debt and I want him to learn that debts must be repaid and that there are consequences to neglecting repayment."

On the final due date, my grandson came to play and had great fun with his Lego City. I didn't mention the train issue when we went to lunch at his favorite pizza cafe, went for a walk by the river, and returned to my house for more play and dinner. After dinner, he requested a box. I asked about what kind of box and how large. He said, “A box big enough for my new train.” I supplied him with a large plastic bin, and in a few minutes, he asked where I would like him to put the bin. He dutifully put the bin with the new train set under my desk. It only remained there until his next visit, however, when he returned with money from his allowance and was ready to pick-up limbs from the back yard. Of course, the train became his immediately when he finished. He’s in college now, but has never forgotten the dilemma of creating debt he cannot repay.

When presenting logical consequences, it’s essential to follow through if the behavior is not changed. Just as the train had to spend a week under my desk, consequences must be implemented. That’s why it’s essential to use only *logical* consequences that are safe but unpleasant for the child. It’s important to simply *present* the logical consequence but *never use as a threat*. Another device that must always be avoided is the threat to tell the parent because they might not respond the way you want. It also places the parent in an inappropriate position. Besides, children typically respond to threats the same way that a military dictator reacts. He’ll test you every time. Then, you’ll be forced to follow-through, or worse, acquiesce and teach the children that your words are meaningless. It can even become a “dare” and they will feel a compelling need to see if you’re serious and force a follow-through. Rather, make suggestions, such as Holly’s grandfather did, as in, “Is it time for us to leave? Would you rather go home now? Would you rather go sit on the steps and take a time out?” If the misbehavior continues, however, you must follow-through, but that’s unlikely to happen often.

During my decade as head of St. Nicholas School, a logical consequence to the rare discipline problem was a visit to my office where the child and I would have an analysis of the problem and a discussion about appropriate responses when something happened that the child didn't like. The talk was followed by my insistence on an understanding that the behavior was not acceptable and could not happen again.

On the unusual occasions when a teacher brought a child to me with a discipline problem, no matter the age, I just asked the child to explain what had happened. The usually contrite child would begin to explain something like, "Well, I was using the math balance and Joey knocked my numbers off—so I hit him." With great disbelief, I would ask, "You what?" Then the child in a soft, and sometimes hesitant voice would repeat, "I hit Joey." At that point, I would go further into my disbelief and refusal to understand how the other child's doing something inappropriate was met with a fist. After probing for further explanation, I would add, "Joey should not have knocked your numbers off, but when it happened, did he offer to help you replace them and tell you that he was sorry?" The sheepish reply was typically, "I don't know." Then, I would suggest that the child could tell Joey that he/she didn't like that and it should not happen again. Only with reassurance from the child of a total understanding about what went wrong, and that there would be no repeat performance with the fists, would I calmly walk with the child back to class and suggest an apology to Joey. Then, I would confirm with Joey to be certain that it was an accident, and that Joey also knew how to resolve problems.

It became apparent that the child's having to analyze and explain the behavior was both a revealing and an appropriate consequence. Trying to get me to understand about the behavior was so difficult that I guess the children decided to never go there again as it was rare to ever have a child in my office with a problem, and certainly not the same child on a repeat visit.

A big part of teaching self-discipline is directing the child's behavior. Sometimes, it's just a matter of the child's being focused and busy. At Saint Nicholas School, parents would often ask what kind of discipline program we used. I would reply simply, and probably to their frustration, "the curriculum"—but it was true. A busy child who's deeply engaged in learning is demonstrating appropriate behavior. It was very unusual to have a behavioral problem with those children. When I visit the school today, I still see very happy children who are busily engaged in learning.

Perhaps the worst, most severe consequence at St. Nicholas was a suggestion that, if the behaviors were not appropriate to learning, the child could be sent home because there was no point in being at the school if there were no interest in learning. It was not a threat, just a mere suggestion of logical consequences. In my years in elementary education, I only sent one child home, one time. His very cooperative mother provided a boring afternoon, and it never happened again. Incidentally, today that brilliant and very charming little boy is a successful lawyer. I guess he had to test the limits even at age seven.

The logical consequences of having to explain the misbehavior worked with those children because their basic needs were met and they had been blessed with educated and devoted parents. Such an approach would be less effective with abused or neglected children. It would be difficult to explore the logic of misbehavior with children who have little impulse control and are operating primarily with an emotional brain. Further, social needs seem to be of little importance when the child's basic physical and security needs have not been met.

The other side of logical consequences is found in the positive rewards for desired actions and behavior. When the child is cooperative and responds appropriately, then it may be useful to reward the positive behavior. Although this is sometimes known as bribery, it's really just completing the process. If we present negative consequences for inappropriate behavior, then we can present positive consequences for appropriate behavior. Cooperation, completing chores, or learning assignments may be rewarded with a compliment, a trip to the playground, swimming pool, or toy store. Quiet, cooperative behavior in church or when visiting adult friends may be rewarded with a stop on the way home for frozen yogurt or other kind of treat. We reward good behavior, and as much as possible, ignore the undesirable behavior. The key to rewards, however, is that they must be intermittent. If we hand them a cookie, or constantly say, "Good job", the rewards become meaningless.

Presenting positive consequences is as important as allowing the child to experience the negative results of decisions or behavior. It's essential for the child to learn that when we do good "stuff," we increase the likelihood of good results. When our behavior is negative, or we make bad choices, we enhance the chance of negative consequences. What we're really doing is preparing the child for a lifetime of smart choices and decisions that lead to emotional stability and success.

The Goal of Discipline: Self-Discipline

If we think about what we're trying to achieve in disciplining grandchildren, our thoughts probably range from "Survive until his parents return," to "Well, I want her to behave but still like me." Choosing the right approach can be confusing. As grandparents, we often rely on how we were disciplined or how we disciplined our children and make assumptions about how well that worked. Some of us think about our strong desire to be liked, and retreat from anything that the little darlings might regard as too strict. But then, we hesitate because we don't want them to think of us as simpletons—such a dilemma!

Often, the term *discipline* conjures up images of punishment. Older grandparents may have grown-up in an era when spanking may have been an accepted form of enforcing discipline, but today, that would not create a beautiful memory. Although our parents may have dispensed ample spankings, it's hard to imagine spankings and punishment creating beautiful grandparent memories. We say, "Remember when we were punished in school?" meaning that we were penalized for some infraction of the rules. For many of us, discipline is synonymous with spankings, demerits, or being sent by the coach to run laps around the track. Such punishment *interrupts* the behavior, but it is rarely effective in *changing* the behavior. In our quest for enhancing the child's learning, we endeavor to stop and change inappropriate behavior, teach the child appropriate behavior, and encourage the child's learning *self-discipline.*

From the beginning of our discussion, we've agreed that our greatest grandparent goal is to nurture independent, stable, successful young people. We know from many studies of high achievers and successful leaders that one dominant mark of their personalities is that such achievers demonstrate a high degree of *self-discipline.* When we consider our goal, we realize that discipline isn't something we *do,* or impose on our grandchildren. Rather, our goal is to help them learn *self-discipline.* It's ever so much better when the child recognizes the impending storm and gets out of the swimming pool at the first sound of thunder, than our having to drag the kid out of the water. It's ever so much better when the children pick-up their toys when they're finished playing with them, rather than our having to nag them.

Memories are ever so much better when the children are cooperative rather than coerced. How do we accomplish this? The same way we taught them to walk and talk—by encouraging, rewarding, and being a role model—by showing them how to be. Although sometimes, when we're tired, and the parents have left the child with us longer than expected, the good discipline seems for our convenience, but it's really an integral part of growing effective grandchildren and making beautiful memories.

We begin the process of teaching self-discipline with the basics of decision making. The first part of decision making is learning to make choices. From the toddler stage, we offer the child two choices—never between right and wrong but always between two right choices. It's often about which toy do you want to play with first, or which book shall we read first. Then, we progress to clothing, and it becomes, "Do you want to wear the red sweater or the green sweater—never the bathing suit or the ski suit?" As doting grandparents, it's easy to fall into the trap of providing everything and making all of the choices for them, but this is one of our first opportunities to begin developing good decision-making skills. Asking such simple questions as, "Which of these two shall we do first?" is the beginning of a process that will continue throughout childhood and have major benefits in the teen and young adult years (more in Chapter 9).

An important part of self-discipline is what psychologists call *impulse control*. That is, acting without consideration of the decision or its consequences. Life is filled with the impulse to immerse ourselves in all sorts of ineffective activities. I have the impulse to stop at every doughnut shop, every ice cream store, and every barbecue restaurant that I pass. Of course, we don't give-in to these impulses because we know that such must be only a rare treat. Excessive indulgences would not be in keeping with good health and nutrition.

Unfortunately for most of us, impulse control is not inborn, but rather, an understanding and a practice that must be learned. In the same way that we learned not to acquiesce and imbibe in every savory or sweet treat, we learned not to react to the impulse to procrastinate on completing tasks. Instead, we learned how to break big projects into portions of work that we can tackle, then ultimately complete the whole project. These are the pieces of impulse control that we can gradually teach the grandchildren through our examples and our stories. Even though it takes place over years, learning impulse control enhances their success in the workplace and in adult life. As we discuss in Chapter 10, learning impulse control is a major factor in helping children progress through adolescence, free of the burden of addiction and other life traps.

Regardless of the rules and discipline that the child receives at home, grandparents can be a major influence in the child's life by demonstrating effective self-discipline and talking through decisions that show the importance of self-discipline. We can be good role models and help them see the value of self-discipline. When children become self-disciplined, they gain impulse control. They don't eat too much junk food because they understand the difference between a treat and gluttony. When children have self-discipline, they understand the consequences of doing their homework or leaving it undone. Self-discipline reflects their thoughtful decision making rather than impulsive actions. When children are self-disciplined, they are equipped for success in life.

We teach self-discipline over time. Just like we clapped and made a big deal the first time we saw the grandchild walk alone, we encourage the child's positive behavior. The child was motivated by the need to be independent and act like the grown-ups with those first steps. We continue to incentivize positive actions.

Summary

The purpose of disciplining grandchildren is not to make it easier for the adults, but rather, to help the children learn self-discipline and to thrive. It is possible to be both the encourager and the teacher of self-discipline when we use logical consequences. We're obvious with our unconditional love, and opportune with feedback for desirable behavior and performance. Then, the child has no doubt about our feelings and is confident in our love. The child may enjoy pleasing the grandparents, but it is more effective not to make behavior about pleasing us but about learning and decision making. We focus on seeking cooperation. Rather than compliance, we teach decision making skills, and foster self-discipline.

We'll be more effective when we focus on what the child needs, rather than on how the obnoxious behavior is annoying us. I can recall with regret the times that I lost patience with my grandson or didn't handle a situation well. It was usually when I was tired, distracted, or had been working too many hours before I saw him. Just as being aware of the child's needs, we must also be aware of our own needs for sleep, food, and rest. Self-care isn't selfish but essential to our own self-discipline and well-being. We must be primed and ready to give our best selves to the most important people in our lives.

Allow me to share the most important principles I've learned about discipline.

- *The goal of discipline is not compliance, but cooperation and self-discipline.*

- *Teaching self-discipline is more effective than trying to impose discipline.*

- Punishment interrupts behavior, but learning consequences can change behavior.

- *We only need to attempt to control that which is out-of-control.*

- *We humans have a tendency to do what works for us—and we keep on doing what keeps on working for us.*

The last somewhat colloquial phrase is the most important cue I can share with you for changing behavior in children or adults. The quickest route to changing behavior is to somehow interrupt the "what's working for me" because as long as what I'm doing gets me what I want, I'm likely to continue the behavior. If we want the misbehavior to stop and be replaced by desirable behavior, then the misbehavior must not get the desired result. With the toddler, it's often merely a matter of distracting or moving the child's attention to something else. With older children and adults, we must be increasingly clever as we change the "what's working" part.

Discipline is not as effective when it is imposed, but rather, when *self-discipline* is learned. Grandparents can be great role models to help grandchildren learn the value of being self-disciplined—especially with life skills, such as the way we manage our time and money—and the advantages that self-discipline brings to a thriving quality of life. Moreover, this self-discipline will become a bulwark when the child enters school, college, and can be a major factor for career success in the workplace.

Beautiful memories can be obliterated when we mishandle behavior situations. Since even the most "perfect" grandchild will occasionally misbehave, we must be prepared. With some thought, and the goals of seeking cooperation and teaching self-discipline, we can avoid creating regrets. Most of all, the grandchildren's learning better behavior rarely takes place when we or the children are angry or exhausted. Rather, it must be an on-going piece of the love and encouragement that becomes part of the memories that we create.

Rather than focusing on *disciplining* the grandchild, we'll be more influential and successful if our concentration is for an on-going process of teaching *self-discipline.*

Chapter 4

Influence During Childhood

To support the development of character

Perhaps the only time that can rival the moment we first held each of our children, is the first moment that we held each grandchild. Those are some of the most significant memories of our lives. As we think about the special days in our years, our perspectives now, and what those significant moments have meant, we realize how they have shaped our lives.

I'd gotten passed the fear of the grandmother image and was excited about the anticipated birth of my new grandson, but then, he was born premature, four pounds, and in November, not at Christmas. It was very scary. I was concerned about the newborn and terrified about my daughter's health. Although I was at the hospital almost daily, I didn't touch the baby for a month, but the first time I held him, it was magic, and we were bonded! He came home from the neonatal intensive care unit (NICU) at five weeks and only five pounds. I remember walking the floor with this tiny bundle nestled under my chin—and a 15-pound monitor hanging from my shoulder. That first year was intense, but an awesome mother and some very competent physicians nurtured him through, and he began to thrive. Even through the anxiety, from the very first moment I held him, we were bonded, and the memory making process began.

From that first instant, I forgot about my original disappointment that I would not have a granddaughter. I forgot about the frilly dresses and dolls I'd once anticipated buying. I forgot about shopping trips and playing princess. Every shred of any disappointment dissolved into joy that this beautiful little boy had survived and that we would have a glorious future adventure together. We grandparents may have silly preconceived notions about whether we want a boy or a girl and how we will be with the new grandchild. When that magical moment of the introduction arrives, however, all of that fades in our excitement and anticipation of the commitment to this wonderful new member of the family.

Because of his precarious beginning, I spent considerably more time with my grandson than would be typical under normal circumstances. The hours of holding, rocking, and walking the floor were certainly no sacrifice and a necessity to give my exhausted daughter a few quiet moments in her week. But as his growth overcame the early problems, and his mother's needs became less critical, I continued the habit of spending as much time as possible with this fascinating child. Regardless of what else was happening in my life, he was and is "the light of my life." From that first time of holding him, I became committed to doing everything possible to influence his becoming a happy, successful citizen of good character. I like to think that I've been a good role model, but he's probably had as much influence on my character as I've had on his development.

Character Development

Our nation's founding fathers viewed strong character as a necessity for the young democracy. Benjamin Franklin said, "Only a virtuous people are capable of freedom." Virtue, the art of doing what is good, is a part of character that enables people to flourish. In the past, it was postulated that virtue is necessary to attain true happiness. During our country's first two centuries, when religion and a liberal arts education were emphasized, the Christian virtues of *faith, hope,* and *charity* were a part of most young people's learning. In addition, the cardinal virtues of *prudence, fortitude, justice,* and *temperance* (the latter often confused with abstinence), as derived from Plato, were a part of every learned person's enlightenment. The importance of these seven virtues is even more crucial today, but now, virtues are more likely learned from family and grandparents than from school or society.

It's easy to assume that children will become people of good character when they come from families of character, but unfortunately, character isn't an inherited outcome. Instead, character development is the result of an environment that's filled with daily examples of good character, often with religion as a component and interactions with people who guide, encourage, and model character development.

A hundred years ago, family members and religious activities provided the child's primary environment, but that was a different society. In the past, character building and learning "right from wrong" was considered to be a parental duty and easier to accomplish at a time when there were limited other influences. Today, our grandchildren are bombarded with information from countless sources, and despite our best efforts to limit what gets to them, they hear and see actions from self-centered people with little concern for integrity or for others. Although some schools make an admirable attempt to foster character development, grandparents have a unique opportunity to make character building personal. We can help the parents nurture the child's values and character.

A beginning place for grandparents to foster character development is in being a solid role model of *integrity, honesty, accountability,* and all of the other components of what we regard as good character. Although it isn't always easy for us, the first way the children learn honesty and right actions is by watching others. As children watch and listen to us, they must never hear us in dishonesty or breaches of integrity, especially when we joke or think they're not listening. They must never see us cheating, degrading others, breaking the rules, or violating the law.

When younger, my grandson could see the speedometer from his car seat and constantly monitored my driving, making the most obnoxious alarm imitation whenever I exceeded the speed limit, to which I would reply, "Thank you," and lower the speed. One day when my daughter was in the car, she scolded his disrespectful behavior. But I had to explain that he and I had an agreement and I appreciated his letting me know that I was breaking the rule—even with his annoying alarm sound. I explained to his mother that I was preparing for his teen driving years. She smiled and agreed, but begged me not to speed and to spare her my grandson's irritating vigilance.

Children learn from the stories we tell and the books we read to them. There are some excellent resources, such as *The Berenstain Bears Tell the Truth.* We can be more effective when we talk about it afterwards, pointing to the pictures of the characters, asking why they were dishonest, and what the child thinks about similar situations. It's also useful to follow-up in everyday life with references to the story and the importance of truthfulness.

It's not uncommon for children to relate their own version of something as they are capable of gross exaggerations. Instead of chiding their honesty, it may be more appropriate to say, "Let's talk about the facts—what really happened." Then, lead them through their tall tale including only the facts. Accuracy in truthfulness is not inherent, but a learned practice. When they hear our being truthful, they will learn to be truthful.

It's not only what we say, however, we must also attend to the matter of honesty in our actions. Because young children's brains are often operating out of the emotional, self-centered part, their actions and decisions typically reflect that. Young, and without impulse control and self-discipline, they will sneak a cookie when no one is looking or grab a toy that is not theirs. Through our repeated teaching, "No, this is not yours," they will learn. We must not be angry or regard their actions as stealing. Rather, it's all part of their learning. We continue to teach them about distinguishing between what is really theirs and what belongs to others as we guide their development. We must instill in them that honesty prevails, even when no one is looking. We want them not to be tempted to cheat on an exam for fear of being caught, but rather, not to cheat because they are never dishonest. If we want them to grow into an adult who does not steal post-it notes, cheat on the expense report, or goof-off on the job, we begin the emphasis on honesty when they're very young.

Character Traits

In addition to honesty, there is a huge opportunity for grandparents to teach *responsibility*. Occasionally, in our Disney Grandad and Fairy Godmother roles, we can become so lenient and indulgent with the children that we miss the chances to teach them the importance of responsibility. When we gently coach them to put their toys back on the shelves as they finish playing, when they carry their dishes to the kitchen sink or to the dishwasher after meals, and when they pick-up their clothes at bath time, they're learning responsibility. When they help us put items into the grocery cart, we're nurturing responsibility. When we take them to the park or playground and they obey the rules that we set for them, they're being responsible. These are all very small things that become the foundation for helping them to become responsible people. When they perform those tasks for which they've been responsible and they make efforts to do them with skill and commitment, then they're becoming accountable for their actions. Today, it's easy to see places in which employees dodge accountability and decrease the performance of their organizations. Grandparent guidance can set-up children for becoming highly valued professionals, workers, and crafts people who will be prized by organizations and others. Learning to be conscientious not only adds to adult job security, competence, and trustworthiness, it also adds to the child's sense of self worth.

Teaching *philanthropy,* giving, sharing, and concern for others begins in childhood. It's really a part of developing empathy, EQ, and being able to relate to others. We teach it by our own examples of kindness and sharing. We also teach it as a part of money management (Chapter 9) when we give the child two coins—one to keep and one to put into the offering plate or the Salvation Army bucket. When we just give the child one coin to give away, the child is only executing our generosity. But when we give the child two coins and say, "This is yours to keep or spend, and this is yours to share," we're beginning to teach the child the importance of giving.

When children see us take food to an elderly person or to a sick friend, they see us sharing our time and effort. When they see us contributing to the community food pantry, they see our generosity and concern for others. Often, we're busy and distracted by the many tasks in our lives and we just give the child a can or a package of beans to place into the collection bin. That's when we miss an opportunity for teaching the child about sharing and giving to others who are less fortunate.

These are very small ways that we model and teach generosity, but if we want the child to understand the importance of philanthropy when he or she becomes wealthy, it's the way we begin. If it's part of our religion, we connect our actions of sharing by talking about why giving to others is important. We talk about how we have been blessed and sharing those blessings is part of our beliefs. Even if faith isn't important to the family, developing empathy and awareness of others is a part of nurturing EQ.

Although we typically think of philanthropy and giving in monitory terms, it's also related to *kindness* and being perceptive and thoughtful of the needs of others. Another part of the development of EQ, kindness reflects empathy and the ability to understand other people's needs and emotions. We begin encouraging kindness when we treat the toddler's stuffed animals with gentleness and encourage care and kindness to live animals as the child grows. Teaching children how to care for pets and how to be safe in the presence of all animals also helps them to learn responsibility.

Teaching the child *forgiveness,* how to stop being angry with someone who has hurt or been unkind to the child, is not an easy task. It may not be completely accomplished until adolescence. With young children, we teach them to accept the offending child's apology with an acknowledgement or simple "thank you." With younger children, we're usually trying to teach them the importance of saying, "I'm sorry" and apologizing for accidents or their inappropriate actions. As the child grows, perhaps in adolescence, we may have a more complex concept to help them understand. At the same time that we do not want to minimize their hurt, we also want to teach them not to carry a grudge or resentment and bitterness. This is when we teach them that forgiveness is about us, that we say to ourselves, "That was wrong! That shouldn't have happened. I'm very angry with that person or situation, but I will forgive because I don't want to keep my anger and bad feelings."

We can be a role model of showing the difference between forgiveness and excusing someone's bad behavior in the way we relate to friends and family members. We show the teens that we don't hold grudges because that isn't productive for us. Unless there's a lesson or a "teaching moment," we don't discuss family incidents that happened years ago. We show the children that, unless there is something illegal or a breach of integrity, few family bonds are strengthened by withholding acceptance or constantly probing old wounds. Unless we must protect family members from a law breaker or an immoral relative, we can become a role model in demonstrating forgiveness.

With an incident involving older children, we analyze and talk about what has happened. We talk about anything that the child can do to avoid such hurt in the future. We discuss how whatever happened should not have occurred, but we continue to emphasize that part of the healing from the hurt is the forgiveness—being free from anger, resentment, and bitterness. It's essential to help the child distinguish between excuses and forgiveness. It may be appropriate for the young person not to want to excuse the wrong, and even though some acts are inexcusable, the forgiveness may be a way of healing. Although this may seem another word game, it can be helpful in developing the child's emotions and keeping him/her from falling into the downward spiral of feeling like a victim.

If the child has been a real victim of abuse, neglect, or major harm, it becomes vital to help the child channel feelings of anger and pain. By differentiating between not excusing the perpetrator's act, but being able to release the feelings and achieve recovery through forgiveness, the child avoids *feeling* like a victim. There is more about the victim mindset in Chapter 10.

Teaching about the virtue of *justice* is appropriate during the adolescent years, when children learn about our legal system. Even very young children, however, can sometimes seem obsessed with the concept of *fairness.* How often, when we watch groups of children playing games, we hear one proclaim, "No fair!" at a violation of the rules or loss of an advantage. From a very early age, some children develop strong concerns for equity and adherence to their interpretation of the rules. Although we certainly want to encourage their sense of equality, it's often difficult to help them understand that not everything can be what they see as fair. In these circumstances, and often through their tears, we must do our best to explain what has happened, help them to analyze the situation, and learn from it. Unfortunately, there are times when we must console them with something like, "No, that was not fair, and you didn't deserve to be excluded." We tell them that someone else's actions were very unfair, but that the best thing to do is disregard what happened and move on. Yes, one of the perplexing facts that we must help children overcome is that not everything in life is fair, but perhaps that reality requires years and maturity to comprehend.

Such traits as humility and courageousness may also require more maturity than younger children possess. Because of their lack of experiences and situations to relate to the words, it's easy for the young child to misunderstand these components of character and risk safety to demonstrate courage or believe they should have lower self-confidence to achieve humility. Instead, perhaps an excellent way to introduce these is through discussion of literature. When older and reading such classics *Number the Stars* or *Red Badge of Courage* we can talk about how people in the story demonstrated various traits of character and how we can demonstrate character in our lives.

Fortitude, Perseverance, Gumption, Grit, and Resilience

Whether observing entrepreneurs, students, or average people, we know that the ones who reach their goals are the ones who demonstrate a generous amount of perseverance, especially during the difficult times. Controversial British writer, Claire Fox (2016), has referred to today's young people as the *snowflake generation* because they seem to melt under the slightest bit of heat or pressure. Sometimes, we point to the excessive praise and adulation given to the Millennial Generation as conditioning them for an entitlement to ease of success. Supervisors in numerous organizations complain that the younger generation "needs a trophy for just showing- up." Their bosses lament that these young employees are educated but lack the character and purposefulness to prevail when working on tough or demanding projects. Worse, they may be quick to quit when the job is tough or something else seems more slightly more appealing.

We know the importance of steady practice and "keeping on keeping on" to improve success at soccer, the piano, or great innovations. As grandparents, it's easy for us to praise children for their brilliance, but it's better to encourage their efforts. When we exclaim, "You made an A! I'm so proud of how smart you are," we may make them feel good at the moment, but we might also make them falter when they encounter difficult subjects. Then, they may doubt their intellectual ability. We serve them better when we encourage their efforts and say, "Wow! That must have been tough, but you continued to work on it, and look what you accomplished!" The latter communicates that continued effort can lead to attainment.

Grandparents can be highly influential in encouraging effort and the ability to be undaunted when faced with difficulty. It's a quality that is sometimes referred to as "tough mindedness" that we want our grandchildren to develop. At the same time we want to teach them about perseverance, we also need to help them learn about *fortitude*. This is the virtue that lies between the courage to continue trying and the waste of effort in chasing a lost cause. Helping children to gain the wisdom to know when to keep trying and when to quit can be very useful.

The current favored term in education to describe this quality in children is *grit,* referring to a combination of passion, tenacity, and perseverance. In the South, there's another familiar term. When asked in an interview shortly after the release of the book *Gone With the Wind,* about the theme of her book, author, Margaret Mitchell said,

> . . . it's about what quality lies within those who survive and those who go under. The old timers called it *gumption!* So I wrote about survivors. I wrote about those who had gumption and those who didn't. (*Atlanta Journal,* 1936).

Regardless of today's attitudes about her book or the times, it is an intriguing chronicle of how the characters, including the somewhat frivolous Scarlet, were forced to prevail through incredible hardships and adversity.

My favorite illustration of gumption—this mix of perseverance and fortitude—came from Ray, a deceased World War II veteran. He was a highly successful electrical engineer who worked all over the world but liked to tell the story of being a struggling freshman at Auburn University. He said that his rural high school and service in the Air Force had not prepared him for the rigors of Auburn's engineering classes after the war. Ray said that he felt so overwhelmed in the middle of his first year that he decided to quit.

Feeling like a victim, he packed his bag on a Saturday morning and rode the bus to his family's farm north of Birmingham. When he arrived, he found that no one was at home. Feeling incredibly lonely and discouraged, he walked outside and plopped down on the trunk of a fallen tree. As he sat there wallowing in his misery, he remembered his late grandmother and the times that he'd followed her around the farm when a child. Then, a particular memory flashed into his awareness. He looked across the backyard at the depression in the ground where the root cellar had been and remembered a time when his grandmother had brought a load of potatoes from the field. Grandma told him to put the potatoes in the cellar and cover them with straw. He remembered that when Grandma returned from milking the cow, she was upset that the young boy hadn't unloaded the potatoes as instructed. Ray remembered whining, "Grandma, I can't put all those potatoes in the cellar." But he said the elder retorted, "Of course you can, boy. Ain't you got no *gumption?* You gotta put that cart-full into small loads you can carry. Take your basket, fill it up, dump it into the cellar, and keep going. Don't look at the big cart. Just look at the one basket that you can carry at a time. Then, you'll finish the whole job in no time."

Remembering the scene, Ray said that's when he knew how to get through Auburn, one load at a time. Incredibly, having been at home for only a short time, he said that he walked to the highway, caught a Greyhound Bus back to Auburn, and never told anybody he'd decided to quit until years later. Ray liked to say that he conquered the demanding engineering program at Auburn with honors, because he had gumption.

Regardless of whether we call it grit, gumption, or perseverance, one of the most useful traits that we can give our precious grandchildren is the will to continue effort for a worthy endeavor and determine how they can approach a problem with energy and determination. To equip them for overcoming failure and becoming discouraged, we can tell stories, talk about our own experiences, and show them how to be clever in finding ways to apply their energies and efforts to accomplish big goals. Perhaps a precursor to confidence building, this grit, perseverance, and "plain old gumption" can prepare them for success.

Although resilience isn't typically regarded as part of character, perhaps it's the *result* of developing fortitude, perseverance, gumption, and grit. It's the ability to "bounce back" from adversity, illness, a poor home or school environment, and other factors that diminish normal growth and development. As Margaret Mitchell mused about how she wrote about survivors, we too can observe the difference between the child who succeeds, despite a stressful home environment and children who succumb to a terrible atmosphere of poverty or neglect. Even though children are subjected to negative influences, we know that many respond to encouragement, to having someone in their lives who cares, and expresses confidence and hope.

Instead of giving them flowery words about being strong or smart, we can motivate their resilience with such comments as, "That must have been difficult for you, but you kept trying until you got it!" or "That couldn't have been easy, but wow, you worked until you succeeded!"

Encouragement, confidence, and a reassuring grandparent can aid in building resilience.

Trust and Trustworthiness

Being able to *trust* adds to a child's sense of security and is critical to children's sense of well-being. Knowing that they have people on whom they can rely and who care about their safety and security is basic to their needs. One of the deficits of the child of an addicted teenage parent and an absent father is having adults they can trust. Without being sure of an environment of ethics and reliability; then anxiety, anger, or withdrawal and depression can result. Without an anchor of trust, children have little chance of school success or developing a secure sense of well-being. Without being able to trust, and without role models of trust, they are less likely to develop integrity or their own trustworthiness.

Trustworthiness, is taught over time through our being a role model and in the interactions of our relationships with grandchildren. They need to be able to believe in our integrity, benevolence, and our love. That's why it's essential that we acknowledge our mistakes and apologize for them. We grown-ups make many mistakes, both in our competence and in our intentions. Although it may be easier for others to overlook our incompetencies than our breaches of integrity, nonetheless, we must always admit, say, and mean, "I'm sorry" to the children. In doing so, we give them an important role model.

A key component of trustworthiness is predictability. We make it easier for the children to trust us if they have a sense of how we might respond. If we're casual and ignore their misdeeds today, but explode in anger tomorrow; they will be confused and their trust in us will be diminished. If we're attentive and comforting at one problem and ignore them another time, they can't be sure of our intent. They will not believe that they can depend on us if we fail to do what we say. Whereas, consistency in our demeanor, actions, and responses is the beginning of being trustworthy and a "rock" on which they can depend.

Helping children learn how and when they can trust others is a huge asset toward keeping them safe and contributing to the development of their EQ. They learn who can be trusted by observing that person's words and actions. The child learns who is trustworthy and becomes comfortable connecting with that person in friendship. They see and experience the consequences of associating with trustworthy versus untrustworthy people. Learning who can be trusted, in time, they learn the importance of being trustworthy. As they grow into adulthood, they develop the part of character that makes them highly valued in relationships and employment. Feeling such trustworthiness also adds to their sense of self-worth.

Respect and Manners

Teaching respect is an important part of teaching children what we refer to as "good manners"—the outward behaviors that carry our respect for others. Traditionally, respect was demanded of children and always given to older people, regardless. That assumption may not be a part of today's society. Instead, respect is a reciprocal attitude that is earned and best taught by practice. People who are regarded as having a high EQ are considered to be respectful of others.

Using manners is one way of interacting with others in ways that give regard to their space and movements. We teach respect through being a positive role model in being considerate, both to the child and to others. We model respect in the way that we interact with others. We teach respect in the care and concern that we demonstrate for others' needs and possessions.

Until a virus called Covid19 impacted our culture, teaching a child the importance of an effective handshake was a part of learning about manners. It was an important non-verbal form of communication in interpersonal skills.

From job candidates to business dealings, the handshake was attached to meanings beyond the mere touching of palms and fingers. Once a part of man-to-man greeting, it became an initial encounter for both genders, especially in late twentieth century business. The firm grasp, but not too tight, with eye contact and a smile, conveyed much. Learning this art in childhood was very useful in adulthood as the handshake was often the beginning of effective interpersonal interactions. The pandemic of the twenty-first century and the need to control infectious diseases, however, impacted our culture in many ways. At times, the rapid spread of diseases can make close personal contact too risky. Instead, we can teach grandchildren to smile, make eye contact, and make a kind-of wave with the hand. Some elders prefer the Indian custom of *namaste,* or the *wei* as it is done in Thailand. Both are similar with a gracious nod and slight bow with hands clasps just below the face. We also might prefer a gesture of respect and greeting from a safe distance. When there is no danger of transmitting germs, we may teach grandchildren the proper handshake and tell them about life before Covid.

While the rules of how we interact in society have changed drastically in our lifetimes, it's interesting to note that young people who know how to greet others, *write* a thank-you note, and demonstrate good interpersonal skills, command a huge advantage over others who have only equal technical skills.

Formal dinners may be superb opportunities to learn good table skills and effective social interactions to practice everywhere. Because my grandson has a severe allergy to nuts, we are always cautious about "dining out." When he was young, we were restricted to two small neighborhood restaurants that knew my grandson and practiced safe kitchen methods to accommodate him. Any dining not at home was in familiar places. I didn't realize how I had limited his opportunities, however, until we were on a trip in Florida when he was about eight. I splurged on a restaurant with a beautiful tropical view, live music, and all of the accoutrements of fine dining. My grandson thoroughly enjoyed the experience and his ability to demonstrate carefully cultivated table manners. It was a lesson for me about what I had overlooked. Although his parents and I had taught him table manners that were used at home, we had neglected to provide occasions for him to enjoy demonstrating his skills in an elegant restaurant.

Shortly after the Florida trip, a friend shared a story that confirmed the value of efforts toward civilized table manners. My friend said that her 25-year-old daughter had called to report on a first-date she'd been quite excited about. When her mother asked how she liked the young man, her daughter said, "Well, Mom, he made me appreciate you and Grandmother." Puzzled, the mother asked, "How's that?" The reply was, "Well, I guess he was okay, but I could never seriously like this guy because we met at a restaurant, and well, he was just disgusting." Of course, my friend started imaging all sorts of things and quickly asked, "How was he disgusting?" She laughed in relief at her daughter's quip that the two-year-old cousin had better table manners than this guy. The mother asked if the young man had other redeeming qualities, but her daughter said that she couldn't imagine sitting across the table from this slob, regardless of other qualities. The young woman ended the conversation with, "Even though it was a dull date, it made me appreciate Grandmother and you and how you taught us to hold a fork and not talk with a mouth full of food!"

Meal times aren't just a chance for teaching the young ones how to hold a fork, it's also a great time to model and teach conversation skills. Today's busy households may not contain adequate opportunities for calm, pleasant table conversation. Yet, mealtimes can be a prime time for connecting with the grandchildren, using stimulating topics and interesting questions. Other situations in the child's life may be focused on nutrition and just getting the children fed, but mealtimes at grandparents' home can be elegant, inviting, and opportunities for polite manners and engaging conversations.

Often, manners must be systematically and conscientiously taught. We grandparents can become accustomed to doing everything for the toddler—holding doors open, buckling them into car seats, and helping them into a booster chair at the dining room table. Just as with the control/independence issue illustrated in Chapter 2, it's easy to continue these chores when the child no longer needs assistance. I remember learning to be more aware when my grandson became big enough to handle large doors in public places. He especially liked "being a gentleman" and opening doors for Gran. I must admit that it was a bit of a jolt on the day when he opened the passenger car door for me and announced that he would drive me to our favorite coffee shop—gleefully demonstrating that he had become a *gentleman*. Although not typically regarded as a mark of character, the consideration conveyed in good social graces often communicates respect for others.

Demonstrating respect for others also includes consideration of their possessions. When children are allowed to be careless or to abuse another person's belongings, it sets them up for problems in school and in life. That's why we do not allow children to run amok when we visit friends. Some may advocate that it is up to the owner to set boundaries for what's permissible, but I contend that such an approach may threaten relationships. Preparation for what the child may do, where the child may play, and what the child may touch is essential for teaching how to be a good guest. It's a beginning of teaching good social interactions. Visiting friends provides another great opportunity for the GO BAG described in the next chapter. With young children, it's useful to take along a blanket or play mat that can be spread in an open space on the floor at the friend's house. This defines the play space and makes collecting toys and possessions easy when grandparents are ready to leave. It can also be insurance for preservation of the adult friendship.

Many courtesies, from opening doors for others to giving a seat to an older or disabled person when on a bus or tram seem to be somewhat universal, while some manners are regional or ethnic in origin. It's often said that when you hear the response of "Yes, Ma'am," you know you're in the South, but when the response is, "No, Madam," you know you're in the Northeast. Whatever your culture reflects, and whatever is important in your world, model it and teach the practices to the grandchildren from the time they're very young.

The familiar axiom, "When in Rome, do as the Romans" is probably good advice for social acceptance as social skills are often reflective of culture. If you grew up in a family in which the knife was placed horizontally across the top of the dinner plate when not in use, your children and grandchildren probably do the same. If you were part of a European tradition, the knife was probably held in the one hand and used to push food onto the fork.

Remembering another principle, that we are most comfortable when among people who reflect us, who are somewhat like us, it may be wise to make older children aware that it's polite to reflect others' manners. This is also a good time to talk about how "fitting-in" is useful in times when it makes others comfortable, and has no cost for us. The discussion can lead to crucial conversations about not conforming when it might result in a loss of values, or our own identity. Knowing when to "blend-in" or when to be a "stand-out" become critical lessons.

Unfortunately, television and media rarely provide good role models for children. The dancer from twentieth century movies, Fred Astaire is credited with observing that the hardest job kids have is to learn good manners without seeing any. We often laugh at the scenes in a movie or TV comedy when one of the boorish slob characters blunders into a situation and utters some obscene impolite comments. It's funny in entertainment because it's so inappropriate. Intentionally, there is little display of manners or demonstration of respect in today's comedies and entertainment because what makes us laugh is the irony and stupidity of the actions. Although it isn't funny when such incidents happen in real life, these scenes too often become the role model for our grandchildren's actions and communications.

Even though we do not have control of everything to which they're exposed, we can be supportive of the parents' teaching. We can be good role models of manners, respect, and exemplary social interactions when they're with us. We can be a support for their busy parents and present a different view of society.

Manners Are the Antidote to Harassment

Not many teens and young adults will be comfortable discussing sexual issues with their grandparents. They may not realize that we've had uncomfortable experiences—the professor with creeping hands and dirty jokes or the date who kept saying, "No, stop!" Actually, we may be as uncomfortable approaching the subject as they are, and yet, it's an essential topic that we may need to confront. It just requires an astute, crafty, and savvy approach.

We find the right moment when we're talking about the disrespectful behavior of a public figure. Then, we move to the subject of how we like to be with others who show us respect through their manners, and we can say:

> "Perhaps that most harassment issues that we hear so much about in the media would just disappear with good manners—if people treated each other with respect."

> "Manners are about respecting other people's space. If we demonstrate good manners, we don't bump into

people or touch them in ways that make them uncomfortable. We respect their space."

"We show others respect by giving them what they like. If you're with someone you know likes strawberries, you like giving them strawberries. But of course, if they say, 'Stop, I've had enough.' You don't cram berries at them. That wouldn't be respectful."

"When somebody is pushing strawberries, avocados, or anything that *you* don't like. Stop them and escape. You don't want to be around anybody who shows such poor manners and little respect for you."

"I like it when you hug me, but I don't want somebody that I dislike or don't know to hug me or touch me. That's presumptuous and disrespectful. You never want to be or be with one of those people who makes a competition out of seeing how much disrespect they can show others.

"When we find ourselves with people who have no manners or respect for others, it's just smart to distance ourselves and find friends who are more like us."

Conversations about sex are not easy for grandparents, and perhaps talking of strawberries seems silly. If they giggle or tell us that we're antiques, that's okay. Don't worry, strawberries or anything that eases the conversation and gets the point across can be useful. We must remember that the changes in social morés are significant from when we were their age, but some elements are the same. We humans are sexual beings, but we also like being in control of our own bodies, lives, and actions. We don't want anyone to intrude on our space or take away our control. Regardless of how we approach the conversation, whatever metaphors we use, or how silly we seem, we add to the young people's grasp of appropriate behavior when we increase their awareness.

Irrespective of our comfort level, we can be significant in reminding our grandchildren about the importance of respect and being respected. We can help them realize that manners are just a way of communicating that respect. We can also help grandchildren recognize that it's okay to decline unwanted and disrespectful behavior. We can help them realize that no matter how attractive and popular, or how much they like the person, if it's not a reciprocal, respectful relationship, it should be ended immediately.

Some psychologists point to a lack of relationship skill as the basis of much of what brings young people to counseling. They have difficulty in social and family relationships. They can't distinguish between romantic love and casual sex. They struggle in the workplace because they don't recognize that people who do quality work usually enjoy quality relationships with their colleagues. If we make exceptions for the "Eddie Haskell" types from the 1950's TV era of *Leave it to Beaver,* we usually find that people with what we call "good manners" also demonstrate effective interpersonal skills and respect. When we consider the overall impact of relationships to long-term success and happiness, it becomes impossible to minimize the importance of manners as one indicator of character and consideration of others.

Character and Career

As we attempt to guide the four-year-old, and as we try to influence the teen, we're looking ahead to the adult that this grandchild will become. We know how character and being a good person will impact their adult lives and happiness. We also know that long-term career success is more likely when built on a strong foundation of character.

As I've reflected on the importance of character development and social skills in children, I'm reminded of how often, when involved in hiring decisions for organizations, I've advocated consideration of character over skills. I've frequently said, "Go with evidence of good character." You can teach skills to the thirty-year-old, but we won't be able to teach integrity." In every selection/interview/hiring program that I've developed, I've always included a restaurant component for upper level candidates. One way to determine how an executive will interact with customers and supervise employees is to observe how he/she interacts with restaurant staff and hourly employees. In such situations, one test of character is to see how the person interacts with people who don't seem to matter and whether their manners demonstrate respect for others, regardless of rank or position.

Business writers, from the late Warren Bennis to Pat Lencioni, all seem to advocate similar attributes in promotion and hiring—character, competence, and ambition. Even though they have different names for these dimensions, in one way or another, they all look for the ability to "do the right things right, for the right reasons, to look for learning and growing in the future, and to treat people with value and respect." Perhaps one source of my zeal for character development comes from observing successful leaders. From schools to *Fortune 500* companies and the U.S. Department of the Interior, I've had the chance to see up-close the long-term different results that leaders of character produce. Although other people with less concern for honesty, accountability, ethics, and employee well-being can flourish for a time, they seem to achieve less satisfaction and less sustainability. Such people don't appear to be able to maintain long-term success. Often, they've neglected their families, taken some unfortunate short-cuts, and carry many regrets. Character is an important component of hiring and an essential ingredient of success.

Shared values are critical to career partnerships. Whether the fifteen-year-old wants to go into the lawn care business with a buddy, or the adult is forming a business partnership, mutual values matter. If the buddy is only in it for the money, is happy with a slip-shod job just to get paid, the responsible fifteen-year-old will be unhappy with the arrangement. In the same circumstances, if business partners don't share some values, the partnership is doomed. We can enjoy going to dinner or watching a movie with people of a very different value system, but if we must interact with them on a frequent basis, such as at work or in marriage, the relationship is usually more successful with people who share similar values. (More about clarifying values in Chapter 11)

Summary

Sometimes, it seems that, as a society, we have decided that virtue is an outdated concept and is no longer relevant. Yet, when we consider our culture, the lack of virtue appears to be very relevant to many of the problems that we see among us. Perhaps appreciating how crucial virtues are to a highly civilized and functional society, we grandparents can give our precious ones this enormous asset that can make a significant difference in their lives.

Character development is about establishing a system of beliefs that govern and guide actions. It doesn't happen overnight or with one lesson, but rather, begins in early childhood and is fortified through the years. Grandparents' influence in that development is a necessity to counteract the diverse onslaught that young children have from elements of society that are very self-centered, materialistic, and secular in emphasis. When we add to their parents' emphasis on character development, the children will grow into adults with integrity.

It's easy for us grandparents to focus on games and treats, assuming that our precious ones will learn character and life skills in maturity. Yet, one of the major attributes that will ensure success in school is that of perseverance. It's that grit to continue working and studying when the subject becomes difficult. It's that gumption to continue practicing when learning the skill seems overwhelming. Developing this tough-mindedness will be an asset all through life and a source of resilience through adversities.

We want grandchildren to find trustworthiness and security among family members, and recognize that other relationships are *optional.* We want their character development to be so strong that when their friends, classmates, or fraternity guys are engaging in unethical, questionable, or risky behavior, our grandchildren's sense of integrity will prevail. We want them to be stronger than the temptation to go along with the crowd. We want them to remember that if they find themselves with friends whose character is lacking, they will look for new friends, remembering to associate only with people whose presence motivates their best. We want their sense of character to be so indomitable that they will choose not to participate in anything immoral or illegal.

Our challenge is that we can't delay to start building that character. Their parents need our help in character development from early childhood. Since psychologists tell us that the basis of character is established by age six, we cannot afford to miss any opportunity to be influential. We can instill in them the essence of a quote partly attributed to newspaper publisher, Horace Greeley, about how fame, wealth, and popularity are fleeting, but *character* endures. Character is essential to success in life and grandparents can be significant to that success.

Grandchildren can be a mirror image of us as they model the traits of our character. Let's make it an exemplary reflection. When we grandparents do our part, the young people develop a solid character from which insight and discernment direct their actions. Then, all through their lives they will hear our voices saying,

Do what's right!

Let their memories include the importance of character.

Chapter 5

Special Opportunities for Grandparents

To foster their love of learning

As we hold the sleeping newborn, we contemplate the wonderful adventures we'll have, the exploring we'll do, and all of the learning we will experience together. In just a short time, we'll teach this little one to stack blocks, to catch a ball, and to enjoy the books that we'll read together. We smile as we anticipate all of the exciting time our relationship will bring. Then, we think about how precious this little one is and how important and productive the learning will be.

Making Time for Opportunities

Expressing unconditional love, caring, and interest is easy when all the baby does is look at us, coo, and smile. It's easy and great fun to clap and encourage when baby is able to roll-over, takes those first steps, or stacks one block on top of another. We can be generous with our encouragement during these early days. We can be liberal with our applause for the cute toddler, especially if we can return the child to the parent for any difficulties. Our challenge is to continue the expression of unconditional love and finding ways of communicating interest and encouragement as the child grows.

By the time the grandchild reaches what's sometimes known as "the terrible twos" stage, we may wonder what happened to the cute baby that we could cuddle in the rocking chair. Instead, we're faced with an often cranky, constantly in motion kid who is said to have a vocabulary of 200 words, but only says one—"NO!" At that point, it becomes easier to be busy when we're asked if we'd like a visit from the little monster, or to simply proclaim that we don't have the energy to provide a safe environment. We could just suggest that pictures be sent instead. It seems like the easy and smart way to simply wait until the child is older to see if we really like this kid because it's certainly different from that adorable infant who delighted us only yesterday. Although we joke about such reservations, we do secretly hope the child will become civilized so that we can begin to live out the imagined activities that we expected to have with this "whirling dervish" that may carry our genes and hold our hopes for the future.

While it's easy to abdicate all activities to the parents at this time, it's really the wrong decision. Just as when our children were this age, the stage of beginning independence must be encouraged and also endured. Although much patience may be required, it's essential to remain in contact with the two-year-old and continue cementing our relationships. It isn't possible to take a time-out in our relationship building just because we don't relate well to that age, or that they're too much trouble at that stage. Rather, it's essential to continue to build our bond of guidance and nurturing, regardless of the age or challenge.

Sometimes, it's easy to allow our opportunities for learning and making memories to degrade into child care, just watching the grandchildren to be sure they're safe, without much thought as to what they will do while with us. Anyone who's tried this approach has probably learned that, if we don't focus their activities, they'll make their own—not always the best for them or for us. Instead, it's more productive for everyone if we plan our time with the child. For example, we don't invite a friend to visit, and then just try to ensure his/her safety. We don't invite one of the guys over, turn on the TV, and ignore our friend. Instead, we invite friends to lunch or dinner, to watch sports, play cards, or to do something. When we issue invitations to others, it's usually with a purpose, plan in mind, and we interact with the guest. Visits from the grandchildren should not be different. They need a reason and activities for every visit.

As indicated in Chapter 2, ideal grandparent time is one-to-one. These focused interactions are impeccable for building influential relationships at any age, but can make indelible impressions on young children. If grandparent time is limited, restricted by geography or other circumstances, it may be necessary to see several grandchildren at once and with more than one grandparent; however, that may not the best possible arrangement. Since part of the magic of grandparent time is the focused attention, it's easier and usually desirable to see one grandchild at a time. At least, some the time should be with just one grandchild and one grandparent. If two grandparents are together, the other adult may be a distraction from the child focus. If there are two or more children, they may compete for grandparent attention.

We can make our time with grandchildren awesome. We can make it enjoyable for them and for us. Much of the time with them can become actual learning experiences. In the last fifty years, science has shown us the importance of a rich stimulating environment for brain development. The more we learn about how the brain matures, the more we see the need for the child to have stimulating surroundings. In addition to an invigorating atmosphere, brain development also requires care and protection.

We know the results of a stress free pregnancy with no alcohol or drugs for the mother, along with safety and protection from concussions during childhood and adolescence. When I read the research about brain development in young children, however, it made me want to wrap my grandson in bubble wrap and protect him from everything. Then, I remembered the issue of plastic and bisphenol (BPA) and decided that a plastic bubble wouldn't work either. I'd have to be more clever in protecting and stimulating his development. When I read about brain development and listen to lectures about how the brain works, I quickly concluded that my brain is not capable of comprehending most of the information. What I have gleaned, however, is that growing good brains is much like growing a garden. We look for and maintain ideal growing conditions. It seems that the best growing conditions for in utero, infant, childhood, and adolescent brains are simple —intellectual stimulation, exercise, good nutrition, adequate sleep, and no disease, alcohol, drugs, or stress. Just like plants must be protected from adverse conditions that jeopardize their growth, brains need protection too.

Be Alert for Safety, Improvements, and New Ways

When the first grandchild arrives, we must make some minor modifications in our households for this new family member's visits. Grandparent homes should be safe, inviting, and amenable to the grandchildren. Coming to visit us will not be pleasant for them or for their parents if everyone must be constantly alert for the open stairs, grandmother's antique glass, grandfather's gun collection, and the deck railing that the toddler can slip through. One certainty that we know is how quickly time flies through childhood. The joys of pleasant and stress free visits are made possible by the small sacrifices of storing the fragile and dangerous stuff. There will be plenty of time for displaying the antique music box and the delicate china figurines when the children are older. Such small accommodations make our homes more welcoming to little ones and their parents during this relatively brief time.

We must also renew our knowledge about infant care and safety. Should the sleeping infant be placed on back or stomach? Is baby safer sleeping in adults' bed or in a crib with slats that could entrap the tiny head? Should the baby be swaddled or blanketed? Yes, there are changes in practices with each new generation. As a child, I recall hearing my elderly grandmother talking about preparing toddler food in the days before much commercially produced baby food was available. When my daughter was born, I remember hearing my mother exclaim that the new high chairs and other furniture were a great improvement over what she'd had when my brother and I were young. Yet, when my grandson was born, I assumed that I was totally informed—until I was introduced to the "mothering chair" that replaced Grandma's rocking chair. That's when I realized that with each generation, not only do the tools and furniture change, there are many new advantages. I wonder what my Granny would say about the "Smart Sock" that monitors baby's heart and oxygen rates to prevent sudden infant death syndrome (SIDS). I also wonder if the smart baby monitor with wall mounted camera and high definition video/audio, sleep tracking, night vision, temperature, and humidity sensors would have made a difference in my own sleep deprivation during that first year of motherhood. As the tools and practices change, it would be easy to scoff at the new apps and the technological innovations, but really, anything that makes babies safer and parenting easier should be applauded. Okay, maybe we have a bit of envy that some of the suffering and anxiety has been removed, but we're really happy that each new generation has advantages.

Most recently, it's become essential for grandparents to be vaccinated against long forgotten childhood diseases, such as whooping cough. But there are many other safety precautions that grandparents must take, sometimes, before the new family member's first visit. Although great-grandmother might have positioned a napping baby on an adult bed and put pillows all around, today, there are better ways. The purchase of a portable crib and other equipment may be a good investment, but as soon as the child becomes ambulatory, it's critical to conduct a safety inspection. Even if there are infrequent visits, new grandparents must be especially cautious because it may have been many years since we've been in the "safety mindset." Sharp corners, electrical outlets, dangling appliance cords, household chemicals, gate locks, furniture that can tip over, stairs that must be blocked, and anything that could become a hazard to a young child must be checked. If there's a swimming pool, fish pond, or any water space, we must consider purchasing a surface alarm. Children under age three can drown is less than 30-seconds, much faster than older children or adults. Since any amount of water is a magnet for little ones, children must be totally supervised when near water in any amount greater than for drinking. In addition, it's imperative to program emergency numbers into cell phones, including the nearest poison control.

Appendix A contains a list of possible hazard reminders for use to prepare grandparents' home to make it safe and hospitable. Because young children like to jump, climb, and explore, it's wise to remove hazards that will attract their play. It's imperative to remain alert to possible hazards because of the difficulty in predicting what a quick and determined grandchild can sometimes make into a threat to their safety as the 13-month-old in this photo. Children with behavioral or developmental issues may be at even greater risk for accidents.

One of the threats to children's safety that we may overlook is how to keep them away from food borne illnesses. Hand washing and food preparation safety become even more important for younger children whose immune systems are not fully developed to combat pathogens. By never retrieving a pacifier from the floor and sticking it into the child's mouth, we may be preventing unnecessary discomfort and illness for the child. Floors can be very dirty places, especially in public areas. It's amazing what a toddler can scoop up and put into the mouth.

Preventing young children from excessive touching in public areas becomes even more critical during outbreaks of communicable diseases. Yes, anticipating the problems these grandchildren can encounter requires considerable effort and trouble, but it's all worth the effort to care for their well-being.

Another serious hazard may be the docile family pet that has never harmed anyone. Most often, a cat will hide from "that creepy dubious little stranger," but we cannot depend on Sylvester's good behavior. Cats can be unpredictable. A dog may also have an unexpected reaction, especially to a toddler. The first problem that the toddler presents is that it may be of similar size and on the same eye level as the dog. The child may be delighted and fascinated by the furry pet that looks like many of his/her toys. The dog, however, may regard the intruder differently and could even become suddenly aggressive with the child. More than one pediatrician and emergency room physician has told stories of mangled faces and hands caused when a crawling baby reached for the family pet's chew toy. Until the child is old enough to interact appropriately with pets, understands where to touch, and how to move around the animal; it may be best to keep critters outside or restrained during the grandchild's visit. Even though we may consider the pet to be a member of the family, the pet may not be eager to accept an unpredictable child. It would be difficult to continue to live with and enjoy a pet that harmed a grandchild.

When considering the evolving changes in both equipment and accepted practices, it becomes apparent that grandparents must be alert, well informed, or defer to the parents in order to provide the best practices for nurturing that precious new life in the family. Even though it's easy to "fall back on" our own childhood or parenting experiences, it's better for the family when grandparents learn the new ways or concede and cooperate with the parents. We may scramble to learn new methods, adopt new practices, and modify our concepts to accommodate grandchildren and parents' practices, but the outcome is certainly worth our compromises. Unless addiction, abuse, incarceration, or death necessitates that we must assume full custody and responsibility for the child, the parents must always be the primary decision makers and the ones who set the standards and expectations.

Every Moment with Grandparents is a Time for Learning

For some older people, there may be a tendency to assume that the routines we knew or the way it was during our childhood will be good enough for our grandchildren, but times and society have changed considerably in the decades since our childhoods. A century ago, a child might visit a grandparent's home with no agenda, but in those days, there was much to explore, and children were usually free to roam safely. Recently, my cousin reminded me of how our grandmother showed us how to play hopscotch on the sidewalk and "rock school" on the porch steps. Granny had no Legos or Lincoln Logs, but she entertained us with a box of odd buttons and a Crisco can of clothes pins. Today, we cringe at the mere idea of the choking hazard of giving buttons to small children. Just as the world's environment has forced changes in what children can be allowed to do, the changes force us to be more resourceful, to plan, to think ahead, and develop activities and an atmosphere that allow us to focus our attention on the child. We need time and spaces to interact with the young ones and to nurture the discoveries and learning.

The key is to consider the child's needs. The first year requires our full attention for the baby's every waking moment. The second year allows few moments when we can turn our attention away for even a minute. By the third year, we've learned, and the child has certainly learned, that the focused attention and our time together is too much fun to allow distractions to diminish the joy. In the past, when grandparent time was primarily for baby sitting or child care, the goal was to make as many situations as possible where there weren't opportunities for the kids to be too noisy, too active, or present too many problems. However, if we regard our role, not as caretaker, but as influential grandparents, instead of this being a "driving-me-crazy" time, we can make it into a great opportunity to interact with the child. We can begin the practice of one-to-one time for grandparents in many fun adventures together. From simple play activities, everything from pouring water into different measuring cups to walking around the back yard, can be fun. Anything can become an exploration and an adventure. This is when we begin to send the message to the child that grandparent time is a wonderful time for learning. Almost everything is new and can be made into an exciting introduction, especially for very young children.

Holidays present special opportunities for fun and learning. Halloween for young children is an exciting opportunity for playing dress-up. For young ones, it cannot be about "All Hallows Eve," ghosts, or goblins. It's all about *pretending* and imagining being different characters. Christmas presents weeks of crafts, art, and kitchen activities. Every holiday can be made into a grand adventure. It's important, however, to distinguish between a religious significance and secular celebration. We dye eggs and laugh at the story of the Easter Beagle, but we don't want the little ones to expect the Easter Bunny at a Passover Seder. We certainly delight in reading *The Night Before Christmas,* but we're careful not to confuse Santa with Jesus or dilute the real meaning of these holidays.

With some ingenuity, we can do more than just provide safety. We can ensure that they thrive by providing activities, adventures, and bright sunshine where their love of learning takes root. We can make every experience with us a delightful adventure for discovery.

Activities at Home

Recently, I saw a young woman who'd been a student in the Early Learning Center at St. Nicholas School where I had designed the curriculum long ago. She said that she thought of me when teaching her young son how to close a door quietly. I laughed as I remembered those first-day activities for four-year-olds. After greetings and helping every child to be comfortable, I walked around the building with each group, reading every EXIT sign. Learning "the way out" was the important first word for them to read. The second lesson was being able to turn the handle, close the door, and gently release the handle so that it didn't make a loud disruptive noise or pinch little fingers. It was the beginning of their learning independence in being able to leave the room to go to the bathroom safely. And you guessed it, the next lesson was about going to the bathroom and completing those needs. As I also thought about how I taught them to stand behind their small chairs, safely lift and carry them from the back, I reminisced on the many practical and useful tasks they were taught.

Most of my philosophy of teaching independence in everyday skills came from the early twentieth century Italian physician, Dr. Maria Montessori (1914). In observing children, she noticed how frequently they were drawn to learning practical tasks over playing with toys. By being able to gain control over the little things in the environment, they gained confidence and independence. For example, being able to put on and take off a coat without pulling the sleeve lining out can be a delightful achievement when it's time to go outside. Gaining mastery over everyday living tasks gives children a great sense of pride.

Over and over, I'm reminded how easy it is for us grandparents to fall into a pattern of assisting and doing tasks for the child that the child can do independently. It isn't appropriate to do everything for the child. Instead, we must teach the child to do. Countless times in leadership development, I have said, "The leader must do for the team only what the team is not yet ready to do for themselves." Maybe I'd learned that from working with young children.

*We grandparents must do for the grandchildren only what they are not **yet*** ready to do for themselves.

It's that gradual evolution of independence that we discussed nurturing earlier. We learned it during our parenting years. Now, we re-learn it all over again.

It's amazing how much fun and enjoyment little ones gain from learning simple tasks. I've never been a fan of the efficiency engineers of the Industrial Revolution era, or of applying those theories to education or grandchildren, but one practice that can be useful is the concept of *task analysis*. This idea of breaking every task into each part and considering how to make it as efficient as possible is a great boon for children. For example, it's very difficult for a three or four-year-old to put a coat or jacket on a coat hanger in the same way we grown-ups do it. Instead, we show the child how to lay the coat on a low bed or play table. The child can slip the hanger inside of the jacket, and voila, it's ready to be placed in the closet or on a low hook. Of course, it's easier and safer to avoid a wire hanger and use a small plastic hanger instead.

As we think about how to analyze and systematically teach children to perform other household tasks, we contribute to their long-term independence. At the same time, we learn how many steps they can follow, one-at-a-time. In the coat example, we would say:

1. "First, let's lay the jacket on the play table with the sleeves pointing out so that you can see the front."

2. "Then, let's slide the hanger into the open front."

3. "Let's check to be sure that each end of the hanger is inside of the top of the sleeve."

4. "Now, pick-up the curved top part of the hanger."

5. "And wow! You can hang your jacket on the hook and it's all ready for you to go outside again."

Don't be surprised if the child wants to repeat the process as children typically like to practice a newly learned skill. Other fun tasks are learning to fold hand towels or T-shirts, putting groceries on shelves, along with sorting socks and utensils. Young children seem to enjoy anything new that grown-ups usually do. The key is in choosing tasks that interest them and that they can succeed in completing. If the task is too easy, it will be of little motivation. If it's too difficult, their attempts will be thwarted and they could become discouraged.

It's tempting to jump into giving the child too much help too soon. Instead of interfering, when we see the child struggling, we offer gentle suggestions, but keep "hands off." As long as the child is persistent but not frustrated, we must allow their trial and error. We begin to encourage their perseverance from the time they are toddlers and applaud their continued efforts. That's how they learn.

Perhaps in previous generations, we thought that by doing everything for the children, we were being dutiful grandparents. What we did, however, was to make them dependent upon us. What we've learned is that by helping them to become independent, they have better memories, a more solid sense of responsibility, and greater gratitude for what they've learned from us.

Kitchen Activities

Playing house should not be gender related but independence related. When we reflect on favorite memories of our grandparents, it's likely that there's something about preparing a special food, playing with pots and pans, or splashing in the water at the kitchen sink that was fun. Maybe it's because grandparents seem to spend much time in the kitchen or maybe it's because the children like what we create there, but the kitchen seems to be a favorite play area for grandchildren. Especially in winter months, the kitchen can be an inviting place for some home activities that will captivate the child's attention and furnish interesting discoveries.

Kitchen activities can make incredible memories. Perhaps because I have such warm memories of my grandmother's sugar cookies, these photos of my daughter

sit on my desk. The first is when she was proudly displaying her cookies baked at grandmother's, and the second, when she was a college student in her own apartment kitchen and I arrived to find her icing cookies. The little girl grew, but the overalls and delight in baking cookies remained. It's difficult to say whether the greater fun is in the baking or eating treats with grandparents. Regardless grandparents' kitchen is an incredible place for making lasting memories.

Appendix B contains some activities that are really *idea starters* about enjoyable pursuits that focus the child's attention and can be great resources for learning. These are simple activities that can take place at home, and adjusted to be appropriate for the child's age. Generally the activities require minimal financial investments. Of course, you could hand the kid an iPad, or new video, but it's better to save such passive activities for when you need to prepare a special dinner or take an important phone call. When there is a video, then talk about it, ask questions about what the characters did and what made it fun to watch.

Make the most of the child's time with you. Make it really *with you*—a time when your attention and interactions are completely focused on the grandchild. Those become the memorable times. Unless you're cooking over an open fire or doing something potentially dangerous in the kitchen, invite the child to join you. Many children delight in kitchen activities, such as making cookies or baking bread. If your home arrangement can accommodate a frequent visitor space in your kitchen, create a small area where young ones can have child sized equipment that they can use to "cook" with you. Kitchen activities can also be a great opportunity to expand the diet. When children have learned how to break asparagus tips at the right spot or slice a banana with a plastic knife, then they may be more open to tasting what they've made. A plastic apron, small cups, pitchers, and the kitchen sink can provide endless

diversions. Even if a couple of dish towels are necessary, it's a small inconvenience to the delight of the child's discovering how the water swirls as it goes down the drain and learns the new word, *vortex*.

Kitchen activities can accommodate all sorts of learning and fun. For example, when the child is learning to count, the kitchen can provide endless objects—everything from spoons, cans, and potatoes, or anything that will not be a choking or safety hazard. A way to cultivate an interest in reading is when the child begins to recognize letters. Pour a box of salt into a simple tray and shake until the tray is covered. Then guide the little fingers into making shapes or capital letters. Although it seems natural to proceed in alphabetical order, it is easier for the child to begin with the first letter of the child's name, saying the letter and its name as you make it. Then, gently shake the tray and begin again. When that letter has been mastered, continue with H, I, L,T, and other letters, one-at-a-time, that are easy for the child to say and shape, saving the curved ones for later visits. Then, when driving, shopping, or doing other activities, look for the new letter that's been learned on signs and in other places.

Don't worry about the child's understanding correct alphabetical order. The nursery song seems to take care of that bit of learning. What makes the salt letter activity good for the child is not only the precursor to writing, but your closeness, your guiding the little hand, and the wonder of the discovery. The same tray and technique can be used for drawing simple shapes and saying the names of square, triangle, and circle. Incidentally, if some salt is spilled, it's easily wiped away with a damp towel. This kind of activity can be taken outside in pleasant weather and done with sand. Having used a large plastic tray on my deck, filled with sand, I can tell you that it's very adaptable and a fun learning tool, but best to keep the sand outside!

For children of ages four through twelve, and even beyond, holidays often provide terrific opportunities for kitchen adventures. For example, making a gingerbread house can be as simple or as complex as you desire. It can be constructed from store bought graham crackers, candies, and prepared icing or as elaborate as the Greenbrier Hotel or Williamsburg Inn's version. The product isn't as important as the fun of building it together. The holiday cookies and treats you've made together can become more memorable when consumed in ceremonious tea parties that take place at a child size table and with the proper small tea set. Independence Day, Flag Day, and summer picnics are wonderful opportunities for making round, square, and triangular shaped sandwiches that may be packed in a basket, only to be consumed in the backyard or the nearby park as you celebrate together.

Another kitchen activity that's great fun is playing with dough—any dough. Making and kneading bread dough is exciting. Of course, cookie dough is fun to slice or drop. Play dough can be fun and presents a good opportunity to teach young children that we never eat dough. Perhaps a preferable play dough is one of the home-made recipes that use soda, salt, and water or cooking oil. This dough is easy to make and can be used for shapes with plastic utensils or cookie cutters. (See Appendix B)

Learning table setting is great fun for the five or six-year-old. It's easy to begin with inexpensive plates and important to teach the child how to handle utensils to keep them clean and germ free. This skill also develops a sense of responsibility as the child can offer help, not only at your house, but also at home. Although first attempts are not likely to rival the formal dining room at Downton Abbey, such tasks can build self-confidence.

Preparing and enjoying a *tea party* can be great fun, especially to brew chamomile tea and read Beatrix Potter's story of *Peter Rabbit*. Baking cookies or small cakes can be

an added treat. The daffodil adds to the festive springtime celebration, and also shows the scale of a tea party appropriate for ages three to seven.

If baking is not your thing, then cutting small pieces of sliced white bread, spreading with a bit of butter, and sprinkling with a mixture of ground cinnamon and sugar will make a fine substitute, especially if the child can do the spreading and sprinkling. A few moments under the broiler, or in the toaster oven, and these tiny tidbits make a nice complement to your tea party. Consuming the goodies at the kitchen counter makes a pleasant treat, but moving the party to a child-size table and chairs makes it delightful, especially when accompanied by attentive eye contact and conversation.

For members of the older generation, it's easy to fall into the gender trap of thinking of the tea party as a girlie activity, but when that little boy grows up and is studying or working in England, he'll be expected to be familiar with the tea rituals. Tea sets need not be frilly and can be appropriate and enjoyable for masculine settings, but if tea is not your thing, try having a *Chocolate Party* for your grandson. Pouring hot chocolate over tiny marshmallows can be just as much fun. What contributes so much to these rituals is that you're pouring from a small tea or espresso pot, drinking from the same small size cup as your grandchild, and sitting in a small chair at the child's eye level—even though your knees are cramped. It's this eye level communication and interaction that creates an emotional intimacy, even for the very young child. Of course, we must always arrange such settings so that spills or accidents don't ruin the mood. By avoiding having a tea party on our best rug, or with fragile china, the

inevitable spills just become the inevitable wipe-ups. Incidentally, the teapot, demitasse pot, cups, saucers, and placemats in the photos were just junk shop finds that were less than the cost of a toy set.

Regardless of the culinary product, and occasion for consumption, most children enjoy being able to take home a tin of cookies, a bowl of grilled veggies, or something to show, share, and talk about with others. It becomes a way for them to extend the fun of time in the kitchen with you. Just as they enjoy baking cookies, icing cakes, and peeling fruit, they will learn to enjoy the clean-up. Even though we may not treasure the drudgery of loading the dishwasher or wiping pans, the child must not be deprived of finishing the whole project. Allowing the child to be a part of the clean-up is part of how we teach the cycle of play, projects, and much that we do—with completion.

In time, we soon learn that it isn't the activity that is as important as the interaction. Giving a child crayons or markers and paper can capture his/her attention for a while. Drawing together, however, is far more enjoyable. As the shapes, colors, and purpose of the art work are discussed, the activity becomes more meaningful.

It's not unusual for busy men to relegate child rearing to women, and therefore, miss the chance to develop a strong bond with young grandchildren. Just as Holly treasured her time with Papa, every child should be given the chance to enjoy both grandparents. It's easy to assume that it isn't safe for young children to be in a man's basement workshop or present in other typically male activities. Yet, some of the best memories of my grandfather were our walks in the woods and my time in his woodworking shop where I would draw in the layer of sawdust on his workbench and build structures from his wood scraps. Both boys and girls often enjoy driving large nails into a piece of soft fiberboard with a small hammer. With some instruction and minimal supervision, and after the major hazards have been decommissioned or unplugged, Grandpa's shop may be a wonderful place to practice eye/hand coordination. The key to making it a pleasant and safe experience for everyone is to eliminate possible safety problems before the child enters the shop. Such experiences help to build the child's confidence and enhance the relationship with grandfather.

One reminder is that we now live in a less gender discriminating world than we may have experienced as a child. We cannot surmise that time in the shop, working in the yard, or playing golf is only for grandsons. These can be great experiences for granddaughters, grandsons, and grandparents.

Just as in the kitchen, it's important to remain attentive and alert to prevent accidents in the workshop. Unfortunately, it's easy to assume that time is being spent with the grandchild, but when we're really focused on our other activities, the child doesn't feel our companionship. With younger children, and especially when potential hazards are present, it is critical to be *with* the child, not doing our own thing *in the presence* of the child.

Making a Space for the Grandchildren

When grandchildren are frequent visitors, we can soon acquire an array of toys and materials to support their activities and guide their attention, all of which can quickly become a storage issue as the collection grows. Having toys unique to grandparents' house is all part of the excitement of the visit. Having the house look like a disaster area when the child leaves, however, is highly unsatisfactory for us and not a good habit for the child. Instead, this too can be part of teaching self-discipline. From the toddler stage, teaching the child that choosing the toy, playing with it, and replacing it to its designated storage area all becomes part of the cycle of play. One way to encourage this practice is to avoid the words, "clean-up," or "put your toys away," at the end of the visit when the child is tired and time may be short. Instead, try the suggestion of, "Finish playing

with the toy." That means replacing the toy to its storage place when choosing another toy. To make it easier for the child of any age, open shelving is preferable for storing their toys and activities. This enables easy access and return and is far preferable to the old-fashioned toy box with a lid that smashed little fingers. Although a big toy bin that can be stashed out of sight when not in use may seem logical, open shelving in the area where the child spends the most time at your house will produce the best results for play. It will also leave a neat play space ready for the next visit, and most important, teach the child responsibility, independence, and self-discipline. Upper shelves can be used for storing holiday items or toys that are waiting to return to the resale shop.

These neatly arranged shelves are a magnet for the curious child, and at the same time, begin the process of helping him/her learn the value of an organized environment. Learning this follow-through and organization skill will be a tremendous asset all through the school years and into the workplace. Learning this bit of self-discipline is easier for some children than others. The key is to make the suggestion of "Finish playing with this toy before you choose another," and gently help the child with replacement on the shelf. Even though complete learning may not be accomplished quickly, it is an important ritual that will be significant to the child in many ways. It also helps to verbally acknowledge the child's routine replacement, especially in the beginning stages of teaching the process.

As the child grows, and a variety of building and construction toys become part of the repertoire, inexpensive plastic bins or boxes that fit the open shelves may be useful for organization. If all of the toys and materials are thrown together, they may appear overwhelming to the child, and seem less inviting for play. Wooden puzzles with pieces askew aren't nearly as inviting as a rack or stack of the same wooden puzzles that can be taken apart and reassembled. Incidentally, very young children like to begin a puzzle with all of the pieces in place. We may be tempted to turn the wooden tray over and dump the pieces out, but a better approach is to help the child remove each piece, right side up, and lay it beside the tray. As they remove each piece, they learn where the piece fits. Again, it's a more structured, inviting way to play with the beginner puzzles as we interact and verbally guide placement when help is needed.

With older children, board games become more important. Many are fun and entertaining, but the most valuable ones teach strategy and decision making. Everything from Tic-Tac-Toe, to *Connect Four, Scrabble,* and the various editions of *Monopoly* can be great fun, as long as excessive emphasis on *winning* is avoided. The child should not be deceived into always being the winner, but neither should a competitive grandparent dominate the game. This may be a good time for the introduction of luck and chance in some games that will help the child to recognize the improbability of gambling or playing the lottery. As the child grows, the importance of introducing and using board games increases. As an adolescent, when friends come to "hang-out," the grandchild will be accustomed to interacting and playing games as favorite activities. It's useful to teach grandchildren to plan recreation with friends and avoid leaving a group of children to "make their own mischief."

Recently, I was invited to the home of a friend to meet her three-year-old granddaughter, a delightful, energetic, and intelligent little girl who I found fascinating. After the child's mother came from work to take the child home, my friend and I chatted over coffee as she quickly told me of her exhaustion from too much child care. Although she adored her only grandchild, she confided that it was becoming overwhelming to keep the child "occupied" while she did her normal routines. She said that the little girl was very attention seeking, chattered incessantly, and that she would be glad when the child was in kindergarten so that she could "have her life back."

I assumed that my task was just to listen to the frustrations of a friend, but she asked for my help and seemed genuinely eager for some suggestions. I asked if we could look at the child's play area and she took me to an upstairs walk-in closet that contained three laundry baskets tossed full of obviously old toys. When I asked about their origin, she said that most had belonged to her son (who was then 35), and that she had kept them. When I examined the toys, I found that many were broken or with missing parts. As I held them, I wondered what the child was supposed to do with them.

As we walked downstairs, I asked my friend how she wanted things to be different during her time with the granddaughter. She just looked at me and finally said, "I don't know. I love her dearly, but I just want it to be easier when she's here." After listening patiently to more of her concerns, I suggested that we look for a place near her kitchen or family room where she would be comfortable with the child. The next afternoon, we found a set of low shelves to fit unobtrusively there. After a trip to the local discount store for six red plastic "dishpans" that became bins for *Duplos* and other playthings with multiple parts, we sorted through the laundry baskets of "toys." She chose her son's special ones that she wanted to keep, the ones to dispose of, and some that could go onto the new shelves. A few days later, the three of us went on the kind of toy buying adventure described in the following section. We began by purchasing two child size chairs and a folding child size play table. Today, my friend still talks about the transformation in her relationship with her granddaughter.

She describes how she actually plays and interacts with the child, how the child will play independently when she's nearby, and how she treasures their time together.

Candidly, this is an intelligent woman with considerable financial resources. As I have watched her frequent shopping trips for new clothes and trips to donate last year's clothes, I was puzzled why she didn't provide more stimulating materials and activities for the child. It was easy to see the problem with the three-year-old—the child was bored! The little one flailed through the laundry baskets of broken toys looking for something to engage her curiosity. When she didn't find it, she followed grandmother around looking for something to engage her attention. To maximize influence with grandchildren, we must be resourceful and use our problem solving skills.

This friend could certainly afford to supply a relevant inventory of interesting and stimulating toys, but we grandparents can provide wonderful toys and activities without spending much money. A favorite example was a fishing game created from a small plastic bucket, along with a 12" plastic ruler. After tying a piece of yarn on one end, and a magnet on the other end of the yarn, we had a fishing pole. I cut fish shapes from colored paper, and made the mouths by attaching large metal paper clips. We scattered the colorful fish on the kitchen floor and called it a pond. Then, I would say to my grandson, "Can you catch a blue fish?" Catching each colored fish with the fishing pole and depositing it into the bucket made great fun. For another visit, after playing fish colors was mastered, I wrote letters on each fish with a black marker and my grandson would catch the fish letter that I named and dump it into the bucket. When the letters were conquered, we would put three fish letters together to "catch" three-letter words. We also made a version using numbers. This was an early introduction to magnets that was fascinating. It's a wonderful learning invention but only if there's no danger of the child's putting the magnet or a paper clip into the mouth.

The grandparents' play shelves anchor joyous times for the countless visits, but the key to making this area an adventure to which the children look forward, is in keeping the contents relevant. They must change as the children grow. In the middle childhood years, such additions as complex Legos, the cubes that make electric circuits, art materials, and articles that reflect the growing child's interests will extend the fascination. For older children, the "toys" may need to be replaced with crafts, art supplies, complex puzzles, and science activities. Whatever the contents, the play shelves will create many memories as long as the contents are focused on the child's interests and needs for learning. We can put vast amounts of money into the contents of the shelves, or we can be clever and thrifty. On-line sources, recycled toys from friends, resale shops, and grandparent ingenuity can ensure that there are always exciting activities there.

Buying Toys

When the first grandchild arrives, it's typical to rush out and buy an armload of cute and pricey rattles and mobiles. I certainly succumbed to that excitement. In time, we remember that, just like the child's clothes, most toys have a short shelf life and are often cast aside after six months to a year. Even though we may continue to purchase *new* holiday gifts, stuffed animals, and toys that can't be thoroughly cleaned, we soon discover the wisdom of the resale shop. In many areas of the country, this is one of the different options available since our own children were young. Resale shopping not only enables grandparents to spend less money, and perhaps, buy more toys, such shops are a great resource for periodic returns. Just as children out-grow clothing, they also out-grow toys. About twice a year, it's useful to note the toys that have become ignored. They can be removed and stashed away for a few weeks. If the child doesn't miss and ask for them, it's time to return them to the resale shop or give them to another child. Although some favorite toys become "keepers forever," most can move-on and bring joy to other children. Open shelving, with an inventory of puzzles, books, toys, crayons, water colors, paper, and materials that are age appropriate, provide on-going insurance of fun times with the grandparents.

A trip to the toy store can be an exciting and entertaining adventure for young children. Although not an option in times of contagion, some stores may offer play spaces where the child can try-out the toy. Just as in any activity, it's important to prepare the child and set the expectations. First, this preparation ensures a pleasant activity for everyone *and* it increases the learning opportunity for the child. As indicated in Chapter 3, we simply announce that we're going to the toy store and we're going to be there for ___ amount of time. We will *look* at as many toys as the child wants to see. We will walk together on each aisle as we look, but we cannot open any of the packages. Finally, the child is free to choose *one* toy to take home. It can be anything that the child likes that doesn't cost more than $___ amount of money.

This is a great place to practice and see the effectiveness of our influence. It's easy to distract the child and guide to better choices. With some clever diplomacy, we can usher the child to the most appropriate toys and prices that fit our wallet. The Bat Man mask can be avoided by diverting attention to some spectacular little train car or Lego kit. Remember, this is the perfect time for our guidance and influence, not our "because I said so" control. There's no need for the child to have a tantrum, because we can be more resourceful. Instead of controlling by swooping up the screaming child, we control the situation with our guidance and clever teaching. This can be a useful time for learning that we cannot have everything we might want and how to make good choices.

Watching the child's play and what attracts his/her attention can be revealing. When not restricted by the threat of contagion, I like to utilize play spaces that allow children to "try out" the toys. In any case, I have a bias for toys that stimulate a long attention span. These are often the toys that enable different options for play, such as building blocks, transportation sets, and miniature structures that accommodate assembling in different ways. Wooden trains, blocks, bricks, doll houses, and play sets that support imaginative play and can be built, erected, connected differently, and that stimulate the child's imagination will hold a fascination much longer than some of the plastic, single-function, brand name toys. The toys that come with a box or a tray for replacing the many pieces are especially valuable because they encourage the child to "finish playing" and are ready and much more attractive for the next play session.

Obviously, the suggested toy store technique may be problematic to attempt with a two-year-old, but by age three or four, if we have gradually taught the child our technique, it can be filled with learning opportunities about time, money, decision making, and delayed gratification. When the child begins to develop basic math skills, it can be very useful to give the child cash in the amount that will be spent before entering the store. Then, when the toy is selected, allow the child to pay for the toy. This is a great time to begin teaching about money, but it's less tangible if a credit card is used. It can also be good for applying grandparents' influence while having great fun, if we remember the necessary hand sanitation afterwards.

Another technique for purchasing toys is to seek an on-line resource. A simple internet search for educational toys will produce selections for different ages. But before making a purchase, it's advantageous to think about what the child will do with the toy, how the toy will stimulate play, and if the toys present any safety hazards. For example, I'm fond of shape sorters, but I'm uneasy about the ones with pegs because if the shapes are not stacked there, those empty pegs can be dangerous to a falling toddler. Young children love rolling things down ramps, but when buying, it's best to choose the ramp toys with little wooden cars or tennis size plastic balls, avoiding marbles or anything that can become a choking hazard. It's essential to also overcome the temptation to go for the toys and activities that appeal to us. Rather, watch what appeals to the grandchildren. The cool art pencils that look terrific to grandmother may have less appeal to the young math whiz who would enjoy fraction circles or an electric circuit board.

It's useful to remove the outgrown and no longer challenging toys. With appropriate rotation, we can keep a new and fresh attraction ready for the next visit. Through watching what captivates the child's curiosity, by looking at how the child learns, and noticing what holds the child's attention, we gain cues for choosing the right toys and activities. If you go a bit daffy in the toy stores, as I frequently did, you can delight the grandchild, but it's also possible to provide equal enjoyment and learning without expensive purchases.

If the grandchild is a regular visitor to grandparents' home, the child will learn that there are toys at home and toys at grandparents' house. Leaving the toys at grandparents' house is a part of learning to adapt to different places. These toys add to making return visits inviting, especially for toddlers who may have occasional separation anxieties. In situations where visits are less frequent, it may be appropriate for the child to take any new toys home after the visit, especially if a return visit is not soon anticipated. Unfortunately, the toy that is fascinating today may be outgrown in the future.

The Sandbox

One of the most delightful kinds of child's play is with sand. At the beach, we can dig, find shells, build castles, and mold letters. With a big umbrella and sufficient sun screen, we can enjoy endless play and fascination. At the grandparents' house, a sand box can provide more sand play. The two-year-old loves to dig with little plastic spoons and shovels, to fill cups, buckets, and molds. As the child grows, the sand box can become a place for creative play, for building cities, and developing budding architects. A collection of miniature houses, cars, and animals can be complemented by sprigs of shrubbery and other objects chosen from the child's imagination to create intriguing landscapes.

I'm a big fan of providing a sandbox and can share some useful tips gleaned from experiences. When my daughter was young, she had an outdoor sandbox that was on the ground. When she played *in* the sandbox, it was a drag for me because I had to uncover, remove any leaves or insects that had crept in, and then, hose her down when she tired of the sand. With my grandson, I learned that the sandbox doesn't need to be large. The toy stores have some nice models, but a large plastic bin with a bag of sand from the hardware store can work well. Even a plastic box could provide hours of fun. There's an advantage in having it raised to a comfortable height for the child, allowing the child to play *with* the sand, but not be *in* the sand. That makes a great difference for the clean-up after the play. I also learned that in some parts of the country, it's better to locate the sandbox on a deck or screened-in porch than to expose the child to insects or the sandbox to debris and visits from the neighbors' cats. Yes, I always had to grab the broom or vacuum cleaner after the grandson's visit, but watching his delight was far greater than any problem from the clean-up. And his clean-up was usually just a matter of

washing hands, whereas, my daughter required a complete bath after every sandbox adventure.

The objection that adults may have to sand play is fear that the child will rub the eyes with a sandy hand or throw the sand. Our vigilance prevents the eye injury and the problem of throwing sand can be eliminated by some cleverness. Simply take a bucket of sand into the garden or back yard and have the child throw handfuls until the enjoyment is satiated. Then, we say,“That was fun, but no more throwing sand, instead, let’s use it for making ____.” That one episode is usually enough to satisfy most children. For the little ones and grandparents, the creative sandbox can be a real winner.

The Special Library

Every grandchild’s toy shelf needs a large space for lots of appropriate books. The importance of reading to a young child and encouraging older children to develop a love of books is a great opportunity for grandparents. Trips to the library and the local bookstore can be wonderful adventures. These can be chances for the child to explore and find new and interesting subjects, especially when accompanied by lots of grandparent interactions. Always having an assortment of interesting books available for bedtime stories and quiet moments is a necessity for stimulating curiosity and building language skills. We don’t assume that the children lack access to books and parents who read to them, but we can provide additional resources. It would be hard to find teachers or librarians who caution against over exposure to good books.

Personally, I’m a strong proponent of utilizing technology for my own reading. The capacity to enlarge the print enables my older eyes to read much faster than in conventional printed books. I like the iPad feature that produces white print on a black background, diminishing the amount of blue light emitted at bedtime, along with the ease of holding the instrument, especially when traveling. I love the highlighting feature that collates all of my important points. I also like that I can carry a complete library of almost every book I've read in the last couple of years in my bag. These days, I find that it takes considerable effort to read print books. Although I'm totally devoted to technology for my reading, I would not advocate a complete conversion to technology for young children. There's still something special about turning the pages and having a personal copy of such favorites as *Pat the Bunny* and *A Wrinkle in Time*. Another reason that, at least, a few favorite books should be in print is that books are not as fragile and the "favorite keepers" in print are not likely to be lost in what may become an obsolete technology in future years. For example, I have a beautiful collection of animated Beatrix Potter stories on VHS tapes that still sit on my shelf, now no longer easy to access, but I can't bear to trash them. Many of us enjoy occasionally thumbing through those special books as we enjoy our own pleasant memories. Perhaps there's an advantage to a mix of print and technology for children.

Resale shops and book exchanges are good resources for buying used books. Many children have a similar attitude about books as they have to favorite toys—some are keepers and some have a limited "shelf life." At the same time that they like new stories, children usually also enjoy familiar books.

It's important to begin reading to toddlers as soon as they can focus an interest in picture books. This is a great way for children to learn the sound/symbol relationship. The kinds of books that have only pictures, or just a few words on each colorful page are very useful for toddlers. They also enjoy the sturdy "board" books that they can handle. We say, "dog," point to the photograph of a dog, and the child says, "dog." That process continues with familiar objects. We proceed with numerals and counting, up to three, then five. After they count five objects in a picture, we move on to counting five fingers, five blocks, and other discoveries. Then later, we learn letters, as we say, "H" and make a breathy "hhhh" sound. From the beginning of our reading together, we establish the practice of reading, talking about what has been read, and applying it to our everyday activities.

Young children usually love the experience of having grandparents read to them. From *Inside, Outside, Upside Down* to *Big Dog, Little Dog,* all of these beginner books are a delight to the curious child. They will sometimes memorize phrases or passages and enjoy making your reading a kind of duet. They may especially like the *You Read to Me* series by Hoberman that they can read with grandparents. As they grow, they may like reading to us, but children generally enjoy being read to long after they've learned to read independently. Regardless of age, they may enjoy looking at colorful pictures and talking about the actions. Discussing the story, characters, pictures, and other features of the books adds to the magic of grandparent reading.

Perhaps even more than the books, many children enjoy the emotional closeness of the experience, nestled in the swing with grandparents, sitting on Grandpapa's lap, or being curled up beside Nana on the sofa, all enhance the memorable involvement. Don't be dismayed or put the book aside if the child doesn't want to cuddle attentively beside you. Not every child enjoys close physical contact, but may still enjoy your reading together. Even if the child wants to play nearby, continue reading and exposing the child to stories and language.

It's easy to pick-up inexpensive books at the grocery or discount stores, but we must choose carefully. Of course, children under six need books with colorful pictures and few words, but we must be cautious about the exact language. All too soon, the child will be in school and required to write passages. Yet, many of the early reader books are filled with incomplete sentences and incorrect grammar. To avoid the children's adopting such a style and writing with sentence fragments when they are in school, we must be discerning. It's best to avoid exposing children to language structure for which they'll be penalized in just a few years. We want books that teach. When reading to younger children, it's easy to make editorial changes to correct grammar and send the right message. When the children have learned to read, it can be very informative to show the child how to correct the script and improve the message. Don't be afraid to mark and write in personal books and promote the use of correct language.

We must also choose grandchildren's reading material carefully because these colorful stories can have a subtle but significant impact. You probably recall favorite stories that were read to you when young. As these stories are very memorable, they can make indelible impressions on the young. When I was in the eighth grade, I found a novel in the school library that was set in the islands along the Georgia coast. That book was the root of my lifelong obsession with the beauty of the Sea Islands.

As most children's literature conveys a message, it behooves us to ensure that the message we want our grandchildren to hear is positive. Counselors often use stories as aids to help people understand their problems. Some counselors may encourage people to explore how their relationship models have been pursued through children's literature. They may be invited to talk about their approaches to life and getting what they want. For example, identifying strongly with the Cinderella story can encourage a passive approach to life—just waiting for someone to come along for the rescue. It can be amazing how often stories from early childhood are used to illustrate adult actions. And it isn't just the reading material for young children that's important. The *Nancy Drew Mysteries* have inspired the fantasy of many young girls, beginning in 1930 to the present. Even with adjustments for time and culture, the series has continued to captivate attention and foster feminine independence. It's a sobering reminder for us to choose reading material carefully.

If distance or circumstances separate you from a grandchild, and your opportunities for reading to the child seem limited, utilize technology to eliminate the distance. From the age of two, or as early as possible, discuss your desire to read to the child with the parents. If they want to read the bedtime stories and choose the books, applaud their attentiveness and ask how you can support their efforts. If it seems that working parents could enjoy a few quiet moments in the evening, perhaps you can enlist their assistance with technology to allow you to read to the child.

There was a time when grandparents would mail several cassette tapes with matching books to grandchildren who lived far away. These wonderful packages required that grandparents record the text, ring a bell or tap a spoon on a glass to signal page turns, and make a few personal observations at the end. Then, the books and tapes were boxed and mailed. The complications meant that the child could only enjoy a few books with grandparent voices, but today, it's much easier to read to grandchildren. Since even toddlers seem to grasp the use of technology, we can use the camera on our phones to focus on the page as we read or we can setup a video or device conference. Even very small children quickly embrace looking at the pages on an iPad or a tablet and listening to a familiar voice as we read. To reduce the light issue that may keep the child awake, we may want to read via electronic screen earlier in the evening. Bedtime stories may be more effective when parents turn the lights off and leave a phone on speaker near the bed so that the child can gently drift off to sleep to the soothing sound of the grandparent's voice.

The time and frequency of "distance reading" must be determined by the parents, since we're really a virtual visitor in their homes. It's the same as if we just walk-in from down the street. We are intruding on their schedule and space at a time that may be hectic for them. With some discussion and planning, however, we can fit into their schedules and be an added resource. If the parents choose to read the bedtime stories, applaud their commitments and ask if there's an alternate time during the week for grandparent reading. In families of more than one child and working parents, our fifteen minutes of easing the evening routine may be an additional bedtime asset. Whatever the routine, we must be certain that it's a support for the parents and a contribution to the child's developing language, reading skills, and a love of learning.

It's easy to place an importance on reading when the child is young and following us around with a book and plea of "Read this to me." Unfortunately, it's also easy to forget to continue the emphasis on books and reading as the child learns to read independently and seems less interested in having us read to him/her. Yet, this is the most critical time for us to continue the emphasis on reading as they become capable of reading longer passages and entire books. We can continue to guide and coach their choices of reading material, not only through visits to the library and used book stores, but through discussions with them about plot, characters, and features of the books. I recall long car rides to the beach when my grandson would read passages from *Charlie Brown* and we would laugh as we talked about the characters. Now, my grandson and I discuss his reading from a recent course in philosophy and what both of us have read on politics and world events. The topics and depth of the reading material have changed, but the delightful and insightful exchange of new learning and ideas continue to stimulate interesting conversations.

Pursuing an emphasis on reading is becoming even more important to our grandchildren's generation. One of the most disturbing statistics about the younger generation is that they will arrive at college having read fewer books than you and I. In addition, today's young people's exposure to technology may have given them less tolerance for reading or writing long passages of text—leaving us to wonder who will be the researchers of their generation as some seem to be limited to short phrases or comments. Just as we introduce the toddler to *Good Night Moon,* we must continue to provide and encourage interesting reading materials at every stage of their development. Appendix C contains some suggestions for age appropriate titles to consider for young grandchildren. School and public libraries are usually staffed with informed professionals who can suggest a variety of books, ways to develop language, and encourage reading.

Fantasy and Make-Believe

The books that we first introduce to children are usually photographs of animals, and familiar objects. We point to the picture and say the name of the object. The next books usually have colorful pictures with very few words that may even tell a simple story, such as *Go Dog, Go* from the *Bright and Early Series.* As we progress from actual photos and real objects, to fanciful drawings, such as in the *Dr. Seuss* series, we begin introducing fantasy into the child's world. As we progress to *Peter Rabbit* and *Benjamin Bunny,* we move into personification and anthropomorphism—giving animals human appearances and behavior.

Some grandparents may prefer to restrict the children's stories to realism, while other people see the value in creativity and stimulating imagination. We may find, however, that it's not about our preference, but the child's liking for realism or fantasy. Regardless of the choice, ensure that the selections accomplish the purpose.

For example, some fables that are intended to teach moral truths may be misleading. When the ancient Greek, Aesop's wagoner's wheels go into the mud, he appeals to the heaven and hears a voice say, "The gods help them that help themselves." Without clarification, young children can confuse the fable with Bible verses. Conversely, if fantasies are introduced without adequate explanation and understanding, other uncertainties can occur. There's always an important challenge in teaching about God because if we aren't careful, the "faith of believing in something that we cannot see" can sound too similar to the fairy godmother's magic wand! Whatever the choice of stories and reading material, children benefit from discussion to aid thorough comprehension about what is a "pretend" and what is real—even though we may not be able to see it.

Puppets

Another appealing way to extend the interest in storytelling and pretending is with the use of puppets. A large leftover moving or appliance box can be easily transformed into a puppet theater by simply removing one side and cutting a large hole in the opposite side at the right height to accommodate the child's hands. The "theater" can then be decorated as elaborately as the child and grandparent choose to make it. The cardboard could be painted, designs could be added, and even a curtain could be suspended using the large plastic S hooks and a rod, available at many closet and hardware stores. Toy stores may offer a nice wooden version, but it can be an expensive investment that may become a storage issue and only be captivating for a year or two.

Although older children might enjoy marionettes, many creative children love hand puppets. They may even enjoy making puppets from old socks. "Stick puppets" that are simply silhouettes cut from any kind of paper and taped onto a drinking straw can be used in a shadow theater. By positioning a lamp in a darkened room to cast shadows on a wall, simple stick puppets can enable imaginative little ones to retell stories you've read or to make up their own tales.

In addition to making stick puppets for the shadow theater, it's great fun to simply use fingers. By holding the thumb and forefinger together, with the other fingers above, the shadow can be made to look like a rabbit, a fox, or other animals. This shadow puppet can be made to talk by moving the thumb and forefinger back toward the hand and outward, or by tapping the thumb and forefinger together. Actually, this movement is superb practice for writing. Too many children grasp the pencil with three or four fingers, requiring a larger muscle movement to write. By practicing the thumb and forefinger motions, we're really preparing the child to learn to write with a pencil. The smaller muscle motions literally lend more control and better penmanship—even though such is rarely emphasized in many of today's classrooms.

Counselors often employ puppets to enable troubled children to talk about their anxieties or problems, using the puppets to rehearse possible responses to distressing issues. Grandparents can also utilize puppets to encourage young children to verbalize topics about which they might be reticent. Whether watching the Muppets on *Sesame Street* or playing ventriloquist with their old socks, many children have fun with puppets, but it's an individual preference. The child who will become a highly concrete, logical adult may have less interest in puppets than the very imaginative child. It's just another individual preference for one type of toy over another.

Music

From the wind-up music box that plays a soothing lullaby for the sleepy infant, to the nursery songs that we sing to entertain the toddler in a moving automobile, music is an essential part of the culture to which we expose the grandchildren. This is an era in which much of what children hear is electronic, and often, too loud. Instead, they need exposure to Mozart, Haydn, folk songs, real music, and your favorite music. In our guitar dominated culture, grandchildren may not be exposed to great music or the piano that was a fixture of every refined living room in the twentieth century.

Whatever is your talent or preference, sing with the little ones, expose them to a variety of musical idioms, including symphony, military bands, traditional jazz, various instruments, and good choral music. The music they hear before age seven will have a strong influence on the music they listen to when teens and adults. Be certain that the children get a good sampling of the performing arts. Outdoor concerts that allow a little more wiggle room can be an especially enjoyable way to introduce them to orchestral music and the large symphony orchestra.

If the children gravitate toward making their own music, encourage lessons or participation in musical groups. Learning to play a musical instrument is a great intellectual stimulation, and at the same time, enhances self-discipline. Acquiring a love of music is part of developing a young person of culture and distinction. For the adult, great music can also be a lifetime source of relaxation and inspiration.

Adventures on the Go

As the child matures, it becomes enjoyable to mix time together with adventures outside of the home. We grandparents can be very resourceful in finding interesting places to take the children. When we begin with an attitude of "anything and anyplace can become a learning adventure," we make memorable times out of all that we do with the grandchildren. We find parks and places to go that are free or relatively inexpensive.

From the time my grandson was about six months old until I moved away when he was 12, one of our most favorite places was the nearby tennis courts. Rarely used by anyone else, and surrounded by trees, it was more than a surface for hitting balls over a net. For us, it was a magical island! Our adventures there began when he was a baby and I pushed his stroller around the perimeter at nap time. A short time later, it became a great place for running and games. It's where he learned to kick a soccer ball, hit a soft ball, play dodge ball, and oh yes, hit tennis balls. There was a succession of wheel toys, bicycles, and scooters. One of my fondest memories is of his sitting in my lap or snuggled beside me as we sat on the bench and "watched the stars come out" after a vigorous playtime. What a fun place it was! And it was free—if we omit the cost of the balls, wheel toys, and other accoutrements. Some of the most memorable and enjoyable activities were not about the place, but about our interactions and the loving relationship.

There are many places away from home that can be a superb destination for adventures and making memories. Of course, the trips to historic Williamsburg, *Disney World,* amusement parks, and the beach are all great fun, but there are more places to go that are free or the cost is minimal. Sometimes, these places hold more potential for enjoyment than the expensive excursions because they may be closer, require less preparation, and be more accessible. The walks along a stream, the adventures through the spring flowers, autumn leaves, and the picnics in the nearby park can be as delightful as the expensive excursions, and perhaps, safer during periods of contagion.

For planning time with grandchildren away from home, an online search of nearby parks and facilities is a good way to begin. Anything and anyplace with the grandchildren can be wonderful if we commit to adequate forethought and make everything a learning adventure. A simple search for museums, walking trails, nature preserves, botanical gardens, and an alert for special events can produce many delightful experiences with children.

If funds are limited, or even if grandparents have unlimited funds, appropriate verbal preparation can be an opportunity for teaching self-discipline. For example, if the exit from a museum is through a lavish gift shop, tell the child what to expect before you leave home. You might say, "At the end, we will see lots of toys and goodies for sale, but we will only look at them because today is not a toy buying day." Another appropriate preparation might be, "The place where we're going sells lots of popcorn and candy, but we will not be buying any because later, we're going to get your favorite chocolate cone at the ice cream shop. And you remember our rule—only one sweet for one day." Such preparation will spare everyone a lobby meltdown, disappointment, or a tummy ache. More important, it contributes to the development of self-discipline.

There's no better example of the advantage of preparation than being ready for the children's museums or play places that contain a water play feature or sand play. If the child isn't aware, it's easy to detour around the water area and leave that until the end of the visit, but if the child is familiar with the place, it's better to tell the child that you'll visit the water area last so that he/she can avoid spending the rest of the visit in wet or uncomfortable clothing. With proper explanations and reminders, most children will be cooperative. Although perhaps we're thinking about the clothing, the outside temperature, and extra socks, we must also be aware that proper preparation facilitates learning self-discipline in the delayed gratification of waiting until the end for a favorite activity. But in the event that it isn't the day for self-discipline, it's best to pack some dry clothes for emergencies.

Truthful preparation is best, even if we get some toddler pushback. My daughter still likes to tease about her deceptive mother. She remembers my telling her that all of the candy, gum, and junk foods at the grocery store check-out were on-display, *and not for sale.* By the time I was pushing my grandson through the check-out aisles, I had learned the importance of honesty in teaching character and told him that we did not buy from that display. He accepted the reminders, just as my daughter, but happily, he doesn't have memories of my dishonesty.

If potential problems are anticipated, it's an advantage to prepare the child for what will happen and to reassure the child of security. Cautions about the best way to navigate your outing are helpful, whether the child will be free to roam and interact with the environment or whether it will be necessary to stay in the stroller or walk holding your hand. There is nothing as stressful to a grandparent as realizing that the child who was standing beside you a moment ago has vanished. Although it's good for the child to feel and experience independence, in today's world, constant vigilance is a necessity in any public place.

A bit of thinking ahead about scheduling adventures around nap and meal times is essential. It's also important to anticipate where clean restrooms might be found, along with needs to pack snacks, water, sanitary hand wipes, and extra clothing. Anticipating items that might be needed can make a huge difference in whether it's a grand experience or an exhausting outing for both adults and children. Most of all, it's important to give notice as to when the adventure will end. Ideally, it's nice when the activity can continue until the child finishes, but unfortunately, that isn't always possible. We don't like being ripped away from something delightful, and neither does the child. As indicated earlier, even with very young children, it's wise to tell them something about the time and schedule, then give them several notices about the ending times. It seems that the more enjoyable the activity, the more important it becomes to warn the child when it must end.

Long walks in the neighborhood and hikes in natural areas, local parks or in our state and National Parks can be very memorable adventures. Of course, a trip to Yosemite or the Great Smokeys can be terrific, (and remember, when grandparents visit National Parks with a senior pass, everyone in the car is usually admitted on that pass), but there are many opportunities that may be closer, less expensive, or even free. As we share the beauty of the spring flowers, the falling leaves, and the colorful sunsets, we enhance the grandchildren's curiosity and sense of aesthetics. These are also opportunities to teach the young ones about environmental responsibilities and the importance of leaving no litter, only footprints.

We can expand the learning as we teach the children how to be safe in nature and in areas of inherent risks. Instead of just demanding that they "stay away from the edge," these are opportunities for teaching about erosion and unstable rock formations. Instead of commanding that the children "stay close to me," we can ensure their nearby presence by engaging them in discoveries of plants, insects, water flows, and the countless other intriguing uniquenesses in nature. Immersion in nature provides great opportunities for children to learn about the fundamental dangers in wilderness areas and how to be alert and safe when in the natural environment. At the same time that we're teaching them about the dangers of the wilderness, we can also introduce them to the sensory experiences available—the clouds, the trees, the view of a sunset, the feel and sound of a breeze, the call of the birds, and the beauty of the silence.

Adventures in nature are wonderful explorations and enhance so many characteristics that we want to encourage, from inquisitiveness to regard for our planet. Even what might seem to be incidental—a rock, a weed, the shape of a barren tree against the winter sky—all of these can become wonders when we explore with a curious child. We never miss a chance to expand the children's horizons.

I was reminded of those adventures in nature many years ago, of teaching my grandson to identify trees and birds, and calling his attention to the silhouette of trees in the night sky. Recently, I noticed a framed print from a just completed photography class that was hanging on his wall.

It was a crisp, striking, black and white photo of a large oak tree against a winter sky. I smiled as I recalled similar sights that we had shared and was pleased that he, too, remembered and saw beauty in the scene.

Even though trips with young children require some planning, preparation and equipment, adventures are worth the effort. Complicated car seats, big heavy strollers, bicycle helmets, and an equipment bag large enough for a professional football player seem to be necessities for today's outings with young children. Yet, it's all worth the time and trouble when we hear the squeals of delight and see the happy faces as the little ones enjoy our planned activities. As they grow, and we can see the results of our efforts, any expenditure seems incidental when compared to the significance of keeping them safe, happy, and learning.

With all of the planning and equipment necessary for grandparent adventures, it seems that there's little time left for documenting the memories. Yet, when the children are older, it's delightful to reminisce as we reflect on these special times that will never come again. There are fancy and complicated methods of scrapbooking that are admirable for everyone who knows the techniques and has the materials. If, like many of us, you have limited time or resources, make a point to collect the digital photos that you've made into virtual "albums" that identify the people, dates, and places. All of these tasks are automatic on many of our devices, but sometimes, it's helpful if we add details. The other easy way to maintain an "Adventure Book" is to simply collect the drawings, brochures, and keepsakes that accumulate into a box or a binder. Regardless of what fits your style—fancy, organized, or other—it becomes important to document many of the special adventures and wonderful memories. Whatever method you choose, the only caution is to be alert for acid-free papers, glues, and sheet protectors. It's amazing how quickly our mementoes can deteriorate. Such memorabilia may seem trivial today, but your great-great-grandchildren may have a different attitude. I certainly treasure the letters that my great-great-grandparents wrote to each other in the 1880's. Whether they become trash or treasure, we can let descendants make the decision, but in the meantime, we'll enjoy the collection that prompts happy memories for us.

When Grandchildren Must Go Places That Are Not Fun
(And when they can't be the center of attention)

It's preferable for much of the time that we're with grandchildren to be focused on them, making eye contact, talking, and interacting with them. We can make many of our activities interesting learning adventures for the children. Even when we're in the grocery store, we can discuss the items we're putting into the cart and talk about good nutrition. Sometimes, however, we may need to have the children with us, but be unable to focus on them. Occasionally, the grandchildren must go with us to visits, meetings, church, synagogue, medical appointments, and other places that aren't especially enjoyable for them. It's ironic that in our careful preparation, we'll anticipate the need for diapers, snacks, water, and extra clothing—caring for the *physical needs.* Yet, we're oblivious of the *intellectual needs.* Didn't we agree that our grandchildren are brilliant? They're wonderfully curious and are very responsive to learning opportunities. With such mental capacity, we must not miss any chances to stimulate their inquisitiveness, to occupy their awesome brains, and of course, to keep them safe and busy, especially when our attention needs to be on something else.

We've already acknowledged that the days of the compliant child belong to the Victorian era. But remember, a child of today, born into this noisy, busy world with its excessive stimulation is not likely to sit quietly with hands folded because we need to talk to a friend or listen to a speaker. Regardless of the child's age, when not in an interesting environment, a clever tool is needed! It isn't necessary to invest lavishly in the contents, only to be thoughtful and prepare for activities that will engage the child and diminish need for attention or discipline issues.

The GO Bag

On these "not so fun occasions," it's imperative that we have a "GO Bag" in the hall closet, ready for any trip. Adapted for various ages, this is a tote bag filled with quiet toys, books, art, writing supplies, and quiet electronics. It is only available for boring times away from your house. If you don't find anything else in this book that benefits your relationship with your grandchildren, this is guaranteed to be a plus for both grandparents and the grandchildren. It's for those times when the child cannot be the center of our attention (when we need to ignore the child), yet keep the child safe, quiet, busy, happy, and in one place.

Any opaque tote bag with a closure will suffice. Fill it with safe and engaging materials. For young children, it is essential not to include anything that might become a choking hazard. Remember, the goal is to occupy the child's attention but require minimal attention from us. For the toddler, small soft books, stuffed animals, and manipulatives are good. Show the child how to take one book or manipulative out, play with it, and then, choose another. Discourage the child from dumping the contents out, all at once as this diminishes the time that the contents will captivate the child's attention. Some of the items shown in the photo would be appropriate for a child from two to four. In many circumstances, and especially for toddlers, it's useful to have a place mat, or a dish towel,

as in the photo that can be unrolled and become a defined and *clean* area for the child's play with the bag contents.

The GO Bag for older children could contain age appropriate books, manipulatives, and a stuffed animal or two, but it can also contain crayons, paper, or an inexpensive sketch book. If the child uses an iPad or tablet, that could also be included, but be sure not to add anything that makes noise, requires assistance, or your involvement. Little farm sets, miniature train sets, small cars, dolls, and small toys that are not a choking hazard are a great addition, but anything with smaller parts works best if a small plastic tray, box lid, or something that confines the little pieces is included. If the GO Bag is used very often, it becomes essential to add new surprises to the contents in order to keep the child engaged. Just as with the toy shelves at home, it's important to keep the GO Bag fresh and interesting.

Suggestions for older children could include puzzles and activities that are easy to transport. When the child is mature enough that pointed objects are not a hazard, colored pencils, other art materials, and electronics may be included. The caution for electronics is to be sure that the child's screen time is not excessive and that ear buds are included for any sounds.

When it's necessary to take more than one child to places where they must be quiet and not distract you, it may be important to pack a joint bag with quiet games and activities for two or three. If it is important for the children to be quiet, however, try packing a smaller bag for each child with the understanding that each child will play with the bag contents, replace everything into the bag, and then, exchange bags at a specified time. The good news is that neither bag must contain the same or as many objects as a singular bag. Again, this is an opportunity for the children to learn sharing, impulse control, and delayed gratification as they know that they will have a chance to draw or play with the manipulatives they want.

To make church attendance as pleasant as possible, it's useful to have a small *Go to Church Bag* that's only for worship services. Crayons, paper, and drawing materials are especially useful, along with age relevant religious books to keep the child quiet and appropriately occupied. I saw an especially enterprising grandmother whose *GO to Church Bag* included a Noah's Ark set of tiny fabric stuffed figures. In December, the same child quietly arranged a Nativity set on the pew beside the grandparents. By preparing, interacting, finding hymn numbers, and emphasizing the need to whisper, we can ensure the child's enjoyable participation. It's critical to make worship as pleasant as possible if we want the child to continue attending when in college and a young adult. We don't want their only memory of church to be the boredom of listening to the loud voice of an adult talking about something that the child couldn't understand. We must make church attendance relevant to age and capabilities.

It isn't necessary to invest large amounts of money in these bags, just keep them interesting and only use when needed for time away from home. But if you do a great job of providing captivating contents, don't be surprised if you get pleas for play with the bag at home. This will require a firm, "No, the GO Bag is only for when we GO." The denial is another great opportunity for teaching impulse control and delayed gratification.

Just as preparation for adventures away from home is important for the child, it is essential for grandparents. We need a GO Bag to accommodate the unanticipated necessities. Think about possible needs for water and snacks, along with a disposable placemat, paper towels, or clean dish towel that can be placed on a restaurant table to corral a small child's food and hands. (I cringe at the microbes transferred to a child's hands from that much used rag the waiter grabbed to wipe restaurant tables.) An extra set of clothing for accidents and an extra jacket for a sudden change in weather are also essentials. Don't let a perfect day be ended because of a spilled water bottle or a perfect mood spoiled by a hungry child. If permitted by the facility where you're going, it's likely that the food you take will be more nutritious and cost less than what you could buy. When possible, save the purchase of food for treats and occasions for intentional dining to avoid fast food and inappropriate restaurants chosen out of necessity.

An absolute essential for the grandparents' bag is a package of sanitary hand wipes. Although the liquid and sprays are useful, little hands frequently benefit from the recyclable cloth-like wipes and may be safer for children's use. Emphasizing hand washing, especially before meals is a good habit to encourage, but even more essential when away from home or in an era of highly infectious diseases. With increasing concerns about communicable diseases, such as the Covid virus, emphasizing hand sanitation, has become very wise. During epidemics, it can even be a matter of life or death. Because we're frequently taking grandchildren to playgrounds, parks, and places visited by many children, we may find them to be a magnet for germs. Sending grandchildren home sick after an adventure doesn't create a good memory for the child or the parents. And besides, they may share their newly acquired germs with us!

The Car Box

A similar adaptation of the GO Bag is the CAR BOX. Regardless of age, when the child is in the car for more than a ten-minute ride, there should be a plastic, safe box

or bin within easy reach of the child's car seat that contains age-appropriate "distractors." This is especially essential for young children to have some form of diversion because the safety seats are very confining for energetic, wiggly bodies. Although I like being able to point to various scenes that we're passing, and talk about the journey, at some point, the views may be insufficient to hold the child's attention. Soft stuffed figures, puzzles, crayons, and notebooks will occupy the child's attention and make travel more enjoyable for everyone. The car box in the photo reflects the needs of an older child for a long car trip. Magnetic puzzles, mazes, flash cards, books, and art pens can hold the older child's attention for long periods. It can also be very useful to prepare a journal that they can use to record scenes along the way and increase their value of the experience.

If the car ride will be a long one, or the return will be at nap time, including a small pillow and a fleece blanket can be especially comforting to the tired child. In the photo, the curved hippopotamus neck pillow sits atop its cloth bag with a small fleece blanket below. The Snoopy puppet to the right makes a snuggly companion for naps while riding. Keeping both clean in a bag at the bottom of the car box can make the difference in an adventure that ends beautifully or one that ends in tears. Be sure to use a cloth bag instead of plastic for small children.

The key to success with the CAR BOX is that its contents are only available in the car, that they are soft, safe in motion, and may be rotated and changed as the child's interests grow. Think of these as planning tools for means of ensuring the child's mental stimulation, your "peace of mind," and good memories for everyone. In addition, an unhappy, screaming child can be a distraction to grandparent's driving that must be avoided. As mentioned earlier, today's car seats are confining to energetic bodies. It's essential that we keep the little ones distracted and happy when traveling. The GO Bag and the CAR BOX are small but very thoughtful ways to make all of the time that your grandchild is with you engaging and memorable. Of course, we can always add a phone or screen to the mix, but stimulating learning toys can be appealing alternatives.

Additional Grandparent Strategies

We grandparents have considerable experience and observations that fuel our cleverness. When my grandson was young, I noticed that he paid no attention to the smaller Christmas presents that he received. Thinking that it would give him the fun of opening more presents, I wrapped the new box of crayons, a book, and even a new pair of socks for Christmas morning, but I soon learned that these were not properly appreciated and were quickly ignored, as the trinkets in the stocking were ignored. I also observed that the days post Christmas were a "let-down" after the much anticipated excitement of Christmas morning. I decided on a different strategy. Buying the largest stocking I could find in the "after Christmas sales," I was prepared for a better approach for the next year.

Just as the Advent Calendar marks the anticipation leading up to the big celebration, I decided that an "after the big day" transition was needed. I wrapped all of the small and incidental gifts, including a quarter, and put stickers on each with the numbers 1-12. Being familiar with the old carol about *The Twelve Days of Christmas*, he delighted in having something to open each day. I found that it seemed to make the transition from the excitement of Christmas Day to ordinary days a bit easier. The Advent

Calendar was religious and marked the days before Christmas, whereas the Twelve Days marked the season between Christmas and Epiphany, and at our house, was an extension of the festivities.

From the time he was four, he loved having a little surprise to dig from his stocking and open. He would call me each morning in great excitement to tell me what he'd found for that day. When he was older, I would get an email thanking me for the small gift. He still enjoys Twelve Days of his favorite treats, money, and small gifts. And yes, I still wrap and label each one from 1 to 12. Will he outgrow the tradition? Not likely—until the great-grandchildren.

Another tradition that is fun and memorable is purchasing a special Christmas ornament for the tree. Some years, I was able to find a suitable ornament that contained the year as part of the design. Other times, we chose something special that the child liked and added the date to the back or on the hanger. Just as I smile when I look at the silver glass bell that my grandmother purchased for me at Woolworth's Five & Dime, the younger generation may also enjoy the mementoes. Although they have mostly crumbled, I still have the soda and salt dough ornaments that my grandson and I made one Christmas when he was about six. We clever grandparents can find pleasure in any strategy that brings joy to the young ones and maintains their connections to us, regardless of age.

When my daughter grew older, somehow, it seemed easier to maintain the Easter Egg tradition with her than with my grandson. She enjoyed decorating the eggs and making fancy cookies. I had to be more discerning as my grandson grew, he still enjoyed baking cookies, but I filled the basket of plastic eggs with Legos, coins, and we omitted the Easter afternoon egg hunt. Although older children may be reluctant to admit their affinity for childhood treats, they continue to love the traditions. The smile that was produced by finding a dollar bill in the "golden egg" was an inexpensive reward and made a very happy

memory for this grandparent. In our beginning conversation, we mentioned grandparents' fondness for indulgences and I freely admit that I greatly enjoy providing treats, especially at holidays. Maybe sometimes, we grandparents make memories for our own collection, as well as for the grandchildren's.

Pets

In our discussion about safety, I expressed my concern about mixing pets and crawling babies. Perhaps a better time for introducing pets is around ages 5, 6, or 7. At this point, children can learn how to interact appropriately with pets, how to feed, walk, and care for animals. Pets present an excellent opportunity for teaching children about responsibility and dependability. When anticipating getting a pet, we must consider its purpose, who will care for it, what it will mean to the child, and who will benefit from its companionship. Grandparents may get a pet for the child to enjoy during visits, but if a pet is provided for the child's home, it must be with full parental agreement. Any animal may provide fun and learning opportunities about pet care, but parents must be in full accord.

Cats, birds, or other animals may be preferable pets for some grandparents, but dogs are often the best choice for a child because certain canine breeds can provide companionship and be energetic playmates. In instances where the child has suffered a loss, a move to a new school, or an emotional trauma, the dog may provide a wonderful source of unconditional love and companionship.

Breeds that are patient, yet energetic, such as, Labradors, beagles, and standard poodles can be good choices, especially for growing boys because they love to play with a ball and to be helpful. Border collies and

Shetland sheep dogs are wonderful companions, but they are work dogs that need a job, such as loving and herding a young child. Shelties are known for their energy, intelligence, and shedding. A mixed breed may prove to be a superb companion if it's the right size and temperament. Whatever the size or breed, be sure that it is appropriate for the child. We grandparents may prefer a Yorkie, Jack Russell terrier, Chihuahua, or other small dog, but these may not be the best choice to bond with and be a child's companion. Although it's less expensive, and admirable, to choose a rescued animal, the dilemma is in sometimes not knowing the dog's background, how it has been treated, or if it has been abused. Perhaps a somewhat more expensive, but safer choice, may be to secure a puppy from a shelter or reputable source and let the child and dog grow together. Beginning the companionship with a puppy also diminishes the chances of the young child's having to deal with the death of an older beloved pet. The unfortunate demise is more likely to occur when the child is a teen and better able to cope with loss.

Whether provided at the parents' home or at the grandparents' home, pets can be a terrific source of fun and companionship for young children, especially when they take an active role in pet care and bonding. A dog, like grandparents, can be a dependable source of unconditional love for any child.

Summary

How well did I succeed at persuading you of the importance of planning focused activities and making everything about learning and your relationship with the cherished grandchildren? Toys and activities need not be indulgences or objects just to "keep the kid busy." Rather, all provide experiences and all provide opportunities for learning and to influence the child's development.

Did you find the immense advantage of having some low shelves for toys with bins for the toys with small parts to accommodate younger children? You probably noticed how much more inviting it is to have an organized play space for small visitors.

When I became annoyed at the clutter in my kitchen or having to step over a maze of small cars in the living room, I simply thought about when my grandson would have too many other activities and distractions to want to spend time with me in the kitchen or playing on the living room floor. It was an instant reminder of my priorities. When our children were at home, we closed the door to their rooms because we didn't want to look at the chaos, but after they left for college and became adults, we closed the door because the emptiness was sad. So it is with grandchildren. We must make enticing spaces for them and enjoy every moment of their all-too-brief childhoods.

Play is an integral part of the child's brain and physical development. Watching, interacting, and guiding their play, whether at the park or the kitchen sink, is our opportunity. Whether an occasional visit, or extensive child care, making time for real interaction and one-to-one focused attention is our opportunity.

It isn't necessary to spend big money on toys or elaborate trips. It isn't what we do or where we go with grandchildren that's as memorable as our being together, how we react to what we see or do, and most of all, what the child learns. As the children grow, the wooden puzzles are replaced by elaborate picture puzzles. The stacking cubes are replaced by Legos. Then, come the microscope and the brain teasing board games. *Bedtime for Francis* and the collection of *How Do Dinosaurs* books are replaced by *The Chronicles of Narnia* and volumes of Shakespeare.

All too soon, the toys are replaced by animated conversations with the grandchildren, and time for them to help us with our technology devices. The tangibles and the activities change, but the learning, the interactions, the relationships, and the memory making continue.

Chapter 6

The Instant Generation

As we strive to guard against our own
defensiveness in the face of change,
Help us to develop a reasonable optimism
when confronted by the new.

We can do everything to build and enjoy close relationships with our grandchildren when they're young. We can have long low shelves of interesting books and toys that capture their interests when they visit. We can play endless games of tic-tac-toe and chess. We can take them on trips to Disneyland, to the beach, parks, museums, and playgrounds. We can teach them botany and entomology while exploring the backyard. We can become very influential in developing their character. We can be ideal grandparents through childhood, and yet, lose them during adolescence.

It's frightening how the children who cried and protested when having to leave or miss a grandparent visit suddenly have no interest in seeing us or even taking our phone calls. It's sad when they scheme and complain that we're so old and boring or that they just don't have time for grandparents anymore. When this transpires, we grandparents cannot feel dismissed or alienated. We cannot sulk and express our pitiful feelings of rejection. Instead, it's merely a signal that those cute little ones are growing up and that we must not become obsolete in their world. We must change our approach. At this point, their interests and needs for independence are growing exponentially. Just as we changed our technique and the environment that we provided when they learned to walk, it's now time for other significant changes.

We must change the home activities. Instead of having toys on the special shelves, we must have different board games and content, such as classic books to discuss or new apps on our phones that help us connect with them. The chess set that was used when they were young should continue to be a challenge as their thinking skills develop, but a more mature appearing version may be needed. The *National Parks Monopoly, Metropolitan Museum Monopoly* and other versions may continue to capture their attention occasionally. *CandyLand,* and *Mouse Trap,* however, may need to be replaced by *Diplomacy, Catan, Apples to Apples,* or other games.

Although we might miss the enchanting afternoons of sipping camomile tea from the Peter Rabbit tea cups, the menu may need to change to popcorn, lattes, and food that pleases their taste for accompanying grown-up style conversations. It's important to think of interesting topics and thought provoking questions to have ready for their visits. Just as the face-to-face and eye-to-eye conversation with focused attention was important when they were five, it's equally as essential when they're fifteen or twenty-five.

It's time to share more of the world in which we've lived, and at the same time, show them that we understand and are relevant in their world. It's time to build our ongoing credibility. The credibility that was once achieved by ice cream cones and bedtime stories must now include a demonstration that we're savvy and can relate in today's world.

Grandchildren Live in a Very Different Era

In the nineteenth century, schools were not available for everyone, but parents could ensure their children acquired the necessities of a good life and would be successful if they taught their children a responsible work ethic, and to read and write. In the twentieth century, schools were larger, had a longer calendar, and took over the responsibility for teaching children to read and write, along with the acquisition of many facts about history, economics, literature, and language. In the twenty-first century, however, technology has changed what's needed in the curriculum. Instead of acquiring knowledge, technology puts all facts at the fingertips of every student. Therefore, the schools are needed to teach the students *how to find out and how to learn.*

Just as our teen years were vastly different from those of our grandparents, our precious grandchildren live in an environment that is characterized by technology, and often, a very different family structure. They may not enjoy the support of nearby extended family, lots of siblings, cousins, and other relatives and family friends for a social life. Concerns for safety require that they can never roam the neighborhood with other children or walk to a playground alone. Instead, news of violence dictates that we keep them close and carefully monitor where they are and with whom they are at every moment. In times of contagion, they may even need to wear a mask when in public. Although the state of our world has dictated a more protective environment for them, it may have also resulted in a lonelier place, but grandparents can be a great compensation for their isolation if we remain relevant.

Rather than roaming and exploring the vicinity, today's children cruise the internet. Although they may miss bicycling around the neighborhood, playing kick ball in the street, and wading in the nearby creek that we enjoyed, they have the world under their fingertips. The internet basically gives them access to the world's information—*in an instant.* They can find out anything, see anything, and go virtually anyplace in an instant—both a marvelous intellectual advantage, and possibly, an emotional and physical deficit.

This instant accessibility is why I like to call the children born after 2007, the *Instant Generation.* Other writers (Twenge, 2017) use the term *iGen* as in the iPhone, the iPad, and to reflect the *i*nternet technology. Regardless of a label, these children are growing-up in a very different world. The emphasis on their physical safety, along with their mastery and extensive use of technology, has shaped much of their attitudes and outlook for the future. If we are to relate to them, to continue our influence in helping their parents shape character and equip them for success, we must learn about them and increase our knowledge of and connections to their world.

When my grandson was about nine, I recall an interesting conversation about his great-grandfather who was 96 at the time. The three of us routinely had dinner together on most Saturdays. During the drive home after one of those dinners, we talked about the many world changing events that had happened during Great-Grandpa's lifetime, from the sinking of the *Titanic* shortly after he was born, through the World Wars and various military conflicts. Having been on several plane trips, and taking everyday air travel for granted, my grandson marveled that Great-Grandpa was born during the infancy of powered flight and had lived through the moon landing and the International Space Station.

When Great-Grandpa talked about his family's first car, the child realized that he had also lived through the infancy of the automobile to cars that would not even need a driver. As we discussed the changes in technology, the child discovered that Great-Grandpa had used a hand cranked adding machine when he worked in a grocery store during business college. The fact that Great-Grandpa grew-up on a farm without electricity and didn't have a telephone until he was grown was perplexing, but what really impressed the child was the fact that Great-Grandpa didn't have an electric typewriter until he was 65 and didn't get the Mac Computer or a cell phone until he was nearly 90. Great-Grandpa had not really known technology that was familiar to the child until long after the elder's retirement. That discussion was a huge reminder to me of the increasingly rapid changes in our world.

Another experience that jolted my realization of this revolution happened one day during a conversation with my daughter. I told her that a mutual friend had suffered an aneurysm. She expressed concern and asked, “What’s the difference between an aneurysm and a stroke?" I stared at her and replied, “I don’t know.” Then, I turned to my grandson, who was probably 12 at the time and said, “What’s the difference between an aneurysm and a stroke?” ...click, click, click, “An aneurysm is the rupture of a wall of an artery whereas a stroke occurs when brain cells begin to die from lack of oxygen," he read promptly from his iPhone. Now, if I had even known the word aneurysm at his age, much less how to spell it, to get that information would have been more complex. Anything that I couldn’t glean from a dictionary or encyclopedia, would have necessitated a walk to the bus stop, a city bus-ride to the downtown public library, a scan through the card catalogs, and a search of the books to maybe locate the information before I walked to my father’s office to ride home at 5:00. That’s how we got information in my generation. The knowledge that would have taken a half day to find, my grandson could locate in seconds—and he didn’t even have to know the correct spelling of aneurysm!

Something similar happened when we were discussing the music we were hearing that I couldn’t completely recall. “Click, click, click” and my grandson produced a complete copy of the music and asked if I’d like to order a printed paper version. No, I didn’t have to ride the city bus downtown to the library or go to the music store, my grandson could put the music in front of me on my iPad tablet with just a few clicks!

Remember the days of maps, highlighters, and getting lost on trips—no more because Siri or your global positioning system (GPS) will take you wherever you know the address. I’m so old I can even remember “getting dressed-up," driving downtown, and going from store to store in search of an item that I wanted to buy. Now, technology lets me find it in a few minutes and have it at my front door in a matter of hours. Remember our lengthy phone conversations with that special girl friend or boy friend when in high school? Well, this Instant Generation spends even more time with their phones, but instead of communicating with only one person at a time, they talk, text, *Tweet, Snap,* and send photos to countless friends and strangers. Their whole world is connected *in an instant!*

Even if you're a young grandparent, you may have lived without a cell phone, unlimited TV channels, a personal computer, a microwave oven, and many of the technological conveniences that our grandchildren enjoy as necessities. And then, there's email, Google, Amazon, Instacart, drones, and the many resources that have become contemporary amenities.

There were very few computers in my hometown when I was a teen, and only computer scientists could use them. When I was working on my masters degree, the computer occupied almost the entire basement of an academic building on campus and used punch cards for processing. Now, I wear more computing power on my wrist than existed in those early computers. The speed of change is becoming what we call *disruptive*—when innovation breaks an industrial or societal usual course of events. A familiar example is what the automotive industry did to makers of buggy whips. It's what white boards and markers did to classroom chalk boards. It's what CD's and DVD's did to tape recordings, what the cloud did to CD's and DVD's, and what the Covid pandemic has done to what we once called "normal life."

We could go on and on reminiscing about how we had to learn parallel parking and remember phone numbers. It can be fun for us to recall the stuff of our youth, but the more we talk about it, the more we realize how foreign and quaint our world must seem to the Instant Generation. These stories of "dialing" a phone call can seem funny and entertaining *if* we summarize with examples of how we've adapted and now relate to their world. In our reminiscing, we must not seem out-of-touch or irrelevant. Not only is this important to our maintaining credibility with the young people, it provides an excellent role model of adaptation for them as there is every indication that this speed of change will continue, and perhaps, even accelerate. These rapid and disruptive changes are not only a challenge for grandparents, they will ultimately challenge the *Instant Generation.* Certainly, equipping the children to cope with the changes in technology and the environment, while still maintaining their faith, values, and aspirations will prepare them for their futures.

The challenge is that this *instant* connection of everyone and everything through what we call cyberspace has created a virtual world with no legal or moral authority. With the speed of change, the domination of technology, and the many disruptive innovations in our lives, we cannot afford to become irrelevant to the most important people in our lives. Interestingly, one of the few things we've seen return to the old way is the current fascination with vinyl recordings, but I'm not sure that we grandparents can risk being like vinyl records.

Birth of the Instant Generation

Although authorities don't agree on an exact date that the technology generation began, we can see major changes in the late 1990's with the availability of the *World Wide Web,* email, *eBay,* and *Amazon.* Cell phones became more convenient during this time, but they were big, expensive, and often unreliable. Despite preceding one of the worst economic recessions since the Great Depression, 2007 was remarkable in that it was the year of the introduction of the *iPhone, Android,* and *Kindle.* That year, *Google* bought *YouTube, IBM* created *Watson,* its artificial intelligence system; then *Facebook* and *Twitter* went global, and *Airbnb* was founded. The year 2007 was also the beginning of an exponential rise in solar energy, wind, biofuels, LED lighting, the significant electrification of vehicles, and an emphasis on energy efficient buildings.

For simplicity, we call children who entered the workforce around the turn of the century the *Millennial Generation*. I refer to those born after 2007 as the *Instant Generation* or the *iGens*. We may even call children born after 2019 the *cGens*, as the Covid virus caused another disruption in society—in the economy, the way we live, and even the way we greet each other. Regardless of the label, today's young people exist in a rapidly changing world. We can debate the effect of excessive screen time on them, just as our parents were concerned about the amount of time we watched television, and their parents probably worried about too much time listening to the radio. It seems that many technologies come into common use before the impact is thoroughly understood. Then, time seems to be needed before society really understands the consequences.

When we were teens and committed an infraction of the rules, we could expect to hear, "You're grounded!" meaning that we were confined and isolated from everyone except for attending school. Today, when parents exclaim "You're grounded!" they must also remember to include the caveat, "Go to your room, while I lock away your iPhone, iPad, notebook computer, smart watch, disconnect the wifi, and remove the TV from your room." Of course, that's no longer a threat because the misbehaving teen can retort, "But I need them to do my school assignments."

Recently, we've become aware that, although today's children are connected by technology, they are not always positively engaged with people, especially during times of quarantine or social distancing. We can worry about possible vision or hearing damage from too much screen time and ear phones that blast loud music, but the real concern may be how technology can so easily replace human interactions. Since humans seem to need some contact with other real people, the absence of interactions can be deleterious. Different personalities and people of different ages may vary in their needs for contact, but no technology is an adequate replacement for human interactions. That's where we grandparents can supplement and replacc some of the screen time. We can have captivating conversations over their favorite Saturday lunch, offer a pick-up from school on Friday for some miniature golf, a favorite activity, or simply connect via an interesting phone call. Their screen time is a huge technological advantage and a part of their world, but they still need interactions with us. Any excuse or function that produces positive interactions and makes a good memory is a contribution to their development.

A very intelligent, articulate friend met me for lunch one day with the opening exclamation of, "Steve Jobs must be burning in hell for what he's done!" Quite surprised at the uncharacteristic pronouncement of this very conservative physician's anger, I replied, "Well, considering that he was an atheist, but what did he do that's made you so angry today?" The quick reply was, "He's hijacked my granddaughter, along with almost every other adolescent! He provided these young people with something that's as addictive as cocaine!" Then, she went on to lament that her granddaughter seemed to be withdrawing and was always either "thumbing her iPhone or glued to her iPad."

As much as I depend on the technology that Steve Jobs led the development of, I had to agree with my friend about the tech effect on teens. From my first Mac computer in 1986 to the MacPro on which I'm writing this treatise, I love the Apple tools. But perhaps, that's the difference, whether using the innovations of Steve Jobs, Bill Gates, or some other techno-genius, we adults utilize the technology as tools to accomplish something. Instead, the adolescents use their iPhones, iPads, and computers as a way of life—a lifestyle that diminishes their human interactions, good manners, and their use of correct language. These technologies may subject them to cyber bullying, lead to depression in adolescent girls, and even cause a lack of sleep. How can we, as grandparents, adapt to this technology, and at the same time, help our grandchildren to use it effectively? How can we ensure that these tools are for their advantage rather than their detriment?

First, we must acknowledge that the technology is as much a part of the grandchildren's world as the electric light bulb is a part of ours. Our great-great-grandparents might scoff at our regard of electricity as a necessity if they never experienced it. We can see movies and read about life before the electrification of homes, but it's hard to imagine life without this convenience, and besides, who would want to exist without electric lights today? Isn't it called an *emergency* when a storm takes out the electricity? Could this be how our grandchildren regard their technology? Just as we've never known life without electric lights, our grandchildren have never known life without instant access to the internet.

Perhaps the ancient Romans complained about the innovation of scrolls instead of the familiar stone tablets, just as we whine about how technology has replaced our familiar books and print media. When my grandson heard my complaints about kids being glued to their screens, he asked an interesting question about what people did on the bus or when they were alone in a restaurant before the days of mobile technology. After a moment, I replied, "Well, they might have read a newspaper, or perhaps a magazine." Then he said, "Gran, isn't it the same? Have people just replaced their reading instruments? When they're alone, they read from their phones, just as Great-Grandpa's generation read the newspaper, right?" I nodded, wondering where he was going with this one. Then he added, "Screens or phones are only a problem when it becomes easier to text people nearby rather than actually talking with them. It would be like four friends sitting at a restaurant table, all reading their newspapers instead of having a conversation, or like someone who always had his nose in a book instead of interacting in the world, right?" I smiled and nodded at his observation.

Although it may be beneficial to limit passive screen time, especially at the dinner table, perhaps we should analyze the technology and its benefits and detriments. Completely eliminating technology use from the Instant Generation could be compared to our being forced to live without electricity. Instead, coding, building robots, using technology for creative writing, graphic skills, and even non-violent games can simulate young brains and be useful. But just like a steady diet of any one kind of food can be unhealthy, an unlimited diet of screen time can be a harmful influence.

Grandparent Credibility and Remaining Relevant

The rapid pace of today's change in so many different areas can seem overwhelming and disorienting. But it isn't essential for us to embrace every new *app,* drive an electric car, or install solar panels on the roof to demonstrate our relevance to the grandchildren. Rather, it's our *attitude* toward the new that's critical. We cannot be obstinate and recalcitrant. Instead, demonstrating curiosity with an open mindset and being interested in learning about the new is important, not only to maintaining credibility, but also to being a positive role model for the children. When talking about a new app, it's easy to be an old mumpsimus and say to my grandson, "Oh, that's too complicated for me, and besides, I'd have no use for it." But then, he might take the same attitude about learning statistics or pursuing a graduate degree. Such a dismissive comment could send the wrong message, like the comments I heard when young that "math is hard for girls." We cannot allow our superfluous comments to cause the young ones to reach discouraging conclusions. Even though we may have no interest in and no idea about their recent discoveries, we must not dampen their curiosity and creativity toward positive pursuits. Instead, innovations can become a means to engage them in interesting conversations.

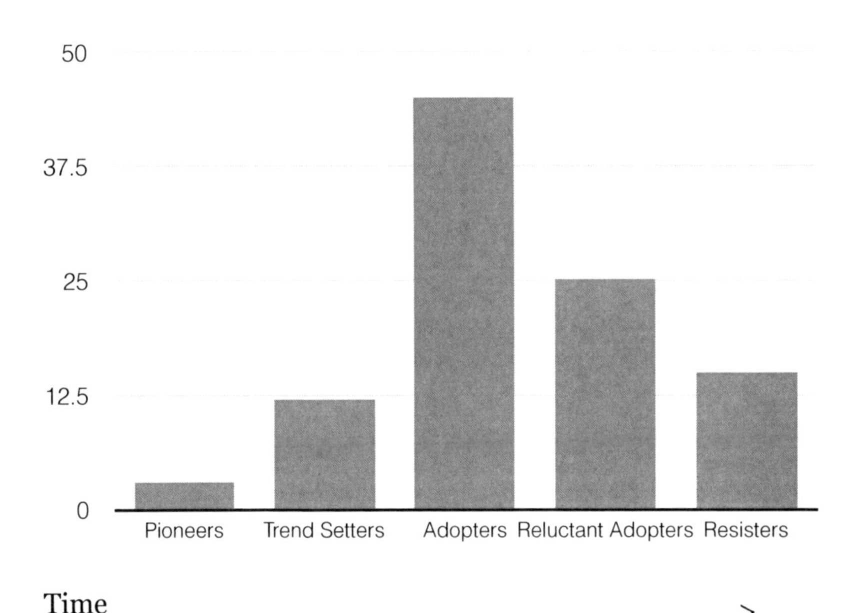

ACCEPTANCE OF CHANGE AND INNOVATIONS
(Distribution Estimates)

When did you become interested in a smart phone or digital photography? What prompted you to get an email address or investigate Bitcoin or a smart watch? Where would you be on this graph? Where we take action, if at all, is not as important as our attitude toward change. Although we may not have the interest, resources, or use for every innovation, it's important to show the children an attitude of curiosity. Although we need not be a "Trend Setter," we must not demonstrate the attitude of reluctance as we brag about how much we liked our old "flip phone."

It's interesting that young people often assume that older people are automatically "out-of-touch Reluctants," but it's fun to change their assumptions.

On the evening of June 29, 2007, I was in the long line outside of the Apple Store in Atlanta, waiting to buy the "about-to-be-released" new iPhone (my flip phone had just died). Several teenage boys in line with me would ask, "Who are you holding a place in line for?" and I would smile and reply, "Me!" Their somewhat puzzled response was usually, "Cool!" or "You, really?" Now, had I been a Pioneer, I would have bought the original IBM smart phone in 1994, but that would not have been a wise decision because the *Simon* was taken off the market in only six months. We want to help children learn the difference between a fad and an innovation that changes an industry or society. We can do that by showing them how to investigate, consider, research, and learn about the new. Although we want to demonstrate an inquiring attitude toward change and innovation, we need not jump on every change, just maintain our positive inquisitive approach. We can resist change vehemently when clinging to our values and culture, but for matters of technology, innovation, and process improvements, we can remain relevant and credible with our attitudes.

Older people may be tempted to cling to the old ways, but just because something is familiar, doesn't ensure its superiority. Concomitantly, the Instant Generation may assume that old is inferior and that all new methods are superior. As in many situations in life, when we attempt to make everything either/or and good/bad, we miss opportunities. Instead, it's better for us grandparents to make judgements based on merit and set a good example.

Although the old rotary phone that hung on the wall in the kitchen of my parents' home when I was young was familiar, reliable, and made their lives easier, its potential for making my life more efficient cannot be compared to my smart phone. Yet, when the *iPhone* and *Android* were first announced, many of us grandparents probably regarded the idea of paying several hundred dollars for a complex telephone as lunacy. Then, we learned that it was a phone, a camera, calendar, calculator, computer, an information system, an instant letter delivery system, much more, and we adapted.

Children are often fascinated by tales of what life was like when we were their age, but to maintain our credibility with them as they grow, it helps to be able to also relate to and function in their world. When excited grandchildren talk about what they're developing at their maker space, it's important to listen and relate to the young innovators.

We wouldn't expect to maintain a relationship with someone who came to visit from another part of the world if we rejected everything about them—their food, clothing, hairstyle, or interests. In the same way, we cannot reject or act disinterested in our grandchildren's world. Even though they may sometimes seem a bit foreign, we'll maintain our bond if we express interest—even when everything inside us screams disapproval because it's so different. We can disapprove breaches in character, but show interest in innovation. We'll be more influential if we take an inquisitive approach, rather than declaring immediate rejection. Sometimes, it helps to remember how obnoxious we may have been at the same age. That's when we choose a short-term annoyance in favor of remaining relevant to them as we pursue a life long relationship.

Educating the Instant Generation

The pace of change was slower when we grandparents were in school. What we learned in high school and college was relevant and remained applicable for our foreseeable future. When we were in school, Pluto was a planet, an occasional 16mm film was a treat, and DNA wasn't even mentioned in our old tattered biology textbooks.

Perhaps the best example of how much faster knowledge and relevance has changed is the use of deoxyribonucleic acid, DNA. The cell material that now seems to be the center of every crime scene investigation is the molecule that carries genetic instructions used in the reproduction of cells. After discovery in 1953, decades were needed before it was used in criminal trials to identify a perpetrator. In 2003, it cost about a $1M to map one person's DNA. A decade later, it could be done for less than a $1,000, Today, its use has become commonplace.

Another interesting example is *germs*. These pathogens were postulated by the ancient Greeks, but it wasn't until the mid-nineteenth century that their role in the spread of disease was considered. Throughout the twentieth century we became aware of the necessity of sterility in medicine. Yet, only in the twenty-first century did the requirement for hand sanitation in some hospitals become standardized. The Covid pandemic taught us how quickly viruses spread, the value of a mask, and the importance of frequent 20-second hand washing. These simple examples forced us to realize how the speed of change has been compressed in recent years.

Technology, and this ever increasing speed of change have obliged today's students become life-long learners. As there is increasing competition for jobs, there will be increasing pressure for learning and developing new skills, especially in the technology area. Consider the colossal changes that have occurred during the last four or five decades in how we shop, travel, work, get information, and function in other aspects of life. Yet, let's look at the changes in how we educate children.

Many students begin some type of school experience at an earlier age. Most classrooms are air conditioned, accommodating a different school calendar from what some of us knew. Instead of heavy desks bolted to the floor, some students sit at tables, on the floor, or in desks on casters that even have a cup holder. The dust of chalkboards has been banished in favor of white panels and brightly colored markers. Yet, other aspects of the school classroom remains the same.

If we analyze the structure of traditional schools, we find many facets from the schools of the past when education reflected the needs of the Industrial Revolution. In the 1960's when society placed a strong emphasis on having every student complete high school, some standards were lowered or adapted in order to make that possible. A result of the 1970's was a move away from the classical education model of western civilization to a more global approach. Yet, none of these incremental changes fully reflect the needs of today's students or economy.

Even in many expensive private schools, there remains an emphasis on the traditional educational model. Students' common question is, "Will this be on the test?" Such schools readily meet the needs of visual and auditory learners who develop savvy test taking skills, but the more creative and divergent thinkers may be left behind. From Henry Ford, Thomas Edison, and Winston Churchill to Elon Musk and Steven Spielberg, none of these accomplished men made good grades in school. Perhaps divergent thinking boys either "act out" or "check-out," whereas girls who think differently may become depressed or mediocre students. Many biographies of successful people note their dropping out of school to pursue their passions. School simply didn't capture their interests or feed their creativity as it was all too often about *the right answer*. In too many places, the public education of the past is too much like today's schools. If we are to invest 13-14 years of every child's life in schools, then we must be certain that this educational environment stimulates their learning, nurtures their abilities, develops their thinking skills, and exposes them to new horizons.

Relevance of Traditional Education

Just as in the 1800's, modern traditional school classrooms need the students to be compliant. Much of the learning has been expected to occur through the student's passive listening to the teacher or reading from a book or working from a tablet. To a great extent the purpose of this learning is about memory—memorize the multiplication tables, name the Great Lakes, recite the States and their capitals. Even though the requirements in many school systems have been expanded, somehow young people seem to know less. An enterprising TV reporter did interviews on several college campuses asking students the name of the current U.S. Vice-President, the dates of the Civil War, and the difference between the Reformation and the Renaissance. Numerous respondents made the viewer laugh, but the students' ignorance was more pathetic than funny. When state requirements have often been increased for public education, how can students know less? When a major classroom emphasis is on memory, how can college students have such limited knowledge and often require remedial tutoring?

With enormous expenditures for U.S. education, it's perplexing that we're not enjoying greater return on the investments. Many classrooms have more than one teacher or a teacher and an assistant. The old ruler of corporal punishment is long forgotten, but yet, discipline continues to be an issue that impedes learning in many classrooms. Some children thrive and some classrooms are superb environments, but there may be a problem with consistent quality. When we explore failing schools and inferior quality in education, the results are often a blame game, the objects of which range from lack of parental support, to lack of quality teachers and adequate expenditures.

There are examples of innovative and highly successful classrooms or schools, but American education is not what we'd like it to be for every child. Rarely have we been able to improve the whole system. While the last century has seen indescribable gains in so many areas of life, the public education system has remained too much the same. Even though it's efficient and economical, there has never been any proof that putting a number of children of the same chronological age in a room with one or even two adults and some visual materials can result in quality learning. Usually, the curriculum is presented to groups, or the entire class, and everyone is expected to grasp and retain the knowledge the same way and at the same time. We have invested little research in examining how children learn in order to develop corresponding environments that support individual learning. Worse, there has been limited consideration of the full potential of how technology can be utilized for learning. Instead, when the pandemic forced online learning for many students, the same traditional classroom methods were simply transferred online.

The story of how quickly students seized on Salman Kahn's series of videos in 2006 to supplement their learning, and how quickly Kahn's tutoring efforts became a free resource, is fascinating. Although not perfect, *Kahn Academy* was embraced by students all over the world. In a few places, the Kahn videos have reversed the way that teachers work. Instead of lecturing in class, then assigning practice homework, the students first watch assigned videos on their computers that illustrate the concepts at home via the internet. Then the next day, the teacher uses class time for discussion and individual help. This method ensures consistency in the presentation of material, while giving students more individual and "hands-on" experiences. An advantage is that engaging visuals and illustrations make the homework less pedantic and arduous. In addition, if the student didn't achieve comprehension with the first exposure, or needs review of the material, the video can be repeated at any time. With its success, and even despite some critics, it's interesting that this method has not made a greater impact on the average classroom.

With the speed and ease of information access, students often ask, "Why do I need to know that?" I often ask the same question. Today, students need to know *how to know*. In the future, perhaps a mark of intelligence won't be knowing the answers as much as having developed the ability to ask the right questions. Perhaps the mark of a true genius will be the ability to analyze, solve problems, and make effective decisions.

Today's students may already have developed the technical skills to research and find facts, but those skills may be directed toward gaming and going places on the internet that are not safe or productive for them. Maintaining an emphasis on memory—knowing the answers—we cling to a form of education focused on taking-in information and remembering the right answers for a test. With today's concerns about high stakes testing, it's not surprising that students seem to be more intent on the exam grade than on what's they're actually learning. After all, college admissions applications don't ask for a demonstration of analysis and decision making skills. There's no question about how the student will apply previous learning to the college experience. The simple question is, "What's your grade point average (GPA)?"

It seems that we have placed the only emphasis on the acquisition of knowledge and have forgotten the importance of understanding and comprehension within the larger context. Instead of focusing on analysis, synthesis, application of knowledge, and full utilization of technology in education, in some instances, we've told students to put away their smart phones and tablets, and use pencil and paper for worksheets. Unfortunately, one of the deficits of this Instant Generation is that their technology has shortened their attention spans and made them impatient with writing and reading printed books.

In the past, two decades were often required between proof of process or technology and its accepted use in the classroom. Perhaps there are a couple of reasons for this lag. First, it is sometimes expensive. For example, by the time that schools were building computer labs in the early 2000's where groups of students, in turn, were given introductory instruction to computers, many students had experience with their own personal or family computers at home. More significant, the limited time and group use often had little impact, but perhaps the biggest problem was that, in the time required for adoption and installation, many of these computer labs quickly became computer dinosaurs, making schools even more reluctant to further invest in technology. Although Covid quickly forced utilization of technology, there was little time or strategy in its most effective use to change how the curriculum is pursued.

The second reason that change and improvement in education occur so slowly is the issue of familiarity. When adults walk into school classrooms, we seem to prefer a setting that we recognize. We may be more comfortable to see a conventional classroom of desks in neat rows in a commonplace setting with which we can identify. Especially in rural areas, this expectation of "school and homework like I had" often pressures teachers toward traditional education, even though it may not be the most appropriate setting for today's children.

Whatever the setting, the curriculum, or the teaching arrangement, perhaps the most important focus for today's schools is to create an energy and zeal for learning. An excitement in explorations can nurture an eagerness for much reading and ability to communicate, inform, and persuade verbally and through composition—what we called "writing." Developing a positive approach to math can, not only result in enhanced thinking skills, but can create a pathway to the new curricular emphasis on STEM —science, technology, engineering, and mathematics. Immersing young children in nature helps them learn to value the environment, and stimulates their future interest in biology, botany, geology, chemistry, and other areas of science.

More urgent, skills for today's students in the "learning how to learn" category must include study skills. We can no longer assume that, just because the students recognize all of the words in a reading passage that they completely understand and can use what they've read. When many students are impatient with reading long passages and may even struggle with independent learning, study skills become critical. Being able to find the important points in a passage of text, gaining complete comprehension of the text, and being able to apply, analyze, and evaluate can make the difference between a struggling and a successful student. The same skills that foster students' focus and effective study habits also become important for test taking. As we continue to measure worth, achievement, and potential for college admission and beyond by performance on exams, the students who can perform well on different kinds of tests will excel.

Another Opportunity for Grandparents

In reality, study and test taking skills can make a crucial difference in the child's school success at any age or grade level. When they're young, we can help by reading with them and talking about the important points in paragraphs or short passages. By discussing what we're reading together, we can help them comprehend what has been read. When you and I were young, we were taught to take care of our books and never write or mark in them. Today, we've learned the value of underlining or highlighting important points and gleaning the essence of our reading material. Unless using a library, school book, or a valuable antique first edition; don't be hesitant to underline and show the child how marking the reading material can be useful for recall and understanding. Library and school books must be preserved in pristine condition, without underlining or highlighting. In situations, where the child does not own the book, instead of underlining, yellow sticky notes can be used to mark or record important points. Both techniques can eliminate the need for re-reading and enable a quick review for comprehension.

When reading from an iPad or tablet, showing the child how to highlight important points by touching the words, and how the device assimilates the notes, can build essential skills for comprehension and higher level thinking skills. The children can be shown that underlining, highlighting, inserting sticky notes, and having a special journal for major content, can help to concentrate on comprehending the essence of what has been read. Regardless of the educational setting, a full complement of study skills will enhance the learning.

In one of our delightful Saturday dinners with my father and grandson, the child was shocked at Great-Grandpa's comments about the importance of cursive writing. In an era when cursive writing is not a part of the national common curriculum and no longer taught in many schools, this business of cursive writing seemed foreign to my grandson. Grandpa explained that, in the nineteenth century and much of the twentieth century, cursive writing was an indication of being educated, ambitious, and even a mark of good character. Yes, Great-Grandpa lived in a world quite foreign to his great-grandchild who, like many of the *Instant Generation* is adamant that he has no need for writing anything and can be totally competent with two-fingered keyboarding. I maintain, however, that another part of this "learning how to learn" should include the early introduction of keyboard skills. We can debate the stupidity of the "qwerty" arrangement of letters and its origin to prevent typewriter keys from colliding, but today's technology still uses that same arrangement, regardless of its relevance.

Even though many young people insist that they don't need what we grandparents called "proper keyboard skills," I can compose or input text faster and more accurately than anyone using the "two finger method." Until speech-to-text software is perfected, I'll still encourage my grandson to use the same keyboard method that I learned in high school and to write legibly in cursive. Our great-

great-grandchildren's world may need a "Rosetta Stone" to be able to read their ancestors' letters that were written in cursive. Actually, they may also marvel at the need to use those antique computer keyboards because their generation will be able to just "think or say" the instructions as the technology grows.

Although the method of "writing" has changed, there is an increasing value for "thought presentation." From the classroom to business and the political arena, there is an emphasis on the need to be persuasive and influential. We must be able to develop, speak articulately, and present projects and ideas. Unfortunately, many classroom experiences don't foster such skills. Even the casual grandparent conversations can encourage thoughtful expression. When we give them reasons to draw and show us their ideas, and when we cultivate their thinking skills, we're supplementing vital proficiencies that may not be available for them in school.

Ideally, every educational experience should include art, music, and activities that encourage and enhance the creative potential in every child, but when resources are limited, opportunities may not be available for every student. In such circumstances, these could be experiences that grandparents may need to provide. Since not every school includes a chance to study or actively participate in art and music, perhaps we can include more concerts and trips to museums in our activities. We may need to provide instruments, materials, and perhaps, even pay for lessons that enrich the lives and development of our grandchildren. At least, we can play classical music in the car, play card games that use photographs of great art, and express an attitude of appreciation for great art and music.

Since schools are a series of group settings, it's become a major function for them to teach positive student/human interaction as sports have become a tool for learning to be part of a team. Although some schools have an excessive emphasis on athletics, it's vital for children and adolescents to have adequate physical activity. When too many of our youth are becoming obese, their physical activity must be encouraged.

The emphasis on collaboration in many workplaces has echoed the importance of team sports. These can be awesome opportunities for youth that fulfill physical, interactive, and collaborative training. If these are inappropriate or not available for the teens, here's another opportunity for grandparents. We can coach and shoot basketballs with the children. We can follow them around the golf course, the batting cages, pay for tennis lessons, or take long walks and hikes with them. Regardless of team or individual sports, our role is to introduce, encourage, and support vigorous physical activity throughout their lives and establish patterns of exercise that keep them alert and robust, even when they're our age.

Perhaps one of our major contributions may be in encouraging the grandchild's safety in physical activity, in avoiding the head injuries so prevalent in some sports. If dad was a football hero or mom was a cheerleader, the parents may see no problem with football or soccer. Yet, as we grandparents continue to read the research on sports concussions, and look at how many of the football players we knew in high school and college are now gone, we may not have the same enthusiasm for such sports. The cheerleader who just jumped and waved her arms around in our day is nothing like today's cheerleader who has become a gymnast and is bumped and thrown through the air. Worse, we see the statistics on how many young athletes become addicted to pain medications after a sports injury, then seek illegal drugs to feed their addiction.

Rather than cause a needless family conflict by loudly voicing our concerns, a better approach may be in the early introduction of tennis, golf, track, swimming, or other individual sports. By creating an enthusiasm for a non-contact sport, we may avoid the issue. Although accidents can occur in any of the alternative activities, still, there may be less danger than in tackle football or the head shots of soccer.

Sometimes, the best approach to solving a problem can be an indirect approach. If we focus only on our goal—preventing head injuries—and not on our role in defining the problem, we're more likely to be successful in maintaining our grandchildren's safety. We don't need to enumerate the dangers or to get credit for outlining the risks. I know that I'm *right* about the inherent risks in activities that can result in head injuries and health risks, but just being right isn't enough. I must be diplomatic, articulate, clever, and carefully prepared if I am to be *effective*. I must always remember Rule #2, it isn't about just being *right*. I must also be *effective*.

The Learning Environment

As you can ascertain from my description of traditional education, I have major concerns about the environment that we offer children. When I left educational leadership and moved to a career in organizations, the focus of much of my work in the adult world was the same as it had been before—to solve problems, help people learn new skills and thrive. In the world of adults, however, there's a requirement for providing a variety of interesting and energizing learning experiences. Although I usually suggest a selection of articles and books, I would never consider lecturing about leadership to executives and sending them home to get the rest from a book or complete a series of mindless work sheets and return the next day with a total grasp of knowledge. In adult education, it's a necessity to provide interesting, interactive, and engaging activities. Many adults like to learn by doing; therefore, their learning opportunities must be relevant, experiential, self-directing, and involve all of the senses. Think about how awesome such an approach would be in every classroom. It perturbs me that, despite the fact that we know how effective experiential, interactive learning is for adults, opportunities for this kind of learning diminishes with each succeeding grade level in school. What is intolerable for adults must be endured by children.

Countless people, when confessing that they were not good students will say, "Well, I was excited about school when I was little. I loved pre-K and kindergarten. Mom said that I cried at the end of first grade, but somewhere into second or third grade, I just kinda checked-out." When we examine the curriculum and what is actually happening in the classrooms, it's easy to see the problem. From third grade onward, there is greater dependency on learning through visual and auditory channels, i.e. listening to the teacher and reading from a book or on a tablet. With few "hands-on" activities, the experiential learners' opportunities are diminished. Yet, these learners often excel in art, music, and laboratory courses, especially if they can have some measure of self-direction to learn at their own pace.

After second grade, public school classes are generally larger and the need for compliance is increased. Many classrooms become less stimulating places and everyone is supposed to learn the same subject matter in the same way, at the same time, and in what teachers often call the "lock-step" method.

It's typical to meet the school age child in the afternoon and ask, "Whad-ja do in school today?" but that may be the wrong question. Instead, we can ask, "What did you do today that was interesting and exciting?" If that doesn't spark a stimulating conversation, perhaps we can follow with, "You've been in school all day, so was there anything that you didn't get enough of or anything that you want to know more about?" We must always be alert to academic or behavioral issues that might trouble the child, but we should also be ready to provide extensions of the learning and ignite the child's discovery in other ways.

Traditional education is an inferior system for the twenty-first century where teachers often work in less than desirable conditions. It’s a world with much emphasis on grades and test scores. And yet, our dear grandchildren must spend a decade in what may not be an ideal environment for them. The good news is that they have us! We can supplement their needs without ever verbalizing our feelings about the rest of their world. We can stimulate their curiosity, creativity, and energize their enjoyment of learning. We can avoid asking about grades and test scores and say, “Tell me about what was interesting that you’ve learned this week." We can listen to their frustrations. We can provide what’s missing in their world. We can express interest in what they’re doing. And most of all, we can support and encourage their efforts.

Teacher Focus

It's unfortunate that teacher training includes more effective methods of facilitating learning, but the circumstances under which they often work may make it difficult for teachers to implement the improvements. Although it seems ridiculous, teacher education and teaching practice could be compared to learning technology skills in college, only to be sent to a workplace of typewriters or picks and shovels.

For teachers, there’s often an issue of student behavior. Because some children may have difficulty focusing attention, those students require additional time as the teachers struggle to maintain a learning atmosphere. Such children may arrive at school with hyperactivity, attention deficit disorder, other learning and physical disabilities, on medications or without a diet of nutritious food. According to the U. S. Department of Health and Human Services, more than half of the births in many states, and 42.3% nationally in 2018, were paid for by Medicaid, indicating that many children were born into poverty. When the children of needy or addicted parents reach the public school classroom, they may struggle with focusing attention, or retaining information. There are few options for appropriate responses to behavioral issues as many teachers and school systems may be under threat from our litigious society.

From about age eight onward, greater compliance is needed from "good students," to accommodate others. Because some students may not demand as much attention as the discipline problems, and if their primary learning styles are not visual or auditory, they sink quietly into mediocrity. Actually, the problem may be that they're starved for the right learning opportunity to meet their needs. Their environment of required compliance, large classes, teachers distracted by the unruly kids and bogged down by administrative tasks, limits many "good students." When teachers must be focused on the disruptive children, and there are limited interactive learning opportunities, school can become a turn-off for those who learn differently. With so many classroom complications, teachers have little time or opportunity to even think about our grandchildren's preferred learning mode, much less to provide for it.

In addition to much administrative work, many classroom teachers must be attentive to children with special needs. These children face such adversity that the classroom can be their escape, their haven, and sometimes the teacher, their only adult friend.

Although accountability for teacher performance in traditional education is sometimes thwarted by unions and other forces, many teachers are dedicated to their profession. They accomplish as much as possible under the circumstances. They invest their own money in teaching aids and classroom materials. Most make every effort to enhance the children's experience, despite conditions that are often not conducive to learning.

Schools may not be a perfect place for children, but neither are they a state of nirvana for teachers. Maybe we can teach the grandchildren how to approach teachers and appropriately seek help. We can encourage the children to be cooperative and respect their teachers. We can be clever in finding ways to make our grandchildren's educational world better without castigating the world of schools.

The Social Atmosphere of Schools

We wonder about the effects of the stress of deprivation, emotional trauma, and home inconsistencies on the children who will sit next to our grandchildren in the classroom. We're concerned about the influence these stressed children will have on our young ones who've enjoyed a relatively stress free life. We have concerns about how these unfortunate children will become part of the fabric of our grandchildren's society when they live in the upheaval of a revolving door of family members, constant bickering, and even violence.

Despite the child's age, grade, location, or economics of the school population, there is no guarantee or way to anticipate what the students surrounding our precious children will be like. Whether they will be kind, tolerant, cooperative, of good character, use proper language, or have a positive demeanor is important. They will have an enormous impact on the overall school environment and on our grandchildren. We can help children develop good social skills for interacting with others and help them make decisions about choosing friends who will be positive influences in their lives. A major challenge, however, is to help them function effectively in a world of others who do not have the love and advantages that we are giving our special grandchildren.

Social Comparison

We humans often fall prey to what may be called the *social comparison mindset,* wherein we measure our own social and personal worth on how we compare to others. We seem to be more comfortable when surrounded by those who appear to be most like us and indicate their approval of us. As older adults, we've experienced these feelings in life and learned to measure our worth against our own standards, rather than being ruled by status or how well we stack up against others. Our grandchildren, however, may still need to learn those lessons, and they may benefit from our help in getting there. From infancy, we give them our support and encouragement. We use every opportunity to build their confidence and help them construct their own self-identify, free from definition by their peers. We unobtrusively help them to develop social skills that will lead them to positive influences and choose social interactions that contribute to their development. It's been said that the quality of our friends is a good predictor of our future. As devoted grandparents, we certainly want to do everything possible to ensure that our precious grandchildren are equipped at every age to choose friends of good character who will be assets to their everyday interactions and their futures.

One of the worst threats of being with undesirable people is that they're often intimidating and subject others to bullying—physical or verbal abuse. Most of us can recall the bigger kid who took out his or her frustrations on others. We soon learned how we could avoid the bully and stay out of the path of the taunts and torment. One of the unfortunate realities of the Internet Generation is that it isn't possible to run away from cyber bullying, hateful comments posted on social media. The hate, vitriol, and evil that some people can propel via the internet, anonymously, and from afar is astounding. Perhaps a well known example of what has become known as cyber bullying is Monica Lewinsky, who in a 2015 TED Talk described what happened after her tryst with President Clinton became public. Even though the President was able to recover his reputation, the years of cyber bulling continued for Lewinsky. In her TED presentation, she revealed that it was only through her family's support that she learned to cope with the cyber bulling that perpetuated her youthful and life-changing mistakes.

Although there may be little that a grandparent can do to actually stop a grandchild from being bullied or cyber bullied, we can listen, offer comfort, and help the child to think of ways to avoid the bully. Most of all, we can refute the hateful comments and help to build a more accurate and positive sense of self-worth. We can make an undesirable situation into an opportunity to further develop the child's EQ. We can help the child recognize the bully's irresponsibility and lack of empathy. We can talk about the harm that the bully does with no regard for others. We can also talk about why the bully is so mean and suggest that this need to hurt others may come from the bully's own insecurity or lack of feeling loved. Even though we're not always in the position to take actions that remove the bully from the child's environment, we can always listen, comfort, and offer support. If the child spends the day being taunted by others, it's imperative that we provide a safe haven, a place that refutes the insults with positive, caring assurances.

When a young person is struggling in school or in life, whether from academic, social, or physical causes, we must be alert for signs of depression due to bullying or abuse. Continued sadness, hopelessness, blank stares, decreased energy, and loss of interests are a few of the signals for which we grandparents must be alert. If we see these signals, it may be time to discuss with the parents and diplomatically urge or provide professional support.

Sometimes, grandparents loudly advocate teaching the child to "take care of yourself, hit back, and punch 'em in the gut," but that would only further complicate the child's situation today, probably causing punishment or school suspension. While too much of traditional education clings to the past, one major change is that today's schools cannot tolerate any kind of physical violence. With many schools employing a police resource or security presence, advocating that the child become involved in a physical ruckus, or use recently acquired karate skills, would not solve anything for the child. Physical defense and what might have worked for grandparents would be totally unacceptable for a youngster of today. Yes, grandfather could probably fight the bully and might have even had a gun as a teen. He knew how to use firearms, but he thought of them as instruments for shooting pesky squirrels or tin cans and was incredibly aware of firearms safety. It would never have occurred to a student of his generation to take a gun to school or use it for salving his anger. Today, we must help children to develop skills to navigate peaceful means and protect them from violence.

If the child's physical safety is not threatened, such undesirable circumstances as bullying can be used as learning opportunities. If we've been successful in helping the child to develop perseverance, grit, gumption, and tough mindedness, then we can build on those qualities to guide the development of coping skills. As much as we want to remove the children from it, learning how to cope with unpleasant and frustrating situations can be an integral part of learning life skills. Unfortunately, this may not be the only time that our precious grandchildren will be in the presence of undesirable people. We can make a difference by helping them to know when to ask a trustworthy person for help and how to develop the skills to avoid or deal with bullies. Even if our grandchildren are not the target of bullying, we can contribute to their development of empathy and character when we help them to discourage the abuse of others by showing kindness and compassion to children who are being mistreated.

Sometimes, it's not just the school's social environment that concerns us. We may be alarmed by the general disarray in traditional education. We may have doubts or concerns about the learning environment, but we must always remember not to be critical of teachers or the school in the child's presence. The child doesn't have the ability to change schools or teachers. We must remember that, unless we're in the parental role, our ability to influence change is limited. If we have serious concerns, we may express them in private to the parents, but we must be sure that we don't break the child's trust in communicating what's been shared with us. When talking with the parent, we must also be cautious that we don't appear to be critical. If the parents are already aware of problems, our comments may only add to their worries and make them feel inadequate that they can't fix the child's difficulties. Unless we have the financial and other means to offer an alternative school, our role is to listen, be alert, give encouragement, supplemental lessons, positive experiences, or materials wherever possible.

Year of the Covid Pandemic

Inventions are not the only causes of major disruptions in society. When most businesses, workplaces, and all but "essential" functions came to a screeching halt in early 2020, many people found themselves working from home or at home without work. When the schools and colleges were forced to close in fear of the highly contagious virus, it sent teachers and parents scrambling to supplement the sudden life changes. Although many children arrived at home with workbooks and traditional assignments, many moved to learning from home via technology. Others, may not have had enough assignments to keep them busy while parents worked, prepared meals, and managed the stay-at-home family. Many teachers were forced to quickly convert the curriculum to an entirely different mode of teaching. With this time of online learning, assigning independent projects, and conducting classes via various video technologies, many students began to learn differently. In some situations, there seemed to be less pencil, paper, and listening to the teacher. Although the expertise with which these new technologies were employed varied, the pandemic forced numerous teachers to better utilize the technologies and a different mode of facilitating learning. Just as color television made it difficult to enjoy black and white TV, and computers made typewriters obsolete, this utilization of technology was forced upon education in many places. It became an alteration of immense magnitude that could be the revolution that moves education from the influence of the Industrial Revolution into a new exciting and effective era of learning.

This forced distance learning, along with some in-person classes also evidenced the fallacy in presenting the curriculum in a "lock-step" method. Children whose parents were attentive and involved benefitted from greater use of technology. Having greater control of their learning, and probably more adult involvement, these lucky kids moved ahead. Unfortunately, children whose parents could not be engaged in their learning, or who did not have the benefit of technology may have fallen further behind.

Perhaps even more important than the extensive use of technology was this greater involvement of some parents. Whether monitoring the online activities, or being directly engaged in helping with the lessons, many parents became more aware of the learning tools and how vast improvements could be made in the use of the child's time. An addition to parental involvement was the boost in parent/child relationships during this "stay at home" time. Although not every parent could be involved, and not every parent enjoyed the additional responsibilities, the Covid era certainly increased every parent's awareness of the role of school in the child's life. The pandemic certainly forced new uses of technology, greater parent involvement, and different approaches to education. Unfortunately, not all of the approaches were effective, resulting in significant learning deficiencies for many students.

In situations, such as the pandemic, grandparents may themselves highly involved in childcare and as a substitute teacher. Although these circumstances may be caused by stressful events, any time with grandchildren can become a marvelous opportunity for love and learning.

Summary

We can find historical records of people who became anxious and depressed about the speed of change at the dawn of the twentieth century. The transformations of Thomas Edison, Wilbur Wright, and Henry Ford seemed scary. Yet, our culture has adapted. We are no longer frightened by cars, electric lights, or airplanes. Just as our grandparents and great-grandparents learned to cope with what seems to be no big deal to us, we can adapt and be role models of solid growth and development for our grandchildren.

If progress is described by what we no longer have to think about, then I'm overwhelmed with the difference in my life today and that of my grandparents. As I contemplate the things that occupied much of my grandparents time and priorities—laundry, cooking, heating, keeping cool, growing and buying food, etc.—I think about our progress in the last century. I realize that none of my grandparents' primary issues take much of my time or thought. The laundry and ironing that required hours of my grandmothers' and their helpers' time, takes only minutes of mine. The coal burning fireplace and furnace that required my grandfather's attention doesn't even exist in my world. I can adjust the temperature with only a finger on the digital thermostat. The letter writing that occupied their Sunday afternoons takes only minutes for my emails. This fascination begs the question, "What do we think about and spend time on, that for our grandchildren will be incidental? Whatever it is, we must prepare them to approach it with curiosity, adaptability, perseverance, good character, and the blessings of God.

Although we live in a different world from our grandparents, education is much the same. Perhaps there's too much emphasis on *education,* and not enough on *learning*. If we are to continue to compete globally, we may need to advocate significant revisions in our system of traditional education. If we are to stay ahead of the robots,

Chinese, and other smart foreign competitors, we may not be able to get there by perpetuating a method of educating children that was developed for the Industrial Revolution. Although there has never been any research to prove the validity of the traditional education model for the full development of each student's potential, too much of the method continues. When we think about the gains that have been made in other areas of our world, it's scary to realize how little has changed in traditional education. We have only to look at the advances being made in technology, and especially in the area of artificial intelligence and virtual reality, to be jolted into the realization that the traditional classroom cannot be depended upon to give our grandchildren the preparation they need to be adequately prepared for their futures.

I will be thrilled to be told that my criticism of the use of the traditional model in schools is inaccurate, irrelevant, and invalid. Being wrong about my assertions that too many classrooms are inadequate would be my delight. I would be so happy to know that every student has an opportunity to learn at an optimum rate and in an environment that challenges and nurtures individual potential. If I'm not wrong, however, grandparents are still needed to supplement and support learning opportunities.

As grandparents, we may not be able to change the traditional education system, but we can enrich the lives of our grandchildren. As devoted nurturers, we want everything in our grandchildren's world to be perfect. We want to fix all of their problems and provide every toy, book, skill, and experience that will make them happy and develop their potential. We want them to have the benefit of everything we've learned and all that we have assimilated. We want them to explore with energy and curiosity. We want them to be creative and adaptable as we make their lives easy, happy, and wonderful. But wait, can we really do that? Isn't a part of life the learning of how to overcome difficulty? Yes, as much as we want to spare them from everything unpleasant, perhaps our greatest gift is in helping, encouraging, and supporting their learning to prevail when faced with adversity. Maybe instead of perfection, our biggest and best gift can be in an enthusiastic approach to learning, regardless of the school, the environment, or the circumstances. Showing them how to learn with energy, excitement, and curiosity; that's a magnificent gift. Teaching the value of persevering in the face of adversity—that becomes a blessing.

One of the concerns that we frequently hear about the younger generation in the workplace is that "They don't know what they don't know." By emphasizing curiosity and an eagerness for a lifetime of learning, we will give our grandchildren an advantage over many of their generation.

On one of my last days in elementary education leadership, I chatted with a group of "graduates," the students who were moving on to middle school. We discussed their favorite topics, what they had enjoyed, and what they would remember. After animated talk of subjects, activities, and field trips, a beautiful little girl with brown eyes and flowing brown hair gave me the best professional compliment of my entire career. She looked at me and said, "I'll remember that you made learning fun!" Nothing that I could ever do anywhere else could make me as excited or feel as gratified until my grandson verbalized something similar.

Making learning fun, effective, and developing a curious pursuit to become a life long learner—that's a gift that we grandparents can give our precious heirs.

Ancora imparo

"I am still learning"

(Attributed to Michelangelo when he was 87)

Chapter 7

Grandchildren's Personalities

Help us appreciate and honor their differences.

Sometimes, grandchildren's personalities are similar to a parent or grandparent's personality, but not always. It may be convenient and easier to relate to children whose demeanor, style, manner, and personalities are familiar and comfortable for us, but when they're very different, it can be challenging. This is when our toleration and appreciation of diversity is required. Perhaps the quote attributed to Carl Jung expresses our challenge, "Everything that irritates us about others can lead us to an understanding of ourselves."

Considering a child's personality and preferences not only helps us to better connect with the child, but it can help us nurture the child's individuality. Even though it's easy to develop chemistry with a child whose demeanor is similar to ours, we must be aware of the child who is different. Maybe we're aware that the affinity isn't there, that the bonding doesn't come easily, but we're not sure what to do about it. The child may sense that difference and see it as disapproval or rejection, a situation we grandparents must avoid.

There are numerous approaches to studying the child's temperament, but perhaps the easiest is to simply be aware of our own preferences, of the child's preferences, and how they are similar and different. We can just ask ourselves some questions about what we observe and how the child is like us, or not. Instruments listed in Appendix D can be helpful later, but may not be necessary for now. Simple awareness is the place to begin.

Exploring Preferences

Many factors make up the human personality—the type, set of emotional qualities, ways of behaving, etc., that make a person different from other people. Some are attractive qualities that make someone interesting or pleasant to be with, while other attributes may be less desirable or perplexing to us. We know that much of what constitutes personality is innate. We can even see it beginning to develop in the early part of the child's life. Sometimes, we see what pleases us, the emotions or behaviors with which we identify. Other times, we may observe something puzzling, but this is part of the challenging delight of being a grandparent. This is an opportunity for our learning as we help to nurture the child's development.

There has been considerable research into personality. It's been studied and written about since the time of the ancient Greeks. There are numerous instruments and materials available that attempt to define personality traits and predict behavior. These systems range from labeling personalities with various colors to the online questionnaire that identifies you with a cartoon character, but these may be of limited use for our purpose.

Perhaps the best source for considering the budding personalities of our grandchildren and supporting their development comes from a century of what began with the Swiss psychiatrist, Carl Jung (1875-1961), and Americans, Katherine Briggs (1875-1968) and Isabel Myers (1897-1980). Through the subsequent decades of work at the *Center for Applications of Psychological Type (CAPT)* and publication by the Myers Briggs Co., Myers' original research and development of the *Myers Briggs Type Indicator® (MBTI®),* has been continued. They keep the instruments' language current, expanding the supporting resources available, and making the materials relevant and very useful for today. If you're familiar with the key to unlocking Jung's ideas, the *MBTI,®* these concepts will be easy to apply to understanding the grandchildren. If not, there are resources in Appendix D for learning more about these extraordinary tools for children and adults. This material is not about psychopathology or Freudian analysis. Instead, the instrument uses everyday language and is a simple means of beginning grandparents' observations, awareness, and thinking about our special young people.

As a cursory introduction to considering how certain preferences make up a portion of our personalities, we can explore, in a very basic way, the four pairs of preferences in the *MBTI®*. Jung observed that much seemingly chance variation in human behavior is not due to chance but is the logical result of a few basic, observable differences in mental functioning.

The first is about our focus and the source of our energy. Psychological energy is like a power source that's constantly being depleted, but is refilled in different ways.

Think about just one grandchild at a time, in normal circumstances when the child is not hungry or tired. Choose a time when you can relax and reflect on the child. Think of what you notice in typical everyday situations, not of how you want the child to be or what the child might have learned. Then, circle the most likely response—what you observe most of the time. If your choice isn't immediate, just skip it for the moment, and think about that observation later.

There is no good or bad in any of these preferences and no correct score. Our main task here is to simply increase awareness.

Re-energizing

1. Would you ever think of this child as a "chatterbox," interacting eagerly with strangers, other children, and adults? Yes No

2. Does this child appear to be energized by being with people and interacting with the world? Yes No

3. Does the child initiate interactions with others, rather than hesitating to engage other people? Yes No

4. When the child was in a stroller and you were at the park or the grocery store, did the child respond to seeing other children or people who smiled and waved at the child? In the grocery store, was the child chattering and reaching for familiar items? Yes No

5. When the child was in a stroller and you were at the mall or the grocery store, was the child usually quiet, gazing studiously at people and objects? Yes No

6. Does this child appear to be quiet and thoughtful, carefully checking out situations before participating? Yes No

7. Does the child talk more comfortably in familiar situations to which the child is accustomed and with a few others who are very familiar? Yes No

8. Does this child enjoy solitary play or activities and prefer some quiet time alone? Yes No

The responses you just gave are about behaviors related to how the child might *re-energize.* If you circled *yes* to 1,2,3,4, and *no* to 5,6,7,8, these are indications that the child may prefer *extraversion,* indicating that he/she is re-energized by interacting with the external world of people and actions. Conversely, if your responses to 1,2,3,4 were *no* and *yes* to 5,6,7,8 these are indications that the child may have a preference for *introversion,* being re-energized by interacting with the internal world of thoughts and ideas. After observing and considering a source of the child's energy, look at your responses. If the responses were mixed, you may continue your observations, consider where there were more *yes* responses, or simply defer the observations for now. It isn't important to find a label, only to increase our understanding and observations of the child.

Extraversion——***Re-energizing***——Introversion

Although some extraverts are talkative and some introverts talk less, it's not about how verbal the child is. Rather, it's about the source of the child's energy. Unfortunately, there are common misconceptions about these preferences. It is a recurrent assumption to label the less talkative introvert as "shy," but that would be a mistake. Children with a strong preference for introversion like to pause and think before they speak, and often, like to mentally think through things before they take action. Conversely, the extravert may not know what he/she thinks until it's verbalized. Both can be effective.

Although there may be more extraverts than introverts in the world, the important factor for us grandparents is in recognizing the child's preferences, accommodating, and honoring them. Although it's tempting to tell the extraverted five-year-old to be quiet and give grandparents some peace, or to insist that the introverted two-year-old be immediately comfortable and talkative when introduced to new friends, that would ignore the child's innate needs.

Perhaps it's easier when the child's preference for *introversion* or *extraversion* is the same as the grandparents, but if not, we must return to our Rule #1 of grandparenting—*focus on the children with unconditional love*. If we are to give them all that we intend, and if we are to effectively nurture their development, then we must accept them as they are, and for whom they are. The last thing we would ever want to do is to try to change this aspect of personality because we know that it's inborn. To attempt to make an extravert out of an introvert would be like insisting that the left-handed child develop a dominance for the right hand. Actually, the preference for one hand over the other is often used as a metaphor for type and preference. We use both hands, but we prefer one over the other, and we are more comfortable using the preferred hand in certain situations.

My favorite example of this re-energizing preference is the party story. If you take two grandchildren to an exciting evening party where both engage in lots of activities, talk, and play with numerous other children, both having an equally good time; the difference is observed at home. The introvert will likely go home and be ready for bed immediately, eyes closed almost the minute the head hits the pillow. The extravert, however, may get into pajamas, but will insist on a snack and an animated conversation, recounting the people and activities of the party. The extravert has become *re-energized* by all of the interactions at the party, while the introvert *used energy.* In the quiet, and with the lights out, the introvert can re-energize by calmly thinking through the party experience and gently falling asleep while the extravert needs to unwind because the child was so energized by the party experience. To deny either would be to deny their needs. Even though it may not be what we need, or what we think they should need, the attentive grandparent supplies the child's needs.

Fast-forward to the teen years. If we want to know about the fifteen-year-old extravert's world, who his friends are, what he does when away from home, and what he's thinking, we may have to listen to endless childhood chatter from the extravert from the time he's a toddler. For children with preference for extraversion, we become a great source of enjoyment and re-energizing when we listen intently to the stories and constant narrative of the child's world. Then, as a teen, we're likely to continue to hear about the grandchild's world when that bond of engaging conversation was established early.

Conversely, it may seem convenient to have grandchildren who are introverts during the childhood years because they're often happy to play alone, and they will leave us alone when they are in our care. The challenge comes, however, when they are teens. If we have not established ourselves as a supportive resource during their childhoods, if we have not gently asked open ended questions, and if we have not been patient with the pause before their responses; they will be less likely to share their concerns, activities, or problems. It's easy to diminish the relationship with an introvert during the teen years.

Regardless of personality and their preference for *introversion* or *extraversion,* it is imperative that we develop an effective communication style that's built on our solid supportive relationship with grandchildren. We must recognize and accommodate their communication needs at every stage of their development.

The question is often asked, "Will type change?" The answer is a definite "No!" We adapt to different situations, we use both hands, but the leftie doesn't suddenly morph into a right hander. We are talkative and quiet, but we get re-energized from interacting with the external world or from the internal and that doesn't seem to change. As adults, we learn to develop the skills to perform with our less favored preference, but that doesn't change our dominant choice. Somewhere in our days, however, we are happiest when we can be who we are and in our preferred world.

It must be emphasized that for Jung, Myers, and Briggs, the descriptors have specific meaning within the context of their concept. For example, within some psychological instruments, extraversion is positive and introversion is somewhat negative; however, that is not at all how Jung or Myers used these descriptors. In her writings, Isabel Myers (1980, 1995), constantly emphasized that there is no good or bad preference and that the strength of a preference does not indicate excellence. She stressed that it's only bad when one's type is not recognized and respected.

Taking-In and Using Information

This preference is about how we find-out, take-in, and use information. The preferences are for *sensing* and *intuition.* As with all of the terms in the *MBTI®*, these labels have meaning within the concept. They're different from some of the familiar meanings to us. They relate to whether we prefer to start with concrete facts and details *(sensing)*, or we like the big picture and connections *(intuition).* This preference may not be as apparent in early childhood, but it has enormous impact on the learning environment. As we watch the young child grow, we can gradually see signals of this preference. Circle the response that you observe most of the time.

1. Does the child focus on the here and now? Yes No

2. Does the child like real stories, about animals, and adventures of real people more than unreal or fairy tales? Yes No

3. Does the child prefer concrete facts? Yes No

4. When the older child is assembling a model airplane or new set of Legos, does the child look carefully at the directions and proceed step-by-step? Yes No

5. Does the child become impatient or frustrated with complicated or future oriented tasks? Yes No

6. Does the child like fantasy, pretending, and make-believe? Yes No

7. Does the child enjoy imaginative fairy tales and stories about animals with human characteristics? Yes No

8. Does the child like exploring creative adventures? Yes No

9. When the older child is assembling a model airplane or a new set of Legos, does the child look first at a photo of the finished model before considering the step-by-step directions. Yes No

10. Does the child like to work in bursts of energy but become bored or try to avoid maintenance or repetitious tasks? Yes No

A "yes" to the first five questions indicates a preference for *sensing,* while a "yes" the last five are focused on *intuition.* Again, the numbers are irrelevant. These questions are listed only to stimulate grandparents' observations. If you're not certain, continue to observe the child's actions and preference indications. As in all of the preferences, there is no advantage or disadvantage. One way is not better than the other. It doesn't matter which comes first, the facts and details, or the whole.

Although we take-in information through the senses—sight, hearing, touching, etc.—we may like to use that information differently at first. To put it simply, it's useful to be aware of whether the child gravitates to basic facts or likes to start with whole concepts, the big picture.

Sensing—***Taking-in and using information***—Intuition

An example of this preference in school could be found in the old familiar rhyme, "In 1492, Columbus sailed the ocean blue." Does the child prefer the simple facts of Columbus' exploration in 1492, or does the child first need the "why" and the bigger picture?" Would "In the fifteenth century, Spain helped Columbus search for a new route to Asia to expand their trading and riches" give the child a better understanding on which to learn the facts? We can observe whether the child prefers to begin with the facts,

“1492” before considering the big picture of why Columbus sailed.

It's not about an *either/or,* rather, it's about where the child likes to begin when taking-in, learning, and using information. When the child gets a new toy, does the child like to look at the directions or just “dive right in?” What leads the child to ultimate effectiveness as an adult is in being comfortable with where he/she begins, then considering the other preference.

MBTI® researchers indicate that the population may be about 70% *sensing* and 30% *intuition.* If teachers are focused on the majority of the classroom, it will not be accommodating to all learners. That could put the child with a different preference at a disadvantage. By being aware of the child's preferences, grandparents can supplement or translate for the young child whose preferences are less accommodated in the classroom.

Even with little children, it’s useful to be aware of their preferences in our interactions with them. For example, in a phonics lesson, when a kindergarten teacher asked the class to draw a picture of their favorite word that ended in the “ap” sound, she expected to see crayon pictures of a *cap, map,* or from the creative students, a cat taking a *nap.* A very clever, literal little girl with a preference for *sensing*, however, drew a picture of an iPad with the YouTube “App” in the middle.

When we give instructions, we’ll be more effective with *sensing* preferences if we just use the concrete facts and avoid needless details. When giving instructions to children with a preference for *intuition,* we’ll be more effective and avoid frustrating them if we put our instructions in the context of the whole—how what we’re doing is important to the entire issue. Grandchildren can be exasperating and seem disrespectful when they become frustrated with too much information because they have a preference for *sensing*. Others may question our instructions with a seemingly impertinent, “Why?” Yet, with a preference for *intuition,* they may be only asking for more information so they can understand how what they're supposed to do is relevant to all that's involved.

Again, there is no advantage in either preference. There is a disadvantage, however, if we grandparents fail to understand the young people's innate needs or fail to help the grandchildren understand that, even though it doesn't matter which comes first, they need both the basic facts and the whole context.

Deciding

The third pair of preferences is about where we go first when we make decisions. This pair of preferences is called *thinking* and *feeling*. People with the *thinking* preference first consider the logic and rationale in a decision, then the human impact. Whereas, those with a *feeling* preference first consider the people effect, then the logic and rationale. It's important not to regard the *feeling* preference as "emotional" and *thinking* as "cold." Rather, they are part of the function through which we come to conclusions and reach decisions.

Effective decisions that involve people are not achieved by using one preference alone. It doesn't matter where we begin as long as we are thorough in considering both paths. The key is in understanding what we prefer and where we begin. We can get into trouble, however, when we make decisions only considering our preference—forgetting the logic or overlooking the impact on others.

Thinking———***Deciding***———Feeling

The *thinking* preference is often associated with males, as it fits our stereotype of the objective, logical, and steady man. Whereas, the *feeling* preference fits our stereotype of females, caring and people oriented. Perhaps these stereotypes exist because a majority of females seem to demonstrate a preference for *feeling* and more men may express a preference for *thinking*. The result of our stereotypes and expectations is that when girls have a *thinking* preference they get negative feedback because they "aren't soft enough" or they are too masculine in their thinking. Boys who have a *feeling* preference may also get negative feedback because they don't fit the usual expectation. Myers (1980), repeatedly emphasized the importance of accepting and honoring people as they are.

The *deciding* part of the concept is introduced here because this preference is often observable in older children, however, it must be emphasized that emotions of the moment often dominate children's decisions. The ability for logical, rational thinking and the capacity to analyze all facets of the decision may not be fully developed until much later. As we understand these preferences, and as we observe the children, we may begin to see one choice over the other. Just as we can't determine a preferred hand in the infant, we can see it in the five-year-old. We watch for the development of preference in deciding during childhood even though we don't usually see full development in decision making until much later.

When grandparents recognize and respect preferences, we encourage the child's confidence and self-knowledge. One of the negatives of not understanding our preferences is that we fall prey to poor choices and ineffective decision making. For example, the people with a *thinking* preference can make decisions that seem cold and calculating because they may convey a disregard for people, even though the issue might seem very logical to the decision maker. People who don't understand their *feeling* preference can become too dependent on harmony and the need for approval. Because the *feeling* preference is so focused on others, it's easy to be manipulated by the constant need for approbation. This can be disastrous for the teenage girl, especially when dating and attempting to be part of a social group, She will benefit from a grandparent or caring adult to help her understand this preference. Knowledge of the *feeling* preference can prevent her from being manipulated or becoming prey to underage sex just because she has such an inherent need to please. It's as if people with the *feeling* preference are allergic to rejection.

When we help children explore their preferences and learn how to use both *thinking* and *feeling* for making decisions, they are more thoughtful and their choices are usually better for them. They don't succumb to bad decisions because of a lack of self-knowledge or self-worth. They remind themselves, "Oh, I don't like being rejected, but I can deal with it," or "Oops, that seemed like a good idea at the time, but I forgot about the other kids." Instead of criticizing the child's lack of concern for others or whining about being left out of a game, we understand how they got there and can guide their better decision making.

Living and Organizing

The last pair of preferences, implied in Jung's work but made explicit by Myers, is about how we like our environments to be, how we want to live, or how much order we want in our surroundings.

Judging ––***Ordering/Living***––Perceiving

As you've already surmised, the first pair of preferences about how we like to re-energize, is easier to observe in children than the taking-in information or deciding preference. As with the first, this preference for how we like to organize is somewhat easier to observe. The trap that many people fall into, however, is misunderstanding the descriptors. The preference for order, schedules, sequence, systems, etc. is the preference for *judging*. Too many people assume that the description of how we make judgements about the way we want to be in the world, is the same as being judgmental, critical, and biased.

Don't allow the descriptor to be misleading. It really explains how we make judgements about the amount of external order we want in our lives. Perhaps, more than the other preferences, this can be an issue of interpersonal friction in families and an impediment to grandparent and child relationships as different choices for order collide.

Remember those low shelves for toy and book storage we discussed in Chapter 5? If your little ones have a *judging* preference, they will find the shelf arrangement very comfortable. They will also appreciate regular meal times, consistent routines, and knowing what to expect. This predictability will be calming and add to their sense of order and security.

The other preference, *perceiving,* (not about what we call being perceptive), describes an alternate way of making choices about how we want to live. People with a preference for *perceiving* enjoy flexibility and keeping their options open. They like spontaneity and find too much structure or planning to be confining. They are adaptive and open to change and new opportunities. They are often stimulated by new possibilities.

For some of us, *perceiving* is a kind of internal sense of order. Because we may order things internally, it's irrelevant how they are in the external world. Whereas, people with a preference for *judging* prefer order in the external world. For example, eight-year-old Greg, who has a preference for *judging,* likes to keep his socks matched, folded, and in the top drawer of his bureau. He likes to read the dinner menu that's posted on the refrigerator so that he knows what to expect. In contrast, his cousin, Emily, another eight-year-old, frustrates her parents because they sometimes see her as such a slob. With a preference for *perceiving,* she is spontaneous and open to changes. She regards socks that are not on her feet as irrelevant. It doesn't matter where they are—in a drawer, in the laundry basket, or under the bed—who cares! She finds that a rigid system of planning family dinners for a week is frustratingly confining because she can't know on Monday what she would like to eat on Friday. Emily likes to keep her options open.

Initially, we might see Greg as a preferable personality and Emily as lazy and slovenly, but this preference is not about neatness or self-discipline. Clearly, there are assets and what might seem to be negatives to both preferences. The key is in understanding and teaching both how to be effective in the world. For example, we would rarely need to remind Greg to do his homework and have his back pack by the door, ready for school in the morning, but we must help Greg to not waste time obsessing over arranging his papers, then being upset because there isn't time to read the most important part of his assignment. With Emily, we may need to help her organize her backpack because she became so intrigued with the geography assignment that she did an extra project.

It's possible that there are more people with a preference for *judging* than those with a preference for *perceiving,* but it's difficult to prove exact statistics. Some have speculated that these preferences are somewhat drawn to geography, pointing to how the trains run on time in Germany and Switzerland, but the buses in Egypt and Mexico are not so predictable. Although interesting to observe and speculate, preferences and ways of being in the world are not as easy to project as on-time train and bus performance.

Neither of the preferences is better than the other. The key is in observing and helping the child understand how to use the preference effectively. Myers (1985, p.15) indicated that type development is a lifelong process.

When Grandchildren's Preferences Are Different From Ours

When we put aside our own convenience and think about the child's preference for *judging,* we understand the importance of telling the child about where we're going, what we will do, and preparing the child for what will happen. When we disregard our own needs for neatness, we understand why the child with the preference for *perceiving* delights in spreading the art materials across the kitchen floor. Just as the first child likes to have a sense of order over what's happening, the other child likes having the option of any and all art materials readily available.

After thinking about our grandchildren's preferences, we may become more aware of our own preferences—how they are like the child's or very different from the child's. When referring to romantic relationships, we often use the common axiom, "opposites attract." In social relationships, we may be fascinated by people who are very different from us. Yet, the more exposure we have to others, the more that social comparison force seems to prevail and we want people to be like us. We're comfortable with people who have a similar demeanor and attitudes. If they are different, there's a temptation to want to change those differences, to correct what we may see as deficits, and to make them reflect well on us. Although we can accept or reject our social relationships, when it comes to grandchildren, it's imperative that we accept them for the budding personalities that they are. As discussed in other chapters, just as we must help them to develop their skills —social, math, or physical—we must help them to understand their preferences and develop their personalities. Even though it might be convenient for them to be more like us, such as being more talkative or more open to options, we must help them develop their innate preferences and nurture their own individuality.

The four pairs of preferences that we've discussed can be combined in sixteen different ways and lead to sixteen different *types* as described in the *MBTI.*® To really expand understanding of type, it is highly recommended that grandparents either review the *MBTI*® that was completed many years ago in a business or college setting or consider one of the resources listed in Appendix D to utilize the instrument. If the *MBTI®* score comes from decades ago, you may find that, although your actual *type* will not change, your scores may be different because maturity tends to make us aware of whom we really are. Unfortunately, in our youth, what we've learned or think we should be, may contaminate or camouflage our responses on the instrument. If you're hesitant about your scores and the type that you identified long ago, or want to know more, you might consider the various materials available. For a more in-depth understanding of type, grandparents could consider the *MBTI® Step II* that explores five facets in each of the preferences. In addition, there is a description of an instrument for ages 7-16, the *Murphy Meisgeier Type Indicator for Children (MMTIC®).* Our main purpose in this cursory overview is to simply increase awareness of grandchildren's preferences, of how they are like or different from us, and perhaps, to spark interests in knowing more about this wonderful resource of the *MBTI.®*

When Preferences Clash, Resulting in Family Tension

As we have emphasized, there is no good/bad or effective/ ineffectiveness in the preferences. We all have some of each, but we use or rely on one more than the other. Negativity only happens when we attach criticism to a preference. It can be annoying for an introverted grandfather to have an energetic extraverted four-year-old granddaughter, or for a highly logical grandmother to deal with a sensitive people-focused grandson. In such circumstances, the differences can be frustrating, but these preferences don't usually cause major problems.

When we make the issue about us, instead of recognizing another family member's different preference, however, we cause the tensions to rise. For example, a grandparent, whose strong preference for *judging,* and a child who has a *perceiving* preference, will likely clash over the child's apparent lack of attention to order. The grandparent may see the situation as an issue of character or discipline and say, "This is a negligent, careless child who has no respect for me." Yet, the child is clueless about why the grandparent becomes upset because attention to order, schedules, and such can be less important to this child.

We avoid this kind of needless difficulty when we understand the underlying causes and educate ourselves and others. For example, the *perceiving* child can be taught that there are simple rules about where toys, books, clothing, etc. must be kept. Even though the child may not have the same innate need for this organization, the child can be guided to a bit of order and will enjoy being able to find things easily with having more options. At the same time, the child with the preference for *judging* can be eased into transitioning from one activity to another with preparation and time alerts. Life is ever so much better for everyone when we can avoid emotional distress by guiding, coaching, and helping children develop skills.

Even though life may seem to be easier when our grandchildren have preferences similar to ours, we are often challenged to love the different. This proclivity for being with people who are most like us, who do things the way we do, who seem to think the way we do, can cause us to reject those who are different. Instead of appreciating their uniquenesses, we can easily slip into the trap of concluding that their ways or ideas are wrong. When we reject such innate qualities in the child's personality, we send bruising messages that are harmful to the child and damaging to our relationships. Although we would never do this intentionally, we can reject without realizing. When the child with a preference for *feeling* is upset about being left out of play groups or if the 13-year-old is depressed at not having enough "likes" on social media, we cannot disregard their concerns. If we say, "Oh, you're just being silly," we deny a part of their personality. Even though such superfluous worries may appear illogical to us, it's better when we understand and say, "It's so unfortunate that you feel hurt. Tell me about what's happened." Sometimes, people with a preference for feeling seem to have an insatiable need for approval, acceptance, and reassurance of being loved.

We must also be aware of our own preferences. My friend, Beth, can feel rejected by her young *introverted* grandson. She says he probably has preferences for *sensing, thinking,* and *judging*. It seems that he's uncomfortable hugging her upon every arrival, departure, and several times in-between. She says that, even before the days of social distancing needed for the pandemic, he was reluctant to express affection. Such emotional reticence could leave this *feeling* grandmother experiencing needless rejection, as it's sometimes easy for *feelers* to fall into the trap of personalizing everything. That's when Beth says she must remind herself of Rule #1 *Focus on the child. This isn't about me, I'm the grown-up.* She says that she smiles as she thinks, "Oh, he told me that he loves me months ago, and for him, nothing has changed!" Understanding type is helpful in so many ways.

People with different preferences do the same things but for different reasons. Teaching the young child to "finish playing with the toy" and replacing it on the shelf is easier for the child with a preference for *judging*—external order. We do the same with the child with a preference for *perceiving*—internal order, but it has a different appeal to the need for options and spontaneity. For example, early mornings are much easier for everyone if the closet is neatly organized. The child with a *judging* preference will like having the clothing grouped by type and color—shirts, pants, skirts, jackets. The child with a *perceiving* preference will also benefit from an organized closet, but for different reasons. The child will like being able to open the closet door and have all of the options in front, readily accessible. The choice is pleasant as the child can immediately see all of the possibilities. With some help, both types can learn to maintain an organized closet. Incidentally, some *perceiving* children benefit from choosing clothing, preparing lunches, and assembling materials the night before. Mornings with too many options may require more time than is available.

There is another trap that we grandparents can fall into when we confuse the preference for *judging* with "neatness" or when we regard this preference as ridiculous obsessiveness. People with a strong *judging* preference may not be deemed to be neat by you or me. They may have their own system of order, organization, schedules, and systems, but not appear neat or efficient to someone else. When we confuse the issue of the preference for living or order with neatness, we may be imposing our needs on the child. It's important that this preference is about the child's *judging* how he/she wants to live and with how much order in the environment. If we impose our need for our kind of neatness or randomness, it can become an unnecessary source of family tension.

A similar trap occurs when we put endless pressure on the child with a preference for *perceiving* because we can make the child feel inadequate. The child may simply not see the value in the tidiness that we're demanding. The solution lies in not regarding the issue of required order as a behavioral or a discipline problem. Rather, it's another learning opportunity. When we consider the child's view, we can see how to teach the child in ways that appeal to the individual needs. For example, we know that people are generally more successful who have a certain amount of order in their lives. Their possessions are not lost. They pay their bills on-time. They keep appointments. And they enjoy a sense of control over their lives. As grandparents, we can make a major contribution to the children's development by guiding and showing them how to organize their possessions and their lives. The key to success is in showing them how to make their preferences accommodate their needs for successful living.

Without understanding and commitment to honor the child's preferences, this *judging/perceiving* preference can cause tension in other ways. A simple trip to the ice cream shop that was intended to be a surprise treat has the potential to become a stressful adventure if we aren't aware of preferences. The late Otto Kroeger (1994) liked to joke that people with a *judging* preference "moan." He indicated that they complain about everything, even the things that they like or want to do. I maintain that this moaning is caused by their agenda. It's as if these *judging* preference people have an agenda that's carved in stone. If I suddenly proclaim that we're stopping for an ice cream cone, the little *judging* preference in the car seat is likely to respond with, "Why are we stopping? Will we be late getting to the playground? Mom says I've had too much sugar this week." It's not that the little one doesn't want ice cream. It's as if he must get out his hammer and chisel to re-carve his agenda that's written in stone. If we don't understand the preference, we wonder why we bothered. We're annoyed with the unappreciative, obnoxious little moaner in the back seat! When we understand, however, we just smile and reassure the child that it will be okay. After a bit of moaning that we ignore, he'll adapt, and we can continue on a pleasant adventure as he enthusiastically licks his favorite chocolate cone.

Children with the *perceiving* preference can be equally frustrating from their love of random options. Actually, they love different options so much that they can generate more options than we want to deal with. When I announce a stop at the ice cream store, I'll get squeals of delight because, even though the *perceiving* preference has an agenda, it's as if it's only written in pencil on paper. Since it's quite easy to change, there's no problem, but yes, that *is* the problem. Before I can park the car, the little one is saying, "What about frozen yogurt? I like frozen yogurt. Do you like frozen yogurt? Or, what about soft serve cream? It's good, but Mom says it's messy." And once inside, there can be endless exploration of the different flavors, especially if it's a shop that offers samples. By this time, I'm wondering why I thought this would be a treat because I'm exhausted.

Just as we disregarded the moaning from the *judging* preference, we can relieve any tension in this situation by simply helping the *perceiving* child to reach closure. We say, "Wow, you have lots of possibilities, but we're here, so we'll have ice cream today." After watching the child's complete survey of the many possible flavors, we can say, "Choose two flavors that you would like. . . Then, decide which one of those you don't want today. Now, you've found a yummy choice." We simply help the child narrow the possibilities because it's sometimes easier for people with a *perceiving* preference to decide on what they *don't* want, thereby narrowing the possibilities to what they *do* want. By ignoring the first child's moaning and helping the latter to obtain closure, we solve the problems and avoid any tension.

You may have noticed that it isn't just children who moan or generate options. If you invite me to lunch and ask where I'd like to meet, I'll likely reply, "Anywhere except tacos or burgers." I have a firm sense of what I don't like, but everything else is a possibility. In contrast, when I ask my grandson if he's available for lunch on Saturday, I'll get a hesitation as he mentally checks his calendar and decides how he can rearrange his schedule to make time for Gran. By accommodating what's happening in each of our personalities, we remove the possibilities of misunderstanding or tension in our relationships.

I wonder if, as brain research continues, and we learn more about the connections between our bodies and our personalities, if we will find another connection. I've noticed that many people who indicate a preference for *judging,* also describe themselves as being "instant on" in the mornings. When they wake, all of the systems kick-in, they're ready to get-up and get-going immediately. I've also observed that many people who express a preference for *perceiving,* describe their mornings as a bit like the old television sets that required a warm-up period and began functioning only gradually. Their systems begin operating at a slower pace, requiring a bit of slow moving time, and perhaps a bit of caffeine to get-going. Although we're certainly not going to give the grandchildren caffeine to speed-up morning routines, maybe this knowledge that their doodling around may have a physical basis will give us more patience. When we realize that they're not slow just to annoy us, but that their bodies are slow moving for the first few minutes, then we can adjust our morning routines appropriately. I have no statistical proof, just a collection of anecdotes. Even though, it's just my theory, watching for such indications in your grandchildren may make the mornings after sleepovers more serene, especially if the child is an "instant-on" and you awaken more gradually.

Knowledge of preferences allows me to better manage me and enhance my interactions with others.

Extraversion ———***Re-energizing***———Introversion

Sensing—-***Taking-in and using information***—-iNtuition

Thinking ———***Deciding***———Feeling

Judging———***Ordering/Living***———Perceiving

Perhaps grandparents can copy this little graphic from the book and stick it above the kitchen sink or on the bathroom mirror as a reminder of preferences and how we can nurture the uniquenesses in each grandchild.

One note about the *Myers Briggs Type Indicator,*® it is not considered by some academics as a favorite instrument. First, it was not developed in a classical university research setting. Instead, it was developed by two women, a mother and daughter, in their living rooms. Second, even though both were college graduates, neither had extensive formal training in psychology or methods of statistical research. Nonetheless, mother and daughter were a brilliant team who produced a valuable legacy.

Today, the *MBTI®* is the most widely used and thoroughly researched, instrument of its kind. Unlike much of psychology, it focuses on normal people. Most psychologists and psychiatrists must concentrate on abnormality or those with serious mental issues, and use such instruments as *Minnesota Multiphasic Personality Inventory (MMPI),* instruments to determine anxiety, or depression and projective tests. Unlike such analysis, the *MBTI®* doesn't fit the paradigm and usual approaches of clinical psychology. But then, you and I aren't interested in diagnosing or labeling grandchildren. If they have special needs, are struggling, or require medical or psychological assistance, we certainly want to encourage the parents in obtaining appropriate help. Although we seek any information that will assist our quest to support the grandchildren, we quietly resist unproductive tests or labels. Rather, we're interested in tools and concepts that help us to be effective in our relationships with them and to nurture their growth and development.

The Comfort Zone

Recently, when a young executive was sent to me for a session on leadership development, I asked his CEO what was the most important thing I could do for this man. He replied, "Introduce him to the *Comfort Zones!"* He said, "The *Myers Briggs* will give him understanding, and your invention that you called *Comfort Zones* will enhance his self-concept. Then, he added, "Even though it was 20 years ago, when you showed me why some things that others do easily were a struggle for me, it was like magic. I understood why and how I had to approach some areas with more energy and perseverance. I better understood myself! That's what I want for this colleague."

Even the growing child recognizes that some endeavors come easier to one person than to another, especially in learning environments. When differences are accepted and honored, children learn to seek help when struggling and to help others who are floundering. They learn from those who are better and share with those who need help. One of the most important advantages for the child's understanding of preferences comes in the realization of what's needed when circumstances are outside of the preference. Instead of feeling stupid or inept, the child concludes, "This stuff is harder and will require more time and effort because it's not how I like to learn." Instead of concluding, "Math is too hard for me," the child thinks, "I must figure out a better way to learn this."

Even for very young children, grandparents can plant the seeds of understanding that we can't be good at everything, that not everything comes easily for all of us. In middle childhood, it may be possible to give the child a more in-depth understanding this concept of some things coming easily and some endeavors requiring more effort.

At the right time, and when the older child is open to learning, you can begin by talking about comfort, about what makes us feel comfortable, and giving a few examples. At the top of a blank sheet of paper, write the words COMFORT ZONE. In the center, draw a small circle, and in its center write the word CORE. You can say, "We'll call this your core, like the core of an apple, the little inside part that holds the seeds. In that small circle, draw three or four physical characteristics to describe the child, such as an R or L to describe a preference for which hand. You can use a crayon to represent hair color and a happy face with a big smile. You can say, "These are the things with which you were born, your beautiful hair, smile, and liking to use this hand to draw or hold a fork." Next, draw a larger circle.

The Comfort Zone

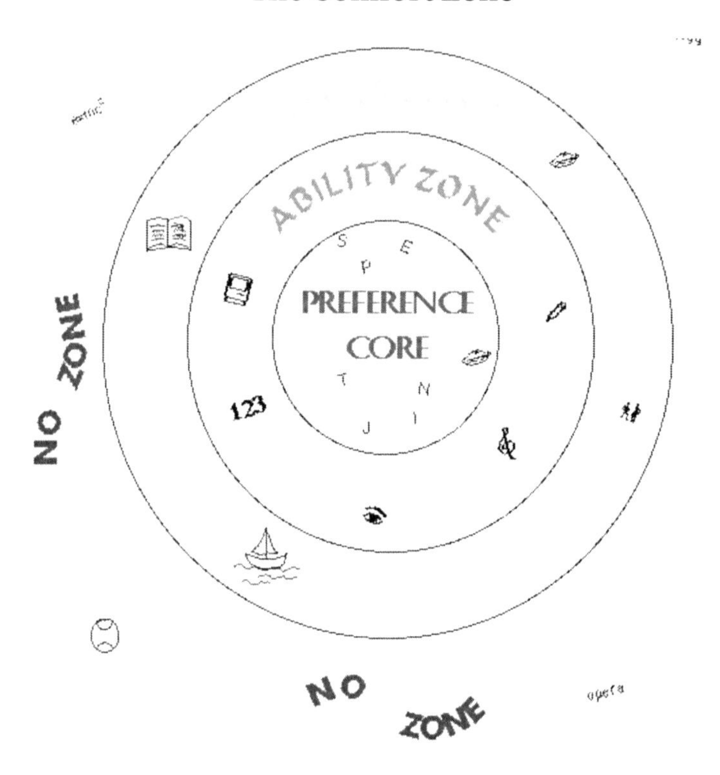

To enlarge on a computer monitor, see
https://zelmalansford.com/making-memories/
and click on *Myers Briggs* in the menu bar

around the outside of the core, and at the top, write *Ability Zone*. Then you can say, “Because you like to use your right hand, it was easy for you to learn to draw with that hand.” Now, you draw and write using that hand without much thought or concentration because your brain works easily with that hand. That’s what we call an ability. Let’s add some other things in your Ability Zone, actions that come easily. Then, draw or describe whatever the child describes as facile or effortless.

Next, draw another larger circle on the outside. At the top of that circle, write the words, *Skills Zone*. In that circle, write the L or R, to indicate the less favored hand, and say, “Now, what if I told you that I would give you a zillion dollars if you learned to write with your other hand? (Smile as the child laughs and you acknowledge that you don't have a zillion dollars.) You could learn to do it, but it would always be a little more difficult. It would always require a bit more concentration and effort. It might even take longer for you to write the same words with that hand than your favored hand. With practice and extra effort, you could develop this other handed *skill.* That's how it is with skills. They don't come as easily as the things in your *Ability Zone.*" Then you could add something like, "I've noticed that _____ seems to be in your *Ability Zone.* You seem to enjoy studying and learning _____, and it appears to come very easily for you. You don't have to work hard to learn ______." Look for cues from the child for confirmation. If confirmed, write or draw something to describe it in the *Ability Zone* circle and encourage the child to indicate other subjects or activities that come easily. Then, you can add, "I notice that, while that comes easily, _____ requires more work. Can we put _____ in the *Skills Zone?*" Again, look for the child's confirmation. Then, together think of some additional areas that don't come easily and require extra time, effort, concentration, or practice, inviting the child to contribute to the drawing.

This makes a great opportunity to help the child understand endeavors that come easily and others that may be more difficult. Developing the conversation, a discussion can ensue about how we seek help, work longer, or figure out ways to increase the skill. We can also talk about how we can help others with areas in our *Ability Zone,* that might be in their *Skills Zone.* We can reinforce the understanding by talking about what's in grandparents' *Ability Zone,* then describe what's in the *Skills Zone.* We could use an example such as car maintenance and talk about how we recognize that since "mechanical" is not in our *Ability Zone,* we depend on a good car mechanic. I would talk about how technology wasn't really in my *Ability Zone,* but that it's so important to what I do that

I've studied and learned that skill. I say, "It helps me to know that when I have complicated work on my computer, I must have quiet and time to really concentrate because this kind of work doesn't come as easily for me as it does for some other people." It's important to delve into the conversation as necessary to show the child how abilities vary for different people and we must approach the areas that are not easy with patience, perseverance, and clever ways to succeed.

In such circumstances, grandparents can reinforce with my favorite example of, *Nobody can be tall and short.* I like to use a story such as, "Uncle Riley is tall and never needs a step stool to reach the top shelves in his workshop, but did you notice that band aid on his head? His height means that he must take care to avoid colliding with low hanging objects. But look at our friend Jennifer. I've never seen her dodge low hanging objects, however, she keeps a step-stool nearby for reaching things on the upper shelves. If we're tall, we have no problem with *this,* but we must be aware of *that.* If we're short, we don't worry about *that,* but we must be alert for *this.* Neither tall nor short is a strength or weakness, just a way of being. None of this is about strengths and weaknesses. Instead, we all have areas where we excel and we all must remember places that need extra tools or effort."

With older teens, it may be appropriate to sketch the title *No Zone* in the corner. We can describe a few areas that are not of interest and represent no ability or skill development. I might give an example by saying with laughter, "Rock climbing and nuclear physics are in my *No Zone*. I have no knowledge of nuclear physics and no desire to develop any skill because I have no use for such. I don't have the upper body strength to pursue rock climbing and that's ok because I can't imagine wasting my time just climbing rocks, although other people might thrive on the challenge." Then, we might probe for similar areas for the teen. It's better to exaggerate in this area than to confuse difficult or strenuous endeavors with what we might put into the *No Zone*. Nothing pronounced as a *No Zone* topic should restrict the child's future, and actually, this may be part of my concept that is best reserved for maturity.

If the child insists on putting inappropriate topics or endeavors into either the Ability or Skills Zone, it may be an indication that the child is not ready for these concepts. Insisting on being great at everything or good at nothing may point to defensiveness or the need for more self-understanding and self-confidence. Rather than making a fuss about accuracy, just postpone that part of the discussion until the child is more mature. In the meantime, be alert for indications of a lack of confidence about abilities and skills.

Preferred Ways of Learning

Another part of our individuality is somewhat related to our preferences and determines how we learn most effectively. As discussed earlier, there's a variety of preferred learning processes. For example, if you've determined that your grandchild is an *extravert,* you may be aware of how the child seems to enjoy the interactive discoveries that you make when exploring nature and talking about how to solve a math problem. You can see the value of discussing the child's learning, not only to enhance the remembering, but also to encourage the enjoyment. At the same time, the child with a preference for *introversion* may be content to simply gain knowledge from reading the book and thinking about it with no further discussion.

If you've observed that the child prefers *sensing,* a concrete step-by-step approach to problem solving, first gathering all of the facts and analyzing them, you can encourage the child's use of this ability as you read books and play games. You can show the child how to maximize that preference in the classroom. You may find that the acquisition of facts comes easier than the connections between facts and their interpretation. It's easier for those with a *sensing* preference to learn about what's real than to learn symbolic concepts. This is where you can enhance the learning by helping the child to make those connections.

If you're aware of the child's preference for first understanding the whole, the concepts, and the big picture, you can supplement classroom experiences by showing the child how skills learned in the classroom can be put to use in everyday life. Especially for the extravert, conversations about how to apply facts learned in school can complete the child's learning. Talking about the facts can also be very useful in helping the child who needs the "big picture." Although diversity in learning styles is usually acknowledged, the different needs of children are not always accommodated in traditional education. Unfortunately, some children conclude that they struggle because they are not very smart, when in reality, their main learning style is just not available in the environment. When unconventional arrangements necessitated by situations such as a pandemic force children into learning situations that are not ideal for them, grandparents can be a tremendous support.

There is considerable research and information available about how children learn. It can be a fascinating discovery for grandparents to pursue. But unless you have unlimited research time and vast resources, the most practical approach may be to simply observe and become very aware of how your grandchild seems to learn most effectively. Watch how the child takes-in, understands, remembers, and uses information. Then, utilize those observations in your activities. If the child is a "hands-on," interactive learner, there will be considerable benefit from time and activities with you when learning can become wonderfully fun and exciting. It can be a needed contrast to the time spent in the classroom if the child's most effective ways of learning are not available.

As we become aware of the grandchildren's preferences and learning styles, we can increase our benefit in supporting their learning. We can accommodate their most effective ways of learning in the adventures and activities that we do with them. For example, when we recognize that the child is an interactive learner, we can encourage underlining important points in their personal books that we read together especially when the materials are about science, history, and other fact focused subjects. For the older child, we can show them how to take notes, thus strengthening the study skills for the child whose preference is not for auditory learning. Although some auditory learners thrive from listening to the teacher, interactive learners need to convert what they are hearing into some kind of “doing." We can show this child how writing the key words that describe what the teacher is saying can enhance the learning. Then, discussing it with us extends the understanding and memory.

As with adults, many children learn best by “doing." I remember a time when my dining room table was covered with a big world map. On top of the map were tiny historic sail boats that had hand lettered labels taped to the tops and various colored yarn stretching from the boat and the areas of discovery on the map to the explorer’s country of origin. It was a conglomeration of labels, plastic ships, and tiny pictures, but certainly not to scale. Nevertheless, it was a fun activity that taught my “hands-on” grandson about early explorers, a subject about which he had little interest when presented with a history book. Somehow moving the boats with the trailing yarn fed his curiosity and made an exciting and memorable experience, rather than a memorization exercise. For a child with a visual learning preference, this could have been a silly waste of time when the information was readily available in the book. We grandparents must be resourceful as we supply the child’s individual needs.

We can compensate for learning opportunities not available in the classroom in different ways. Regardless of the initial taking-in of information preference, both children and adults seem to benefit from applying their learning, especially in ways that stimulate analysis, problem solving, and new ways of using their learning. My best example of how grandchildren can delight in being able to use their new learning came a few days after one of my grandson's new vocabulary words was "destitute." We were in the final stages of a game of *Monopoly,* when despite no intention on my part to let him win, he had acquired all of the property and I had incurred considerable debt. With one final, colossal move, he popped up on his knees in the chair, flung out his arms, and with a gigantic grin proclaimed, "Gran, you are destitute!"

We also know the difference that careful, self-disciplined preparation can make in career, college, or kindergarten. Yet, some types seem to learn this easier than others. The meticulous child who routinely does homework and places the organized backpack by the door before going to bed, is on the way to success. This same child, however, will be paralyzed by the sudden requirement for a task without proper notice. Another child will be spontaneous and adept at momentary improvising, although often needing reminders for proper preparation with homework and organizing other chores. Both types have their assets, and both have their *Skill Zone* wherein they need development. Instead of being impatient with the area that is not yet developed, this is our opportunity to show them ways to be successful when life requires operating outside of our *Comfort Zones.*

We may not have been aware of the information on learning styles, or had the time to accommodate when their parents were young, but using grandchildren's preferences and their preferred learning styles is something that we can do to help this generation. These are areas where we can support, encourage, and make significant contributions to the quality of our grandchildren's lives.

Summary

The total personality is made of many qualities, emotions, and behaviors. We have only discussed four aspects in this cursory introduction to the fascinating journey of exploring preferences. As you have seen, these are very simple concepts, but with enormous depth and complexity. Here, we have only attempted to point to the importance of enhancing awareness that these little people have a distinct way of being in the world and that it may be like ours, or maybe not. Grandparents can extend the knowledge and experience with the *MBTI.*® Our observation process begins during the first few months of their lives, and although probably never complete, our recognition and appreciation for their individuality is an awesome discovery for us grandparents. By realizing how they learn, re-energize, take-in information, make decisions, and like their worlds to be, we supply needs and understanding that may not be available to them elsewhere. Simply recognizing their differences and being aware of their individuality can significantly enhance our relationships and our influence with them. At the same time, this knowledge becomes a stimulus to their development.

Clarifying preferences can make grandchildren easier to understand and nurture. By observing and being aware of their budding preferences and personalities, we can sometimes separate what is a behavioral issue from a simple preference. We will not see a discipline problem and issue a "time out" because the den floor is strewn with toys. Instead, we recognize that the child may not see a problem, but if we want to change the situation, we will need to guide the child toward neatness. With coaching, but no admonishments, we can "talk" the child through restoring the order that we need. Preference is never an excuse. Rather, understanding preferences is an opportunity for nurturing growth.

It is both unnecessary and inappropriate to put labels on our grandchildren. A better course is to use our awareness of their preferences and nurture their development. Until the grandchildren have the opportunity to use the MMTIC© or are old enough to utilize the *MBTI*® we can enhance our relationships by simply becoming aware of their preferences, how they are similar or unlike us, and how we can increase our effectiveness with them.

Whether the grandchild's personality is like ours, or very different, we must remember Rule #1. As the adult, it's our responsibility to understand their uniquenesses and nurture our relationship with grandchildren. They don't always know how to talk to us, how to relate to us, and how to initiate interactions. These are our opportunities. Whether the children seem similar to us and are easy to engage, or whether they are quite different and more of a challenge, nevertheless, we love and nurture grandchildren as they are.

It is my fervent belief that authenticity is an essential element in EQ, happiness, emotional stability, and success in life. It gives us the ability to truly know who we are, be accepted for whom we are, and function in everyday life as our real selves. Perhaps understanding these preferences in ourselves and in others will help us to achieve that empowering sense of authenticity to be our best selves.

Isabel Myers' associate, Dr. Mary McCaulley, (personal communication, March 15, 1998) told me that when commenting on the contribution of her work, Isabel said, "The *Myers Briggs* allows people to smile and joke about what once caused them upset and hurt feelings." Her goal was to help people be happy and effective. Like Isabel Myers, *happy and effective* is what we want for our special grandchildren.

Chapter 8

Communicating with Grandchildren

Prompt our words,
that they may be acceptable in Thy sight.

Our communications with the grandchild begin with the first smiles and lullabies as we hold that newborn. These communications, both verbal and nonverbal, are a vital part of our relationship. We choose our words carefully to ensure that we're sending the right messages. We listen intently as we facilitate their development. We communicate our interest and unconditional love.

If we want the grandchildren to have confident, appropriate interpersonal skills, if we want them to have excellent command of English, and if we want them to avoid dependence on foul language for expression, we begin work toward that process from the first day we meet them. Although media, friends, and other sources may influence their language, and they may pick-up expressions from many places, still, positive communications within the family can be the greatest influence on the grandchild's language and the way that the young person interacts with others.

Communication skills have permeated this discussion in every chapter, beginning with how we talk with the parents—our adult children. We've emphasized the importance of making our intentions known, giving attention to our choice of words, and of not putting others on the defensive. Perhaps we can summarize how our communications need to be by simply saying, "Let's make our words always reflect the love and concern that we have for our grandchildren and our family."

Effective Communications

The beginning of appropriate and successful grandparent/ grandchild relationships is this foundation of how we talk with the young ones and how we communicate our love. The first rule of communicating with children is to save the "baby talk" for pets, but talk to grandchildren the way we speak with a colleague or anyone that we respect. Even with babies, it's important to be articulate and use an extensive vocabulary. Sometimes, children are more perceptive than we realize, and nobody likes being "talked down to," so from the beginning, it's better to converse with them at a respectful level. If they don't get the vocabulary, they'll ask, and that's a good way for them to learn language.

Researchers have observed mother and baby interactions in various socio-economic conditions, theorizing that disadvantaged mothers talk to their babies less and are less articulate with them. It may be that poor children develop less language skill and develop it later than more affluent children. Certainly, talking to and interacting with baby is an essential part of the bonding and parenting process. When mom needs a break, is employed, or other conditions prevail, we grandparents can step-in to provide that language stimulation for the child. Not only can we grandparents aid in the development of language, this caring relationship may stimulate brain development in other ways that enhance thinking skills and lessen the tendency toward emotionally driven aggression.

For some time, pediatricians have discouraged having babies under one year from being in the room with a television set due to the white and flashing light levels emitted by TV. More recently, some pediatricians have discouraged television for children under age two, believing that it delays the development of language. Regardless of age, what we know is that too much screen time from any technology is not as effective for language, emotional, or thinking development as animated focused conversations with caring adults. Knowing that not many of today's children will grow into adulthood without exposure to video, perhaps the best way to use it is sparingly, with discernment for the content, and thought as to the purpose. Are we using it as a substitute for us or as an enrichment? I cannot imagine having deprived my grandson of the wonderful Beatrix Potter video series or some of the other videos that exposed him to classical music and beautiful scenery. I must confess, however, that he was deprived of all video when he was a baby and some of the popular animations with loud guitar soundtracks.

Grandparents' key to language development and effective communication skills is related to our purpose—to enrich and influence the lives of these precious children. Like everything else in our relationship, we approach it with care, concern, and our intent to be a positive influence for our grandchildren.

Preparation and Intent

In working in leadership development in organizations, I've often used the phrase,

We must not let what we can ***do***
be diminished by ineffective things we ***say.***

Of course, what we can do for our grandchildren is monumental, and the commitment to them is greater than to anything in our working careers, so why would we put less thought and preparation into what we say to the most important people in our world? Often, it's only a matter of awareness that brings us to the reality of our priorities. When we're planning an adventure to a museum or a park, we can think about the stimulating questions we'll ask. When we're driving to pick-up a child for the playground adventure, we can give thought to topics of conversation. We think about how we can guide the conversation and the main points that we want the child to get. Just moments of preparation can make our communications with grandchildren pleasant and incredibly more effective. When we're aware of our intent, we can make it easy for the children to trust us and what we're saying.

This issue of thought and preparation is incredibly important when the grandchildren are teens. If they're awkward or uncomfortable in social situations, we can make a major difference in their comfort level and their communication skills when we show interest and have some insightful questions to ask. Grandparents typically ask about school and sports, but it's very useful to go beyond the obvious and mention current events, their activities, and the child's interests. When we do this with teens, it helps to develop their skills with peers as they get ideas of how to positively engage others.

We often joke that when we don't know any other subject, people talk about the weather. Yet, the weather can sometimes be a superb topic. There was a period in which weather was a topic of fervent interest for my grandson, and therefore, led to captivating conversations. It was a long period of intense interest in meteorological conditions. We had many exciting conversations about hurricanes, tornados, drought, and climate change. Several times, we drove to an out-of-town museum that had a weather feature with all kinds of measures and instruments. His interest was further stimulated by an "expo"sponsored by the *The Weather Channel* where there were in-person meteorologists, storm chasers, climatologists, along with all sorts of displays. He was even able to record a TV weather forecast just like "for real!" His growing-up years have been marked by the phases of his interests, but topics of conversation were especially easy during the weather time. We laugh and call his cyclical interest phase a genetic tendency as it can be compared to other family members who've enjoyed evolving interests. Just as the days of a life-time career are gone, there's no longer a need for a life-time hobby. Today's world contains too many possibilities for such restrictions. We must express interest in whatever captivates the grandchildren's attention for the moment.

Knowing people and grandchildren's interests can make conversations easy as they usually like to talk enthusiastically about what captivates them. We must always be alert to their keen interests and engage them, learning why they're attracted to something, what they're learning, and how it is adding to their development.

Conversation Is Not a Contest

For many Americans, there is what we often call the "competitive spirit," a society in which everything is a contest and every communication is an attempt to win. When we hear something from a friend or a grandchild that we don't like, we may feel a strong need to enlighten them to our point of view. We approach everything as a right or a wrong, whether or not it's a religious or moral truth. Taking such an approach with our adult children can cause conflict as they may feel entitled to have their own opinions. Taking the same approach with grandchildren can cause them to withdraw and avoid talking to us freely.

Perhaps a better method is to *approach conversations seeking learning*. If we listen and encourage free discussion on all sides of an issue, we may even learn something new. At the very least, we'll each better understand why the other holds a particular opinion. With friends, when discussing politics or sports, sometimes we just agree to disagree and there's no issue. With family, however, we may feel that it's our duty to bring them to the right place, whether or not they want to be there. That's when we can appear to be obstinate and controlling, whereas, if we assume a learning approach, there is no rise in discomfort on either side, as discussed in Chapter 2.

A friend said that she loves her father dearly, but is forced to keep their communications short and trivial because, as a retired lawyer, he approaches every discussion as a summation to the jury in which he's compelled to convince everyone of the correct conclusion. When our communications with our adult children and our grandchildren reflect such a win/lose attitude, we are not laying the best foundation for our relationships. Rather, we're forgetting Rule #1 and making everything about us. We're forgetting our prayer for acceptable words that enable effective communications.

Questions

When communicating with grandchildren, questions are a great tool, not for interrogation or making the child uncomfortable and defensive, but for expressing interest and stimulating the conversations. We can ask many insightful questions, the kind we call "open ended," questions that illicit something beyond *yes* or *no*:

> "What do you think about what happened?"
>
> "What's the best way to handle that?"
>
> "What did you like about that?"
>
> "What can we learn from this?"

Positive questions are not only a way of interacting and conveying importance, questions can stimulate the child's thinking, and most of all, convey interest in the responses and value for others. If we ask questions that are too vague, or that the child hears too often, we may be confusing.

Instead of

> "What do you want to be when you grow up?"
>
> "How did you get to be so tall?"
>
> "What would you like to do today?"

Instead, try

> "What are you doing when you're having fun?"
>
> "Tell me about your interests, what do you like to do?"
>
> "Which of these would you like to do first?"

Questions can also engage the child, but we must remember to avoid prying and the "why" questions about their choices or actions that may put grandchildren (and adults) on the defensive, such as:

"Why did you do that?"

"Why do you feel that way?"

"Why do you like him/her?"

"Why don't you do what you're supposed to?"

Instead of the above, some examples of statements said in soft tones that might get a better response are:

"Tell me about what happened."

"Talk about what's happened to cause those feelings."

"Describe how you feel when you're with that person."

"Let's talk about what happened that prevented you from what you were responsible for doing."

These statements require more words and more thought, but they usually stimulate a more informative response, and without defensiveness or anger. They are also likely to get more accurate information and increase the child's comfort.

To avoid making the child feel that it's an interrogation, we intermingle our probing questions with declaratives that have the same intent, such as:

"Tell me about . . ."

"I'm interested in that and would like to hear more."

"You must feel excited about that, tell me the best part."

We save the "why" questions to stimulate thinking skills and for learning adventures:

"Why does the frost form at daybreak?"

"Why is this full moon sometimes called a blue moon?"

"Why was Columbus interested in exploring the Atlantic Ocean?"

If we get avoidance responses, such as:

"I don't know."

"Well, I'm not sure."

These responses might indicate that the child is hesitant or fearful of giving the wrong answer. Such avoidance can be frustrating and annoying for grandparents, but it may simply mean that we need to approach the subject in a different way. Perhaps we need to inquire in a less direct manner, or in a way that doesn't assume there's a correct response. It could even indicate that we're asking the wrong question. That happened to me during my days of educational leadership when I was trying to engage in conversation the brilliant, logical nine-year-old, Walt. I simply asked, "What's your favorite cookie?" and got the reply of, "I dunno . . ." Not being easily assuaged, I said, "Oh, come on Walt, there must be a cookie that you really like." That's when he politely smiled and said, "Chocolate chip, but that's not what you asked me." Flummoxed, I said, "What?" The cute kid replied, "You asked about a cookie that I really like and it's chocolate chip. But the first time, you asked what's my favorite cookie and I can't tell you that because I haven't tasted all of the cookies available, so I can't possibly know which would be my favorite!"

Yes, sometimes we can ask the wrong question. Although I was tempted to chastise the kid for what seemed to be a sarcastic response, I realized that he wasn't being disrespectful, only operating in his logical genius world. That's when I recognized that this was my opportunity for learning better questioning techniques.

We've all had to deal with how ghastly boring and uninteresting it is to be subjected to someone who talks only about himself/herself or the obnoxious prying person who asks too many questions. Thus, asking appropriate questions or engaging statements expresses interest in the other person and makes it a two-way conversation that children respond to more than listening to our monologues. Especially, if the child's school experience is a traditional classroom, he/she spends far too much time being quiet and listening to an adult. Rather than more passive listening, when they're with us, grandchildren need to be engaged. Asking their opinions and making observations convey respect and interest. In our responses, we may even sprinkle our views, values, or other tidbits, but these engaging conversations help to develop their verbal skills, their interpersonal social skills, and their ease in communications. By teaching them how to converse with others, we're giving them an important lifetime skill.

Listening

It's intriguing that we teach children to talk, but we give little thought to teaching them to listen. When we listen intently to them, we model what we want them to learn. When we make eye contact, and nod to let them know that we've heard them, we model good habits that they will reflect. When we're reading to the five or six-year-old and we underline the main points (but not in library or school books), we're also giving them listening cues as we indicate what's important. When the seven or eight-year-old is telling about some event or something that's important to the child, we can jot three or four key words to model note taking and indicate our attention. Listening is a key skill that we want them to develop. And, it is a skill that we can model for them.

As indicated numerous times, if we want the 15 and 25-year-old to talk to us, if we want to be a part of their lives, then we must maintain the relationship through years of conversations that may be interesting—or not. If we have not listened to their stories, even when trivial, we cannot expect them to listen to our chronicles. If we have not been interested in their tales, we cannot expect them to listen and implement our wisdom.

The subject of listening usually includes the art of what we call "active listening." This is where the listener, not only hears what has been said, but gives the speaker feedback through gestures and comments that the speaker has been heard. We've all experienced the frustration of trying to tell somebody something important only to have the person gaze into the distance, and tell us with a blank facial expression of total disinterest. This is an experience that we must not give our grandchildren. Instead, to let them know that they've been heard, we give eye-contact, smiles, nods, and simple verbal responses, such as:

"Hmmm. . ."

"Yes, go on . . ."

"Wow! Tell me more . . ."

"Interesting, what else happened . . ."

This is what we do when conversing with a valued colleague. How could we do less with the most important people? Even though they may be young, and seem less urgent at the moment, we cannot miss even a single opportunity to converse with them and help them to learn effective listening skills.

Another valued reason for intense listening is in looking for cues—listening for needs, problems, difficulties, and opportunities. This is what a skilled sales person does in inviting us to talk about our needs, then showing us how his/her product can solve our problems. We can do even better for our grandchildren when we are alert to any difficulties they may have. We probe with statements and questions that don't put them on the defensive.

"Tell me about it . . ."

"Talk more about that . . ."

"How did you feel about that?"

"How can I help?"

We listen to engage, we listen to support, and we listen to help. Sometimes, we must do more to confirm that we're really listening. We must also convey understanding and empathy. When the older child is describing problems, anxieties, or hurt feelings, it can be useful to clarify with a statement:

"In other words, you're feeling _____ because _____"

After the child is able to articulate the emotions and the cause of such feelings, it may be helpful to gently probe further by filling in the blanks of the above statement and adding,

". . . and you want _____."

Allow the child to make any corrections and repeat the statement until there's indication that you're hearing correctly. When the child nods, or confirms that your description is correct, continue with an acknowledgement, such as:

"Let's talk about some ways you can get what you want."

"I understand your feelings and what you wish could happen."

"Let's talk about how it might not be possible for you to get what you want just now"

"Since what you want isn't possible now, let's talk about how we can find some better feelings for you so that instead of feeling____, maybe you could feel ____."

Being able to put the problem and the feelings into words is very helpful for some children, especially those who have difficulty with language or connecting with others.

There are times, however, when we state the problem correctly, but there is little we can do to solve the problem or change the situation for the child. That's when a grandparent's empathy is helpful. During times of grief and loss, young children may be feeling pain but not have the capacity to express their anguish. Certainly, during times of quarantine, pandemic, or difficulty, any isolation or disruption in their routines can be very confusing and frustrating for them. In such circumstances it's important to help the child move beyond feelings of despair. It is in these times that the grandparent relationship is critically influential. This is when our phone call or video chat can make a significant difference for their emotions (and their parents' tranquility.) We might respond with:

> "I hear you. I understand how you're feeling. I feel some of that sadness too.
>
> "What can we remember to help us feel better?"
>
> "What can we do to change these feelings? Let's talk about it."
>
> "What are some things you can do for others who may have your same sad or frustrating feelings?"
>
> "Talk about what you'd like to be doing on a sunny day when your world is better."

Sometimes, young children may express their feelings through drawing rather than through words. Whatever their preferences, of most importance is the relationship that they can depend on to hear their concerns. We listen, we let the children know that they have been heard, we comfort, and when possible, we help with problem solving.

During the Victorian era, it's said that a conventional punishment for children was putting the offending child *in covenant*. No one listened or responded to the miscreant, thus isolating the child. As we know the negative effects of solitary confinement on prisoners, one can only imagine the damage to children who were isolated and ignored. That's why it's so important that the child has some place to be heard and someone who really listens to the child's chatter, stories, and feelings.

When we practice active listening, we let grandchildren know that we hear and care about what they're saying to us. The Biblical instruction in James 1:19 to be "quick to listen, slow to speak, and slow to anger" is very useful, especially in times of grief, anxiety, or disappointment.

One-to-One Time

Throughout our discussion, I've made numerous references to the advantages of one-to-one time with grandchildren. There are many benefits. It's easier, calmer, and contains fewer opportunities for conflict or jealousy. There is no competition for our attention and it is not divided. Most of all, however, the advantage of periods of one-to-one focused attention comes from being able to listen to the child without distraction or interruption. When we sit in the uncomfortable child size chairs, across a child size table, it's easier to make eye contact. We can listen intently. We can practice active listening and model all of the skills that we want the child to develop. Most of all, through this wonderful focused attention, we communicate importance, value, and unconditional love, for the child of any age.

There was a time, before the pandemic, when I was a strong advocate of taking the child to a fast food restaurant because it presented a great opportunity to sit across a small table, make eye contact, and listen to the child over a treat. After many restaurants added loud music and noisy playgrounds that distract from grandparent time, however, fast food places became even less accommodating for conversation and nutrition. There may be restaurants or outdoor areas that accommodate good communication time, but the best places are often in grandparents' home where we can somewhat control the distractions. It is for this reason that, when space allows, a table and two chairs of the child's size are recommended for a convenient location. Often, by putting the table near the open toy shelves, this can also become a suitable place to sit with the child, not only for tea parties, chocolate parties, and games, but for an inviting play space. Again, the advantage is the focused attention, eye contact, and the all important one-to-one active listening.

It's important to make this one-to-one time with the children totally focused on the children. The environment needs to be calm and quiet with no TV or music blaring in the background. Especially at a time when many children have difficulty focusing attention, it is critical to remove all sounds and distractions, making it easy for the child to engage in your conversations. In today's crowded world, many children live in circumstances where they rarely experience silence, thus making the quiet world of an emotionally intimate grandparent conversation a rare treat.

Seeking the child's eye level and making the physical conditions comfortable for the grandchild are important, but also, grandparents must be emotionally available. If we've built an ideal relationship with the grandchild, if we've been a great resource for support and encouragement throughout childhood, we have a sense of calm, ease, and enjoyment of being with the child—regardless of age. When we become aware that our "head is somewhere else," however, that's a cue that we need to break away from work, distractions, or whatever keeps our attention and our listening from being at our best. It's part of that commitment to always give our best selves to the people who matter most.

The powerful ingredient in these one-to-one times for focused attention is the eye contact. It begins with the toddler and continues as the grandchildren become adults. The chair sizes may increase, but the importance of the listening, eye contact, and focused attention does not diminish. Today, when teens are adept at communicating via technology, but struggle with interpersonal skills, we can equip them for success in life as we give them role models of eye contact, active listening, and engaging conversations. Even when geography or dangers of contagion dictate that we cannot sit nearby, we can make phone calls or video chats that give them the focused attention and active listening essential to their development.

If there is more than one grandchild in the family, and if geography determines the logistics of grandparent relationships, it may not be possible to manage when, how, and under what circumstances grandchildren visits or phone chats are made. Instead, we may have to schedule visits around family, activities, and other factors. Although not always possible, it's highly preferable to have grandchildren visit separately in order to give each child some individual attention. It becomes easier to give each child the chance for some one-to-one active listening.

When, at least, some grandchildren's in-person visits are separated to give one-to-one attention, there is less opportunity for jealousy, resentment, or sibling rivalry to occur, especially if the children view the visits as "equal" in content. As we've indicated repeatedly, one-to-one visits greatly enhance grandchild/grandparent communications and relationships. Even though it may not always seem as convenient for time and transportation, one-to-one is best for modeling communications and interactions. For long-term family bonds, it's essential that grandchildren do not perceive disparity in time and treatment. Even though we may see some children more frequently, and some may be easier to enjoy, each grandchild must feel special and loved equally. Otherwise, we cause a lifetime of harm and miss a lifetime opportunity.

Conversations with Extraverts

Recalling our discussion in the last chapter, if your observations indicated that a grandchild might be an extravert, you're probably seeing indications of re-energizing in the external world and interacting with others. This child probably thrives on being able to talk with you. Expressing interest and giving one-to-one active listening to an extravert is an enormous gift to the child, especially if school and other family circumstances limit the sources the child has for psychologically re-energizing. The challenge is in giving the extravert many topics to explore and focusing the chatter. That's when having some useful questions in our inventory is helpful.

It's often said that introverts ask, "Why don't you think before you speak?" The extravert's answer is, "But sometimes, I don't know what I think until I say it." It's as if the extravert has a direct connection between brain and mouth. That's why we grandparents can be especially supportive of extraverted grandchildren when we listen to their ramblings and guide them through problem solving or exploring something that's bothering them. Because extraverts will occasionally blurt out something inappropriate, sounding impulsive or thoughtless, they may need our patience and guidance. Instead of chastising the child, by understanding this very natural tendency, we grandparents can help the child develop a kind of "appropriateness filter" that improves social interactions and social acceptance. By increasing the child's awareness of how the words might have made others feel or by bringing attention to how logical or necessary the comments were, we guide the child into better communications. Instead of restraining the child's verbal nature, we nurture the child's skills and interactions.

It's not uncommon to see a wide disparity in research about how much of the message is carried in the content and how much is in the non-verbal. The portion is probably related to whether we're describing extraverts or introverts. For the extravert, much of the message is carried in the tone of voice, facial expressions, hand gestures, and other non-verbal cues. Whereas for the introvert, much more of the message is in the words and less in the non-verbal.

It's easy to be annoyed when an excited five-year-old is trying to tell us something and can hardly stop jumping up-and-down long enough to talk. Because many of the extraverted child's gestures are exaggerated, it's understandable for us adults to become impatient and disregard them without realizing that it's just the exuberant expression of an extravert. When an introverted grandparent has a grandchild with a preference for extraversion, it becomes important to remember that the child may be looking for approval and other messages in our faces. That's when we remember that, regardless of our own preference, it's sometimes helpful to reflect the other person in our conversation. This affirming reflection can be useful with adults, but such an accommodation is especially important with grandchildren.

There is nothing about me that is anything but an extravert. Actually, I have a zero on the introvert score, but I know that I need quiet. Even though it isn't energizing for me, I must have quiet to do much of my work, and most of all, I need some quiet time every day for thinking and planning. Silence isn't energizing, but it's a necessity.

After sharing my strong preference for extraversion, I'll also tell you that my grandson is as much an extravert as I. Today, when we're together, I am thrilled by our lengthy and animated discussions of everything from politics to technology. I always learn so much from our time together, but it's the culmination of many years of such conversations, with topics that ranged from the heroic acts of the mice in the *Tailor of Gloucester,* to *Hot Cars* and *Legos*. Yes, he was always quite verbal. I can recall one particular exhausting day when he was spending the weekend with me. I had just buckled him into the rear car seat for a trip to float his toy sail boats in the nearby stream. As I hurried around the rear of the car toward the driver's side, I recall thinking, "Well, this is the only quiet moment I'll have today." Although there was rarely any silence between us, I treasure every moment of our time together. Even though occasionally exhausting, I'm glad that I understood the dynamics and my own needs. Otherwise, I might have attempted to suppress the child's natural chatter instead of trying to make our wonderful memories.

If we repeatedly tell the child to be quiet, we send the wrong message. When there are circumstances, such as church or visits, where quiet is necessary, it's imperative to explain ahead and prepare the child. Just telling the extravert child to "Be quiet!" in a loud tone never creates a nice memory. And if the little extravert also has a preference for feeling, the child will likely feel rejection from the grandparent. By observing and understanding the child's nature, we can nurture the extraversion and be a major source of delight for the child. Even if it must be through phone or video conversations, taking time to listen to the young child may mean that you'll be a comfortable source of support and guidance for the child when a teen.

Conversations with Introverts

If your observations have led you to describe a grandchild who might be an introvert, then you probably have a child who enjoys playing alone, who may be very talkative at times, but only when he/she has something to say. This child may be more comfortable and interactive on a one-to-one basis or in small groups. Most of the child's message will be in the words with less in the non-verbal area. The child may also receive messages based primarily on the words, ignoring most of any non-verbal communications.

The young introverted child may not have begun speaking as early as some children in the family and may not be comfortable talking when in the presence of numerous adults. Some uninformed adults might label the child as "shy," but again, that would be a mistake. In the truly shy personality, the hesitation or quietness results from depression or lack of confidence in the situation. Introverts may be silent simply because they have nothing yet to say. They're busy thinking and interacting with their internal world.

Just as we must listen and interact with the extravert, we must enjoy the quiet with an introvert. As we understand their needs for silence and time for their own thoughts, we also nurture their language skills by asking questions and by enjoying conversations with them at every age and stage of development. One of the differences is that, instead of unending chatter, there will be pauses and periods of quiet. When we ask a question, we must sometimes become comfortable with a moment of silence before we get an answer. Introverts don't always speak instantaneously. There may be a pause before the response to our question while they think it through.

An introverted grandfather will probably be very comfortable with a granddaughter who's also an introvert. If the grandparent's type is different from the child's, and if there is no understanding and accommodation, the relationship is likely to be less at ease.

Introverts are sometimes easier to manage when they're young, but that doesn't diminish the need to establish a strong relationship and a foundation of open communications for later. To be engaged in the introverted teen's world, we must be certain that we've established a basis of easy communications. If bullied, stressed, or experiencing adversity, it can be easy for the introvert to withdraw and become depressed without our noticing. It can be too easy to ignore the signals of depression or withdrawal in the introvert, and fail to provide the support needed.

When the grandparent bonds are strong, the child is likely to adapt to the grandparent's preferences. The child senses grandmother's quiet, and especially when older, will reflect a less talkative style when with her. Occasionally, children are more accommodating than we adults. Adapting our conversation to the style of others can be most effective. It's when we try to change the child to fit our preferences that we can damage.

As with all of the preferences, it's important to let the child be who he or she is, to be with them and nurture them as they are, regardless of our preferences. We can't really change them, but if we're uninformed about the introvert/extravert preferences, we can make them uncomfortable, insecure, and not create beautiful memories of their time with us. They may be too young to identify what's happening in a kind of uninformed clash of preferences. They may not be able to identify their feelings, but they could easily feel discomfort and rejection from our communications with them.

Techniques for Adolescents

As we may recall from our own experiences, adolescence is a time when the child's need is to be independent. Not being ready for independence, however, the need tends to collide with parental rules and emotions. During such times, it's imperative for us grandparents to be a source of listening, understanding, patience, and guidance. This is a time when it's especially critical that we listen for depression, emotional upheaval, or difficulties that might need professional help. We achieve this capacity only through years of gaining credibility through example and open communications.

All of the techniques for effective communications previously discussed are helpful skills for interacting with teens. Just as when they were younger, it's important to communicate respect in our conversations with them. Adolescence is a period when it's as if the teen is required to question authority. The relationship that we've built with them avoids that kind of superior/inferior status. Thus, there's no need for them to challenge our power. Instead, when we convey value and interest, just as we would with a long-time trusted friend, we enhance the teens' self-esteem.

Because this is a period of heightened emotions and a possible emotional dominance in decision making, we must find the right setting and opportunity for conversations. We must give extra preparation and thought to our words that can so quickly wound or cause the teen to withdraw. Because adolescence is often a time when they seem to have strong needs for social acceptance, teens are frequently alert for the slightest hint of disapproval or rejection. Being ready to make our intent and purpose known at the beginning of our remarks can add clarity and effectiveness.

Begin with Openness

Although we sometimes don't like what we're hearing from grandchildren, if we oppose or condemn too quickly, we may miss the chance to clarify, and perhaps extend or even modify, the child's view. It's an important part of nurturing the learning process to practice openness without pre-judging what's being said. We listen intently and actively without protest. If we're too swift to object or disagree, we can shut down the teen and end the conversation.

Another reason for modeling and encouraging openness is that we want the child to be amenable to accepting various information. Such receptiveness enhances learning. We can't learn if we don't take-in the information. If you've ever tried to have a discussion with someone who only wanted to argue and be right, you've experienced the futile and unproductive results. We walk away saying, "That person just won't listen. It's like trying to reason with a stone wall." We constantly hear phrases, such as:

> "But don't you think that . . ."
>
> "Wouldn't you agree that . . ."
>
> "But of course, you must concur that the truth is . . ."
>
> "Let me tell you . . ."

Obviously, we must avoid such with our grandchildren because these qualifiers aren't inquiries but only requests for validation and agreement. When we hear these words, we're aware that others are not really asking questions but requesting our affirmation.

In our conversations with grandchildren, we must model the objective to exchange information, and perhaps, to learn something. In the long-term, it's important that we teach them the skills to avoid or adroitly manage the people who don't enjoy a pleasant conversation. Since such people seem to only want to dominate the conversation or win the debate, they do not make a good social environment. In modeling our communications, we can avoid such relationship wreckers. We certainly don't want to be the authority figure that teens often feel compelled to rebel against. Instead, we can engage them in challenging discussions that stimulate learning.

Several years ago, I was attempting to describe Carl Jung's concept of the ego to my daughter, but was frustrated with my ramblings of how the ego is the manager of the personality and can inhibit or enhance the flow of information. She returned with some creative visualization. Her clever illustrations show the OPEN mindset in which the ego manager is a cute little elf who encourages new information, feelings, perceptions, and

ideas to be received. There is no hesitation about incoming messages. There is no barrier to new knowledge. The ego welcomes new information into the brain.

When the mindset is open, the ego is like a playful little elf who swings the gate open wide to invite new, challenging facts, and knowledge in search of learning.

Once inside, the information can then be sorted, pondered, and analyzed for use, memory, or disregarded. Just because the information is allowed to enter for consideration doesn't mean that it will be automatically accepted. Rather, contemplation is the first step for careful analysis. By practicing and encouraging this openness, we enhance our grandchildren's amenability to learning and a growth mindset.

We encourage development of critical thinking skills, of analyzing, evaluating, and considering different aspects of the information. Thus, it becomes both openness in communication with openness for consideration and discernment.

We've experienced the frustration of trying to discuss something with people who are being as dense as a stone wall. They interrupt what we're trying to say. They tell us that we're wrong. They insinuate that we're stupid. And they clearly don't want to hear what we're trying to present. Their gate is closed behind the monster ego and will not allow any new information or ideas to penetrate their big ego. It's as if they have a closed mindset and they're not open to anything different.

A big ego can reduces openness. By blocking the entrance of anything that doesn't fit with what's already there, the ego protects a fixed mindset. Some facts, ideas, and information that comfortably align with the beliefs and concepts already firmly established in the fixed mindset are allowed to squeak past this biased ego manager, but only if they conform. Everything else is rejected.

The fixed mindset becomes deaf to anything that is new or different. This indignant little elf portrays how the ego of a fixed mindset carefully monitors and rejects anything unlike what is already known—what is already inside the gate. Obviously, this is not the model that we should give to children. It can cause us to display an attitude of bitterness, irrelevance, or of being "stuck in a rut." Instead, we must model the little elf's openness for young people.

Recalling the importance of credibility and relevance discussed in Chapter 6, we can't afford to allow our egos to keep us relegated to the past by only operating in and advocating a world that's familiar. We must be open to our grandchildren's world. Even though the new phones can be frustrating and the hairstyles seem absurd, we set a better example when we model openness. We laugh at period movies that depict little old ladies being fearful of electricity and being afraid that harmful vapors might escape from electrical outlets. Yet, that's how we might appear to the younger generation if we restrict ourselves and talk about only what's familiar to our world.

The openness of a growing mind, not only enhances learning and developing critical thinking skills, it gives the young people a sense of control over what they hear. It empowers them to know that they can analyze, consider, accept, tuck away for future reference, or summarily reject anything that contradicts their values or character.

The little elf shows them how they can deal with free speech because they have power over words. They need not run from free speech. They don't need protection from micro aggressions. They have power over what they hear. This power gives them the freedom of thought and freedom of ideas.

Pronouns

Since it is imperative to ensure the adolescent's comfort when talking with us, we can make a small adjustment in our verbal style that makes a huge difference in impact. We can drop the inappropriate personal pronouns—I, me, my. For example, I battle the tendency to begin my conversational responses with, *I think*. *"I think* it's time for dinner." *"I think* you would enjoy this book. *I think* you need to put this toy on the bottom shelf." Yet, I'll set a better linguistic example and enhance my chances of being effective with a sensitive child (or adult) if I simply drop the thoughtless emphasis on me. I can just as easily say, "This toy can fit on the bottom shelf. It's time for your bath. This is an interesting book." By eliminating these small insignificant conversational phrases, I can implement rule #1, *Focus on the child.* It's not about me!

With very sensitive people, or tense situations, it's useful to drop another personal pronoun that might sound accusatory—*you*. Instead of *"You* need to do this," we can simply say, "This needs to be done." Instead of *"You* made a mess," it can be "The mess needs to be cleaned-up." Especially if the child is emotionally vulnerable, we don't need to add to guilt or stress by inferring blame. Although we may make these unfortunate accusations unintentionally, we can greatly enhance our verbal skills and set better examples for the children by being alert to our use of pronouns.

There are times when pronouns are very appropriate, when we say, "I need your help. Please get the ____ for me." Children often enjoy being cooperative and helpful. In these instances, we want our words to be intentional, to express our purpose and what we really mean. With a bit of thought, we use better language and plant the seeds for a future worker or professional who is equipped with excellent verbal skills. The boss might say, "I need you to do ____, but in a pleasant tone the astute leader says, "This is the task that needs to be done. Let me know if there are any questions or help needed from me?" This is a leader whose team members are likely to appreciate respect and enjoy collaboration. Yes, we can teach leadership and interpersonal skills from a very early age as we are intentional with our use of pronouns.

Apology or Acknowledgement

Especially when a teen is emotionally upset and feeling vulnerable, it's useful to distinguish between a needed apology or acknowledgement of the undesirable. For example, we often apologize for everything that happens around us.

> "*I'm sorry* that you don't like to eat spinach."
>
> "*I'm sorry* that you didn't earn an A in that subject. "
>
> "*I'm sorry* that it rained on your parade."

We should not trivialize our apologies, however, by making them when not appropriate, or when we have not caused the problem. Neither should we assume responsibility for something that's not ours. A better response would be,

> "*It's unfortunate* that spinach is distasteful to you. "
>
> "*It's unfortunate* that you didn't find time to study and missed making an A in that subject."
>
> "*It's unfortunate* that it rained on your parade."

Although we shouldn't fail to apologize if we've caused harm, neither should we encourage responsibility for circumstances that were not caused by our actions. In addition, the expression of inopportune circumstances can prompt positive follow-up actions rather than a dead-end of sympathy.

For teenagers who have a preference for *feeling*, saying "I'm sorry" frequently can be a habit that undermines their self-esteem. Without realizing, they may assume blame or accept fault for something that has nothing to do with them. Especially for young women, helping them to make a small adjustment in language supports a positive influence on their self-esteem. We know how vulnerable people with the *feeling* preference are to assuming guilt for what's happening around them. By establishing early language and thinking patterns, we can diminish the likelihood that others will be able to manipulate them with guilt and make them feel sorry for something that has no relation to their actions. This is another small way that we can empower our grandchildren to become independent, self-confident, and immune to others' attempts at manipulation.

Although this may seem to be a ridiculous word game, it can have huge consequences for depressed teens. It helps to distinguish between harm that they have actually caused and other unfortunate circumstances. Learning to say, "I'm sorry," only when they have transgressed or are expressing sympathy, restricts the area of their guilt or responsibility. By saying, "It's unfortunate," when they are only an observer, the adolescent learns to express empathy and compassion, but without the remorse that is sometimes hazardous for teens. This small alteration in our language can have an astounding difference on their self-talk and their self-confidence.

Words that Wound

As we explored in Chapter 7, children with a preference for *feeling* may be a bit sensitive to what seems to us adults to be a straightforward statement. At the same time, we can frustrate a *thinking* grandchild with our passion and lack of logic. What may sound like a logical uncomplicated communication to an adult with a preference for *thinking* may sound critical to a *feeling* grandchild, or the reverse, child to grandparent. Remembering how important approval and harmony are to *feeling* types, we're more successful in our relationships when we acknowledge their feelings and values. Our words will be more compelling when we're aware of the children's preferred styles of communications. With only a bit of knowledge and thought, our words can be effective rather than unproductive or hurtful.

There have been many changes in the world since you and I were teens. Even though we may not understand or accept it as valid, the attitude toward speech has dramatically evolved since our youth. Many of these changes are puzzling to us as we label them ridiculous and quickly disregard such. In our youth, when we heard or saw something that we rejected or didn't like, we tended to ignore it or object to the offense. Many of us recall the common phrase that armored us against taunts on the playground, "Sticks and stones may break my bones, but cruel words can't hurt me." That's how we may have dealt with verbal insults. Today however, many teens regard any speech with which they disagree as an assault from which they must flee or be protected. For example, someone wrote the name of a political candidate on sidewalks at Emory University one evening. Regardless of the politics, if you or I didn't like what we saw, we would likely have ignored it, rubbed it away with our shoe, or if we were really offended, poured a bucket of water over the chalk letters. Instead, a group of the college students immediately challenged the university president that they were in pain and didn't feel safe from the chalk assault.

Some in this younger generation are very emotionally sensitive and may regard anything with which they disagree as hate speech. They call any objectionable words, *micro-aggressions*. Although the term was originally used to describe hate speech or ethnic insults, for many teens it now describes any language from which protection is demanded. Whether you and I are tempted to laugh and agree with the label "snowflake generation," or simply shake our heads in bewilderment, we can do neither. To the teens, this is serious business and they feel disrespected. When you and I would say, "I disagree," these young people say, "I don't want to hear it!" Further, they may demand that they should not have to hear anything with which they disagree.

When we discuss topics that seem ridiculous to us, but not to the grandchildren, we cannot display our disregard. When we are dismissive or say, "You're just being silly!" or "That's ridiculous!" we shut-down the conversation and miss the chance to understand the origin of their views and the opportunity to share our perspectives. Instead of repudiating their views and concerns, we must endeavor to understand their perspective and use the chance to teach them how to handle such situations and emotions.

Regardless of how we feel about the legitimacy of their circumstances, we must first recognize that they live in a very different world—a world in which language and free speech have different meanings for them. Nevertheless, we can help them cope with their fears and anxieties that come from words, taunts, or insults. We must encourage them to share their feelings while we withhold our judgements and comments. We can listen actively and intently, no matter how trivial the teen's concerns seem to us. They are very real to the grandchild. Just as we calmed and soothed the crying infant, we must calm and soothe the upset teen. Then, we can teach the young person how to develop positive self-talk that will be an armor for the next verbal assault or micro-aggression. We can remind them that the little elf of openness welcomes new information, but it also allows them to toss out or disregard anything after it's been analyzed, reviewed, considered, and evaluated. We can give them *word power*.

Self-Talk

Regardless of the grandchild's age, the most vital conversations are the ones that take place in the child's head—the self-talk. Several times during this discussion about grandchildren, we've mentioned the impact that our mental conversations have on us. As the child grows, an important part of development is the growing ability to associate words with feelings and develop thinking skills. We grandparents can influence the substance of what the children tell themselves about their feelings, perceptions, and who they are.

Grandchildren learn language by repeating the words they hear and associating the words with visual images, sounds, cues, and feelings. They learn to talk by hearing the words we say. Just as we can influence the language they use to communicate with others, we can influence what they think—the internal language of self-talk.

In the beginning of our discussion, we agreed that our goal is to help the parents grow happy, stable, and successful people. Certainly a key component of that is in teaching the children useful internal messages. If we want them to have a "can-do" spirit, to be responsible, assertive, and independent, we can help to make that happen through the consistent use of words and phrases of support. A basic technique is to instill in them a mental state that's governed by the right words to enable them to pursue what they seek and be accountable for their actions. If we want them to have a "can-do" spirit, to be responsible, assertive, and independent, we can help to make that happen through the consistent use of words and phrases of support. A basic technique is to instill in them a mental state that's governed by the right words to enable them to pursue what they seek and be accountable for their actions. When something happens that displeases the two or three-year-old, their typical response is immediate tears. We comfort them with hugs and reassurances, but we must recognize that our words of comfort may be adopted as they learn to comfort themselves.

A funny ruse that we grandmothers sometime use to comfort toddlers is to spank what upset the toddler. If the two-year-old has bumped into a table, we will pat the table and say, "Bad table. You should not hurt my granddaughter." It's an easy way to distract the child, but it begins the practice of blaming anything but the child's actions. In doing this, we put the wrong words into the child's vocabulary of self-talk. A better, although not as funny way to handle the situation is to say, "It is very bad that you were hurt when you bumped into the table. Let's move the table so that you'll be safe." We show the child how to take a positive action in response to the harm. While we must use every opportunity to build self-confidence, at the same time, we can develop responsibility by the subtle way that we help the child respond to positive and negative situations. Beginning with the toddler, we teach the child the kind of self-talk that will build responsibility and self-esteem.

When grandchildren are excited and happy about an outcome of something they've done, we want the self-talk to be positive and self-affirming. But instead of a message of, "Wow! I'm great!" we want the message to be "Wow, I did it and it was worth all of that effort and practice." It's important to their emotional development to be happy and feel good about their successes. That's why instead of always saying, "I'm proud of you," we say, "Wow! You must feel really terrific about what you accomplished!" or sometimes we say, "Wow, you did it! How does that make you feel?"

We can give them effective ways of responding to positive outcomes. At the same time, we want them to develop the emotional fortitude to handle the times that they're not successful or when things are not going well. We want the internal messages to reinforce their perseverance so that, when they don't immediately succeed, they tell themselves, "I need more practice," or "I need a different approach." As mentioned earlier, if we constantly tell them how smart they are, we risk that their internal message when they don't succeed might be, "That wasn't smart, therefore, I must be stupid, or I'm supposed to be smart, but maybe I'm not. . ." When they come-up short, we want them to recognize that it was due to their lack of preparation or time invested—something that they can control and change. In essence, we want them to see themselves, not as a victim, but as a victor as illustrated in Chapter 9.

From literature and science fiction, we tend to think of one "possessed" as the description of one whose mind has been invaded by the devil or evil spirits. Literary descriptions of the results of being possessed by evil spirits are usually about abnormal behavior or saying things that don't make sense. Maybe I'm exaggerating here, but the wrong self-talk can create little voices in our heads that possess us and make us do and say things in ways that are not really who we are. A teen can become possessed by being liked by certain friends or trying to reach a high score on a video game. This "possession" is usually driven by self-talk that says, "I must get this person to like me. I'll just die if this person rejects me!" or "I feel stupid in school, but if I can make this level of the video game, it'll prove that I'm not stupid." All of these wrong messages floating around in their heads make them see things incorrectly and send them in the wrong direction. A strong sense of reality about what is real and accurate is critical.

Internal messages must not be inflated or degraded. When our grandchildren experience adversity, we want the self-talk to be something like, "I'd really like for that person to like me, but if not, I'll pursue other friends." Or, "That shouldn't have happened! I didn't deserve that, but I need to figure-out how to avoid such crud next time!" The self-talk directs much of the mood and emotional response. By helping the children develop a positive self-talk vocabulary, we nurture their growth in emotional intelligence (EQ) and help them to avoid the pitfalls of mental depression.

Perhaps the most important "conversations" we want them to learn are the ones they have with themselves. It's essential for us grandparents to remember that teaching positive self-talk is a process that begins very early, and never really ends. Although we always want to be a source of encouragement with confidence in the grandchildren's ability to succeed, it's not effective if we make them dependent on our approving communications. Instead, we must instill effective self-talk that builds a realistic sense of self-worth. Besides, if we are too profuse with our praise, even though we do believe that they are the smartest and cutest kids ever, we'll lose any credibility. Constant "Good job, good job" loses meaning. There is an additional discussion about the self-talk regarding fears and emotions in Chapter 10.

If prayer is an important part of the grandparents' life, modeling the self-talk can be a great opportunity to introduce prayer into the child's life. In addition to evening prayers and asking the blessing at meals, you may choose to add small conversations with God. Along with the celebration of an achievement, perhaps we can begin the talk with, "Thank you God for the strength to practice more." In the children's mental conversations, we can show them how to include their talk with God, especially with thanks for His blessings.

Children and prayer can be a challenging lesson. As we attempt to teach them how to converse with God, we must keep them from assuming that they can negotiate with God in the same way that they sometimes attempt to negotiate with us. When we advocate giving thanks for the good outcomes, the child can assume that when the outcome wasn't what was wanted, that God is punishing or has abandoned them. Nevertheless, we must prevail with care in teaching prayer as part of their spiritual development. Like many of the other lessons, it doesn't happen overnight but over a lifetime.

Communications and Social Interactions

One of the most profoundly important things we can do for our grandchildren is to assist them in developing social skills. Teaching them how to meet people, how to converse, interact with others, and how to write a thank-you note are all parts of the communication skills of success and will considerably enhance their accomplishments in the world.

As mentioned earlier, social graces are emphasized less in today's world, and yet, those who know how to conduct themselves in business and social situations have a decided advantage.

If grandparents are not comfortable teaching social skills, live too far away for repeated social opportunities, or if there are other impediments, video resources can be found on-line, and some are even free. Certainly, the systematic teaching of social skills is to be encouraged. Yet, perhaps the grandchildren learn most readily from their observations of us. Not only is it important for them to see how we interact with others, of greatest value is how we interact with them.

In an era when one rarely receives a personal note or letter through the USPS mail, teaching children to send a card with three or four sentences in gratitude is teaching them a useful adult skill. Today, when handwriting is no longer taught in some schools, children may balk at the prospect of having to write a note—"What Gran, you mean with pen and paper?" Having their own stationery or note cards can increase the enthusiasm. Dictating or copying your suggestions may give them more confidence. If absolutely necessary to avoid a meltdown, we can surrender to technology and suggest an email that, at least, acknowledges a bit of gratitude.

A highly respected lawyer commented that in her family, no one was allowed to use or play with a gift until after the thank-you note had been written. The ritual established an attentive thoughtfulness that has contributed to her incredible career success. Perhaps a good motivator for the personal thank you is the story told about an eaves dropping twelve-year-old. It seems that she listened with interest to her aunt telling the girl's mother about a considerable reduction in Christmas checks that the two teenage cousins had received from a relative. The aunt said that she could think of no reason for the drastic reduction in the amount from past Christmas gifts, other than the fact that the teens never sent thank you notes or acknowledged the gifts. The girl's mother was aware of her daughter's attentive listening but thought nothing of it until that evening when the girl asked for postage stamps. It seems that by bedtime on Christmas Day, a thank-you note had been written for every present that the young girl had received. Apparently, she wasn't willing to risk any future reduction in Christmas gifts. Acknowledging kindness and expressing appreciation are lifetime skills.

Most children benefit from learning how to meet others, engage in conversation, and become friends. If left to their own devices, however, young children's tendencies may be to go into an immediate "show and tell" when meeting new people. Because much of the child's world is naturally self-focused, they often need coaching on how to make new acquaintances and friends. We can provide an effective role model and teach them how to greet and engage others. We can give them examples of how they can ask appropriate questions or relate a common topic to engage others. By nurturing such skills, we propel them several degrees toward interpersonal success throughout their lives.

I readily admit my passion for teaching children effective communications and interpersonal skills. It's part of relationship building. Although I'm certainly no fantastic example, I've seen the results of young people who were taught these skills. I've also seen the results of those who were not. It's easy to observe the success of people who are adept at communications and interpersonal skills. I've also seen the impact that the lack of such skills can have on elderly grandparents.

Louis is an elderly Army veteran of the post-Korean War era. His career as an officer required moving his family often, including from Germany to Texas to Washington. Louis' dutiful and very passive wife took care of the family of two sons and one daughter. They grew-up in the hippie era of the late 1970's when there was a strong rejection of anything conventional and all traditional culture. Louis' children married and produced seven grandchildren. His wife died several years ago, but Louis continues to live independently in a retirement facility where he volunteers in the community. Although he sometimes walks with a cane, Louis is active, mentally alert, and very intelligent. He occasionally receives phone calls from his three children, but almost never hears from his grandchildren, despite his generous birthday and Christmas checks.

It isn't that any of his children or grandchildren are incarcerated or prevented in any way from communicating with their grandfather. Rather, Louis' family dynamic is the culmination of several factors. He was very focused on his military career and was frequently away from home. His wife was very passive, and due to the frequent moves, did not have many friends. His children were the product of a time when etiquette was regarded as irrelevant. Then, Louis' grandchildren grew-up without exposure to a culture that emphasized manners, appropriate attire, or interpersonal skills. The lack of communications probably contributed to a lack of comfort on the rare occasions when the grandparents and grandchildren were together. They don't really know one another. The regrettable result is that Louis, not only didn't develop a relationship with his children, he didn't build a relationship with his grandchildren. He's related to them, but there's no relationship.

As the elderly grandfather waits for his children and grandchildren to contact him, he entertains younger veterans with his interesting stories of what it was like to live in Germany during the cold war era. He tutors several young children through his church's after school program. But unfortunately, he is not a part of his grandchildren's lives. Their hippie era parents never taught them to call Papa or send him birthday and holiday cards. They were never taught the importance of a thank-you note or an impromptu phone call. After many years of focus on his own career, Louis seems reluctant to reach out to the children or grandchildren. He says that he doesn't really know them and doesn't want to interfere in their lives. Maybe this total disengagement of social skills works for some people, but it can contribute to a great loss, especially for the grandchildren.

Louis is not unusual among older men. If they grew-up in an era of "the man is the breadwinner and the woman takes care of the social stuff," they may have developed limited social skills, especially when it comes to conversations. If like Alex, or Tim that we met in Chapter 2, they are men of limited EQ. They will not be role models of good communication skills as they struggle to have any kind of relationship with their grandchildren. Regardless of the grandchildren's ages, most of these grandfathers' conversations and opportunities for interactions and facilitating learning will be missed. Egocentric grandparents who insist on being self-focused miss chances to know and build relationships with grandchildren because of their tendency to make everything about themselves. They abandon Rule#1 as they talk only of their interests, exploits, and opinions. They not only miss having a relationship with grandchildren, such self-centeredness can also limit friendships and social relations, leaving them as the lonely elderly.

I believe there are two reasons that grandparents' opportunities for teaching effective communications and social skills are so vital. The first is that parents may have limited time and attention for such, and even if they do a great job in initiating the skills, grandparents can furnish many opportunities for reinforcing and encouraging effective social interactions. The second reason comes from my observations in leadership development. Occasionally, when asking the client what their young employees needed most, I've been told, "She's a great performer with tons of potential, but can you teach her about appropriate, professional attire and demeanor?" I've also heard, "Can you teach him how to make a presentation and talk effectively with the people who report to him? Otherwise, there's a ceiling on any higher level jobs." It's often sad to see how the lack of communications and interpersonal skills can inhibit promotions and career ascent. By beginning to teach these skills from childhood, we initiate a future means of success.

Summary

The prayer at the beginning of this chapter begins with the request, "Prompt our words . . ." Perhaps that's the key to effective communications with our grandchildren at every age. We just need prompting—prior thought, consideration, and preparation. And occasionally, we may need different words.

When we're giving instructions, we must be clear, specific, and if possible, make eye contact. If our communications are about something unfamiliar or not desired by the child, it's more effective to talk slower, hesitate, and add a few questions. We must ensure that our communications always enhance our credibility and the trusting relationship with our dear grandchildren.

Remembering whether we might be talking with an introvert or an extravert, modeling openness, active listening, and being aware of how we use pronouns are all important. Helping children learn effective ways of responding to stressful language or messages is a huge asset. Thinking of possible questions, topics of conversations, and trying to plan one-to-one time with each child can be useful. We establish a lifetime communication skill, however, when we cultivate a sense of learning from conversing with others. We teach that every conversation can be an opportunity to gain something new or quietly reject what doesn't fit with other facts and our values. Then, there is no need for winning every argument, or only talking about what's familiar. There's no need to hide from different views because the child becomes an independent thinker. When the young person regards interactions as a chance to learn, this becomes a major life skill.

By instilling optimistic words of perseverance and resilience in the self-talk, we arm the child against depression and begin a foundation for emotional stability. With real and positive self-talk, we equip the young person to rebound from adversity and move forward in life.

With so much to teach the child, and sometimes with limited opportunities, our communications can become too pedantic. That's when we must remember the most effective approach.

Influence rather than constantly *instructing*.

If children's environment is one of always being told what-to-do, how-to-do, and when-to-do, we may not get the results we desire with ceaseless instructions. Rather, we can be more effective by using the same influencing skills that we would apply when attempting to persuade friends or team mates about an important project.

When we use our communications as a major resource for our relationships, we greatly enhance the solidarity of the bond we have with each child. When we recognize that our communications are connected like a chain, from one age and one stage to the next, we place the same importance on a conversation with the three-year-old that we have when coaching the college age grandchild about the dangers of alcohol abuse or indiscriminate sex. There are no casual or unimportant communications with our grandchildren—ever.

Every word is an opportunity.

Every conversation is a chance to model.

Every interaction can make a memory.

Chapter 9

Grandparents' Guidance for Decisions

Grant us insight
as we seek to inspire their decisions.

Last year, I had bit of an educational experience when I went to a somewhat rural area to meet a client at the courthouse on a Saturday morning. Because I'd never been to that area before, I arrived early and was sent to wait on a hallway bench. After watching a parade of people entering a large room, I learned that this was the day for state court. It was the time for people to appear who had been cited for misdemeanors, such as shop lifting, driving under the influence (DUI), possession of small amounts of controlled substances, or theft under $500. As I waited and watched the parade of sad, blank faces, I began to contemplate how these people got into such trouble. It made me wonder, were these people here because of a lapse of character or was it poor decision making skills?

When the client arrived, I posed my question. He chuckled and replied, "Dr. Z, if most people had character and integrity, and if they'd been taught good decision making skills, we could shut down this court!" His laughing reply stuck with me. In Chapter 4, we discussed the importance of nurturing strong character—doing the right things right. But my courthouse experience made me realize that decision making is part of the *implementation* of character.

Decision Making Skills

Earlier, we explored the importance of helping even the toddler to make choices by giving the child two equally appropriate options. We discussed how to ask, "Which of these two do you want to do first?" By limiting their selections, we give them the chance to choose between two rights, before the opportunity to choose between right and wrong. By giving them occasions to make safe choices, we nurture their independence and help them develop impulse control and delayed gratification.

Recalling the diagram about control in Chapter 2, it's very easy for adults to attempt to control situations by making all of the choices. Sometimes, it seems to be the efficient and expedient thing to do to simply make the decisions and force the child's compliance. But when we make all of the decisions, we take away the child's opportunity to learn. By presenting small incidental choices, the child begins to develop the skills to make the more important choices. Then, supported by character development, the child learns to make the *right* choices. Many classic children's books provide terrific material for reinforcing decision making skills. Some of my favorites are in the *Berenstain* collection, but almost any stories, from *The Gingerbread Man, the Beatrix Potter Series,* and *Dr. Seuss* to Sean Covey's *Six Most Important Decisions You'll Ever Make* for teens can provide great teaching moments and good references to mention in conversations with grandchildren.

We grandparents have two assets that the parents may not have. First, we have more years of decision making experience, and second, we may have the luxury of more time than the hurried parents. When Mom or Dad is trying to get the children to school in the mornings, they may not have time to ask which jacket the child prefers. Conversely, grandparents may find it possible to make those extra moments in order to help the children learn how and why they have different preferences, what works well for them, and what might not be as pleasant.

Many years ago, a most perplexing professional discovery came from using the *Myers Briggs Type*

Indicator® (MBTI®), discussed in Chapter 7, with hourly employees in a large manufacturing plant where I noticed a disconcerting trend. It seemed that every time the human resources manager described a troubled employee, it would include an inconsistent attendance record, problems with DUI, domestic disputes, or other unproductive behaviors. Then, when these employees completed the *MBTI,®* I noticed that they had difficulty discerning preferences. Was there a correlation between not having a defined preference and making poor choices? Or, was their lack of preferences influencing their poor choices? Through the years, I've noticed that people who struggle with job performance and life decisions often struggle with choosing, knowing, and having confidence in their preferences. Since I rarely got the chance to work with hourly employees, I have no statistical research to confirm my observations, but regardless, learning how to make choices is the beginning of effective decision making.

Analyzing the Risks

We can help even very young children to make productive choices by verbalizing the positives, and exploring the choices. If we stick a vanilla ice cream cone in the child's hand, just to be done with it, we miss an opportunity to stimulate the child's learning. We miss the chance to teach how to consider the options. If we want them to make wise, informed choices at ages 15 and 25, we must invest the time and patience in developing the decision making skills from the time they're very young.

When talking with grandchildren, it's easy to say, "Why did you choose that one?" Again, with both children and adults, "Why?" questions tend to put people on the defensive because it appears that we're questioning their motives. Then, it seems that they must defend, rather than explain their choices. A good tool for guiding young children in their decisions is to say, "Tell me about your choice. What did you prefer about that one?" This kind of open ended questioning elicits a casual response and gives us insight into the child's choices. Follow-up with talk about the choice, can reinforce positive decisions. We ask *how, when, where,* and *what* questions, but *why* questions that examine our motive seem to annoy humans at any age.

As the child grows, and the decisions become more complex, perhaps with negative elements, it's imperative that we encourage the consideration of risks. It may start with simple games when you say, "Okay, if you remove that block and the tower falls, can you handle that? What will you do?" If the response is a laugh and, "I'll build it again!" Then, we say, "Well, there's no risk. If you can handle the results of everything falling, it's okay." But if there's hesitation, we must add, "Maybe the risk is too great. If you'll be disappointed or upset if your beautiful tower falls, then we say that it isn't worth the risk."

Rather than constantly haranguing the child about staying away from the edge of the fish pond, we can present the consequences. We can say, "I see that you like standing near the edge so that you can see the fish, but if you lose your balance and get your shoes and clothes wet, then you'll be cold, uncomfortable, and we will have to leave. Come, stand beside me and hold my hand. Now, you can see the fish without risk of wet feet."

Ultimately, where we're going with this teaching about risk is getting the child to think of all of the possible things that can go wrong, not to make the child fearful, but to bring-up and assess the possibilities that the child can handle. It starts with considering the positives and negatives, or the "pros and cons." If the child is too attached to the tower that's been constructed, or realizes that wet shoes would be uncomfortable, then we've helped the child recognize that proceeding isn't worth the risk.

It's the same as with the adventure in nature that we discussed earlier. We consider the possible risks, and then, assess our ability to avoid the hazards. If we consistently consider the positives and threats, we gradually build the child's intellectual skills, while at the same time, equipping the child with a major life skill. We avoid the child's developing unnecessary fears because he/she knows how to assess the situation and diminish undesirable consequences. Adventures in nature make a great time to talk about how to avoid a dangerous rock slide by staying away from the unstable edge of the cliff. At the shore, we discuss not jumping into water when we can't see the bottom or don't know how deep it is. We not only point out the hazards, but we also explain why it is a risk, and perhaps, a risk not worth taking.

The challenge in nurturing decision skills is that it's sometimes a bit like teaching a toddler to ride a bicycle or play tennis. At this stage, the toddler simply doesn't have the muscular development to maintain balance on a bike, or the eye/hand coordination to maneuver a tennis racket. When young, the limbic system in the brain is a major factor in the child's decision making. This brain area connects the structures that help control emotions. It involves memory, along with the desire to eat, drink, as well as stimulation that causes aggressive behavior and other functions. It seems that young children make their choices largely from the immediate and their emotions—"I want that toy and I want it now!" Although children are capable of demonstrating impulse control, maturity seems to be required for consistent impulse control that may be governed from a different part of the brain, the prefrontal cortex, that won't be fully developed until age 21-25.

The prefrontal cortex is the area of the brain that contains what psychologists call the "executive functions." These are the more complex thinking processes, such as cognitive skills needed for critical thinking, planning, attention, judgement, decisions, goal-directed behavior, and working memory. These are the skills that allow a person to pause, assess the situation, consider the options, plan a course of action, and execute. It's unusual to see a five, ten, or even-fifteen-year-old demonstrate such executive functions, but there are exceptions. Walt, the brilliant kid mentioned earlier, seemed to have exited the womb with a fully developed executive function. He was thoughtful, attentive, logical, and at the same time, also demonstrated a high EQ, but Walt is very unusual. I recall countless other wonderful children whose sole decision making was based on what looked good at the moment. Children like Walt are rare, and probably have fewer needs for grandparents' coaching, but most other children benefit from time and much guidance for the development of the executive functions, the critical thinking skills, and the knowledge required for effective decisions.

It seems that this executive function is amenable to stimulation and intervention, a rationale often given for the disparity in school performance. It may be that the reason that many middle and upper socio-economic class children perform better in school is that their pre-frontal cortex and working memory are better developed. It is theorized that poverty isn't as much of a direct influence on thinking skills as much as the years of compounded stress. Perhaps it's the stress that inhibits the development of this area of the brain in needy children, rather than just the poverty. One reason that neuroscientists and policy makers are so excited over this discovery is, perhaps, that they see that by providing ways to stimulate the thinking skills and reducing stress in the child's environment, there could be a path to diminishing the cycle of poverty.

Teaching the child to ride a bike is a different process with different children. Some may grasp the balance after only a few wobbly attempts, while others need training wheels and much coaxing and coaching. It's like becoming good at tennis, baseball, or any skill. Becoming really proficient requires many hours of practice.

We begin the process by teaching the child to make simple choices, then we progress to simple decisions where we "talk" them through the process. We move on to consider risks, consequences, and rewards. And finally, through a couple of decades of coaching, we see the young adults make thoughtful effective decisions, but this doesn't usually happen until after the maturity of the prefrontal cortex in their mid-twenties. Before that, we must help them through countless choices and hope that our effectiveness reduces their impulsive adolescent decisions, from drunk driving to underage sex, that can have life changing consequences.

Writers, such as Jean Twenge (2017), in observing today's youth and comparing with earlier generations, pose questions about decision maturity occurring later in the current generation than in earlier times. Today, when we worry about the twenty-year-old's making the right decision about risky behavior, we note that, at the same age, the great-grandparents usually had jobs and may have been married and having children at that age. Whether this change is driven by delayed brain development, more social and economic choices, or changes in society, it is an interesting phenomenon. Did our ancestors make fewer emotionally based decisions because they had to, and their executive functions developed at an earlier age? Or perhaps, were the emotionally driven risky behaviors less prevalent among young people of earlier generations because there seemed to be fewer hazards? Whatever the cause, we know that these executive functions can be nurtured, giving our grandchildren an advantage, both as they grow and as they become adults.

As the child ages, we can introduce more complex decision skills in which we teach the child to state the problem, research and gather the facts and information, analyze the alternatives, and reach the best conclusion. For example, a nineteen year-old grandson has worked during weekends and school holidays, saving his money for a car. He is excited about the possibility of buying a used car. When we see the vehicle being considered, what might be in our head is, "That's crazy. Don't throw your money away on that old piece of junk!" But what we say is, "You've worked so hard and been so thrifty. I can see why you're eager to buy your own car. Maybe we can analyze this so that you can make the best decision for your investment." Then, you verbally guide him through a logical fact gathering such as anything appropriate from the following:

"You're excited! Tell me more about the car. Do you like the color, model, interior, and features?"

"I'll bet that with your technology skills, you know where you can get a history of the car to find whether it was ever in a wreck or a flood?"

"Does the sale come with a guarantee or can you have a mechanic examine it?"

"Do you need to buy a car now or can you continue to save your money and look for other good cars that you like?"

"What will be the result of investing all of your savings in this car?"

"Will having your own car add burdens or unwanted responsibilities? Will it make your life better?"

"What other information will help to make a decision?"

We can begin the discussion with, "Wow! A new car, this sounds exciting, but I hear a bit of hesitation in your voice. Let's talk through the pluses and minuses to help you make a decision." With a few leading questions, we can avoid being the controlling wet blanket that extinguishes enthusiasm. Instead, we can guide the young grandson through the decision with influence, without being critical or controlling.

Because we've been there and made these kinds of decisions, with both positive and negative outcomes, we know the answers, but it's ever so much more effective if we *influence, rather than instruct.* Such an approach helps the grandson to find his own answers and reach his own conclusions. If we just instruct him on the answer, "That's stupid, you don't want to buy that rattle trap!" we crush his enthusiasm and diminish his chance for learning. Instead, calmly asking the pertinent questions that help young people find their own answers is much more effective than just instructing them what they should do. With our questions and observations, we're stimulating critical thinking skills that use a different part of the brain. We're gently drawing the young person away from making solely emotional decisions. Then, our influence becomes effective.

I must confess that I have a tendency to want to jump-in and fix other people's problems—especially when the solution is so obvious to me. I'm thoughtful, informed, and very eager to give advice, but such instruction is rarely effective. Recently, I heard a man say that his wife gave him excellent advice, but that only when someone else, even a stranger, gave him the same suggestion, did he take action. The familiarity of family can sometimes diminish credibility and leave us being taken for granted. When this happens to me, I can feel insulted, however, it's better if I just recognize that my initial attempt had the effect of increasing openness to the same solution recommended by someone else. Although my being right isn't acknowledged, that's when I must smile and take silent pleasure in remembering Rule #2 about being effective.

I want to make everything perfect in my family's world, but sometimes, instead of being the consummate fixer, I just need to listen. I must recognize that my solving the problem isn't as useful as my helping others to figure out their problems and make their own decisions. We may be more effective with asking open ended and thought provoking questions. We gently lead others to their own solutions and help them learn. I cannot always be there to fix every problem that my grandson will encounter; however, I can be here to teach him the skills to become his own effective problem solver and decision maker.

Older children may enjoy being introduced to "decision trees," a kind of flow chart that elicits consideration of possible consequences, resources, and other factors common to operations research. This is another visual exploration that helps us delve into developing additional information about our possible choices.

Whatever the method, it is imperative that from an early age we encourage and practice thoughtful and logical decision making. When that grandson is 23 and considering the offer of a great job, or taking a student loan to pursue another college degree, we want him to make the most informed decision and the one that will be best for his future. When that 22-year-old granddaughter is getting into a car with friends, and realizes that the driver has had way too much alcohol or marijuana to be driving, we want her to instantly weigh the risks. We want her to conclude that the danger of an accident, or likelihood of being stopped by the police, is far greater than her need to go along with the crowd.

Like developing character, making effective decisions begins when they are very young and is one of the most important skills that we can give our grandchildren. Unlike learning to catch a ball or ride a bike, decision skills are not learned quickly or at a certain age. Instead, it is a developmental process that takes place over a couple of decades.

Unintended Consequences

In Chapter 3, we discussed the value of allowing children to experience the logical consequences of their behavior as a way of teaching them to think about what they're doing before they create problems for themselves. If we've been thorough in our use of logical consequences in teaching self-discipline, we've created an awareness as the child grows of what can happen when we are careless and don't "think ahead" or anticipate all of the possible consequences of our actions. We make them aware, not only of the need to consider the consequences, but also how to "back-up" and correct mistakes.

One evening when an elderly lawyer was entertaining friends, he gave a superb example of neglecting unintended consequences with a tale of his youth. He told about being with a group of fraternity buddies during his senior year of college, when after a couple of beers, they decided to join a protest that was taking place in front of the governor's mansion. Soon after they arrived, however, they discovered that it was not a peaceful protest, but that some "rabble rousers" were becoming aggressive and the police were taking threats to the governor's safety very seriously. As the violence escalated, my friend sought refuge by scrambling up a nearby pine tree and being very quiet as he remained somewhat camouflaged by the thick branches. He watched as some of his buddies tried to outrun the police when most of the other protesters were arrested, herded into a bus, and hauled to the large metropolitan police headquarters. Remaining quiet until everyone left the scene, the suddenly sober frat boy descended from the tree, and unobtrusively walked to what was common in his day, a pay phone, to call his roommate to come and take him back to campus.

He described how the others were arrested, booked, and received serious charges. He said that even though he escaped, his close encounter was a major event in his college maturity as he realized how close he came to legal expenses for which he had no money, the likely loss of his scholarship, and what an arrest record would have done to his job prospects after college. He said that, today, it might not be such a big deal, but back then, it would have been a life changing disaster. He said that, at the time, he would have just called it "scary," but as he reflects on it a lifetime later, he said that he would call it "a lesson about unintended consequences." He said that under the influence of a few beers, he and his buddies' only thought was about their bold intent to express disdain for a governor's policy. He admitted that no one considered the possibilities of an arrest or the unintended consequences of a police record. Even though contemporary leniency might save our grandchildren from such a potential disaster, our careful and diplomatic stories about unintended consequences can ensure their safety and better life experiences.

Perhaps there is no better example to help young children recognize the unintended consequences of a bad decision than in the story of the *Berenstain Bears Trouble at School.* It's the delightful tale of young Brother Bear who goofed around and didn't complete his homework. He compounded this unfortunate decision when he hid in the bushes instead of boarding the school bus. Then, he became lost as he wandered in the woods. Fortunately, he found Grandpa Bear who, after listening to a woeful tale about missing school, took him to see an old wagon that was rotting away in the swamp. Grandpa explained that a long time ago, he was driving that wagon and took a wrong turn, only to become mired in the mud. Then, instead of backing up and finding a better road, he just kept going, until finally, the wagon was going nowhere. Grandpa Bear explained that, when we make a bad decision, when we find that something isn't working, we must back-up and find the right road or a better way, instead of just continuing to get stuck! The story ends with Brother Bear's lesson learned and the awareness that it's rarely too late to correct a mistake. This *Berenstain* story provides a simple way to teach childrn how to realize when they've made a wrong decision, when something isn't working, and that recognizing the problem and correcting it is far superior to perpetuating the mistake. This is a wonderful little book that's an essential for every grandparent's book shelf.

Applying the Decision Making Skills

If we do our job well in facilitating decision making, and if we gently encourage critical thinking skills, the grandchildren will remember these little stories and the lessons that they teach. For example, when the grandson is a freshman fraternity pledge, and finds himself in a hazing situation where the pledges are forced to rapidly drink excessive alcohol, he may remember the Grandpa Bear story. Instead of becoming a possible victim of acute alcohol poisoning, the grandson recalls the importance of "backing-up and getting on the right road." Then, he exclaims that he's about to be sick, runs toward the bathroom, and instead, slips out the back door. With some time to reconsider his situation, he concludes that these guys are not really his friends and that he doesn't want to be like them. This is not an easy decision for an 18 or 19-year-old, but it may be a life saving decision. We never know how the memories we create will later affect our grandchildren, but we can be certain that they have good memories and character building memories on which to make their decisions.

Years ago, my father was talking about how he borrowed tuition money and rode the bus to business college. My daughter asked, "But Grandpa, you wanted to be a doctor when you were growing-up. Why didn't you just walk on up the hill to the university so you could become a doctor, instead of stopping at the business college? You borrowed and repaid the money. You made that long bus ride. Why didn't you go on to the university?" He paused, looked puzzled, and said, "Well, I never thought about it, but I could have. I guess I just didn't know that I could have." Then, he smiled and said, "But then, I might not have met your grandmother, so a business life turned out to be good." Still, that was a profound lesson for his granddaughter and me as we both resolved never to overlook a possibility. Yes, sharing our missed steps and our mistakes with grandchildren is a great way of helping them. Our mistakes become less disastrous if they keep our grandchildren from following in our footsteps and making similar mistakes or missing opportunities.

Decision skills are a bit like character, some are taught by osmosis—by children watching our daily actions or being exposed to our stories—and some are taught by our coaching and guidance. We can take a lesson from *Grandpa Bear,* talk about our own mistakes, how we could have made better decisions, and give cues for logical thinking. Perhaps that's how we make progress in our civilization.

Choices for Time and Priorities

Another area where we can make a tremendous contribution to effective decision making for our grandchildren is with their use of time. In Chapter 6 we discussed how much time our grandchildren may choose to spend with their technology. We can make their screen time and other activities appropriate by helping them to learn about their investment of time and learning to prioritize.

Today, children can learn about time and to read clocks much earlier than we did. They have the advantage of digital clocks and the ease and availability of many clocks. I found my first watch in my Christmas stocking when I was eight. Of course, it was gold, fragile, and I only wore it on Sundays and special occasions. Inexpensive watches, clocks, and the inclusion of time on phones and iPads make it possible for children to have their own time reminders and learn the value of time at much younger ages. As soon as children can recognize and identify numerals, it's appropriate to introduce clocks and the concept of time. Although the world is moving toward the digital, like cursive writing, it's useful for the child to be familiar with the old clocks. An analog clock with moving pointers may actually be introduced earlier as it is visual and seems more concrete for the young brain.

When children are in the swimming pool, on the playground, or engaged in favorite activities, it's advantageous for them to be aware of time. We begin by showing them the clock and saying, when the long pointer is at 2, I'll tell you that we have five more minutes to play. Then, when the long pointer is at 3, it will be time for us to leave. Having a concept of time adds to the child's ability to prepare for changing activities. It can also avoid a meltdown when the child is suddenly ripped away from fun. Of course, we're the grown-up. We get to decide when it's time to go, but then, it's better for everyone when we seek the child's cooperation and use every moment as a learning opportunity. Although the "five-minute warning" doesn't always ease the transition from one activity to another, and learning to read clocks won't guarantee cooperation, it is generally more effective than the alternative.

Young children often find clocks fascinating. By fostering an awareness of time at an early age, we can build on this development when we say, "We only have an hour to play. Do you want to _____ or to play ____?" Again, we're helping the child to explore preferences and make choices. Then, we can begin to add, "Which is more important? Do you want to ____ or ____?" As the child grows, the child learns about priorities, what is more important now and in the future—what might be more fun, accomplish more, or be more valuable tomorrow or next week. One of the challenges of teaching time is that children have a very different concept of time than is ours. Everything seems much longer for them and it's difficult for them to see or imagine very far into the future. Yet, introducing this concept of future importance is imperative to their overall maturation.

The ability to recognize priorities, how to separate the truly important from the trivial, will be an enormous factor in contributing to success—as a student, an employee, as a leader, in the family, and in life. Because we often confuse what seems urgent with what is important, it's easy to allow the urgent to overshadow what's really vital in our lives. Helping children learn how to invest their time in what's significant will be crucial to their success in so many endeavors. Beginning at age four or five, and gradually developing through childhood, the ability to see the priorities and manage time will be another huge gift for the child's development.

Sometimes, we launch into activities without thought as the to best approach or what's most important. Instead, we just tackle what's in front of us. Such lack of prioritizing can lead to unproductive pursuits and ultimate frustration with what hasn't been accomplished.

Another trap that can keep us from being fully productive is by becoming overwhelmed. When we send a child to "clean-up your toys," the child may be overwhelmed and leave us furious with the lack of results. If the child has not learned to "finish playing with the toy" by replacing it on the storage shelf, play spaces can become an area of cluttered chaos. In these kinds of situations, the child may not be capable of completing the task alone. That's when a grandparent may be needed to "talk" the child through with a series of cues. We say, "Okay, let's begin by putting all of the Duplos in a bin." When that is complete, we add, "Next, let's put all of the doll furniture back into the doll house. You can arrange it later, but for now, let's just put it into the house. Next, let's put all of the games together on this shelf." Without actually doing the clean-up work, we enable the child to accomplish it quickly, and without drudgery. Our being there to verbally guide the task enables the child to avoid being overwhelmed by not knowing exactly how to fulfill the adults' instructions. Our cues also help the child to stay focused on the clean-up and not be distracted and suddenly engaged in playing with the toys instead of the clean-up. Although we may not have the Mary Poppins "spit-spot" magic for the clean-up, for the child, the results will be the same delight. The best part for the child is learning how to begin the process. Even when it may not be as easy without a grandparent coach, we've begun teaching the process of tackling one task at a time and shown the child how not to be overwhelmed by the whole mess.

Perhaps one of the less effective axioms from the Traditional Generation's era is "Finish what you start." or "Don't start something unless you can finish it." This long-held belief causes some people to attempt to wait until they have enough time for an entire project, thus using time in less efficient ways. Helping children to see how they can break large projects into smaller tasks that can be completed in the time available aids their growth in many ways, from managing time to learning delayed gratification. Because they've learned this skill of "breaking big stuff into small do-able chunks," they will not be intimidated or frustrated by major assignments in school or in the workplace.

Grandchildren will be impressed by how you manage time and any tools that you use. Whether you prefer a to-do list, a paper day planner, or a software calendar and planning software, share it with the children. The best time for introducing such tools varies, but astute grandparents will sense the right moment and seize the opportunity. Children can be shown how to use it for their homework, keeping track of piano practice, ball games, and other activities. We can help them to see that with a few tools and practices, they can make better choices for how they manage their time, and in the process, actually have more time for doing the things that they enjoy. Letting them see our tools for organization is valuable, but regardless of what we use, a small paper booklet may be a good choice for a child, even though technology may have more attraction for them. Some schools require a specific planner or format, but as of this writing, there's not a technology that is as readily accessible or quick to use as a simple small calendar booklet or as efficient as a student day planner.

Because small children's sense of time is such a present focus, it's difficult for them to understand how useful it can be when these calendars or day planners become a life history. Perhaps, instead of talking about our history, it may be useful to pull one of our old calendars or planners from the shelf or out of the attic to share with an older child. We can talk about the professional value of being able to tie our actions to date and time. We can also share the note we wrote on the calendar about the grandchild's first birthday party, or other special events. What a wonderful treasure it would be for us to have a journal of daily events from our grandparents and ancestors. Perhaps we can help our grandchildren create such for future generations. Who knows, maybe a digital format that's user friendly will soon become available and make time management and journaling easier.

Regardless of the format, the key to any planning and time management tool is in its consistent use. Sometimes, a weekly review is useful. That's when, instead of criticizing how the booklet was used or not used, it can be an opportunity to suggest additions. If the child doesn't live nearby, and you enjoy weekly phone or video calls, reviewing the planner can be a great opener for initiating the child's discussion of events of the week.

Helping the child use some kind of planning tool is not easy, and it isn't completed in just one session, but it's usually incredibly easier than teaching an adult. Before the adult can embrace a new tool, the adult must move out of the denial that such an aide is needed. For the child, it simply opens up a whole new world. Regardless of how it's approached, guiding the child to make positive decisions about the use of time will result in a treasured skill.

One of the most useful strengths that we can give the grandchildren is the constant awareness of how their time is invested. If we can "implant" the question, "Is this the best use of my time?" in their consciousness, we will give them an awesome asset. They will not be tempted to waste time with meaningless screen time or other mindless activities. Instead, they will be alert to how they can make the most of every minute.

Teaching about time is useful in many ways, from easing young children from one activity to another, helping them structure their school work and activities, and perhaps, making home life better. Perhaps the most important contribution we can make in helping children with time management is for us to first understand that they usually aren't very good at it. Because their total focus is on the *now,* it can cause difficulty with everything from behavioral issues to their decisions. It's hard for them to grasp the future or to imagine how their present actions will impact their futures. Although it isn't a quick or easy process, we grandparents can give them a future perspective. There's more in Chapter 11 about how we can guide their development of a future focused vision that will be invaluable.

Money

The effective use of such resources as time and money can be an incredible life advantage. Often, we grandparents set-up a savings account or a college fund for the grandchild, but we regard this as money for much later. We may not even make the young child aware that such funds exist. Certainly, supporting the parents' endeavors for education are admirable, but we must not overlook the opportunity to also teach the child about financial decisions.

The first decision that we can make is to discuss money issues for grandchildren with the parents. It's imperative that we're on the same page with them. Otherwise, we can appear critical of their financial management, or appear to be undermining the values that they're attempting to teach the child. As with everything else, unless abuse, addiction, incarceration, or unfortunate circumstances change the family dynamics, grandparents must always be in the happily supportive ancillary role. We must defer to the parents' rules about money.

From taking the child to work with us, exposing the child to how we've earned a living, or simply collecting coins, we begin the process of focusing on financial skills. Over time and in tandem with the child's parents, we can be an immense money management coach for the children. If the child receives an allowance, with the parents' agreement, we can supplement the amount—but not too much. Perhaps we can separate the allowance into three amounts—*saving, giving,* and *spending*. If the child is young, we can separate the periodic supplement into three jars or envelopes. If dealing with small amounts of money, an old fashioned piggy bank, or one of the more sophisticated banks that looks like a small safe will work for the *savings* part. A discussion of how the *giving* portion will be allocated and used may be a good introduction to philanthropy. Then, the child should feel free to spend the *spending* portion according to the child's choice. That doesn't mean wasting the money or not having discussion about the choices, but if the child doesn't feel the sense of choice, then we're missing the whole opportunity for teaching money management.

When making a purchase with the child's own money, it's important for shopping money to be carried in a wallet or change purse that belongs to the child, even if the grandparent "holds" the money while the child shops. If touchless transactions aren't a necessity, it's useful to allow the child to use his/her own cash to make purchases and count any change received. Toy and other such purchases can be the first experiences with money management.

Helping grandchildren learn the value of knowing where their money is going can be another lifetime skill. Children whose preference is for *Sensing* may like having some means to track their spending. Whether it's a list on the bedroom whiteboard, a simple card for listing expenditures, or an addition to the day planner, knowing the result of their purchases can become important to the satisfaction and future success of the *sensor*. If the child shows a preference for *intuition,* having the big picture of a monthly spending sheet can be invaluable. Helping the young person to see income on the same page or screen with monthly spending is critical. It can be the beginning of astute financial decisions and the avoidance of a lifetime of debt. Whatever the child's preference, the tool, format, or how it is accomplished can result in significant money management habits. Helping the children learn about income and spending, then giving them a tool that shows them what they're accomplishing with their money will become a foundation of lifetime financial success.

Although it wasn't as efficient as direct deposit, I chose to give my grandson cash for his savings account at the same time I gave him spending and giving money. He learned to complete the deposit tickets, go to the bank with me, make his own deposit, receive his monthly balance, and feel that the money is his. We call it his "security account." There has never been a discussion of any withdrawal as he has always understood that this is for his future, possibly for law school or graduate study abroad. Changes in banking requirements make such practices more challenging today, but whenever it's possible, children relate to the tangible aspects of cash.

When he was about 15, my grandson and I were looking on my phone at the stock price of certain tech shares. He looked at the history and made some insightful observations about how the price was increasing. Later, as I reflected on the conversation and how impressed I was with his interest in the stock market, I decided that this was a double opportunity. There was a chance to, perhaps, make a good investment, and also to engage the teen in investments in a real way. After discussing the issue with him, I made a small purchase. We always refer to the amount as "his stock" and it has been exciting to watch the value increase. Of course, there was another lesson with the inevitable market tumble, but it's an effective learning about long-term investments.

Some people prefer to give their grandchildren debit cards, and that seems to be a workable solution for many teens, but there is merit to teaching younger children with cash. It seems to have a more tangible, immediate feel. In today's world, there are numerous advantages to the use of credit cards, especially in the safety of touchless purchases, Yet, it can be helpful to refer to credit card purchases as "spending forward," a reference to buying today but paying in the future. Giving older grandchildren a debit card or a credit card with a spending limit may be satisfactory for some, but recalling James and Lori in Chapter 2, it can lead to abuses if we are not careful in enforcing the limits. When using a debit or credit card with teens, it's imperative that they keep a record of what has been spent in order to avoid problems and surprises. As stated earlier, we want to ensure their realistic view of debt and avoid their being oblivious as to what can happen with casual, unaware spending.

In addition to that time management question, "Is this the best use of my time?" perhaps we can also implant the question, "Is this the best use of my money?" The question that we really want to plant in their consciousness is, "Is this getting me what's good for me and what I want?"

Social Choices

In addition to decisions about how time and money are spent, another critical decision is how friends are chosen. Of course, we want to advocate our grandchildren's associating with people who are of similar character and who also make effective choices. We want them to be with people who use good language, good manners, and are respectful of others. In essence, what we seek for them is reflective of the "social comparison" issue that we discussed in Chapter 6. We believe that they will be most comfortable and thrive when in the company of those who are most like them and the culture that they reflect. But then, what about equality, diversity, and being exposed to people who are different, from different cultures, and who have different beliefs? How do we ensure that our little ones are safe, and yet, exposed to the world?

Although we certainly don't want them to learn social, religious, racial, or ethnic prejudices, we do want them to be discerning about the people with whom they surround themselves. As we've emphasized, one way to predict a kid's future may be to look at the people chosen for friends during the teen years.

Yes, it's admirable for the children to see the good in everyone, regardless of color, religion, education, or anything else. But, if there are no boundaries, and no constraints, we may be advocating exposure to questionable or even dangerous influences. Perhaps the ideal method of teaching how to choose friends is through character development and teaching the child how to *be* a friend. When children grow-up in an environment of honesty and integrity, they won't enjoy being with others who are deceitful. When they live in a world that values polite, respectful, social interactions, they will not be comfortable with crude, rude people. Yes, we teach them to see the good in all, regardless of origin, but we also teach them to value what is kind, moral, just, and true. We can also teach them how to quietly distance themselves from people whose moral or social values are not compatible with what we've taught them.

Much of this freedom from social prejudice comes from attitudes that we demonstrate. Much of their learning on this subject comes from watching us—with whom we associate, who we like, who our friends are, and comments that we make. If we are an example in our choice of friends, and the way we regard others, they are likely to absorb exemplary attitudes. If we're concerned about the influence of questionable friends, perhaps we can ask some diplomatic questions, such as:

> "Tell me about your friend _____."
>
> "Talk about what you two have in common."
>
> "What do you look for in friends?"
>
> "What makes spending time with this person enjoyable."
>
> "Does this person enjoy spending time with members of your family? In other words, does this person fit into your world?"

If we are diplomatic and successful, we will not put the grandchild on the defensive, but we may plant seeds of awareness about effective friendships.

Incidentally, if the child enjoys being around adults as much as being with other children, and if these adults are a good influence, then don't be surprised. Especially if the child is involved in honors or advanced classes in school, the child may regard the adults as safer, more predictable, and more interesting. It's typical to expect children to prefer their age mates, but children of the same chronological age may not actually be the child's intellectual peers. If this is the case, don't be deceived by the calendar. Look at reasons for the attraction and if it's beneficial. Before proclaiming, "Go play with the other kids," consider whether the child may prefer listening to or watching the adults."

Decisions about the friends they choose and the culture that is reflected can become pivotal points in the grandchildren's lives.

Decision Review

When we teach the child to "finish playing" with the toy by replacing it on the storage shelf, we're beginning to encourage the child to complete the loop that's important in many of the processes that will be central to the child's learning. After big or major decisions are made, and after its effects are known, it's useful to "finish" the decision with a review. This can be as simple as asking the child if the results were what was wanted. As the child matures, we can add a gentle consideration of "What could have been done differently to get more of what you wanted?" But it's essential to remember that our questions are about leading improvements, not about criticism. Although it's sometimes tempting to add, "Well, I tried to tell you . . ." such sarcasm is rarely helpful. Instead, we want to focus on the process of helping the child recognize the importance of constantly improving our decision making skills.

When older, it may be useful to introduce the grandchildren to a technique known in the military as the *After Action Review (AAR)* and adapted for use in business by the University of Pennsylvania and others. It's a very simple process that we'll call *Decision Review* by asking:

> "What did you want to happen?"
> What was supposed to have happened?"
>
> "What actually happened?"
>
> "What did you learn?"
> "What can be improved the next time?"

Verbally, or in writing, by simply analyzing the parts of the decision and the outcome—expected and unexpected, we teach consideration for improved decisions in the future.

All too often, children make effective decisions, but there's little or no acknowledgement. There may be insufficient feedback to sustain the positive decisions. At other times, young people make unfortunate choices and decisions based on their emotions of the moment. They suffer the consequences of the latter, are admonished or left to feel stupid, and miss the learning opportunity. By taking some of the emphasis off of the negative decisions, we can increase the learning and decrease the chances that the bad decisions will be repeated. The more we can heighten awareness of the consequences of ineffective decisions, the more likely we are to improve the child's decision making skills and move them out of the strictly emotional responses and into more logical thinking. At the same time, we can encourage positive feedback and celebrate the good decision.

Sometimes, parents and grandparents are tempted to review inappropriate decisions when angry or upset, especially if the decision has jeopardized the child's safety or adult stability. If either the child or adults are emotionally upset, any learning that could be gained from reviewing the decision is diminished. Indeed, if our intent is to improve the child's skills, it's imperative that we wait until everyone has regained composure.

Wise and effective decisions are about getting what we want in the most advantageous way possible that doesn't diminish others or jeopardize safety. By helping the child understand preferences and by guiding through simple choices, we lay the foundation of decision skills. By encouraging the child to consider positive, negative, and unintended consequences of the decisions, we increase the likelihood of both safety and satisfaction. By showing the child how to logically review important decisions, we stimulate the development of the brain's executive functioning and contribute to preparation of the child's life skills. Most important, every time we can increase the child's critical thinking skills, even in a very small way, we decrease the chances that the teen will get into the car of a drunk friend, surrender to sexual advances, or accept the taunts of buddies to try this drug "just once."

Analysis vs. Self-Doubt

One of the advantages of the simple, but systematic, review of important decisions is that it stimulates the critical thinking skills from an early age. It also sets a pattern that has another vital influence on the child's development. Through the process of that unemotional consideration in the Decision Review, the child becomes accustomed to simple analysis—the process of separating something into its component parts, to study or examine each. This unemotional assessing of the various issues allows the child to see the different pieces of the decision and to decide what was good or not-so-good, what worked or what didn't work, what went well or what went askew. The key to the Decision Review's effectiveness is that it's a very analytical and unemotional process.

There are some empowering life skills that we're teaching our precious ones through these simple processes. First, we're nurturing the *critical thinking* skills, the observing, reflecting, reasoning, conceptualizing, and synthesizing thoughts. In this very action oriented world, in which the approach is too often "fire, aim, ready," there may be inadequate time and quiet space for thinking. Just as we teach the young ones how to kick a ball and how to read a book, we can also teach them how to think. We can begin by emphasizing the importance of finding quiet places and making calm moments in which to concentrate. We can show them how to observe, develop their observations, and record their ideas. Of course, teaching thinking skills isn't accomplished overnight, but rather, across more than a decade as the prefrontal cortex and logical thinking part of the brain develop.

While we're teaching them thinking skills, we also show them how to react to their decisions, through *analysis* and review, rather than self-doubt. The review creates a sense of action through the conclusion of "This was a good decision!" or "Now, I know what I can do to get a better outcome." This sense of action in response to dissatisfaction with results can play a major role in combating self-doubt or contributing to the victim mindset that we'll see in the next chapter. Self-talk will not be, "That was stupid.

I'm a failure!" or "I wanted him to like me, and I let it go too far." Instead, the self-talk will be, "Wow, I didn't consider that! Next time, I'll know what to do."

When analyzing interpersonal problems or situations, it's very useful to help the child focus on the root cause. When there are conflicts between the grandchild and another person, a good question to pose is,

"Who owns this problem?"

First, this approach allows the grandchild to see who first caused the situation. If the child begins to realize that he/she caused the difficulty, then it becomes easier for the young one to take responsibility. The grandchild can then be guided to apologize or find a solution for the interpersonal conflict. In situations where the child realizes that another person caused the difficulty, the grandparent can coach some problem solving on how to confront and fix the situation, or just move-on and ignore the incident. Once problem ownership has been agreed on, it's important that the child neither shirk responsibility nor unnecessarily choose a passive role. In either outcome, the grandparent may give cues, role play, or help the child determine the best way to deal with such problems in the future. Regardless, that question about "problem ownership" is essential to helping the child gain responsibility and reality in interpersonal conflicts. It is an important means of being accountable for actions and taking steps toward resolution. It is also a mark of emotional development to be able to recognize when we own the problem and when we do not.

Without consideration of problem ownership, and without the action of an analytical review, the misery of a bad situation might lead to self-doubt. Without this careful consideration that produces facts and information, the young person is left with a vagueness and malaise that can quickly turn into uncertainty and apprehension. Whereas, an analysis that delineates the dissatisfaction with decision results can lead to improving future decisions. It's essential to take action and avoid questioning self-efficacy, or leaving feelings of guilt and worthlessness of the *person,* rather than dissatisfaction with *results.*

Self-doubt is a tendency that can haunt and stress an otherwise stable person. It produces a hesitation and vacillation that leads to an erosion of self-confidence. It creates a cancer of uncertainty to impede performance in school, in employment, in social interactions, and in many areas of life. Self-doubt is a disease from which we can and must spare our grandchildren. Analysis is the antidote.

An area in which today's children may develop self-doubt is sexuality. People who are born as homosexuals may become aware of their sexuality at an early age. Whether or not we are comfortable with a child's homosexuality is irrelevant. We must remember Rule #1 and focus on the child. Our love cannot diminish because the child chooses to be, act, and dress differently from our expectations. A loving grandparent is a necessity for any child who appears different to his/her peers. One contribution of the twenty-first century has been the social acceptance of people, regardless of their physical appearance or hormones.

The emphasis in the media and popular culture on homosexuality, however, may cause an unintended issue for some insecure teens. Since children often spend more time with others of the same sex, they may develop a sense of identity and comfort with same sex friends. When this occurs during adolescence, the teens may find it especially comfortable to associate with others of the same gender because it feels familiar and with less chance of rejection. This comfort, and today's emphasis on acceptance of homosexuality, may result in the teens' incorrectly assuming that they are homosexuals. Such gender confusion is only one of the many reasons that teens need a safe place to talk about their fears and concerns. Although grandparents may not be the first choice of a place for teens to discuss sex, we must always be open, listening, and help them to clarify their feelings. If we have concerns about a grandchild's gender confusion, and the child isn't comfortable discussing it with us, we may be able to prompt another trusted adult or find a professional to help the youngster sort through the confusing and often complex feelings. We can help them to stay safe and avoid a life altering context.

This is but another area that needs analysis, rather than allowing self-doubt to lead to an incorrect decision. Even though we may not be comfortable with the subject of homosexuality or gender confusion, this may be an additional time when the gentle, non-judging listening of a grandparent is essential.

Summary

Helping children learn to "tell time" when they're young builds their confidence as they become very proud of their knowledge and skill. An ancillary benefit is that we can use their growing awareness of time to prepare them for moving from one activity to another. As the child matures, we can guide their value of time and money, help them to invest these precious commodities wisely, developing priorities, and managing their resources.

Although we call it problem solving, risk analysis, decision making, and decision review, what we're actually doing is facilitating *thinking skills* in the young brains. As we listen, ask questions, and help the grandchildren work through problems, we're really teaching them how to think.

Despite the enormous advantage that technology is giving our grandchildren, too much time on social media and other screen pursuits may not stimulate critical thinking skills. Yet, quiet, solitude, and thought time are essential for introverts. While quiet thinking time may not be energizing to the extraverts, it's part of becoming skilled. Until they learn the value of quiet thinking time, however, extraverts may prefer to "talk out" their thoughts.

That's another opportunity for us to listen, gain insight, and help their development of critical thinking skills. One of our greatest influences and best gifts to the grandchildren may be in teaching them how to think.

As the child grows and develops these critical thinking skills, more decisions may be made with logical, rational thoughts, enabling the child to rely less on only emotions for decision making. As we saw in Chapter 7, effective decisions are made by using *both* critical thinking and emotional feelings, regardless of which is considered first.

As with much of what we've discussed, if we want our grandchildren to make effective decisions, good choices, and be focused on what's really important in using their time and money wisely, the development of those skills must begin when they are very young. Even though their brains won't be fully developed until their early to mid-twenties, by practicing decision making on simple things and in safe places, they become aware of their preferences and of the advantages in careful decision making.

Whether deciding on a toy, buying a car, choosing a friend, or opting not to participate in harmful activities, we want our grandchildren to make decisions that will benefit them and reflect their good character. Our careful influence can help them develop the skills to achieve powerful outcomes. By teaching them how to anticipate possible risks and review their decisions, we give them the skills of analysis that will immunize them against self-doubt and enable them to have confidence in their decisions. We want them to know when to have the courage to persevere, and when to stop and take a different approach. We want them to realize that when they make a mistake or when something isn't working—like *Grandpa Bear*—they can stop, back-up, and get on the right road.

A crucial mile-post along the road to young people's maturity is learning to make logical, safe, and effective decisions that manage or minimize risks. Grandparents can serve as an awesome guide on this journey.

Chapter 10

Fears and Feelings

Help us to set unnecessary fears aside and recognize our potential for a creative response.

The Source of Grandchildren's Fears

Fear is an anxiety caused by the anticipation of some threat of harm. In our prayer, we've implied two kinds of fear. Some are protective inherent fears related to physical safety, such as the fear of falling. Others are acquired—emotional, and often rooted in a fear of failure. To avoid being overly afraid with paralyzing and unproductive apprehension, we can develop the skills to analyze the cause of this anxiety and learn problem solving to reduce or even eliminate the basis of what may be an unnecessary fear.

Whatever the source of the fear, when very young and vulnerable, the action to overcome being afraid that the child most quickly seeks is a trusted adult. There's nothing so comforting and secure as a parent or grandparent's protective presence or embrace, especially when something scary is looming. For a two or three-year-old, being enveloped in a grandparent's arms can diminish all fears, real and imagined. For the twenty-year-old, more than a hug may be required. The requirements of geography or social distance may necessitate some listening, problem solving, and sharing of experiences that assure our credibility to calm the fear. The results are the same for both, the grandchild knows that we care and understand. Even if we can't fully comprehend the cause of the fear, we can communicate that we're supportive, we understand their concerns, and we're here for them—we care.

Grandparents can be a tremendous antidote to young people's fears. When it isn't possible or appropriate to offer a reassuring hug, we can help them associate words with their feelings. This is a first step in identifying the cause of the fears. Children who've been diagnosed as having certain developmental disorders may not like being hugged or touched and may have difficulty associating language with their emotions. To be effective with these children, grandparents will require specific training to help those with special needs to deal with fears, overcome anxieties, and cope with social interactions. Even though different techniques are required, the accomplishments make the efforts worthwhile.

Cause of Fears

For young children, a most common cause of fear is the unknown, something that they can't see or understand. In my family, we now laugh about one of my daughter's early fears. Just after she had learned to walk, we were enjoying my parents' screened-in porch when Granny brought out a large, brightly colored beach ball that was almost as tall as the small child. Just as Granny set the ball a few feet from the toddler, a slight breeze caused the ball to roll slowly toward her, changing delight at seeing the colorful toy into screams and tears. After we removed the ball, and with considerable comforting, the child finally stopped crying; but the ball had produced real fear because she couldn't understand its sudden, seemingly threatening movement. For a couple of weeks after that incident, the child would point to anything spherical in shape—even a tomato—loudly proclaim "ball," and become very fearful. At the time, it was hard for the adults not to laugh, but that would not have assuaged her fears. The toddler's reaction was typical of what can happen when children are confronted with the unknown. By slowly helping her to be near the sphere, touch the object, and talk about its use for play, the ball soon became a favorite toy.

The imagined monster in the closet, under the bed, or below the stairs can cause fears. A dark, foreboding space makes the unknown into an imagined creature. Calm reassurances and casting light on the unrevealed space, can make the monster disappear. There may be other places in the grandparents' house that are fear producing, especially if the child doesn't visit often. Shining a light into the closet or under the bed can reduce a young child's anxiety. Taking action to reduce the unknown is the best remedy for such fears.

The twenty-first century has brought new fears for children. Terrorism, pandemic, school and church shootings have added to fears of weather related tragedies. While it's easy for us to shine a light into the closet to make the monster disappear, it's difficult to explain other things that we can't see. For example, how can something called Covid that's so small we can't see it require that we stay away from other people and sometimes wear a mask?

Encouraging the children to talk about their fears is the best initial response that we can give them. As we listen, it's important not to try to give too much additional information or to explain how awful things happen because there often is no logic. The best we can do is listen, ask questions about what they need to feel safe, and give assurance for our intentions to do everything possible to keep them secure. During a pandemic or in the aftermath of a national tragedy when there is much news coverage, it's important to be aware of the child's suppressing fears and having no way to express being afraid.

To be fearful is to be human. It's another inborn trait that has kept us from being eaten by a tiger or trampled by a wooly mammoth. Although we no longer need to be afraid of the wooly mammoth, fear can be used to our advantage when it's turned into caution that prompts us to analyze a situation, assess the risks, and determine the best action to avoid hazards. Whether for the young child or the young adult, diminishing the fear comes from gently making the unknown known, analyzing, and recognizing what we need to avoid and what can be overcome. A calm, loving grandparent's reassurances can ease the process.

Coping With Fear

Fears cause an internal anxiety, but they don't always remain internal. The anxiety may be externalized through crying, sadness, irritability, or other behavioral issues because children may not always know what to do with the fear. Perhaps the first coping mechanism that we humans have for dealing with fear is that of language. When we can put words onto the fears, when we can verbalize causes of the anxiety, we have begun to manage the fears.

Because grandparents can be such awesome sources of support and encouragement, we can help grandchildren overcome their fears. Perhaps, by sharing stories of our own childhood and adult apprehensions, we can equip them with tools for coping with their fears. As we give them the tools to cope with being afraid, by teaching them to attach words to their fears when they're very young, we help them identify and analyze what's making them anxious. As they grow, by identifying the fear, we help them to see how they can take actions to diminish the risks and need to be afraid.

An asset for coping with fear is in doing something about it—taking action. When it comes to acquired fears, it's easy to focus on the anxiety but be in denial or oblivious as to the exact cause. An example would be an older child who is fearful of not having friends or playmates. That's when it helps to have a trusted adult to help identify a fear of abandonment or rejection. With a grandparent to guide through the process, the child can be reminded that sometimes, when we're very focused on people, and especially if we have a preference for *feeling,* as described in Chapter 7, it's as if we're "allergic" to rejection. By understanding something about the feeling, the child can gain better control of it. Initial understanding of a bit of the root of the fear is helpful. Then, the child can be guided to think about why having friends is important, what can be done to find and maintain friendships, and what to do in situations where there are no friends available. Through this process, we talk about the importance of *being* a good friend and how to gain friends. We can enhance the understanding and change an undefined fear into action.

If the 23-year-old confides that he's fearful of not being successful at the new job because it requires making presentations to groups of colleagues, we can be the caring grandparent who comes quickly to the rescue. Since many people consider fear of public speaking their number one fear, it may not be surprising to hear this from the young man. Of course, we can reassure him and tell him that he'll do well, but perhaps a better course is to also sit with him at the kitchen table, ask a few open-ended questions, and listen intently to his concerns. As we help him to isolate the source of the fear, we discover that it isn't his fear of talking in public, and he's comfortable with these people, but he confides that he's concerned about failing in the new job. He doesn't want to make a presentation because he's apprehensive that he doesn't know the subject sufficiently and that his audience will soon see his lack of competence. We reassure him and brainstorm some ways that he can increase his knowledge and skills. The product of our attentive listening and asking occasional open-ended questions is that he figures out the real root of his fear. He explores how he can learn more about the subject, and gain the content to be comfortable. Then, we discuss where he can get help and practice for presentation skills. The best part of this approach is that we didn't give the young man a solution. Rather, we facilitated his finding his own solution. In the atmosphere of our interest and concern, he was able to see past his fears and solve his problem.

If we are to nurture and encourage grandchildren's learning, then we must recognize their fears and be ready to help them take action to diminish them. Excessive fears, real or imagined, interfere with the learning, but most of all, anxiety diminishes confidence and the sense of self so necessary for coping with school, career, positive social interactions, and everyday life.

Fear of Failure

Counselors who work with juvenile delinquents often report that these adolescents have an underlying fear of failure, along with a denial about the fear or its results. If the teens experience adversity and an accompanying sense of failure in some area, the fear can take over life—at home, at school, and in all forms of endeavor. In such unfortunate circumstances, a caring adult can help the juvenile define the problem, search for solutions, and enable the young person to see how to move beyond the overwhelming sense of failure through goal setting and actions. Diminishing this fear of failure is essential to a healthy self-confidence so necessary to navigating the teen years.

Freudian psychologists infer that our present problems can be rooted in the past in our unresolved fears (Thompson, 2007). I remember a graduate class experience to illustrate that point. Probably because the professor was fascinated by Eric Berne's research into the connection between children's literature and adult attitudes, the class was given the assignment of writing a story about fears. Candidly, the professor probably anticipated a story for children about how to cope with fears, but since he just said, "a story about fears," I decided to connect the childhood/adult fear idea and wrote about a little boy named Lance Ford. Recalling my own childhood certainty that a large monster lived behind the basement furnace, I chronicled how every morning, this big scary monster would climb the basement stairs and jump out to join Lance as the young boy left for school. All day, the monster, whose name was *Mr. Failure,* would hover over Lance, even though no one else was aware of the monster's presence. Whether Lance was attempting to solve problems on a math test, or trying to catch a ball on the playground, *Mr. Failure* was there to distract, laugh, and cast doubt about Lance's pathetic attempts as he worried about failing second grade. Unfortunately, *Mr. Failure* didn't disappear as Lance grew. Instead, he followed Lance through each grade. When he went to high school, Lance was afraid that he would fail biology and that his inadequacy would be confirmed in his performance as a part-time waiter at the local fast food cafe. *Mr. Failure* convinced Lance that he might lose his job.

Lance's fear of failure was complicated when *Mr. Failure* was joined in his ever present vigilance by partner, *Ms. Rejection*. Then, poor Lance not only had to worry about failing at everything, he also had to worry that he would be rejected. As a child, he was fearful, as many children are, of abandonment. Unfortunately, he didn't develop adequate security in childhood and that fear of abandonment grew into a fear of being rejected, of not having friends or anyone to care about him. As a teen, Lance was so afraid that he would be rejected by his girlfriends that he broke up with them before they might possibly reject him. As an adult, his relationships became flawed. He was miserable in his career, and life was just not good. All was changed, however, when Lance's fairy godmother flew in with her magic mirror. As Lance saw who he really was, and through the fairy godmother's magic wand, was convinced of his considerable capabilities, *Mr. Failure* and *Ms. Rejection* disappeared—"and Lance Ford lived happily ever after!"

As in the story, childhood fears can become patterns that haunt us into adulthood. Fortunately, the professor was sufficiently amused by my approach and the name that I gave the young boy, that he didn't penalize me for deviating from his standard assignment. And of course, I had to endure his questions as to how Freudian it was that Lance Ford was plagued by fears of failure and rejection. That's when I had to confess that, having a *feeling* preference, I could relate to the kid's fear of rejection.

Although I hadn't thought about my creative class assignment in years, I remembered it as an opportunity for us grandparents. As I thought about Lance, I wondered about the "fear monsters" that loom over our grandchildren. What are their fears? If the ten-year-old is afraid that tobacco use will cause him to develop lung cancer like Uncle Ed, or that the long-term effects of vaping and marijuana are still unknown, then these may be useful cautions. Fears that are of real hazards protect us from harm. Whereas, being needlessly afraid can become a barrier to effective living.

If, like Lance, the grandchildren are carrying fears of failure and rejection, then that's an opportunity for us grandparents. We can facilitate their exploring the fear and taking action to diminish it. We can borrow the fairy godmother's magic mirror to show them who they are and all they can do. We can talk about our own fear of failure—how it kept us from opportunities and how we overcame the fear and went on to succeed. The key to making our stories effective, however, is in the timing. We can't wait until the grandson has failed to be elected class president or the granddaughter hasn't been offered an invitation to join a college sorority. It's much more effective when the grandchildren hear the stories and how we responded when they're younger. They need to hear our tales long before they encounter significant failure. Dr. Maria Montessori (1914) maintained that children should not experience failure until they have first tasted success.

Perhaps children benefit, not from failing, but from learning what doesn't work. The real value lies, not in experiencing failure, but in analyzing how the loss occurred, and developing a plan to succeed. We can talk about how we nearly failed second year German in college, but that it was a wake-up call for needing new study skills. We can share how upset we were about being rejected for cheerleading team and how we even talked about wanting to change schools. Then, we smile and confess what a misunderstanding we had, because we thought it was such a big deal—but it wasn't. We can talk about learning that not every endeavor can be a success. We can help the children see that it's not really failure, but perhaps, an indication to go in a different direction.

When we talk about the strong sense of failure and rejection that we felt at not being elected band captain or not making the team, we also share with the grandchildren our misperception in the sense of shame that we felt at being such a "total failure." It seems that some early mishaps become inflated in importance to us because they're the first big endeavors that we attempted. It's unfortunate when these early mishaps continue to haunt us —like a famous scientist whose achievements in electronics were industry changing. Yet, when colleagues tried to praise his accomplishments, he would reflect on the math he had goofed that kept him from being admitted to Massachusetts Institute of Technology (MIT). Perhaps his psyche would have benefitted from the pompous Thomas Edison's approach. It's said that when a reporter asked him how many failures preceded his invention of the workable electric light bulb, Edison replied, "Sir, I never failed! I just discovered 267 elements that did not improve the light bulb." Because I like the story so much, in my several sessions of work with the archivist and historians at the Thomas Edison National Historic Site in New Jersey, I tried to authenticate the anecdote. Unfortunately, I was told that it's apocryphal. Nonetheless, it's an attitude toward failure that we want our grandchildren to know.

We learn from watching the grit of successful people who continue trying, regardless of the amount of effort needed or the likelihood of success. The late Warren Bennis (2009), in his research on leadership, indicated that successful leaders talked about their mistakes, glitches, and projects that didn't work, but they never saw themselves as failures. From many writers and observations of success, I'm convinced that failure is when we don't learn and continue to repeat the same mistake or just quit trying. I believe that *real failure—is the failure to learn.* Instead, we can learn from our mistakes and goofs, as we help our grandchildren find the road to success.

When children are experiencing a sense of anxiety and failure, they need our listening, understanding, and support. Long before they're engulfed in a sense of failure, they need our stories that inform them. We can talk of how we over-rated the importance of a situation and how the sense of embarrassment and misery were unnecessary. Grandchildren need to hear that what we thought were disasters were only "warts on an elephant." They need to know how we were not defined by our mistakes but learned from our blunders and misadventures. We can talk about how we might have been hurt or upset at the time, but we came to realize that we could recover and move-on. Our admissions can help them learn how to avoid being paralyzed by the fear of failure as they will have the benefit of our learning and coping tools to help them move ahead. Long before they need it, they can learn that "what I did, didn't work, but I am not a failure because I'm learning and moving ahead." Perhaps the key is to help them focus on how to analyze what went wrong and how to fix the mistake with a very logical thought process, thereby diminishing the emotional feelings about it as a failure.

When They Struggle

We love these grandchildren so much and try to protect them from all harm, danger, suffering, and tribulation. We may have a desire to protect them from ever seeing any struggles, yet that would be a huge mistake. We must know when to act quickly to rescue the drowning child, as opposed to the child who is just learning to swim. As we teach swimming skills to prevent children from drowning, we must also teach them how to handle struggles, how they can use their ideas and perseverance to rebound from mistakes. Viktor Frankl (1997) delineated how humans seem to learn most effectively when struggling, but that when we understand the problem and can develop a picture of the situation, we can begin to gain control over the struggle. We grandparents must overcome our own need to rescue the young ones from every struggle, for when we do so, we deprive them of the chance to learn, to persevere, and to make their own successes. Instead, we must coach, guide, and help them analyze and evaluate the problem. Our job is not to fix, our job is to help them find their own best solutions.

I think of the numerous young people from very educated, affluent families with whom I've worked. I think about how a few languish in underperformance and low self-esteem, often going from job-to-job in employment and life circumstances that didn't challenge their potential. They've been given every opportunity, but because they've encountered no barriers, and have been rescued from every school failure and every youthful debacle, they never learned to persevere. They didn't learn how to keep going when the going got tough. Although we should avoid exposing children to stress, helping them determine how to push through difficulty can enhance the learning.

We ask how can struggling be so damaging to the childhoods of the poor, and yet some struggling, and learning to persevere can contribute to success? Perhaps it isn't the struggling, but the *stress* that is the root of the problem for the less fortunate. If there isn't someone there to support and encourage the young person through the struggling, the situation can become stressful. Perhaps it isn't deprivation of being poor that is the determining factor, but whether or not the child's life is stressful. With almost half of recent births paid by Medicaid in many areas, that's an indication that of children born into poverty. Just being poor, although limiting, may not be the determining influence. Rather, it's the circumstances of the home life, the absence of routines, consistency, and emotional security that may cause the stress.

When children are born to mothers who are addicted, the normal brain development was effected in utero. The addiction may make the mother incapable of the needed bonding and nurturing for normal growth during the first two years. Then, when the children of these addicted parents reach the public school classroom, they often struggle with focusing attention, retaining information, impulsive behavior issues, needs for food, and other basics. We wonder about the effects of this stress on these children who will sit next to our grandchildren in public schools. We're concerned about the influence these stressed children will have on our young ones who've enjoyed a relatively stress free life. We have concerns about how these misfortunate children will become part of the fabric of our grandchildren's society when they live in the upheaval of a revolving door of family members, constant bickering, and even violence.

We know the threats of such toxic stress to normal development. In poverty, and if under constant emotional stress, children may not thrive or be able to see hope of success or vision for the future. Yet, in the accounts of children of adversity, there are many stories of success. Often through teaching the students to dance, play chess, through tutoring, or other activities and programs, their lives are changed through learning thinking skills and to persevere. Simply by having time in their weeks when they can be calm, focused, and in the presence of a caring adult, the stress can be diminished.

Even though affluent youths may have little worry for their economic welfare, the emotional stress of a tense home life can also impede growth. Perhaps the lesson is to prevent stress, regardless of economics. Then, we support and encourage the children through the struggles to be sure they learn to persevere. The results of childhood struggles that teach perseverance and the struggles of adversity that cause stress and fear are grossly different.

Grandparents' Worst Fear: Addiction

If we listed all of our fears for and about our grandchildren, this little book would be too heavy to carry. We're concerned about everything that will hinder our most important aspirations for them. First, we want them to be safe. Second, we want them to be happy and effective people. We worry about anything that will get in the way of their safety and happiness.

Except for a tragic accident or illness, and the loss of a beloved grandchild, the most ghastly thing we can imagine is losing a grandchild to addiction. Today, perhaps the greatest threat to our grandchildren, to both their safety and the future happiness of these leaders and citizens of tomorrow, is *addiction*. It's the short-term reward that results in an insatiable craving with long-term consequences. We worry about how we can deliver them from becoming addicted to drugs, alcohol, gambling, pornography, sex, and the ensuing depression. We wonder what we as grandparents can do to ensure that our beloved young ones don't ruin their lives by getting into these traps. How can we armor them to combat the many opportunities they'll have to associate with the wrong people who will introduce them to addictive substances, who'll taunt them into trying that first hit of that first vape or cigarette? How do we keep them away from that first exhilarating high of cocaine and from experiencing the depths of addiction? How can we keep them from the images of pornography, when it is so available on the internet? How can we prevent their ruining their lives—and bankrupting us and their parents with the high cost of one treatment center after another? Yes, that's an enormous fear for us grandparents.

Even the most clueless teenager is unlikely to approach that first misadventure with some drug or alcohol and think, “Okay, today I’ve decided to become an addict.” Rather, it’s highly likely that they aren’t thinking at all. There is no consideration of the consequences. Instead, their action probably originates from a fear of failure. They fear being inadequate, so they look for something to make themselves feel better. They fear being rejected, so they go along, trying to be one of the group. Unresolved fears can blind the teen to consequences.

Of course, we all have addictions, but some are just more harmful than others. What are yours? I’ve never used tobacco, and I dislike the taste of alcohol of any kind, but I readily admit that I’m addicted to CocaCola. It’s said that if you think about never having another ___ bothers you, then you’re addicted! Well, I’ve given up eating red meat and it is no loss, but ask me about never having another CocaCola and I immediately recognize my dependence on, not just any sugary fizzy water, but CocaCola. Even though it isn’t a life threatening or bankrupting dependence, I realize that *I’m hooked!* Then, if I think about the possibility of my grandson’s having a craving for gambling, alcohol, vaping, marijuana, illegal drugs, or other harmful substances, and I’m instantly sick! In our lifetimes, we’ve seen the deadly ravages of nicotine, that according to required advertising by the tobacco industry, kills more people daily than murder, AIDS, suicide, drugs, car crashes, and alcohol, combined (U.S.Dept. of Justice, 2017). It seems incredible that almost a century was required, from the time of the first cigarettes, for the beginning of public acceptance that cigarettes are harmful. What are the unhealthy detrimental addictions to which we’re exposing the Instant Generation that will exact a tremendous physical, social, and financial toll to jeopardize their futures? What can we as grandparents do to prevent losing our precious ones to these addictions? I believe that the solution is in the seeds we plant, the messages we send, and the example we set many years before the children’s first exposure to harmful substances.

The origin of the word *addiction* is derived from the latin for "enslaved" or "bound to." Addiction becomes the center of life from which other priorities are excluded. Addiction exploits a long and powerful hold on the brain characterized by a craving, loss of control, and being engaged in it, regardless of negative consequences. The *American Society of Addiction Medicine* (2011) definition of addiction sends shivers all over a loving grandparent and makes us commit to whatever is necessary to prevent even an initial encounter with anything that can have such a long-term detrimental effect on our loved ones futures.

As I write these words, I'm reminded of an exchange with a diabetic 80-year-old. When other people were having a glass of wine at a dinner, I asked if he had missed having wine since his diagnosis as diabetic. He laughed and said, "Not at all, but I'll tell you what I really miss, almost on a daily basis. Sometimes, when I finish a meal or get into the car, I really, really want a cigarette. I started smoking when I was 17, and even though I quit more than forty years ago, I still miss it." If a nicotine craving can last more than four decades, it's easy to see why addictive substances pose such a threat.

The most harmful addictions from which we want to deliver our grandchildren have common features. First, there is a sense of initial pleasure associated with the substance and second, there's a craving characterized by the inability to stop. Third, withdrawing from use of the substance is very difficult, unpleasant, or creates pain. But we ask, how can some people drink alcohol occasionally and never become addicted? Somehow, in their brains, the alcohol didn't create a craving for constant repetition. It's what my friend experienced. He didn't miss the wine when he could no longer drink alcohol, but that was definitely not the same for his many years of missing cigarettes.

Addiction changes the brain, first by subverting the way it registers pleasure and then by corrupting other normal drives such as learning and motivation. Addiction takes over the rational mind. There is some thought that, whether or not we succumb to addiction may have a genetic predisposition. With tobacco and vaping, there is the possibility that the earlier the exposure, the more likely the addiction will take hold. Regardless of either, whether these substances are a choice or cause a disease, the risk is too great to expose our grandchildren.

We're in the early stages of learning about the medical uses of marijuana (cannibas) and the effects of its long-term use for recreation. Whether we live in a state where it's legal, or not, the research is too incomplete for me to be comfortable with my grandson's use. Further, it has been observed that few people who've become addicted to cocaine, heroin, methamphetamine, or other such powerful drugs have never used marijuana. Whether or not it is a gateway drug, whether or not it has valuable medicinal uses, or whether it is an alternative for opioids, I cannot say. But let's return to our decision making model, where we teach the child that the goal is a healthy, happy life. If we consider the risk of marijuana or any other drug, we readily see that the risk is too great.

Teens may be too young to realize that there are diseases for which there is a cure and some for which there is no cure. The scarlet fever that killed many children in the early twentieth century is now curable and controlled with antibiotics. There are treatments for malaria and hookworm that cure the condition.

Unfortunately, there are diseases for which there currently is no cure, such as Parkinson's or Alzheimer's that cause a steady decline, some more rapidly than others. Addiction is such a disease for which there is no cure. There are some interventions such as the Alcoholics Anonymous 12-Step Program or opioid addiction's substitution of buprenorphine that improve the condition, but *there is no cure for addiction*. Teens may not realize that there is not even an effective treatment for methamphetamine addiction. When young, and focused only on the present moment, they fail to recognize that starting—the first nicotine, the first meth, heroin, or cocaine is the beginning of a lifetime of disease. They don't realize that addiction can control every phase of the rest of their lives—health, finances, career, relationships—and especially family. They are probably in denial about the reality of addiction.

Brain Chemicals

Recent advances in neuroscience help us understand more of how the brain works and why the introduction of certain substances hijacks normal, rational thinking. We now know more about how addiction changes the brain by sabotaging the way it manifests pleasure, then degrades learning and motivation. If the attraction for alcohol and drugs is the "feel-good" effect that they may produce when first ingested, then let's show our beloved grandchildren how to make their own "feel-goods," and how to be always in control of their own brains. Let's help them learn to produce their own "feel-good" brain chemicals.

For too long, we've attempted to stop teens from the excessive use of alcohol by control, by keeping it away from kids—and yet, they see it everywhere, in restaurants, in the grocery stores, and perhaps at home. We tell them it's for adults, but wait, isn't that just increasing its allure as children often crave adult privileges—driving, cosmetics, or independence? We've tried to stop the use of drugs by control through preventing their manufacture or importation into the country. Obviously, that isn't working. As we've seen many trends emanate from the West Coast, then blow eastward with the wind, we may soon see marijuana shops in every community. We often hear the phrase, "This ain't your papa's pot," but whether legal marijuana is stronger or weaker than when it became a mainstream aid to recreation, can we risk our grandchildren? Since it's becoming such a tax revenue producing industry, like tobacco, it may become a mainstay in our neighborhoods, but can we risk the long term possibility of harm and marijuana toxicity to our precious grandchildren?

We're horrified by the numbers of people in the West Virginia coal mining towns who line up to get prescriptions of opiods and other narcotics, but we may overlook the desolate, depressing, jobless world in which many of these people live. We're quick to advocate "shutting down the pill mills" that dispense endless opioids to them, but then what? What are we doing to diminish the need for people to find refuge in harmful substances? If they lack the skills to change their circumstances, of course, they want to get their "feel-goods" from a bottle. We must enable our dear young ones to escape such a hellish trap by giving them knowledge, skills, and the resolve to be in control of their own brains without any substance dependence.

In Chapter 1, we discussed the importance of sharing our culture and family history with the grandchildren. One way to plant the "avoiding addiction seeds," may be to talk about any family members who have suffered from substance abuse. Although the connection is uncertain, there is some indication of a genetic predisposition to "the addictive personality." When the child is old enough, it may be appropriate to share the stories of Grandad or Cousin Mary's alcoholism or drug addiction. We can talk with kindness but candor about how the addiction limited the person's life and the disastrous effect it had on the family.

In the past, the shame connected with this disease discouraged family members from talking about it. Today, we understand more about addiction and know the importance of young people's knowledge that, if their ancestors had addiction issues, it is an added preponderance for their being alert to avoiding the first encounter with addictive substances. We can make them aware that they could be gambling with their precious lives. It's hard to impress teens without depressing them because they often have such a strong sense of invulnerability and little ability to see into the future. Maybe that's why they need us grandparents so much! We can keep them alert about where they get their "feel-goods" and what they can do when insecure, upset, or disappointed. It may prevent their falling into the trap of addiction.

Obviously, with the abundant availability of harmful substances, and the growing social encouragement to partake, what can a grandparent possibly do to discourage the trend? One grandparent may not be able to change the culture, but you and I can decrease the negative temptations by teaching our grandchildren, from a very early age, about how their bodies work, about healthful living, and how to make their own "feel-good" brain chemicals. It may even help to understand the *oxytocin, dopamine, serotonin, endorphin*—producers of our feelings of happiness. Then, when grandchildren are older, they won't need to seek their "feel-goods" from harmful sources.

We grandparents don't need expertise in neuroscience or to understand the function of neurotransmitters. There is some information, however, that can be helpful. To examine a few ways that grandparents can stimulate positive emotions, help children to be in control of their own cognitive functions, and avoid the temptations of addiction, let's explore just four that are sometimes called the "happiness chemicals."

Oxytocin

Earlier, we discussed the awesome feeling that flows through us when we first feel that little one hug us. What makes that hug so memorable is the oxytocin, sometimes referred to as the "love hormone." And because it's an emotional experience, that hug becomes a more important memory. Oxytocin is the brain chemical produced when we're bonded to another—the emotion we feel from strong positive relationships. Television journalist, Leslie Stahl, gave an intriguing description of the oxytocin effect on grandparents in her *Becoming Grandma, The Joy and Science of the New Grandparenting* (2016). Recent research into what happens to hormones in older males contributes to the understanding of why some men are more involved with their grandchildren than they were with their children.

When we cuddled that little baby, the result was that the grandchild triggered the release of the good-feeling brain chemicals in us. While the four-year-old is snuggled beside us in the swing as we're reading *Bears on Wheels,* the child is probably also experiencing the release of oxytocin. When we sing the cute little verses in *Bread and Jam for Francis,* we delight and stimulate their playful feelings. We say, "I love you," we cuddle them in the rocking chair when they're young, and help the little ones enjoy those good feelings. They experience a release of the good feelings not only from our relationships with them, but also as we teach them how to relate to other children, how to be a friend, and how to continue to enjoy the feelings that oxytocin produces. As we build the good feelings of our relationship, we build the bond of trust between us. The ability to trust is believed to be modulated by oxytocin.

When children are older, they may not want to sit on our laps, and maybe our arthritic knees don't want that either, but they still need the oxytocin, making it necessary for us to change our approaches. In older children, we generate the good brain chemicals with attentiveness, eye contact, and giving importance to their conversations. We demonstrate interest and coach their problem solving skills. That's why we put so much emphasis on active listening and the communication skills that convey the older children's importance. Being significant to other people, being bonded to key adults, and being shown that someone cares, can produce positive emotions. At the same time, oxytocin may modulate feelings of fear and anxiety. Strong family bonds are not only good for the family structure, such warm bonds produce good feelings for each family member, especially the grandchildren.

Dopamine

Helping children produce their own "feel-goods" is really easy if we think about it, but it's best not left until the teen years. Adolescence is a time when there's an increase in the activity of the neural circuits using dopamine, causing teens to seek thrills with no regard for risks or negative consequences. This attraction of wanting more and more, is likely because of the probable release of dopamine.

This business of brain chemicals is not a secret. The developers of video games keep our grandchildren engaged by triggering dopamine through creating anticipation in their games. It seems that technology organizations have learned the basic principle of the tobacco industry—addiction is good for business. With so many sources competing with us for teens' time and brain chemicals, it's easy to see that we grandparents must be vigilant and persevering in protecting and focusing teens on better pursuits.

A major neurotransmitter, dopamine helps to control the brain's reward and pleasure centers, and perhaps, that is its function as a contributor to addiction. It's that magnetic pull toward pleasure that initiates the addiction. Worse, inhaling or injecting a drug intravenously, as opposed to swallowing a pill, often produces a faster, stronger dopamine signal and increases the likelihood of addiction. It diminishes the sense of pain and increases the insatiable need for more of the substance to obtain that sense of pleasure—an ongoing need.

Dopamine is also related to vital circuits inside the brain that involve pain, memory, learning, and motivation. The term, motivation, stems from the latin, *moveré,* meaning "to move." The child's motivation is critical to performance in school, sports, and other activities. Especially during the teenage years, a lack of motivation can sometimes be perplexing to us as we attempt to get the teen “to move.” That’s why, to ensure a constant supply of dopamine, we encourage and reward their achievements. And I thought it didn’t matter whether I attended his ball games or when I just wanted to sit by the pool and read a book. After all, my job was to be sure that the kid didn’t drown, but my reading was constantly interrupted by the attention seeking of, “Gran, look at me, look at me!” I should have been more aware. He wasn’t just being obnoxious, he wanted to be rewarded with my attention. He was only trying to replenish his store of dopamine by showing-off his accomplishments in the water.

Another way that I can encourage my grandson’s healthful living and production of good brain chemicals is emphasizing the need for getting adequate sleep. Through most of my life—college, grad school, travel to interesting places, and a busy life—I cheated on sleep. Rationalizing that sleep was a use of time that I didn’t need to waste was an unfortunate mistake that I don’t want my grandson to make. It was not until I changed my sleep habits that I recognized what a tremendous difference adequate sleep can make in the way we think and function. Teens need a minimum of nine hours of sleep every night. Unfortunately, the reality is that after-school sports, activities, and excessive homework leave teens little personal time. They’re likely to trade sleep for time with their electronic screens and other personal pursuits. Recently, when a client organization was conducting an online survey with a thousand local teenagers, the researchers were astonished to see how many of the respondents submitted the survey between midnight and 3:00 a.m. Obviously, these teens are trying to cheat on sleep just as I did. Maybe we can encourage them to explore the issue. For example, it may be easier to coax teenage girls to get nine hours nightly when we call it “beauty sleep.” If we can entice them to research the issue, teens may be able to come to the conclusion on their own that they need more sleep—9+ hours. The sleep will not only support their growth, it will also increase their levels of dopamine.

As mentioned earlier, this chemical has a role in how we move. Low levels of dopamine seems to lead to fatigue and memory loss. As adults, we may be more familiar with older people who have been diagnosed with Parkinson's disease. This is a condition with symptoms, such as tremors, impaired posture and balance, uncontrolled or slowed movements, and changes in speech due to low brain concentrations of dopamine.

Serotonin

A chemical that acts as a neurotransmitter to help relay signals from one area of the brain to another, serotonin, impacts both our physical and emotional functioning. Of the millions of brain cells, most are directly or indirectly influenced by serotonin. It's the chemical related to mood, appetite, sleep, memory, learning, temperature, some social behavior, such as aggression, along with sexual desire and function. Even though serotonin is manufactured in the brain, the area of its primary function, serotonin is also found in the digestive tract. Maybe that's why, when the little kids seem upset, we hand them a cookie, and it works. Their moods instantly change. The reason that's not a good practice, however, is that it teaches them to change their moods with food. The unhappy child is rewarded with the sugary treat, and as the taste of the sweet crunch is savored, dopamine is released. As the dopamine is increased, however, the serotonin level is decreased. Since serotonin is responsible for the sense of satiation that is felt, the kid's brain says, "Yum! that was a good reward. I want another!" With lower levels of serotonin, there is less sense of being satisfied or having a full tummy. Let's remember that our job is to teach the grandchildren *positive* ways to stimulate good brain chemicals. Teaching them to become obese is not creating a good memory. Although this messenger chemical can make us feel happy, it can affect our sense of having had enough to eat. This tug of war between dopamine and serotonin can influence obesity when the dopamine message is, “feels good, want more” and there isn’t sufficient serotonin to say, “enough!”

Researchers have found the role of sunshine and exercise to be an important contributor to serotonin. Of course, those trips to the playground are enjoyable and provide a nice diversion, but being outside in the bright light, running, and making vigorous movements seems to stimulate the production of serotonin. And when they’re teens, they still need sunshine and exercise instead of spending too much time in their dark rooms. It’s even better if we slosh on the sunscreen and join them in the bright sunshine. Certainly, interacting with an interested, smiling, pleasant grandparent can encourage this “feel-good” chemical in the brain.

Developing positive attitudes and the production of good brain chemicals is essential to a sense of well-being. Grandparents can provide both the “feel-good experiences” and instill the self-discipline that distinguishes occasional treats from an onslaught of gluttony.

In Chapter 3, we discussed the importance of self-discipline and its role in establishing patterns of nutrition that avoid obesity. As we look at the importance of producing good brain chemicals to protect our grandchildren from harm, we must emphasize the interplay between ensuring proper nutrition and well-being. Even though there is no food that we can put on their plates that will supply adequate amounts of self-discipline and positive emotions, the importance of nutritional food is significant. It is a part of making the positive choices that lead to healthy living.

There is much research and evidence available about the results of lower levels of serotonin. Depression, a condition which we certainly want to prevent in our grandchildren, is affected by serotonin. Although there is still much for us to learn about how the brain functions, what it needs, and what is detrimental to it, we know that there is a connection between a lack of serotonin and the presence of depression. With this condition becoming an increasing threat to our children, and especially to teens, we grandparents must be aware of negative moods and a lack of joy in the grand-child's world. We must be alert to conversations in which the young person talks in low monotones, or is reluctant to talk at all. We must distinguish momentary sadness or frustration from a complete absence of joy in the child's life. We must recognize the differences between everyday frustrations and situations when stress precipitates genuine depression. When the young person doesn't seem to want to talk to us or be with us, it's easy for us to feel rejected and forget about Rule #1, but that may be when the grandchild needs us most!

When busy parents may be accustomed to some grumpiness or conflict with teens, grandparents become essential to maintaining awareness of the grand-children's moods. These times may be characterized by lower levels of *serotonin* and the lack of new brain cells being produced. We must be alert for depression that requires professional counseling, and perhaps, some cognitive therapy. Although such decisions are not ours, we can approach the teen's parents with diplomatic and supportive communications to share our observations. Of course, unless the parents are clueless, abusive, or absent, the role of decision maker to seek professional help is never ours. Instead, the grandparent role is one of concerned support.

If a lack of serotonin contributes to emotional depression, while memory, mood, learning, and behavior are effected by proper levels of serotonin, then we must do everything appropriate to be sure that the youngsters have an ample supply.

Endorphins
Sometimes known as the "runners' high," there are more than 20 types of endorphins to transmit electrical signals. Released from the pituitary gland with physical activity, these chemicals reduce the feelings of pain and increase the sense of euphoria. Their original purpose was probably to help react with the brain's opiate receptors to overcome the distress of extreme physical activity and induce feelings of pleasure, such as outrunning the tiger. It's the release of endorphins that adds to the athlete's sense of pleasure when completing a marathon or making an 80-yard touchdown run.

When we take the grandchildren to a track or open field where they can "run until they drop," they go home feeling tired but happy. Although we don't thoroughly understand the exact process, perhaps as they reduce any feelings of physical discomfort, the endorphins contribute to an enhanced confidence and sense of self-esteem.

A popular belief is that chocolate, music, or pleasant smells increase the release of endorphins. There is much to be understood about these endorphins, but what we do know is that they interact with opiates. Although these opiates are useful for controlling pain in the chronically ill, when used for recreation or "mood enhancers," such use of opioids results in addiction—a costly condition that can control the remainder of life.

Healthy Choices
The early twenty-first century has meant many advantages for the United States. Today, we enjoy freedom from some problems of the early twentieth century, such as the famine of the dust bowl days or limited food supplies due to lack of refrigeration. Instead, there is a greater abundance and variety of foods available to those who can afford them. Yet, this abundance has not completely solved the problems of nutrition and hunger. In the early twentieth century, when the "ice box" held limited ingredients for

mealtimes, children were usually restricted and required to ask permission before taking any food from the family larder. Mothers put appropriate size portions of generally nutritional foods on the plates and children were reminded to eat it. Decades later, the availability of food, fast food, and lots of not-so-good-for-us food has had consequences.

Today, most of us enjoy a sense of plenty, but it's easy to enjoy food without adequate self-discipline or thought as to the consequences. We may have forgotten the difference between an occasional treat and an everyday indulgence.

Much of our population seems to be carrying more weight than is deemed medically normal and appropriate for our bones to tote or our heart and lungs to service. The person who might have been put on display as the "fat man in the circus" a century ago, is now commonplace as we require large size wheelchairs and hospital beds to accommodate the hazards of morbid obesity.

At the same time that a considerable portion of our population is overweight, becoming underweight is also an issue. The onslaught of skewed marketing has developed a warped sense of body image in some young people. We can blame the media and many aspects of our society, but some children and especially teenage girls, have developed a distorted sense of what they should see in the mirror. The result has been a crisis of extremes. In the midst of anorexia and other eating disorders, we have seen a surge in diabetes, high blood pressure, other health problems aggravated by food choices that lead to being overweight.

Much of the problem could be remedied by self-discipline and more education about nutrition. If we want our grandchildren to enjoy healthful living, like many of the other things we do for them, we begin by being a good role model, talking about smart food choices, portions, and helping them learn healthy habits. Preparing children for healthy living is a general and on-going process. Encouraging carrots, nuts, and healthy snacks instead of candy bars and gummy drops or air-popped popcorn instead of chips and junk foods, can make a difference. When we take grandchildren to get ice cream, frozen yogurt, or other sweet treats, we must remind them that it's an occasional pleasure and part of our celebration of being together. We must emphasize that the favorite chocolate swirl waffle cone is not something we can do often. I must confess that it hasn't been easy to admit my CocaCola addiction and my affinity for desserts to my grandson, but it's been better than watching him develop such bad habits. Perhaps in admitting our food addictions and talking about the negative consequences, we can discourage the same trap for our precious grandchildren.

As some of us must battle overweight problems, some statistics point to the lack of food and adequate nutrition for many of the nation's children. Often due to lack of family structure, addiction, and the need for caring adults, these children receive supplemental food at school, from religious and charitable organizations, and from local food banks. It is ironic that, in a society where many of us have a problem with too much tasty food, some of our population suffers from a lack of enough food, and especially, really nutritional food. Too often, the food that is available to these children is high in carbohydrates and low in nutritional value.

Growing-up in an environment that is deprived of good nutrition adds to the adversity some children face and often contributes to their cycle of poverty. These may be the children who could benefit from an extra grandparent. Perhaps we can find a couple of hours a week to share some of what we've learned about being a caring adult in a needy child's life. Perhaps we can enhance their quality of life, not only by listening, but by exposing them to different fruits, salads, and foods high in nutrition.

Getting the Good Feelings

The four "feel-good" brain chemicals, *oxytocin, dopamine, serotonin* and *endorphins,* are needed by our grandchildren for optimal development. We can stimulate them through our relationship and providing positive experiences. The best part is that by being intentional, not just indulgent, we can teach the grandchildren how to create their own good feelings, thereby inoculating them from the dreadful traps of addiction, depression, and underage or promiscuous sex. The exciting part is that the experiences are mutual and provide an increase in the good brain chemicals for us grandparents, as well as for the young people.

We grew-up in an era of less knowledge about addiction, when a popular assumption was that, "if it hurts, swallow an aspirin or something." The response to pain or discomfort was to take action by "taking something." This is a mindset that we want our grandchildren to *never* assume. With the advent of profuse advertising of medicines, we've seen the results of the overuse of antibiotics and other medications. Unfortunately, I had to learn that the side effects of allergy meds were worse than the spring allergies. Although we certainly don't want to teach children that all medications are bad, neither do we want them to seek refuge in "taking something." We want them to learn to save medical intervention for actual medical needs.

Instead of always looking for ways to remove every vexation, every obstacle, and every unpleasantness, we can teach the children how to cope with simple aches or minor pains. This kind of response to any discomfort—"take something"—is what grandparents must replace with "do something." We can teach the children that, when they're upset, instead of ingesting chemicals to mask the pain, they can talk to us; when they're hurt, they can tell us; and together, we'll figure out how to cope with it or make it go away. When they're young, we can help them learn to relax with gentle words, and learn problem solving skills. The following are some effective grandparent responses that can calm discomfort, and at the same time, teach children some problem solving skills:

> "Together, let's help you feel okay. Let's think about what will help you feel better."
>
> "Do you need to drink some water? Would lying down for a few minutes be good?"
>
> "Would you feel better to sit here with me for a little while to talk or read a favorite book?"
>
> "Let's try gently rubbing your ankle to soothe the pain."
>
> "Let's run cool water over the scratch, and then, we'll cover with small bandage."
>
> "Sometimes, children's leg bones can grow faster than the leg muscles, causing the muscles to be stretched and to occasionally ache. Can we rub that muscle for a minute to soothe the stretch?"
>
> "Together, let's close our eyes, take slow deep breaths, and be very calm."
>
> "Let's close our eyes, relax our toes . . . our legs . . . our arms . . . our head. . . and take a deep breath, and let it out slowly, another deep breath, and let it out slowly. Now let's think about something beautiful."
>
> "What do you think would help you feel better?"

As they grow, we can teach them how to manage life, the everyday issues and problems that need to be solved. We can give them words that enable them to feel like a victor over the situation and avoid feeling like the victim, as outlined later in this chapter. When things go wrong, we can teach them the "self-talk" that motivates problem solving. We can teach them phrases that reflect their making choices to be in control of whatever is bothering them. We can show them how to improve their moods. We can give them some of the following useful points for their self-talk.

> "This hurts and I want it to stop!"
>
> "What can I do about this to make it stop and that will be good for me?"
>
> "What have I done before that's worked well, that has helped in times like these?"
>
> "I don't want to feel this way. What can I say to myself that'll help me feel better?"

We empower the children with the realization that they can make choices about how they feel. We can teach them to figure-out what's bothering them and what they can do about it. We know that humans are most effective and have an improved emotional sense when we feel in control of ourselves. With some gentle words and simple coaching, we can empower the children. We can help them learn better ways to be in control than to become addicted to substances that are only a temporary fix and a long-term disaster.

Perhaps the most meaningful learning that I found in all of those graduate classes in counseling was that, when possible, the most effective counseling is to teach the person the skills to become his/her own counselor. In helping others to be aware of their feelings and seeking ways of overcoming negative feelings, adults, and even children, can learn to solve their problems and contribute to their own sense of emotional stability and well-being.

Stress Chemicals

The birthing process is very stressful and babies arrive crying. Parents' comforting arms soothe the little one and the crying eventually stops, but babies cry a lot. Crying, however, is the infant's only way of communicating hunger or discomfort. One of the most important things the parents do during the first years is to help the infant learn to comfort himself/herself. Of course, grandparents are great at helping to comfort little ones. Gradually, the baby develops language and can communicate needs. This process of nurturing the little one's ability to cope with everyday stress is an integral part of parenting. Tragedy occurs, however, when the stress in the child's environment is so overwhelming that the child doesn't learn how to respond or when there is no parent or grandparent to soothe and help the child deal with stress.

When under stress, the adrenal glands release *cortisol*. It's sometimes called the body's alarm system as this cortisol works with the brain to manage the body's use of carbohydrates, blood pressure, metabolism, immunity, and even influences the sleep/wake cycle. Obviously, it's a very important substance on a normal basis. Problems occur, however, when a threat appears. Known as the "fight or flight" hormone, extra amounts of this cortisol are released to boost energy for a physical response. If we don't need to escape from the tiger or battle a wooly mammoth, then that cortisol is left in our muscles and flowing through the body.

Adults have learned the importance of going for a run or straight to the gym for a vigorous workout after an especially stressful day at work. We know that robust exercise, yoga, or some kind of relaxing experience is essential for eliminating that excess cortisol from the body. When young children are upset and cry vociferously, we remove them from the stressful situation and calm them by encouraging them to breathe. This deep breathing helps to dissipate the cortisol that has been released by the stressful event. Our bodies are equipped to handle physical stress, but not very adept at accommodating emotional stress. Interestingly, it isn't always the stressful event that's the big problem. Sometimes, it's the body's response to the emotional stress that becomes very detrimental.

Although awareness of research into the negative effects of stress on health has been ongoing for decades, it's only been in recent years that we've become aware of the consequences of stress and adversity on children and teens. It may seem as if the cortisol constantly flows through the bodies of anxious children. They're always ready for conflict and in fight or flight mode. Even though the children don't need this cortisol to help them escape from a tiger, the constant threats they feel from their lives of adversity propel them into a persistent state of aggression and defensiveness. Perhaps they're looking for a means to protect themselves from the instability and chaos of their environments.

Anxiety and concerns for safety and security can inhibit a child's openness to learning. When children are constantly exposed to tension at home or if parents' busy schedules don't allow sufficient time for listening to the child's concerns or problems, it can affect them emotionally and physically. This can lead to an adverse impact on school performance, but the impact can extend even further. Not only is it detrimental to childhood health, the condition is compounded when the stressed children become adults. Among the many anecdotes of adverse childhood experiences and their negative effects is the account of J.D. Vance (2015). His description of growing up in the dysfunctional world of the "rust belt" is both troubling and encouraging. According to his story, what allowed Vance to escape the revolving door of stressful chaos was having loving grandparents. Uneducated and products of their world, the grandparents lacked the skills and resources to propel young Vance out of their dysfunctional world. The character and perseverance they taught him, however, made a significant difference in his life path. Along with service in the Marines and help from some resourceful professors, he was able to attend Yale University, earn a law degree, and aspire to serve in the U.S. Senate. What could have been another repetition of tragedy became a success story that was made possible by caring adults and devoted grandparents.

When circumstances beyond the grandparents' control do not create the loving, pleasant, inspiring environment that we want for every child, that's when we can supplement the bonding, supportive, encouraging atmosphere that the child needs. In *Hillbilly Elegy,* J.D. Vance recounted an example of this supplement when in high school. His math grades were sinking because he was becoming arrogant and negligent in his studies. That's when his grandmother reminded him how she had saved the money to buy an expensive calculator for his math class. Despite his alcoholic drug addicted mother, virtually absent father, and the bleak surroundings in which he lived, that bond with his "Mamaw," motivated him to reverse his performance in math and in high school. It could be speculated that family support is an even greater predictor of high school graduation than IQ or test scores.

The *Centers for Disease Control (*CDC) has an ongoing program, the Adverse Childhood Events (ACE) to study the effects of toxic childhood stress on health across the lifespan. The statistics collected since the 1990's do not paint a pretty future for children exposed to stress, adversity, and abuse, indicating that as adults, they suffer more health problems and die decades earlier than people with normal childhoods. Over time, the constant exposure to stress can tax the body's ability to regulate itself. Not only can there be an actual change in the chemistry of a child's brain, lowered immunity increases vulnerability to disease. Exposure to constant bickering, violence, or abuse of any kind can have a life-long impact on the child's health, confidence, school experience, and social interactions.

My most important learning about stress is where I allow it to be. When the people I love are in jeopardy, I cannot control the stress. The cortisol flows freely and every fiber of my being experiences anxiety as I *internalize* the stress. Conversely, when there are deadlines, problems, other issues, I am most effective if I keep the stress outside and view it as challenge, opportunity, and the chance to accomplish. Such *external* stress does not cause the same physical harm as the *internal* stress. It's all about what I tell myself about what I'm feeling.

When young, I had no idea how much those afternoon walks through the woods with my grandfather impacted my body chemistry. I remember, however, how pleasant I felt and how the stress and boredom of a day in fourth grade disappeared. Decades later, I realized that vigorous exercise diminished the cortisol. When I was nine, I just called it fun when Grandpa taught me to listen to the birds and watch the patterns of water flowing in a small stream. Today, we would say that he was teaching me "mindfulness." The Japanese have carried this quiet enjoyment of nature to a new level with the practice of "forest bathing." Although it may be practiced with too much "touchy-feely" for some, nevertheless, we grandparents can utilize that calm, intentional focus on elements of nature.

In addition to encouraging the children to run and jump, we can teach them the value of taking a slow, calm walk, breathing deeply, listening to the sounds in nature, and focusing on elements of the natural world. We can show them how to change feelings of sadness or depression with simple calm concentration on the beauty of the trees, the clouds, and the surroundings. We can encourage them to take control of their moods by looking at the wonders in nature and the beauty of God's creation.

Depending upon the latest child rearing fad, parents may insist on letting a toddler scream every night at bedtime to teach the child sleep routines. Perhaps that's when we can diplomatically provide research material or better methods, but without actual interference. Although we must not obstruct parental routines, grandparents may prefer to quietly cuddle that little one in the rocking chair and avoid such needless stress, and gradually teach the child how to fall asleep alone. We can show them how to experience and enjoy being calm, peaceful, and how falling asleep can be another "feel-good."

We can spare our little ones from adversity, and teach them how to cope with unexpected stressful events that we cannot prevent. This is a huge opportunity to increase the quality of their childhoods—and their long-term health.

Expressing Anger

Because we dislike fits, tantrums, and meltdowns, we may send the message that it's not acceptable to be angry or dislike something. Instead, a better course is to teach the child that it's okay to be angry, but there are acceptable and useful ways of expressing the anger. Simply walking away from and ignoring the two-year-old's tantrum may be the best course for the manipulative child. In most instances, however, a better way to deal with the child's anger is to calm the child by saying, "I want to hear what has made you so upset, but first, take some deep breaths, then tell me about the problem." Through the child's anger and frustration, we help the child find better ways to get what is wanted or why that isn't possible just now. Regardless of the grandparent's words, the important issue is, not to suppress the anger, but to find acceptable ways to express the anger. At times, perhaps reading such stories as *Where the Wild Things Are* and discussing Max's anger can be useful. Grandparents can support young people by helping them recognize their emotions, then expressing them in ways that are appropriate and lead to development of a strong EQ.

Avoiding the Victim Mindset

Vigilant for our little one's safety, we usually make every effort to spare them from any adversity, especially the kind perpetrated by irresponsible people. As part of our efforts to support avoiding the traps of addiction and depression, it's useful to help children deal with unfortunate events. We can teach them to distinguish between circumstances in which they are the innocent victims, and situations in which they can take action, be in control and accountable.

Let's distinguish between actually *being a victim*—the object of an irresponsible act or circumstance—and *feeling like a victim.* Being a victim is the result of vulnerability and being at the mercy of someone or some catastrophic event. These are conditions in which, through no actions or fault of our own, we become the casualty of an unpreventable disaster or someone else's negligent actions. When children are the object of physical, sexual, or verbal abuse, they must not be left to feel guilt. Instead, they must be assured that they did nothing to deserve the terrible mistreatment and that the abuse should not have happened. They need comfort, professional counseling, or tactics to recover their feelings of emotional equilibrium.

Feeling like a victim is the emotional state that occurs when someone has harmed us or something has happened that we dislike and we feel no power or ability to change the situation. These are circumstances in which, like overcoming fears, we can help the child learn to take action in order to move beyond an unproductive mindset and feeling like a victim. When we take action, we feel a sense of power or control over what's happening, rather than feeling like a victim of what's happening to us. The *victim/ victor* map that follows illustrates the two paths that can be taken, one to a positive mindset and the other to an unfortunate downward spiral.

In the center of the drawing we see an event, something that happened. At that point, we make a decision about how to react and which path to take. If we allow the external forces to be in control of us, we will be angry or sad and tell ourselves that this wasn't our fault as we blame someone or something else for the event. We're left feeling very much the victim. We may make excuses or be in denial about all of the facts of what has happened. In these circumstances, the results are often feelings of anger, self-pity, and depression as we cannot do anything to help ourselves because we're not in control.

The ancient Greek, Epictetus, indicated that it isn't what actually happens to us that affects us as much as what we tell ourselves about what happened. The same event can happen to you and me, but what we tell ourselves is different. If we regard ourselves as independent, confident, responsible for our own actions, and recognize that the bad event happened because of our own actions, we assume accountability for what occurred. We assess what went wrong, how we can fix the situation, and how we can move-on, not making the same mistake again.

If we realize that our actions did not cause this bad situation, we tell ourselves that this shouldn't have happened, and that we didn't deserve this harm. If we assess that what happened was beyond our control, nevertheless, we focus on what we can do to change or fix the circumstances going forward. When we see ourselves being in control of our lives, even though we can't always be in control of everything that happens to and around us, we can move beyond the bad event. Although we might not feel victorious over the bad situation, we will be the victor over the way we handled it. When adults react this way, we become mature, accountable, and highly sought after in relationships and in the workplace.

Although children can't be responsible for everything that happens to them, we want them to see themselves as competent, capable, and learning to handle some of the problems that come their way. When something unpleasant happens to the grandchildren, we can comfort their injuries—physical or emotional, real or imagined. Then, we can help them to analyze what happened and how, if possible, the event might have been avoided. We help them to see how better actions might have produced different results. In the event that the child did nothing to precipitate the event, we can help the child through the process of the "self-talk" to keep the child feeling some

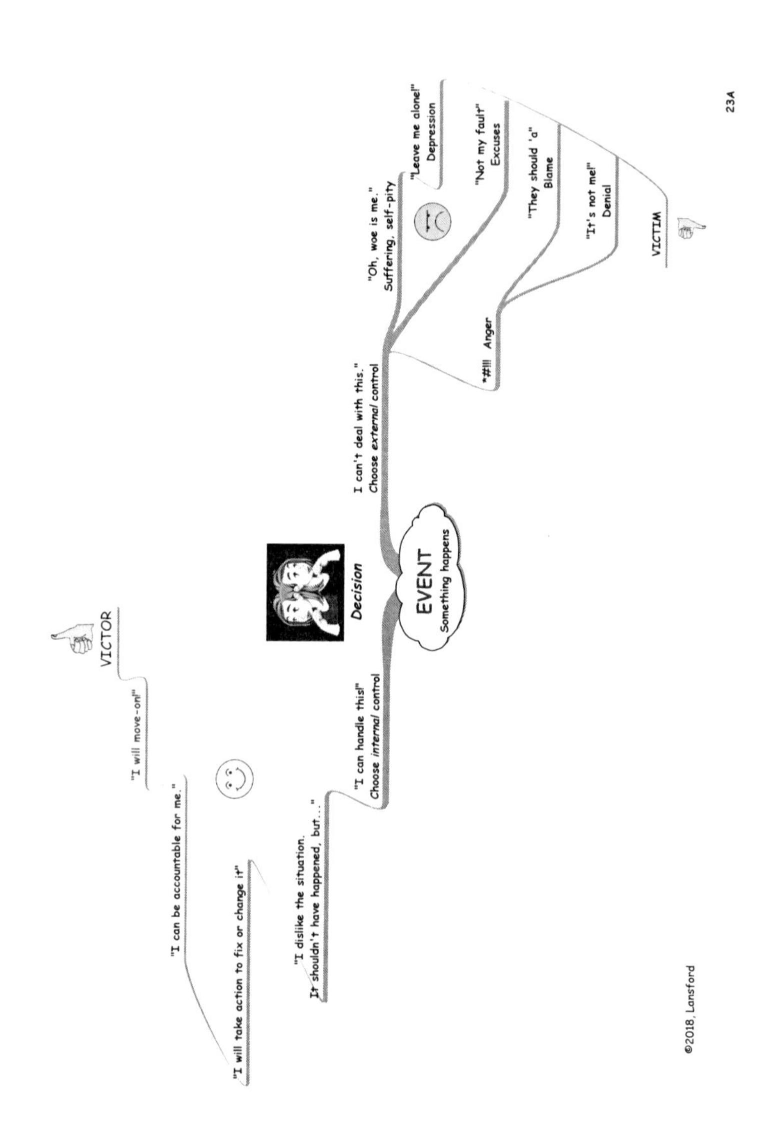

*To enlarge the victor/victim graphic on a computer screen, go to https://zelmalansford.com/making-memories/

control over similar events. By giving the child phrases for self-talk indicated in the drawing, we can equip the child for a more positive mental state. You'll notice that the positive self-talk does not shirk from responsibility. Rather, it encourages responsibility and accountability. It helps us to avoid inappropriate denial, blaming, and self-talk that is not helpful to mood or mindset.

Teaching children how to verbalize their feelings is a first step to their learning positive self-talk. Although sometimes easier for extraverts than introverts, not internalizing emotions is essential to avoiding the negative self-talk that might lead to depression. When we're busy, don't understand the grandchildren's feelings, or just don't recognize their emotions, it can contribute to escalation of their problems.

In situations of abuse, it's critical to help deliver the child from any feelings of guilt or that the child did anything to precipitate the mistreatment. In such deplorable circumstances, by focusing on the actions—"You screamed, ran away, and told a trusted adult" we show the child how the actions help to move beyond the bad situation. Although it is preferable that we will never need such instructions, it's important to help any child distinguish between his/her deeds that may have caused a problem and an adverse condition beyond the child's responsibility. By keeping in mind this simple little victor/victim map, perhaps it will help the next time something happens to your grandchild, especially the times when the child did nothing to initiate the event.

Planting the seeds of the positive self-talk, especially during circumstances of harm or adversity, is planting the seeds of confidence and self-worth. We must discourage negative thinking or critical self-talk that contribute to lower self-esteem. We know that people who don't have a real sense of self may open themselves to all kinds of manipulation, lowered performance, and forms of abuse.

I've often wished for a valid way to measure self-worth. Then, we could determine if there's a statistical significance between low self-esteem and addiction, i.e., "I need the cocaine high to compensate for how awful I feel." Perhaps it's essential to help children recognize that they cannot always control what happens, but they can control what they tell themselves about what has happened. We can help them sustain a strong sense of self-worth through self-talk that can become its own feel-good.

This sense of control can make a monumental difference in results for the grandchildren throughout their lifetime. Even though we can't always control the forces around us, we are free to choose how we react to what happens. We can choose what we tell ourselves about what has happened. Further, this feeling of control and not feeling like a victim aides in helping with forgiveness as mentioned in Chapter 4. Such a mindset is very helpful for us grandparents as we hone our skills in teaching grandchildren the importance of having positive voices in their little heads.

An even greater resource is Romans 5:35, (RSV)

. . . suffering produces endurance, and endurance produces character, and character produces hope, and hope does not disappoint us, because God's love has been poured into our hearts through the Holy Spirit that has been given to us.

Summary

It's human to want to feel-good and feeling good can be addictive. The armor that will keep our grandchildren from being vulnerable to drugs, alcohol, and all sorts of things and people that will not be good for them, is to teach them from a very early age how to make their own "feel-goods and self-talk." We can teach them the self-talk of internal control and responsibility that can be louder than detrimental victim talk. We can help them learn how to be in control of their own brains and their own mindsets. We can be sure they understand that choosing a healthy brain means freedom—being free from the disease of addiction and being free to choose their future.

Regardless of how funny or ridiculous they seem, such as the toddler's fear of the beach ball, we make no contribution to the grandchildren by laughing at what they're afraid of or trying to diminish what they don't understand. Instead of disregarding their fears, we use them as opportunities for learning.

When they're babies, we can calm and soothe the grandchildren, gradually helping them to calm themselves. When they're young, we can soothe and calm the unnecessary fears by showing them how to take action to reduce what's making them sad or afraid. Most of all, we can be alert to childhood fears and lowered self worth that might follow them into adulthood and reduce personal success. We can listen to the grandchildren verbalize their fears, help them solve problems, find actions they can take to diminish their fears, and calm the unnecessary fears.

When teenage grandchildren appear with straggly hair, tattoos, piercings, or inappropriate and unattractive clothing, they may not give us a feel-good emotion. Sometimes, it seems as if an easy goal for grandparents could be to simply survive the period of adolescence and hope that the teens get through it with as few life changing events as possible—addiction, incarceration, pregnancy, or physical harm. It could be easy for us to distance ourselves and not do anything to release the *oxytocin* in them. Yet, that may be when they need us most. Unfortunately, there's nothing more potentially threatening to our precious grandchildren than being bullied into depression, going to school, out with friends, or anywhere, with a depletion of "feel-good" brain chemicals. With such a deficit, they may be tempted by the latest "party pill" and become vulnerable to underage sex, careless decisions, and getting their "feel-goods" from alcohol, nicotine, pills, or through a needle.

Perhaps a better approach is to make this another phase of development for thriving. In learning positive self-talk, and how to develop their own "feel-goods" in the brain, they become less vulnerable to addictive substances. If we have done all of the precursors well, perhaps teenagers can make that thrill and reward seeking of the adolescent brain into positive pursuits of learning, intentions, entrepreneurship, discoveries, and adventures. Adolescence is a time that, instead of being endured, can be nurtured and enjoyed by the grandchildren, their parents, and us.

Perhaps the result of good grandparenting is not just in attending to the children's physical safety, or stimulating their cognitive development, but also being vigilant for positive biochemical maintenance. If we teach them how to create their own "feel-goods" and "self-talk," then we can significantly reduce the likelihood of the ghastly crises of addiction. If we develop a loving, bonded relationship with them from infancy and plant the seeds of good character, resilience, and decision making, we will have shown them the path of virtue. By teaching them what to do when they're sad and how to be in charge of their brains, and emotions we've taught them how to be free of addictions and in charge of their own lives.

In making memories that create good brain chemicals, we can make a difference in our grandchildren's entire lives. We can ensure that they know how to deal with their fears, sadness, and anger, as well as how to feel and express joy, pleasure, and happiness.

Chapter 11

Making Memories That Make a Difference

Please keep us ever focused on the work you have set before us.

It's impossible to know, decades down the road, how a passing remark or some small incident that happens today will impact our grandchildren's future. It may be what we say to them, the experiences we give them, or something that comes from others we bring into their worlds. But it's difficult to know what will be significant for them. What may seem to be trivial or irrelevant to us, may in time, make a major impression on their lives. It's not unusual to hear friends or famous people talk about a chance meeting, simple incidents, or happenstance that changed the direction of their lives or careers.

My daughter is an artist whose contemporary designs are executed through her interests in the ancient metal techniques of the Middle East. She traces the beginning of her passion that led to a college degree in art to a game that was given to her by a family friend. It was a clever board game built around artifacts from King Tut's Tomb. Although I was apprehensive about its ghoulish illustrations and thought it just "one more game to play," she traces her life-long interest to this little game. That seemingly trivial encounter resulted in numerous trips to Egypt and much research into the ancient metal techniques reflected in her work today. How often we think, "If I'd known how important that would become, I'd have paid more attention to it." Perhaps the essence is that, since we can't know what will be paramount to our grandchildren, we must notice and pay attention to what captures their attention at every age.

One big difference in being a parent and being a grandparent is that we know how quickly the children grow-up. We know the importance of every moment that we have with these special young people. Even though our work, interests, and everyday chores may consume much of our time, we may have a more substantial sense of our personal direction than during our young parenting years. That greater sense of life and priorities gives us the perspective that allows us to take the time and focus attention on the grandchildren. When my daughter was playing the mummy game, I was just happy that she was so intent on her diversion. She was safe, happy, and that meant that I had time to do the million tasks that were looming over me. Obviously, if I'd had the insight as a parent that I gained by the time of grandparenting, I would have realized that nothing I had to do was more important than helping her develop her life-long interests. I would have joined her instead of leaving her to play each of the four roles of the game alone.

Yes, what we've learned is how to maximize every moment possible because we can't know or predict what will become important to the grandchild. We can recognize, however, how effective our grandparenting influence can be.

Learning for the Future

Although we want to encourage a lifetime attitude toward learning, it doesn't necessarily mean that the learning must all take place in some kind of formal schooling. In recent years, we've emphasized higher education regardless of the child's interest or abilities. With such prominence given to college, some children's needs are overlooked or they're made to feel less valuable because they like working with their hands or jobs that need a technical school rather than a liberal arts preparation. Although much of future work will be “brain work,” the plumber, electrician, master carpenter and many other such craft jobs are still highly valued and well compensated. In our emphasis on college education, we’ve diminished the importance and worth of the artisans and crafts people. Yet, because their skills are so highly valued, they may be paid more than some jobs requiring a liberal arts degree. Indeed, it’s possible to find people with jobs that we call menial labor who enjoy what they do, even more than the highly paid executive enjoys his/her work. Whether a welder, a farmer, or a truck driver, all are worthy pursuits. Our job is to encourage exploration, whatever the interest of the moment. And it’s okay if the focus changes next month. It’s all part of the career adventure and practice of seeing a future of possibilities.

As grandparents, we smile at the four-year-old’s interest in becoming a firefighter, realizing that the intent is not in becoming a first responder, but the idea of wearing that cool hat, playing with the big water hoses, and riding fast in the big red truck that’s most exciting. Then, the child’s interest moves on, perhaps to pilot, princess, or sports hero. Again, it’s the hat or the costume that may first catch the child’s attention. We understand and constantly expose them to new ideas and new possibilities, knowing that there will likely be many considerations before a final choice. And that’s where a huge difference occurs between their career choices and our grandparents’ life-time jobs. Instead of a career in one area, as was the custom in most of the twentieth century, these twenty-first century children will probably enjoy several different careers as they have more options.

We watch, as many children’s interests change weekly, realizing that it’s not unusual. Our task and privilege is in supporting their interests and expanding their horizons through what we expose them to, the stories that we read with them, and what we talk about in our conversations. It’s not our job to steer them into prestigious universities or a career that will impress our friends. Rather, it's our opportunity to help them find endeavors that bring them success and happiness.

With the realization that life-long learning will be a pursuit of the future, we try to instill curiosity and a zest for study and discovery in our grandchildren. If we've succeeded at our intentions, we've helped the grandchildren to understand that learning can take place anywhere, not just in the classroom.

Although there are myriad reasons to encourage twenty-first century children to pursue higher education, we must be careful about our advocacy. When we older grandparents went to college, there were strict rules that governed our living conditions, social behavior, and that contributed to our safety. With today's recognition of the 18-year-old as a legal adult with privacy assurances, we grandparents may be left with some concerns for their safety and well-being on a distant college campus where there may be few rules or no supervision about how or where the students live.

I must admit that I have a strong bias about the "going away to college issue" for the eighteen-year-old. First, it isn't necessary for many of our grandchildren. Today's world is vastly different from the mid-twentieth century student who, to obtain a college degree, might have been forced to relocate a considerable distance away from home and live in a dormitory in order to pursue quality higher education. Now, for much of the country, the first two years of basic higher education are available in community colleges. In addition, on-line learning, especially during the pandemic, can be as effective, maybe even more so, than sitting in a large lecture hall listening, not to a professor, but to a teaching assistant. Students can pursue much of their central curriculum locally, less expensively, and with more safety. Second, the conditions of college have changed. Many of the faculty who were once focused on tutoring, mentoring, and nurturing young minds are now focused on their own research, publications, and perpetuating their own careers. They are not always shepherding young students to focus on their studies and make effective decisions. Third, as we discussed in Chapter 10, not every eighteen-year-old brain is ready to live independently and function astutely in today's world. Beginning college is a time when the young student needs more focus and self-discipline than ever before. Yet, it's also a time when the late teen has a new freedom and independence. The wild partying on some campuses proves that some teens are not ready to make decisions about their safety and well-being.

Although we don't want to see grandchildren living with their parents at age 30, it may be most appropriate for them to pursue their beginning college education in the stable environment of the family. Such an arrangement not only adds to safety and practicality, it saves considerable money. A less expensive first-two years may facilitate transfer to a university of excellence, and/or lead to graduate school at a prestigious university. Most of all, being very prudent about the first two years of higher education may enable grandchildren to launch into a career and life without the burden of enormous student debt. We grandparents can help by encouraging the young students to be clever and efficient in checking different college requirements to ensure an easy transfer.

Of course, this grandmother cannot overlook the possibility that living at home with partial independence for the first two years of college could diminish some negative risks. At home, the precious young person will be less likely to encounter the threats of excessive alcohol, depression, date-rape, failing grades, and the other threats and distractions that may exist on a far-away campus, alone, with no supervision, no real support system, and with total independence.

Just as adjustments were made in the house and the home environment when baby arrived, when the little one became ambulatory, and when a teen; adjustments must be made for the eighteen-year-old. The grandchild must be acknowledged as a legal adult, regardless of maturity. Acknowledgements and agreements about responsibility, expectations, and independence are essential for the teen and the parents. Although we grandparents may have our opinions, our best role is that of support, resource, and sometimes, diplomatic listener and counselor. Even though we may be tempted to suppose that we're needed less, the college decision, and life after eighteen, are times when we can be of great value.

School and Future Career Choices

Was your fourth grade year as long as mine? My nine months in that crowded classroom with Mrs. Davis was forever. I don't remember learning much, but I vividly remember the long days that seemed unending. If only that year could have passed as quickly as this year is disappearing for me. Maybe it's the way our brains encode new experiences, but not familiar ones, that impacts our perceptions of time. All I remember was that each day with boring Mrs. Davis dragged by, but the afternoon time with my wonderful grandparents flew by. In those delightful hours out in the woods on my grandfather's farm or sitting by the fire, my grandparents gave meaning to my life at school.

Grandparents can show children how school is related to jobs and how they can connect their abilities in science, technology, engineering, math (STEM) and other subjects to what they can explore in these classes. We can pay for a musical instrument, lessons to encourage their creative talent, or simply just applaud their diligent practice and performance. We help them explore school subjects and hobbies in many ways. Recently, when my daughter was conducting a master class in repousse´ someone asked if one of her parents was an artist. She explained, "No, but every time I showed the slightest interest in anything, from art, to cooking, to tennis, my grandmother bought the materials and signed me up for classes. That's how I found my passion, by my grandmother's encouraging me to sample all sorts of things, especially anything creative."

Another indicator for which we must be alert is grandchildren with diverse interests and abilities. These children often encounter major struggles in finding their passion. Because they have been blessed with multiple talents, and can do many things well, they can be successful in a variety of jobs, but often become frustrated in their early jobs. I call such a dilemma the *bell ringer* problem. Just because we can do something well doesn't mean that it "rings our bells" and is intrinsically satisfying. To achieve real career satisfaction, we must be able to perform the tasks well *and* be passionate about what we're doing and what we achieve. We must love the work so much that it isn't work, or just about the money. We must enjoy the endeavor and be so engaged in it that we lose track of time as it "rings our bells." In the absence of a job in which the person can invest passion, there may be success, but no engagement and intrinsic reward. When we detect dissatisfaction or frustration with their early choices of jobs, it's too easy for us to say,

"But you're so successful, why change jobs?"

We know that we will not be successful with judgments or admonishments. We'd just be smashing into their youthful independence with such well-intended comments as:

"Don't be a quitter! I would never quit a secure job!"

"Why would you leave a secure, good paying job?"

"You'd better hold on to that job 'till you get another!"

Instead, we understand. We listen to their frustrations and gently probe with insightful questions and statements.

"Tell me about the most unpleasant parts of the job."

"What are the tasks or parts that you like?"

As throughout their childhoods, we guide and help them explore. With thought, we say:

"Let's think about what you're doing when it's so exciting or engaging that you forget the time?"

"How can we figure out a place where you can be more passionate and enjoy what you do?"

"How can you look for that better place while you finish your present obligation?"

Only after we've listened and explored, can we follow with that last practical statement. After probing insightfully, we may find a root of the dissatisfaction. We can always be supportive. We may even be able to help with problem solving if we patiently explore the difficulty, such as lack of job fit, fear of failure, or dissatisfaction with the culture. For the Instant Generation, these would all be legitimate reasons for job change. As older adults who heard our grandparents talk about life in the Great Depression, or simply remembering the 2008 recession and the 2020 pandemic, we may have a different attitude toward job security, but we cannot put our concerns on these young people. We can, however, be useful in helping them to sort out the cause of their job dissatisfaction.

As older adults, when we're in jobs that we perform well, but are not engaged in or excited about, and receive no intrinsic rewards, we look for hobbies or places outside of work in which we can invest our passion. For example, Haley had risen to the level of vice president in her organization, enjoyed a sizable income, and was a top performer. When her organization was sold and her once challenging job became pedantic and unchallenging, however, she contemplated leaving. Finally, she decided that it would be hard to replace her position and income without relocating. After months of frustration, and with some family coaching, she remembered her childhood passion for music. She recalled the joys of playing in the high school band and singing in the college chorus. Continuing through her boring job, she began singing with a band on weekends and now continues to endure the less satisfying job but invests her passion and enthusiasm as a jazz singer. Today, in addition to her somewhat boring job with the solid income, Haley has a whole new place in which to invest her zeal—in music. She sings in clubs and at events in her home state, and even enjoyed a gig at a prime New York nightspot.

Whether we find intrinsic reward in our professional endeavors, hobbies, or other places in our lives, it's essential to find a place in life where we can experience challenge, enjoyment, satisfaction, and a chance to use our abilities and learn new skills.

Finding Passion in Endeavors

The process of exploration to find our passion begins very early and requires much time and investigation. Gone are the days of routinely deciding on a career at age 16, training, then spending the remainder of life in that one kind of job. Outside of being a physician, there are few careers that follow such a lock-step path of making the decision in high school, going to college in pre-med, then medical school, residency, and medical practice. Although this is the track to become a physician, it's not unusual to find that, even after such extensive preparation, some docs get a law or business degree and move out of, or to the edges of health care. Then, there are the physicians who go into politics or private business. Unlike the past, the twenty-first century career path can take different forms.

Many of our grandchildren may have several vastly different jobs and careers in fields that are unknown today.

We cannot overlook, however, the child who always seems to know the direction in which he/she is heading. We must be prepared for the exception, such as the logical thinker, Walt, from Chapter 9. When he was only eight, he sprawled across the couch in my office at Saint Nicholas School and told me how he planned to use computers to change the world. (When he first talked about Apple, I assumed that he was describing a fruit.) Walt finished high school at age 15, college at 19, interrupted graduate school for a job at Apple, then went to Microsoft, and has since, partnered to developed revolutionary software for healthcare. He's been inventive and highly successful with his computer software creations. He's also an adept artist, musician, and can converse articulately on a variety of subjects, but technology is and has been his passion. Walt is an exception in that, although he has many interests and diverse talents, he's been on a lifetime one-track career course. Without the family and educational environment to accommodate his ambitions, however, he might have been a less happy and accomplished adult.

Another significant contribution we can give to our grandchildren is helping them to know and experience the joy and passion in endeavors. We can help them to see the value of focusing and concentrating on what they're doing, whether practicing a musical instrument, studying history, drawing and painting, riding a bike, or building a robot. We can help them to know the joys of "getting lost in what they're doing."

We help children explore career possibilities when we buy that firefighter's hat and watch them run around the yard squirting everything with the little hose connected to a backpack tank. We sew a fairy costume and crown for Halloween so that the little girl can experience the imaginative fun of dancing around with a magic wand. And even though many of today's young children aspire to become a YouTube star, we read books to them about different life pursuits and talk about what people can do to earn money. We may even be pursuing their career interests when we play silly games about King Tut's tomb!

We share our world with the ten-year-old when we take the kid to work with us. We give them opportunities, not only to see *where* we work, but also, to see *how* we work. We let them see how responsible we are, how we deliver on-time, and show them our attitudes that reflect our character and integrity. We demonstrate how to be an exemplary performer at whatever is chosen. Perhaps some grandchildren may develop interests that are vastly different from ours, but it is not uncommon for them to follow in career paths similar to ours. Even though the circumstances may be different, it's fun when we have a sense of their studies, their part-time jobs, and what their world is like. If not, it's our opportunity to learn about the world of their interests, their passions, and their endeavors.

A very relevant example of how career opportunities change over time is in an old game that you may remember playing. In the popular board game called, *Careers*, girls could become school teachers and fashion designers. Obtaining money and fame were major ways to accumulate points toward winning the game. Today, we place less emphasis on gender specific careers and we've learned the value of worthy endeavors and intrinsic rewards over fame. Perhaps instead of pulling your old *Careers* game from the attic, and using the stereotypical careers, your grandchildren and you can develop your own version. A stack of blank cards, some colored markers, and some imaginative conversation might create a more appropriate and productive learning activity for today's youth.

Whether stories, games, trips, or personal experiences, the children's exploration should include lots of sampling, pretending, and trials. I often comment that I have an undergraduate degree in music—not because of talent, but because of a lack of career counseling. At least, I made the practical choice for a bachelor of arts degree that gave me a broader base of study for my varied career pursuits. Fortunately today, many schools have resources for career counseling. In addition, some organizations allow what's known as "job shadowing" to introduce young people to various kinds of work. An ideal opportunity for both teens and college age is the internship. Whether paid or unpaid, it offers an excellent introduction to the job, along with the chance to know how working in a particular area fits the ambitions and aspirations. Being able to give young people a glimpse of the tasks, skills, and requirements needed is essential. It helps them to choose the career path that fits their abilities, and at the same time, envelopes them in challenges, new learnings, and activities that stoke their energies and passions.

One of the worst mistakes that we can make as parents and grandparents is to assume that because these children have our genes, and they've been exposed to what we do, that they will follow in our footsteps. It's easy to surmise that they'll have interests and talents similar to ours. Although it often happens that way, there's no certainty. The children of many famous people will talk of their childhood years and being asked," Are you going to be an engineer like your father? When you grow up, are you going to be as famous as your mother?" Careless adult words can be such "put-downs." From the Prince of Wales to the little girl next door, no child is helped by constant comparisons and insensitive adult comments about the child's future. That's when a perceptive grandparent must intervene with a clarifying word, "Oh, this wonderful child has talents in many different areas!" and then, change the subject.

If we've helped to build a family business, it's natural to want that to be part of the family legacy, but it may not be a realistic expectation. Fostering their own dreams would create a far greater legacy than binding children to a lifetime of frustration, and perhaps, failure in the family business. Whether they want to follow our path or choose a different destination, our best action is to support, encourage, guide, coach, and help them find the work, interests, and lifestyle that is theirs. Whether the grandchild becomes the President, an entrepreneur in the technology world, or the proverbial ditch digger, what's essential for the child is being able to *see* a happy future.

When Karen's oldest grandson came for a visit before leaving for a job in Asia, he talked about how excited he was about working for a global non-profit and helping to build the infrastructure of developing nations. He commented that he knew his father would prefer that he join the firm of which Dad was a partner, but that Dad just didn't understand his passion for helping people. Then, he looked at Karen and said, "But Grandmother, you understand why I love my job and you've always been supportive." She replied, "Yes, I understand that your values and goals are different from your father's. Of course, he would love for you to join his firm, to see you every day, and to pass on his business legacy to you, but you must follow your dreams and pursue the career that fulfills your passions." Karen knows that we grandparents have the perspective that sometimes compensates for parents' career practicality.

A wealthy grandmother was overheard saying, "I told my 30-year-old grandson that he'll be so much happier, and better able to stay sober, when he's on a payroll somewhere—and not just depending on my bankroll!" She was obviously describing a young man who had not developed character, independence, goals, or learned perseverance from his struggles. The resulting self-image had probably contributed to his difficulty with alcohol and achieving all of which he was capable.

Along with their growing independence as a person, it's imperative that we help the grandchildren develop ambition and achieve accomplishments from which they gain intrinsic rewards. Beyond earning money and becoming financially secure, we must help them find endeavors that are satisfying, enriching, and illuminating. Our support and encouragement can help grandchildren find true passion in their work, rather than just settling for a lifetime of swapping their time for a paycheck.

Stress is a Barrier to Seeing the Future

Physicians often ponder the sometimes unrecognized impact that stress can have on a variety of diseases and conditions. We know that in childhood, stress is incredibly detrimental to normal growth. The upheaval that addiction, poverty, and relationship problems causes in families can assault the growing child's emotional system and physical well-being. When the child can't sleep, does not have consistent nutrition, and cannot bond with at least one adult, the stress thwarts normal development and limits potential in so many ways.

One of the sad realities of children who live in these adverse situations is their lack of ability to imagine a future. They may be too influenced by the limits of their surroundings and distracted by their present circumstances. They often appear to have an inability to see forward. This unfortunate situation dominates their choices as they seem to look only at the present. Their focus is on their present stressed circumstances. They seem to think about only what might feel good at the time or allow them to escape for the moment. They appear to make decisions with the impulsive and emotional parts of their brains. The issues all around them make it seem useless to be concerned about tomorrow. Gangs, drugs, petty crimes, underage sex, and many other vices are strongly influenced by this total focus on the here and now, with little regard for the future—that seems so far away. Too often, the stress, lack of ability to see something better, and this hopelessness become a helplessness that transforms the beginning of a downward spiral and an expectation to see only anguish and despair. Their thinking is constricted by an inability to see options, possibilities, or a better life. These children would probably benefit from a brigade of grandparents to listen-to and care about them.

Even adolescents from affluent families sometimes experience difficulty in seeing beyond the present. Like toddlers, their decisions and emotions may be totally present focused. When school is boring or difficult, when events happen that are perplexing, when others say hurtful things, the teens need help in coping. They can't see beyond the immediate trouble. They may become depressed and need professional counseling, but they can also use a kind, supportive, listening grandparent. It's often tempting to respond with, "Well, when I was your age . . ." but this is typically inappropriate. Just as they can't see forward, they have as much of a barrier in seeing backward. The past seems irrelevant. Grandparents' childhood and anything before the teens were born is ancient history. Although there are many times when grandparent histories and experiences are useful, this may not be one. Instead, when the young person is experiencing stress or depression, it may be a time for much intense and active listening. Our best strategy is to ask open-ended questions about what has happened, about their feelings, and follow with guiding questions about what they would like to have happen. We can coach them to what they can do to make things better and help them generate ideas about how to move forward. Most of all, we can remind them of our unconditional love.

Difficulty in seeing beyond the present predicament is one characteristic of psychological depression. This sense of desolation seems to prevent one from having ideas, actions, or energies that will help get to a better circumstance. A way grandparents can ensure that teenage grandchildren don't fall into the trap that can lead to depression, drug dependency, or other negative behavior patterns is to be alert to the teen's state of mind and what his/her sense of the future contains.

Perhaps one very visible evidence of the difficulty some young people have in seeing the future is their current obsession with tattoos. They don't consider whether the scrolling words or colorful designs will still be relevant and pleasing to them twenty or even five years hence. Worse, they can't imagine how the green seascape that covers the whole arm will look with the distortions and wrinkling of elderly skin. For the children described in Chapter 7 who have a preference for flexibility and options, the youthful tattoos may diminish their choices, especially at ages 40 or 60, but then, they can't imagine being so old. That's why they need us to ask pensive and farsighted questions that gently help their awareness of future consequences. Long before they consider such body art, they can benefit from our insightful conversations about allergies, professional image, and future ramifications. Although tattoos and body piercings may be a stigma for the grandparents' era, attitudes of the younger generation are quite different. While we cannot impose our biases on grandchildren, we can help them analyze and think through such permanent decisions. We'll be more effective in our subtle guidance, however, if we communicate a neutral viewpoint that's only about the young person and devoid of our own opinions.

Helping children of any age to be forward thinking and optimistic about the future is helping them to develop a growth mindset—a valuable asset. Helping them see many options, opportunities, and all that they can do is a grandparent's privilege. It's our job to be positive, supportive, and encouraging. After all, who dares predict what they can accomplish or how far they can go, especially when they have our encouragement.

A former music teacher tells the story of how valuable it can be to approach every young person with an attitude of "It's not my job to determine the child's capabilities. Rather, it's my job to expand their horizons, encourage them to go the distance, and become all they can be." She said that, in her high school chorus many years ago, there was a very shy 16-year-old girl who had a soft but clear, beautiful soprano voice. The teacher described applying this positive attitude with all of the students, but it had an especially positive effect on young Lana. By the spring of the second year, the young girl had been coached to become quite the performer and enjoyed any featured role in musical productions.

After two years, the music teacher moved to another town and pursued a different profession, rarely thinking of her days of teaching high school. Then, 20 years later in the lobby of a theater, a woman recognized the teacher of long ago and introduced herself, the young Lana from high school. Lana thanked her former teacher profusely and talked about how the teacher's gentle insistence and constant encouragement for musical practice and performance had changed her high school experience. She said the self-confidence it developed had put her on a different road in life. The music teacher expressed her delight and walked away from the encounter pleased that her philosophy of positive assumption had made a difference for, at least, one student.

The story of the music teacher is the story of every grandparent who believes in and paints a "you can do it" picture for the child's future. Although we never set them up for failure, we must not underestimate what children can accomplish, especially when we encourage their optimism and perseverance.

Guides For the Future

When working with adults, there are activities we can do to help them clarify their values, to recognize what's important to them, and how their priorities influence their lives. These priorities are often around subjects of the faith, family, vocation, and something of benefitting society or the world. Recalling our discussion in Chapters 1 and 4 about character and the culture that we want to pass on to them, we can have conversations with grandchildren about what's important to us and what might be important to them. Sometimes, we can talk about priorities and why these pursuits are the focus of our lives and energies. Through our influence, we can convey why finding meaning in life is essential.

If an older teen or college student is interested in history, especially the history of World War II, Viktor Frankl's account of surviving a Nazi concentration camp could be introduced. Frankl's famous book, *Man's Search for Meaning,* (1946, 1997) is the astounding account of a Jewish physician's determination to survive, help others, and learn something. It seems incredible that he wanted to learn something from the Holocaust, but indeed, he learned much that can be shared and about what's really important in life. He had plenty to contribute regarding how we feel about what happens around us, how we respond, and how it affects us. He emphasized the value of what we tell ourselves about what's happening and the meaning that we develop for our lives. Most of all, he emphasized the importance of knowing what's important and having a future focus, even in the midst of deplorable and discouraging circumstances.

Actions to Help Focus on the Future

In addition to figuring-out what is of value, one of the most helpful actions for being able to focus on the future is to help the child, from an early age, to prioritize and plan. A key tool in that process is goal setting. Goals can be little markers along the road to the future. In describing goals, a good practice is to "begin with the end in mind." For younger children, writing a simple small goal on the calendar can be motivating. Learning to play a specific piece of music before the end of the week could be a useful goal, but not for a recital or performance, just for the child's satisfaction and enjoyment. Begin with small but useful goals, such as building a specific Lego structure or completing a project for the science fair by Friday.

For the young child, we focus on what the child can do. We help to establish smaller objectives that can be accomplished in a short span of time that build up to a larger, more important goal. After the children understand the concept of goal setting, we can give attention to making the process timely and measurable.

There is a strong relationship between effective time management and goal setting. When we set attainable goals, we're more likely to use our time effectively. When we help a grandchild aspire to hit a certain number of golf balls at the driving range, or to play a favorite selection of music, the child will invest time in that pursuit. When they set academic goals, they will be more likely to invest their time in study and preparation.

Grandparents can help by showing how to set realistic and attainable goals that get to the ultimate aspirations over time. For example, if the teen is barely passing biology, a realistic and attainable goal would not be an A. Instead, an intermediate goal might be a C, then a B, and later, perhaps an A. Although it's possible to go straight from an F to an A, such might be over extending the optimism. A better path is to set a realistic expectation and show the child how to break the study tasks down into achievable parts focused on one realistic part of the goal at a time. Then, we can anticipate possible obstacles and how they might be overcome. All too often, the child may be overwhelmed by the size of the goal. By tying the goal to days and times, then breaking into doable objectives, with a plan for confronting any obstacles, we show the grandchild how it's possible to reach the ultimate goal.

One of my favorite questions, that really excites some people (and may frustrate others) is, "If you could have found three presents under the Christmas Tree when you were eight-years-old that could have had a life changing effect, what would the gifts have been?" When you think of your response, it's likely to be something that you want for your grandchildren. For me, one of the treasures would have been a planning and time management tool. If I had learned at age eight, what I didn't learn until mid-career, then school, life, and accomplishments would have been infinitely easier. That's why I'm passionate about showing children how focused attention, time management, goal setting, and breaking big projects into doable parts can make a profound difference. Although done on a simpler scale, it can impact, not only their accomplishments, but also their satisfaction without stress.

Some children enjoy using a chart or a white board for goals and to track progress. Whatever appeals to the child is the right tool to use. If the practice isn't adopted at first, don't worry. Try again, or choose a different format. Think about how the child likes to learn and adapt something that's appealing. Learning goal setting and tying it to time management can establish a lifetime habit that will ensure much attainment and satisfaction. We need not make the child compulsive, but rather, introduce goal setting as a tool for achieving what the child wants. Learning how to break the bigger stuff into doable parts can be a major accomplishment for any child. More important, is learning how to avoid being overwhelmed by a goal or a project.

We know that few great successes are accidents or sudden surprises. Instead, they are usually the culmination of careful planning and defining of the desired goals.

Two symptoms of susceptibility to drugs and alcohol during the teen years are a lack of friends, or the wrong friends, and a lack of goals or sense of direction. Grandparents can be a guiding beacon to help with both.

Creating a Vision for the Future

In organizations, it's productive to have a strategic plan, a long-term map to guide the future of endeavors. The plan is usually guided by a vision, a concise statement of intended future achievement. Perhaps we add a mission statement to clarify *why* the vision is worthy. Then, we generate a series of goals that reflect big accomplishments in pursuit of the vision and that are aligned with the mission. Those goals are broken down into objectives. Then, both goals and objectives are tied to a timeline. We say that the values point the direction of our vision and the actions mark our progress. Even though we may never fully reach our vision, we go farther because of the pursuit. Now, that's a concise description of vision, mission, values, and goals for organizations and adults. Although the concept is very useful in working with children, the process must be very general, and can only be fully developed over a couple of decades. Otherwise, it can be overwhelming to the child, or worse, set-up an unrealistic expectation that the child feels must be "lived-up-to."

Throughout our lives, experiences, and careers, we've defined much of our own future. We have, at least, a vaguely outlined sense of where we're going. Now, we can take time to help our grandchildren think about their futures. We can help them develop a vision for their future, but we must do it carefully, diplomatically, with much guidance, and no attempt to control or direct. We must be the facilitator, not the conductor.

We often talk about visionary leaders and visionary organizations. We know that people and groups who know what's important and where they're going are more likely to get there—to arrive at their desired destinations and successes. It's easy to find organizational values and visions hanging in corporate lobbies, on brochures, and permeating the cultures. Our grandchildren will thrive when they also have a forward looking, optimistic view of their futures but it can never be hung in the lobby or even formalized. That could easily become an expectation for the child—"something to live up to" that might become more of an impediment than an inspiration.

In the same way that organizations determine what's important in their business, what the priorities are, what they can accomplish, where they're going and why, grandchildren will thrive with the same kind of roadmap. The way that each is accomplished and how each is used, however, is vastly different.

For organizations, we develop the information through much research, discussion, strategic planning, and considering opportunities for the future. We devise a concrete, well-defined vision that, if done well, reflects the organizational culture. With children, however, developing the awareness is much less direct and takes place over a long period. As indicated earlier, children may like talking about various careers and what they might do when a grown-up, but most really dislike being asked about it. Maybe they can't think of being confined to just one job, or perhaps they're uncertain and fearful of giving the wrong answer. Nevertheless, we must encourage exploration, but with an indirect approach. The critical part for children is helping them to see that they have a future and to develop an optimism for their future.

In organizations, we can look at products, services, and customers to focus on expansions, developments, and ways the vision statement can guide the future. With children, however, it is very different as many of the jobs, careers, and activities that will engage them have not yet been invented. When young Steve Jobs was goofing around middle school in San Jose, it would have been difficult to set him on a specific career path to creating *Apple* and changing the way we view phones. When young Larry Page was a five-year-old in Montessori School, it would have been implausible to set him on a path to become one of the founders of *Google*. The best course for both would have been helping them to build character, interpersonal, academic, self-discipline, and decision making skills. They would have especially benefitted from developing the perseverance and grit to push onward through school, through the early phases of their careers and being able to handle both their mistakes and their successes. When we read accounts of their early years (Isaacson, 2014), we can see how many successful people in technology would have benefitted from insightful grandparents, especially in teaching them interpersonal and financial skills.

Even though we can't always help them create a concise vision statement, we can help them to approach the future with optimism, excitement, joy, and a sense of adventure. We can save them from any fears of the future, dread, or uncertainty of how they will cope, what they will do, or what will become of them. Grandparents can provide security for their thinking, that no matter what the circumstances, that they will find ways to cope, to pursue their ideas, and to grow.

On the last day of a session in leadership development for client organizations with future executives, I often introduce a stack of ten sheets of accordion folded paper with a horizontal line going across bottom of the long side. On the first page, participants write the year of their birth on the left of the line and the significant events of their first decade. On the next page, they write the events of their second decade, including middle school, high school, and college. The third or fourth page usually brings them up to their present decade. Then, they're looking at a three or four-page time-line containing the years of their special events. Next, I stretch out the remaining pages across the room so that they're looking at a full century, a page for each decade and a timeline up to age 100. I suggest that they sketch what they want their careers and their lives to be, adding dates, what they anticipate, or want to be significant events. They're often stunned for a few moments, then become energized as they think about and try to describe what the coming years can contain. I challenge them to keep the pages, add to them, and always be forward thinking.

I knew that I'd created something valuable with this activity when I saw Dan, one of my young clients a month after he'd been through the activity. He excitedly told me that he and his wife had rented a cabin in the mountains the previous weekend. Knowing that the weather in the area had been dreadful, I asked, "Did it storm up there?" He replied, "Yeah, but it didn't matter because we were busy with the timeline thing." He told me that his wife had done her timeline, then with a beaming smile he said, "And then, we did our marriage line together and it was REALLY interesting." He said, "Until we compared our lines, neither of us realized that we were ultimately going in different directions. That led to some serious discussion, but because of the weekend, now we're on the same line." he said with a joyful smile.

That was many years ago, but I still see Dan occasionally and always get a family photo Christmas card. He tells me about his wonderful life as vice president of a global corporation, his successes, and usually concludes with, "Yep, we're on the same line and we're on it together!" I share the story of Dan to illustrate the importance of knowing and being passionate about where we're going. It's essential to be able to see a future that's compatible with the people we love and what we love to do.

Grandparenting certainly isn't an exact science and this business of creating an optimism and sense of the future isn't easy. For helping children develop this sense of optimism and forming ideas about their futures, there's no toy, game, or blueprint to accomplish this for us. Rather, it's an on-going process of about two decades in which we plant seeds, listen, guide, coach, and pray for their future. A paper timeline can excite the thirty-something, but it may overwhelm the adolescent. The century-long timeline activity may be more effective when saved until after college. The best we can do with teens is, like Lana's music teacher, broaden their horizons, express confidence and encouragement in their explorations, and always be there to listen for their fears, doubts, and uncertainties. Grandparents can be a major force to help young people move forward with confidence and without fear.

According to Bernstein (2018), the famous Atlanta architect, John Portman (1924-2017), seemed to be obsessed with the word and concept of *entelechy.* He named his home, *Entelechy I,* and his beach house, *Entelechy II.* A term from philosophy, *entelechy is about the realization of potential.* Portman probably borrowed the term from Aristotle and used it in relation to his attempts to expand the thrust of water, shapes, and spaces in his architecture. It's a wonderful concept about how we can take everyday objects and experiences and make them into monumental opportunities to expand horizons and what can be possible. Perhaps we grandparents can use Portman's paradigm in our approach to our grandchildren and their future—helping them to realize their potential.

"Derailments" of the Perfect Grandchild

Many years ago, the head of another school and I were comparing notes of how we'd handled situations with parents of young children. "I don't know how you put up with such nonsense!" the principal of a large high school interrupted. We laughed and asked, "Well how do you deal with parents?" He said, "We don't get the kinds of problems that you have because by the time we get them, the parents have usually accepted that their kids aren't perfect so they're grateful for anything we can do to help them. When you have their little darlings, parents are still under the illusion that they're perfect!"

We laughed, but there was some accuracy in his observations. Young children do seem perfect and we want to keep them that way. We want to avoid the corruption that the world and influences that we can't control have on our perfect grandchildren. Like the high school principal observed, parents may become realistic about the occasional imperfections of teens. Conversely, we see only how wonderful they are. Perhaps that's one of the attractions for the grandchildren's eagerness to be with us. They sense that they're not judged but regarded only for their positives and the potential for always being awesome.

Although we want to see only their promise and their wonderfulness, there are times when we may be smacked by reality. When the three-year-old has a meltdown, we just stop and do an assessment of, "What's needed here? Is the child tired, hungry, fearful, frustrated, or just in need of a distraction and a reset?" The response to the first three are easy—nap, food, or reassurances—actions to fix the problem. If the child is frustrated because he/she isn't getting what is wanted, we understand, apply logical consequences, or use the opportunity for teaching self-discipline. Restoring perfection in the three-year-old is easy when we're thoughtful.

It's responding to the highly emotional teen or college student that requires more tact, patience, and diplomacy than we knew we had. When teens are arrested for DUI and possession of an illegal substance, we want to shake them and say, "What were you thinking?" The problem is that, unfortunately, they weren't thinking! Their decision making took place in the emotional part of the brain, with only consideration of the present here and now. There was little, if any, logical thinking about consequences. There was no glimmer of how such actions would affect their parents or us grandparents. In these times, we may be looking at what appears to be a young adult, but we must remember that the brain has not yet developed into adulthood.

Remember when we were teens, and we saw somebody do something stupid, we would grin, point to our heads, and slowly say, "Nobody's home!" Perhaps that was our simplistic way of expressing what we now know is that, "Due to the delayed development of his prefrontal cortex, decisions are presently being made by the emotional part of the brain, only reflecting his feelings for the here and now, due to the immaturity of this the 'executive function' for decision making." That's what we were saying, nobody was home in the rational, logical thinking part of the brain!

When There Are Problems

Ethan was an adorable little boy whose grandparents took on wonderful vacations, exposed to art, music, and a very stable culture. His parents were educated professionals who made a loving home for Ethan and his older sister. They seemed to be the perfect family with perfect children, until a call came from the high school principal notifying them of Ethan's suspension from school due to failing grades and an encounter with the police that day.

Although his parents were aware that Ethan's junior year had some academic struggles, they thought that all he needed to do was, "try harder." He had complained of the boring classes in literature and that he didn't understand the physics teacher, but the parents had no idea that Ethan had failing grades in both subjects, primarily due to class absences. It seems that Ethan's discouragement had prompted him to leave the school campus, drive downtown, and hang out with some very unsavory people. Being naive and gullible, he was the perfect target for these unscrupulous characters' manipulation. It seems that, not only had he been using marijuana, he'd been selling it to other under age students in a state where it was illegal at any age.

What were Ethan's grandparents to do? Should they blame, counsel, or support the parents? How could they even talk to Ethan? These are usually situations in which perplexed grandparents may be happy to let the parents be in charge and just stay in the background, embarrassed at having a family member who's been arrested.

Feeling like a failure in school, Ethan's unsavory companions made him feel good. His upset, stressed, beleaguered parents, however, needed support and lots of non-judgmental listening from the grandparents. They were torn between their feelings of parental failure, their anger with their son, and bewilderment in knowing how to resuscitate the teen's life.

Sitting with the parents, the grandparents were reminded of what seemed just a short time ago, when the parents were trying to deal with the child's first episode of colic. The parents had no idea of what to do, only that they wanted the infant's pain and their anxiety to go away. Like that time, there was no comfort in platitudes or cliches. The parents needed someone to listen and comfort them. Only when Ethan and his parents' emotions subsided, could grandparents be really helpful. Remembering that it's not grandparents' job to control the situation and provide answers, they were helpful in supporting and aiding in finding the right answers.

It was easy for Ethan and his parents' needs to be subdued by their own feelings of failure and embarrassment. Even though his actions were totally unacceptable, this was when he really needed family and his caring grandparents. Although during adversity, we may succumb to "what will people think?" times like these are when Rule#1, *focus on the child with unconditional love,* must kick-in as we remember our role. This is when we can help by being a role model of calm logic and positive problem solving.

We know that the most difficult things to avoid in these circumstances are verbal assaults on the erring grandchild or family members that will not be helpful and later regretted. Although we can listen, offer encouragement and moral support, we cannot become a rescuer. We must not remove the consequences of risky or careless behavior. We must not over-step the parents' role or step-in to to fix something. Most of all, we must never interfere with the parents' discipline. In private, we might ask the parents to talk about what happened, to hear their anger or concerns, but we must never negotiate on behalf of either parent or grandchild. We assist with listening, clarifying, and helping parents and child to consider the others' perspectives, but unless there is abuse, we do not interfere.

When there are serious concerns about a child's emotional state, it may be appropriate to carefully approach the parents in private about the need for professional counseling. We may need to confront an issue of specific concern, but this is a subject that requires the greatest amount of planning, preparation, and diplomacy to avoid putting the parent on the defensive. Perhaps an appropriate opening might be, "I've noticed a bit of _____ recently. Have you seen anything of concern?" Then, listen and ask leading questions to avoid being overly intrusive or instructive. Although we must never suppress our apprehensions, we can be effective in communicating them, since in most circumstances, the parents must be the ones to take any action. Sometimes, we make a difference by just quietly expressing concerns.

Although we often know what's best for our adult children and our grandchildren, just knowing isn't enough. Simply instructing and telling them what's best, what will work, or what they should do, will not be sufficient. In order to influence them, we must be persuasive and convincing. We must find ways to help them accept, discover, and use the information.

Because of our experience and cumulative knowledge, we often know what's right for the young people, but our being right is not enough. I saw my favorite illustration of this many years ago when working in California's central valley. I was driving through a major agricultural area that is totally flat and was planted with what seemed to be miles of tomatoes. About a half mile away, I could see a giant truck filled with tomatoes zooming down one of the cross roads. As we were approaching the intersection, I knew that, being on the state highway, I had the right-of-way. When I recognized that the big truck was not planning to stop, however, I slowed and let it pass in front of me. Yes, I was in the right, but I could have been dead right! As in this and so many situations, we must remember Rule #2 of grandparenting. *Just being right isn't enough. We must also be effective.* Even when we're right, when we know what's best for our family members, sometimes, we must slow down and take the time for planning, strategizing, problem solving, and determining how to be effective.

Even the most perfect grandchild will get off-track and the most conscientious parent will experience despair. That's when we must express any anger or frustration to a digging project in the backyard or explode to a trusted friend. We cannot dump our feelings on the parents who are probably already upset and filled with self-reproach. This is a time for problem solving and solace, not a time for accusations. This is our opportunity to put our own feelings aside and be there, not only for the grandchild, but also for our adult child—the parent. We listen and guide parents and grandchildren to find their own solutions. We may coach them on how they can correct a situation, fix damages, restore equilibrium, and maintain family bonds; or maybe we just let them know that we're here if they need us.

With our perspectives of maturity, we do our best to make the glitches a bump in the road that doesn't derail the whole of the grandchild's life. We encourage learning, accountability, self-discipline, and moving forward. We give our love as support through whatever the hardships.

Grandparents' Boundaries

All grandparents must have their limits and boundaries, and if we set those limits and boundaries when children are young, we won't face difficulties when our grandchildren are teens. But if the grandchildren are older and there are problems, we can sit with them, preferably in a public place where they can't easily retreat, and in a calm and logical voice say, "Look, this isn't working. We love you and will always be here for you, but you have a responsibility in this relationship too and here are the rules." Then, we can state our boundaries, but always emphasize that our love is without boundaries. It's only the behavior that must have boundaries. Repeat, replicate, reassure, and make it clear that our love is unending, but patience has limits. Because of concern for them, we will not reward inappropriate behavior. We never stop loving them, and we make that clear, but we don't encourage or reward inappropriate behavior—sex, drugs, alcohol, gambling, pornography, or people and activities that are not in their best interests. Always accentuate the love, but we don't compromise values or who we are in tolerating inappropriate behavior, or friends who are not good companions for them.

When we see grandchildren in trouble, perhaps with ugly tattoos, ghastly clothing, suddenly pregnant, and whose demeanor is unacceptable, it's tempting to erect barriers to protect ourselves from young people who seem foreign to us. Although we loved and indulged these grandchildren when they were young, we're astounded at what they have become. This is not what we intended and it's certainly not what we can tolerate, but... Even though everything within us screams, these are not my genes, we must face the reality that something has gone wrong in the grandchild's life and that the barriers that must be erected are not barriers between us, but barriers to the harm that has brought the teen to this deplorable place. Regardless of how we feel about the present, we must be a refuge, a guiding light, and a tough coach to help the child restore stability and find a better life course.

If we want to be effective in such difficult situations, even though we might *feel* indignant, we cannot demonstrate such ineffective behaviors. Instead, we can provide attentive and effective listening. Parents of a troubled youth usually experience considerable anger, frustration, with feelings of guilt and failure. Typically, the parents' own feelings can contaminate their interactions with the teen. Again, we can't solve the problem, but perhaps, we can provide the caring, perceptive attentiveness that may enable them to find their own answers.

Grandparents often withdraw from interactions with a troubled teen, not only because of their own feelings of anger or dismay, but also because of not knowing the best way to respond. Whether on a quiet walk, in a restaurant, at the kitchen table, or on a video call, we begin by listening patiently to whatever the teen will tell us about the problem. Our job is to make encouraging statements, ask probing questions, and help the teen sort out what went wrong in order to develop a better course of behavior and decision making. A few of the following may be useful to get the teen to talk and keep the conversation going, but with care to avoid putting the teen on the defensive.

"Think back to when things first went off the rails, what was happening?"

"Think about what was happening when you made the first decision that didn't work the way you wanted. What was happening around you?"

"How did ______ interfere with what you wanted?"

"What do you think your parents didn't understand?"

"If it worked out the way you wanted, what would be different? . . . better?"

"What are some things you might do differently next time?"

"Talk about what the rewards might be of making it different or better. "

"Describe what the reward would be for you to get that."

"What kind of help would you need to get what you want?" How can I help you get what you want?"

"Can you think of some better ways to get what you want?"

That last question seems to be at the core of many dysfunctional people's issue. *They have limited means or few ideas about how to get what they want.* Relying on the emotional part of the brain and what may have worked for them in the past, they seem to have meager ways of problem solving to meet their needs. Our contribution can be in helping the teen to avoid such a predicament. We can help them see beyond the problem, to take responsibility, improve his/her situation, and find more acceptable ways of getting what the young person wants. Although we certainly can't excuse any legal or moral mistake, our best role is to be a source of encouragement and support that can restore the adolescent's equilibrium and show the precious grandchild how to return to the road to success.

Teens often take parents for granted, but regard for grandparents may be different. Although we don't want to teach them to focus only on pleasing us, perhaps in a pinch, we can use their regard as collateral for avoiding risky behavior. Recalling J.D. Vance's story in *Hillbilly Elegy* mentioned in Chapter 10, it was his respect for his grandmother, and knowledge of how much she loved him, that motivated his academic achievement, keeping him on a path that led to a law degree from Yale University.

Even though we seek and treasure grandchildren's love we can never allow our desire for their love and respect to become a barrier to doing what's right for them. We must focus on the grandchild's needs, even when boundaries are required. We must remember Rule #1, and regardless of our needs, focus on their needs. When their actions are unacceptable, we can be disapproving of the behavior, but we must be always unconditional in expressing our love.

A Better Perspective for Teens

The Performance Review is a common practice in today's business organizations. This is a formal, often numerical, evaluation of an employee's work for the past quarter or past year. It's often dreaded by both the supervisor and employee as it becomes a critique of everything from attire to emails, and can be impacted by rater bias. The worst part is that all of this focus on the past is usually about the negatives. But even when only a small portion is negative, that's the part the person remembers and what often becomes the prominence that obliterates any positives.

Unless dealing with a derelict employee, I'm a big proponent of a *Performance* ***Pre****view* in which the focus is on future performance, on learning about new projects, new behavior, new challenges, and increased productivity. It puts more responsibility on the employee. It's much easier and more effective to paint an inspiring picture of possibilities, than to sit in judgement. Past mistakes can be addressed in terms of how they can be eliminated and not be a deterrent to the future. The intent is that the employee leaves the session with a clear focus of the future expectations, along with the energy and enthusiasm for higher performance and loyalty to the organization.

When grandchildren are derailed, their parents have probably given them a stern review of their lack of acceptable performance. The opportunity for us grandparents is to conduct the *Performance* ***Pre****view,* to help them focus on a better standard with energy and enthusiasm. We can help them feel our quiet support and see beyond present difficulties. We can help them with problem solving and finding better ways to get what they want. Even when grandchildren lose direction, even when they do things of which we disapprove, even when they seem not to need us—they need us. We can be there for them to listen, to support their parents, and help them re-find their future. A few of the following may be idea starters for a *Performance Preview.*

"Talk about some things that are working well for you." (Add some positive observations.)

"Describe some of the high points during the past few weeks or months."

If appropriate, say nothing negative, but just talk about the good stuff and be affirming wherever possible."

"These are some areas I've observed that are recent positives." (Describe some happy moments and appropriate actions.)

"What are some actions to prevent any past difficulties?"

"Name three areas that you can focus on that will make things go better for you."

"As you look at your current priorities, the things of immediate importance, what are the ones that seem scary or most difficult?"

"Talk about what you need to keep your focus, energy, and activities on what you want to accomplish."

"These are my observations of areas that would help your success."

"How do you feel about what I've said?"

"How can I help, support, and encourage your positive performance? What do you need from me that will help you accomplish what you want?"

Don't agree to anything unproductive for the grandchild or the grandparent. Then, conclude with the following:

"You will always have my love. You'll have my support, as you're working hard to reach the goal of ____. But allow me to remind you not to do anything that is a violation of your agreement with your parents or that will disappoint *you* two months from now."

Such leading questions and discussion of positives can spark optimism in the young person and help to overcome feelings of embarrassment, hopelessness, and depression. It's essential to end any such discussion with reassurances and a hug, if the young person is comfortable with physical contact and if geography and social distance permit.

Imperfect Decisions

Several years ago, I facilitated an executive conference that began with a day of presentations by five division presidents of a large corporation. It was concluded with a fancy dinner in a very formal resort dining room. After hours of listening to each other boast about achievements, accomplishments, and astounding financial performance earlier that day, the organization's CEO broke the ice at dinner with an elfish grin. He said, "Well, I've certainly heard about some brilliant decisions, now talk about the worst decision you've made." The silence and startled look on the executives' faces told me that they needed a fast rescue. I quickly clarified, "We've all been teenagers, so it's certain that we've all made some really bad choices and done some really dumb stunts, so maybe we can admit—just to see how far everyone has come." By first focusing on adolescence, everyone could be genuine in their confessions, admitting everything from wrecking the family car to playing leap frog over parking meters—and missing. After some laughter and showing a bit of vulnerability, they were able to share business missteps and ways they had learned to make better decisions.

It seems impossible to get through the teen years without some stupidity. Perhaps we grandparents can be there to ensure more effective decisions and better recovery for our grandchildren. We can be the beacon that helps them navigate growing-up, especially through the challenging teen years. Grandparenting isn't easy, but it can always be a valuable influence, creating memories that make a difference.

Summary

Perhaps we place too much emphasis on *higher education* and not enough focus on *lifetime learning*. When too many young people attain college degrees, yet seem to have less knowledge, fewer skills, but more student debt, it's time to reassess our practices. We must do what we can to supplement grandchildren's learning opportunities. Helping them adapt to changing circumstances is aiding their ability to deal with the evolving world in which they may live.

Career sampling and exploring is important during childhood, but one of the realities of which we must be cognizant is that the careers that our grandchildren may ultimately pursue may not even exist today. With our rapidly changing world and economy, instead of helping grandchildren choose just one interest or one job, we will better equip them for their futures if we help them learn to adapt and reinvent their careers as conditions change. Even when their interests don't seem logical, we must not discourage them or disregard their ideas. Instead, we can show interest in their dreams and aspirations. We can communicate support and encouragement for their abilities to create their own future.

By helping our grandchildren recognize priorities, develop goals, and what's important in their lives, we pave their paths to the future. Perhaps Thomas Jefferson expressed it best in a letter to John Adams when he wrote, "I believe in the dreams of the future more than in the history of the past."

When we help grandchildren create a vision of their future, even though it's very fluid, we teach them not to fear the future but to look forward with optimism. When we help them explore their potential, we're helping them think about something vital. With our help and support to extend their horizons, explore their talents, and develop their potential, we remove barriers and enable our beloved grandchildren to *entelechy*.

Chapter 12

Splendid Results

As we live hopefully into the future.

Let's return to one of our first questions in Chapter 1. *What do we want the grandchildren to remember about us?* Now that we've talked about personalities, addiction, toy shelves, backyard adventures, and all the rest; what kind of influence do we want all of our efforts to have on the grandchildren? What do we hope they'll remember? Is it the love, the relationship, the indulgences, the learning—or all of it?

We'll recall with a smile the details of the four-year-old's Valentine making, the picnics, the birthdays, parties, the chocolate parties, the afternoons of reading and talking via technology or in the porch swing, We'll savor the special graduations, and job and career celebrations. Perhaps we want the grandchildren to recall such pleasant times with happy memories. Maybe what we really want each precious child to remember is the cumulative effect of all of the gifts, occasions, and interactions. Most of all, we want the result to be a stable, happy, successful young adult who remembers us fondly.

Yes, when they're adults, we hope they'll remember and appreciate all of our efforts, sacrifices, and devotion. When they're older, we hope they'll recognize that we happily spent money on them instead of on ourselves. We hope they'll realize that we bought dolls, Legos, and learning experiences instead of new tools or clothes for ourselves. We want them to recognize that we chose trips to Disney with them, instead of a glamorous trip to the mountains or Venice for us. With maturity, we trust that the gratitude they will have for our investments in them will be an example that they'll use for our great-grandchildren and our great-great-grandchildren. We secretly want respect, recognition, and appreciation for our love and devotion, but we accept that it's a matter of delayed gratification. For now, we'll just accept the hugs, Grandparents Day cards, and hope that Hallmark sustains their Grandparents Day invention through the digital conversion from paper cards.

We want the grandchildren's memories, and ours, to make smiles and fond recollections. But more than just remembering, we want to make a difference in every day of their lives. We want to be an ancillary to all the things that they learn from their parents and all of the other experiences provided for them. Even if we must arrange it via mail, phone, or some form of technology, we want to be there to provide the "icing on their cake," the piano lessons, and that extra hug that builds their self-confidence and helps them to persevere. We want their lives to be better because we were there for them.

In the first chapter, I confessed that the metaphor I'd used for this book was an imaginary conversation with you regarding what I've learned about grandparenting and my eagerness to share how we can be highly influential in making our grandchildren's lives exemplary. Together, we've considered how we want them to be happy, healthy, stable people of good character who make a contribution to society. We've looked at how we can give grandchildren important advantages as they grow. We want them to know the joys of discovery, creativity, and the love of learning. We've discussed how we want them to have the benefits of all that we missed and to miss every mistake that we made. We give thanks for them and pray that they receive the many blessings of this life.

What We Want From Being a Grandparent

As we invest considerable time, effort, and money in these young people, it's natural to expect a return on our investment. Even though children naturally relate to the present, perhaps we're more thoughtful of the future implications of our investments. We think about what the advantage of being able to play golf will mean for the future business executive. We contemplate how the math tutor will improve the college admissions test. We know the future joys that art and music classes will bring to the child. As in parenting, we give with few expectations of reciprocity. We nurture them for the sheer pleasure of helping, sharing, and giving. We just want to love and cherish the grandchildren.

We quickly realize, however, that the way we show our affection and the way we go about nurturing our relations with them has a profound effect on the quality of our relationship and on how we are perceived. Mary, who is in college now, said she didn't realize how perceptive her grandfather was until one evening when she was fifteen and at a sleepover with three friends. She said that they were intrigued by the TV advertisement of a local Japanese restaurant and its chef who made little volcanos from onion rings and did all sorts of entertaining tricks at the grill. She told of calling her grandfather and asking if he would come get her friends and her to take them to the restaurant. She told him that she'd call him when they finished to return for them. Mary said that he listened, then responded, "I'll come and take your friends and you to the restaurant, but coming back home, then back to the restaurant is too much driving. How about I sit down at the other end, have dinner, read my newspaper, and take you back to your friend's house when you're ready, and oh yes, how about I pay for the check?" Mary said she responded with, "Grandfather, I think that's a deal I can sell!" Clearly, Mary's grandfather practiced Rule #1. He didn't need to be the center of attention. He recognized that his presence would ensure their safety, but that his distance didn't interfere with the teenage girls' fun.

Ellie's story is quite different. She talked about how much she loved her grandfather and said he was very good to her, but that she never wanted to be with him around any of her friends. She said that he always had to be the center of attention. Ellie said that her grandfather was very proud of a big picture in his senior high school yearbook entitled "Most Handsome" where he was surrounded by a group of girls. Ellie said, "He got too used to being cute and thought he still was." Even though we may prefer our youthful image and not see ourselves as old, wrinkled, and bald, perhaps teenagers prefer to see us as kind, wise, and supportive. Realism demands that if we are to be effective with grandchildren, we must know how to relate to them—not trying to make it about us.

We must think about what we ultimately want from being a grandparent, whether it's to be a source of love and support or the self-delusional selfish source of more fans. When adults really think about it, we take the right approach, but too often without thought, we forget Rule #1 and just do what we did as adolescents—what feels good.

Perhaps what we secretly want is to be regarded warmly, but a colleague told me a story recently that best describes what we all seek and how to get it. She told about going to a concert and seeing a friend who was there with her two granddaughters who were visiting from another state. She joined them and sat beside the seven-year-old. The little girl was thumbing through the program before the event began, when suddenly she sat up, pointed to a little 1 x 1 inch photograph of her grandfather who was featured as a symphony board member and exclaimed, "That's Papa!" My colleague smiled and said, "Yes, it is." Then, the little girl asked, "Do you know my Papa?" My friend smiled and nodded. That's when the child said loudly, and with great emotion, "Isn't he the greatest man ever?" Now, her papa is a very accomplished man—perhaps not of the rank of Washington, Lincoln, or J.S. Bach,—but to his granddaughter, he is—he is a great man!

Now, the story probably describes how all of us want to be regarded—a person of stature to our grandchildren. My colleague tells me that Papa didn't get that esteem because of the recognition that got his photo in the event program, but rather, because of the focus that he gives, the time he invests, and the relationship she's heard about that he has with his granddaughters.

It may be easier for us to think about what we want from the relationship with our grandchildren than to think about all that we want them to achieve from knowing us. For us, it's probably rather simple. We just want to be respected, appreciated, and the chance to watch the young ones grow and flourish.

What We Will Achieve

With such dedication and eagerness for being a superb grandparent, it's unfortunate that there isn't a course of study and some sort of certification to accompany the first grandchild's arrival. I must confess that there's much in this conversation that I wish I had known before... Perhaps my learning will enrich your grandparenting. Certainly, my most important learning is that to ensure the grandchildren's thriving, we grandparents must grow and develop with them.

We've identified what we want to achieve for ourselves, but exactly what do we want this immense investment in time, love, and money to accomplish for the grandchildren? As we've considered the imperative role and opportunity that grandparents have, we've become aware that our grandchildren face challenges that we didn't know. We realize how the impact of technology, changes in social morés, and the onslaught of negative influences present problems for this generation. Although our parents may have carried memories of World Wars, and while fears of the Cold War may have been prevalent in our childhoods, we never had to fear for our lives in just going to school or to the grocery store. We probably didn't worry about gangs, guns in schools, illegal drugs on the corner, or a little invisible microbe called Covid. We may have negotiated with our parents for more TV or phone time, but we had no opportunity to carry them in our pockets. We have only to think of a few of the differences in the world of our youth and our grandchildren's worlds and we quickly become aware of their divergent needs.

Of course, we must encourage proper nutrition, lots of exercise, outdoor play, and appreciation of nature, but we can also supplement experiences that they get at home and at school with opportunities for creativity, discovery, and learning. Along with occasional treats and indulgences, we can supply support and encouragement. Most of all, we can be there to listen to their triumphs and to their problems. We give words to the toddler to develop language and expression of emotions. We give ideas throughout childhood and adolescence to help solve problems and navigate their widening social world. Most of all, we can listen, help them understand who they are and how very much they are loved.

When we grandparents perform effectively, we contribute to ensuring that our descendants, these wonderful grandchildren, will have the foundation for future success—of knowing whom they are, where they are going, and a safe and happy path of integrity to get there.

Physical Health

Our first priority for a long and rewarding life for the grandchildren is to nurture and protect their health. We began that when we diplomatically gave the young mother the latest research on the importance of pre-natal vitamins and avoiding drugs and alcohol. We continued as we emphasized excellent nutrition for the child. We tried to be a role model as we practiced portion control, avoided fatty fast foods, and maintained a healthy weight—or talked about their need for better choices than we'd made.

If we've been consistent in our teaching the importance of wearing a seat belt, bicycle helmet, and taking proper precautions in every sport, we've helped to establish a pattern of safety. We grandparents are also eager to protect our young ones from severe injuries that might be treated with pain medications and ultimately lead to addiction.

If we've been a good role model, and made physical activity and exercise a habit, it's easier to encourage grandchildren's exercise, especially during adolescence. Introducing or encouraging individual sports, not only decreases exposure to head injuries, activities such as track, golf, biking, and tennis may be more attractive when the child becomes an adult. These sports are easier to carry into lifetime fitness than football, gymnastics, or wrestling. Regardless of the means, we know the critical importance of physical movement to humans at every age and make every attempt for exercise to be attractive and sustainable.

One lesson that I learned about the child's health was to *first eliminate any possible physical cause before assuming an emotional problem.* My daughter taught me that when she was about ten and I became frustrated with her irritability. To divert her crummy attitude and attempt to bribe her into a better mood, I took her shopping. Unfortunately, all I did was change the setting of her irritability. Finally, in the middle of her favorite craft shop, I said, "You seem to be constantly upset. Is something wrong? Do you feel okay? How about we just leave the store and go to the doctor?" I thought the mere suggestion would improve her attitude. But she quickly replied, "That's a good idea." With that alert, we drove straight to the pediatrician's office, and in those days, were able to see him almost immediately. As he looked into her nose, throat, and ears, he asked, "What's the problem?" I said, "She's just so irritable." He calmly replied, "Yeah, not being able to hear and breathe will cause irritability." She had an upper respiratory infection. Because she had no obvious physical symptoms, I'd focused only on her irritable demeanor. Instead, I could have been more observant, asked a few probing questions, and paid attention to her physical state. Lesson learned for me!

Mental Health

We know that positive interpersonal interactions are a bit like exercise for us humans. In order to be healthy, every day we have a renewed need for the optimal amount of both. If the child is isolated, doesn't fit-in with the peer group, or has any other reason to feel alone, the relationship with us grandparents becomes even more essential. To maintain good emotional health, children really benefit from having a caring adult who will listen to their issues and support their problem solving.

When they are infants, their only means of expressing pain, hunger, or discomfort is to cry. When we focus only on the irritating wailing, and not on the cause of the crying, we cause stress for the infant and for us. One of our major contributions to baby's development can be giving words and a means of expression to replace the crying. Too often, young children don't know what to do with their feelings. They don't know how to express their sadness or anxiety. Our important contribution is to listen, clarify, and help them to verbalize their concerns. We can help them understand why they have the feeling that they may not completely understand. When we do that, they experience empathy and learn vital ways of dealing with emotions that will be useful throughout life.

Perhaps our greatest contribution to the grandchildren's mental health is in teaching them how to control their thoughts and practice good brain health. Helping them learn how to create their own "feel goods," and avoid the temptations of nicotine, alcohol, and illegal drugs ensures their brain health and inoculates them from the disease of addiction. Giving them positive and realistic phrases for self-talk ensures the flourishing of mental health and aids in avoiding childhood and adolescent depression.

Self-Confidence

Whether we call it self-confidence, self-esteem, or self-worth, it is an essential sense of identity that may be described as "knowing who I am, having a realistic estimation of what I *can* do, and what I *can't* do well." This kind of pragmatic, viable confidence gives young people an ability to trust in their skills, abilities, and judgements. It's a self-knowledge that's invaluable in helping to pursue so many situations. It is also protective information. Knowing what I *can't* do easily, those areas in my "Skills Zone," keeps me from recklessly launching into situations that are "over my head." Although it doesn't prevent me from pursuing tough assignments, it alerts me that I may need more effort, energy, and cleverness to succeed.

When we consider troubled teens, it quickly becomes clear that their poor decision making is rooted in a lack of character and/or self-knowledge. They have little real estimation of what they can do/cannot do well in school, relationships, or the future. The unfortunate result is a severe lack of confidence or an inflated pretense of invulnerability.

The gift of genuine self-knowledge is empowering. When people have real self-confidence, they don't appear to be egotistical, or passively withdrawn. They have a sense of humility that is neither rooted in an underestimation of their capabilities nor rooted out by a big ego in need of impressing others with their greatness. Instead, they project an image of genuineness and credibility. Theirs is not the pride described in Proverbs 16:18. Rather, it's a realistic estimation of abilities, and skills. The usable sense of self enables people to put themselves into situations where they are most likely to succeed.

This very desirable kind of self-knowledge doesn't restrict learning or inhibit relationships. Instead, the confidence creates a person who is very real. Whereas, an inflated ego is the result of a fear of failure and inadequacy. This big ego is needed to conceal shortcomings. The "inflation" is an attempt to hide the fears and deficits behind a facade, a fake image behind which to take cover. There is little openness to new information or experiences. The gate is closed! According to Jung, this inflated ego becomes a barrier to new information, learning, and effective interpersonal relations. (Thompson, pp. 389-391).

Unfortunately, an inflated ego tries to impress everyone with importance, but people with real self-confidence don't need to hide behind an inflated ego. Rather, they have a true sense of self. They put themselves into situations that may challenge and stretch their talents, but usually enable them to succeed because they have perseverance. They know what to do when they encounter barriers and how to overcome them. They know who they are and what they can do—as well as what they don't do well and where they need help or a different approach. They believe in their skills, abilities, and their capacity to continue to learn. They have self-awareness. It is impossible to sustain the level of success that we so desire for our grandchildren without this very realistic and accurate sense of self-confidence.

This self-knowledge and self-confidence, combined with perseverance, empowers the young person's potential for success. As indicated earlier, one of the typical characteristics of troubled youth, many criminals, and dysfunctional people is that they have constricted ways of getting what they want. Whereas, our self-confident grandchildren will have profuse means of attaining their goals. They will learn that, when they seem to bump into a brick wall in their pursuits, they will have the confidence to simply analyze the situation and attempt a different approach.

Self-confidence will also be a tremendous resource as they encounter difficult people who present barriers. The combination of perseverance, along with their polished interpersonal skills will enable them to succeed, even with the most obnoxious people. They will recall the manners that we have taught them, and how hard it is for others to remain angry or uncooperative with someone who is very polite, smiling, and pleasant. They will remember how we've taught them to be *pleasantly persistent* in overcoming barriers. Their confidence, gumption, and pleasant demeanor will go far in propelling their success at whatever their tasks.

Many of the experiences that we give them, from music lessons to encouraging their participation in speech and debate activities, can add to their self-confidence. It's very useful for every child to have some skill, hobby, or interest that differentiates the child and gives a base confidence for feeling distinguished. That's why we support their various interests, because it's impossible to know today what will give them a special edge in life.

Independence and Self-Reliance

We endeavor to ensure that the self-knowledge and confidence we encourage results in resilient and independent young people. Unfortunately, for some, a school or social difficulty during adolescence spawns a lack of self-worth and creates an inapt family dependence.

A term taken from rockets that fail to fly into space as designed, the common phrase used to describe adult children who continue to be dependent and live with their parents is often referred to as a "failure to launch." This continued family reliance often results in under-employment and underachievement. Rather than seeking their own way in the world, these young people cling to the familiar warmth of the family dependence they've known. With each succeeding year and each lack of success, life becomes more difficult for them as they continue to underperform due to their lack of gumption, self-reliance, self-confidence and belief in their ability to be independent.

Grandparents can be added insurance against such "failure to launch." We begin very early as we ensure that the child experiences success in folding clothes, helping in the kitchen, learning to read, and gaining independence in the small things. When the child has trouble in school, we're there to assist and encourage. When distance or subject difficulty makes it impossible for us to help with school work, we locate on-line help, or find it in our budgets to pay for a tutor. Again, we support and encourage the grandchildren through the struggles, but we are not so overly indulgent that we contribute to dependence. We help them understand that, although not every attempt can be successful, there's a sense of reward in just continuing the effort toward worthy pursuits. We guide their struggles toward the goal. We urge accountability when they falter. And when they attain some successes, we're there to applaud their endeavors and independence.

From the days that we were assembling big wooden puzzles with them, to the times of learning to ride a bicycle or figuring-out the complex Lego sets, we helped the child persevere and feel successful. What we've enabled the child to realize is that when something has meaning for us, we pursue it. When we love playing the violin, practice isn't unpleasant because we love the music and we love learning the musical skill. When we enjoy the stimulation and inspiration of great literature, reading isn't a chore. Perseverance isn't arduous when we love the pursuit.

Finding the grit, however, for tasks that we don't enjoy is not so easy. That's when we remember what we observed from the discussion of the *Comfort Zone* and we help the child to look at his/her successes and the things that come easily. Then, we talk about how the task is *not* an area of ease and will require more energy, more concentration, and more cleverness to complete. We never instruct the child to just, "Try harder!" Instead, we look at what the impediments might be, we show the child how to go around the barriers, and express support that the child can do it. From the toddler stage, we begin equipping the children for independence and self-reliance. We help them learn to believe in themselves, in their character, and their ability to succeed. Although we want to be a resource for them, a place they can talk through their problems, or think about the feedback that we may have given them, we never want to be overly prominent in their decision making. Even though we're there for them as they grow and when they struggle in school or have problems on the job, what we want most is for them to be accountable for their performance and take charge of their education and their careers.

The Lesson from Copernicus

A Renaissance era mathematician and astronomer postulated that the universe doesn't revolve around the earth, as had been assumed for centuries. Just as

Copernicus recognized that not everything revolves around us, but that there's a whole universe out there, we are challenged to teach the same lesson to our fabulous grandchildren.

If we grandparents are retired, indulgent, and very devoted to and focused on our grandchildren, it's easy for us to foster their belief that much of their world revolves around them. Early in our discussion, I admitted that my grandson is the light of my life, but my daughter's practical and grounded insistence has always provided a Copernican lesson. She has prevented my falling into the trap of creating an "entitled" grandson. She has been there to sometimes restrain my enthusiasm and excesses. In our delight and devotion, it's quite easy for us grandparents to become manipulated and taken for granted by our wonderful grandchildren. And yet, we're not doing them any favors when we enable them to be dependent or become less than their capabilities. We're not helping or nurturing their growth to become wonderful adults when we lead them to believe that they're the center of the universe (even when they are the center of our universe).

Just as it's important for us to teach grandchildren the Copernican lesson that not everything revolves around them, that's also a good lesson for us grandparents. Too often, I hear elderly people complain that their grandchildren are so busy with soccer, tutors, and school work that they don't have any time for the grandparents. Yet, when I listen to these people, I quickly realize that the problem may not be with the grandchildren's busy schedules. These elderly adults don't engage and interact with others. They just talk! Cindy brags about all of her grandchildren's accomplishments, but then, she talks incessantly about her activities, her opinions, and her aches and pains, to anyone who'll listen. Jason is a retired truck driver who is intelligent and can regale listeners with a lifetime of interesting stories, but that's all he does. He expresses no interest in others. Cindy and Jason are just two examples of people who have somehow become self-centered and self-absorbed in their old age. They've forgotten how to respect, relate to, and engage others. It's not surprising that they have no real interactions or connections with their grandchildren—depriving the children and themselves of what could be wonderful and stimulating relationships.

Often, I hear retired people lament their boredom and lack of challenge. Especially when limitations preclude extensive physical work or activities, many older people need and want to be useful and positively engaged in other ways. We gain from opportunities to be useful. Ultimately, we bring benefit to ourselves as we engage with and give to others. Whether volunteering to read to children at the library, to assist with children's activities at church, or to mentor young people anywhere we find them; building relationships with children can be as useful for us as it is beneficial to the young people. We must never miss a chance to help others as we help ourselves. We soon recognize that it is much more invigorating to be focused on others, than to be self-focused.

When we become the center of our world, not only can we become lonely, but we can miss colossal opportunities to benefit our grandchildren and others because they don't really know us.

Making That Difference

Throughout our discussion of this future generation, we've reflected on earlier generations. We've looked at concerns and chores that occupied our grandparents and great-grandparent's time and attention and compared it with our lifetimes. We've seen that the tasks and endeavors that occupied much of our grandparents' lives have been of little concern for us. Yet, we look at the gifts they gave us with their love, time, attention and guidance. We want that and much more for our grandchildren.

One dimension that hasn't changed over the many years is the importance of just being there for the grandchildren. At every age, when life gets tough, it's nice to know that somebody loves you and is there for you. My grandparents had a welcoming smile when I visited in the afternoons after school. They were always there to listen to my problems, take me on adventures, and supply an occasional treat. Although I had loving, attentive parents, my grandparents were an additional blessing. It was such an advantage to know that they were always there for me, were interested in me, listened to my stories, and always supplied encouragement. They made a critical difference in my life. Today, we offer more nutritious treats than my grandmother's warm biscuits with honey and her homemade butter, but we still offer the same support and comfort.

To be effective in being there for our grandchildren, we must understand something of their world, their fears, problems, accomplishments, and opportunities. We don't need to be adept at computer coding to relate to their use of technology, but we can learn enough to know the difference between the web and the internet. And even if everything seems too complicated for our doddering brains, we can demonstrate an attitude of openness to their world of emerging technologies. We can show interest and the same eagerness for learning that we want them to have.

We're aware of the deleterious effects of excessive fears, stress, and adversity on the growing brain. We're aware of the importance of nutrition, health, and freedom from disease. Even if we must not fix every problem for the child, and even if we can't completely remove causes of stress, we can teach the child coping skills to diminish the damage of stress. *Into the Magic Shop* (2017), is Dr. James Doty's autobiographical account of how the chance encounter with a kind older lady engaged him with snacks and helped him discover the "magic" of focused attention. Then, she taught the young boy the value of mindfulness and to concentrate on his goals. The result was his learning skills that lifted this child of poverty and addicted parents to a new life of becoming a wealthy neurosurgeon. An inspiring account of how one caring person can change the world for a child, this story also illustrates the importance of gaining the coping deftness to become resilient.

As I approach the end of my sharing, I reflect on the critical importance of our relationship with each grandchild, our facilitating their learning life skills, and the immense opportunities that we have to nurture, coach, support, and inspire the young people around us. The elderly lady in the *Magic Shop* probably never knew of the impact that she had on the young boy's life, but the successful adult neurosurgeon never forgot her or the influence of what she taught him. The story is very thought provoking and causes us to focus on the effects of what the special children in our lives are learning from us. It also prompts us to concentrate on what else we can do, other ways we can foster learning, and how we can extend our influence. Most especially, it makes us aware of the opportunity to be a caring guide, not only for our grandchildren, but any needy young person that we encounter. Even our smallest actions of concern and encouragement can have meaning and motivation far beyond our time or knowledge.

Preparation for Great-Grandchildren

A culmination of our nurturing, encouraging, coaching, and all the rest, is helping the younger generation to develop positive relationships. We want to give them the skills for interpersonal relations in the workplace and the knowledge of how to develop genuine friendships. Most of all, we want them to learn how to build their own family relationships. We want them to know themselves and what's important to them. We want them to find a significant other who has similar values, priorities, and who will be a solid mate as they begin a new family and another generation. If we've succeeded at helping them to acquire life skills, such as time and financial management; and if we've facilitated an insightful EQ, we've given them a head start in life. When they've learned to manage their self-talk and to make their own "feel goods" they will have escaped the dangers of addiction. When they've learned to get what they want, without encroaching on others, and when they've learned to communicate and manage conflict, they will have major assets for success in life.

We will have taught them the importance of social and relationship skills. They will know how to conduct themselves at the swimming pool, at church, and in the executive board room. They will have impeccable table manners and conversation skills that are engaging and put everyone at ease. They will appreciate the importance of family dinners and traditions that we've taught them to continue with the next generation.

Of course, we want them to find a mate as wonderful as they are and to have a happy marriage that can become the anchor for our great-grandchildren. In order to eliminate threats to our grandchildren's marriage, we inoculate them against the most common marriage problems that often begin with a lack of self-knowledge and EQ. Differences in values and goals can then lead the partners in opposite directions, and possibly, into money issues. Lack of communication skills results in conflict and a loss of interest in each other, followed by a lack of intimacy and romance. Then, the marriage falls apart and there is no foundation for parenting.

As we review what we've been trying to teach the grandchildren through the years, just to ensure that they become good people, we realize that we're paving the road to their success in marriage relationships. John Gottman's (2019) research at the University of Washington indicated that problem relationships are characterized by criticism, defensiveness, contempt, and stonewalling. With these characteristics dominating the relationship, there are limited means of resolving conflict. As we review the nurturing and relationship building that we're doing with our grandchildren, we recognize that we're teaching them how to interact without these negative forces. When we look at Gottman's structure for a healthy marriage, we see that we're equipping these young people to become great marriage partners and excellent parents. They will have strong marriage bonds and will nurture the succeeding generations.

We will have taught them to understand and value their family culture, but culture isn't just a matter of ethnicity or a nationality. Perhaps, by sharing our observations or experiences as the child is growing-up, we can make the young person aware of the importance of our own culture. For example, my grandparents had introduced me to a love of nature and the outdoors. I had also grown-up in a culture where the extended family enjoyed movies, holidays, picnics, swimming parties, and family celebrations. By the time that I was an adult, my grandparents had passed away, and like too many young people, I wasn't always receptive to my parents' guidance. Concomitantly, when my husband and I were dating, I failed to notice that he didn't invite me to go to movies, parties, or typical dating activities of the 1960's. Instead, we would get a burger and go to the university music practice facility where I would listen patiently to his performance. At the time, I was so intrigued with his talent and expertise that I didn't notice when he declined to be included in my family activities or to invite me to his family occasions. I didn't like his friends, and he resented my friends. That he didn't fit into my world, nor I into his, didn't seem important at the time, but after we were married a few years, the lack of cultural fit became evident. I began to miss the outdoors, picnics, the summer swims, and family occasions in which he didn't want me to participate. As the years progressed, I became disillusioned with his self-absorption and he resented my loss of focus just on him. If only I could have connected the dating activity and his center of attention, it could have been illuminating and informing for both of us. As indicated earlier, devoted love, common values, and culture can provide the foundation for a happy long-term relationship. Whereas, a deficit can result in alienation, despite the romance.

As we grandparents have emphasized the importance of character and having guiding values, we've given the young people a greater understanding of themselves and others. Common culture and values can greatly enhance conflict resolution—whether among nations or family members. As we watch our grandchildren search for lifetime relationships, the cultural understanding that we've given them can support their choices and provide a strong family foundation for our great-grandchildren. We can help them understand what is important to them and what will become important in their adult lives.

When appropriate, at carefully chosen times and in strategically planned settings, we can plant a few ideas and thought provoking questions. With young adults who are considering a lifetime commitment, the following questions give some cues, some ideas for "planting seeds" for thought. They raise critical issues that romance might obliterate. Over time, and without putting the young adult on the defensive, some of these possibilities may be useful.

"Romance is so exciting and captivating. Being in a romantic relationship can make an exhilarating here and now. Talk about how you see your future ?"

"I know that you find this person very captivating today. Are you finding indicators that this is a person who will learn, grow and love you with as much devotion as your family does?"

You're intelligent and curious. Are you're finding signs that this is someone who has your same intellectual capacity and will be able to challenge your intellect in the future."

"Do you have compatible goals?
Will it be a reciprocal relationship?"

"Tell me about his/her family. You must feel comfortable and enjoy celebrating holidays and special occasions with them. Do they like having you around."

"How will this person fit into our family?"

"Just now, you're focused on romantic interests, but if you're thinking of marriage, you're also choosing a set of grandparents for your children. Are these people you want to influence your children?"

"Whether choosing a partner for business or for life, we know that successful partnerships are based on similar values. Does this person share your governing values? Is most of what you value in life similar to his/her priorities?

"It's difficult to look beyond the romance just now, but to enjoy a compatible life together, the cultural likenesses and differences become critical to enjoying a stable married life that is never threatened by stress or divorce."

"At times, we find security and convenience in a relationship for the present. They're pleasant and enjoyable, but not for the long-term, but that's okay when both of you recognize that it's just for now."

"It's probably hard for you to think about it now, but there's a big difference between infatuation and love that endures a lifetime. As your relationship with this person grows, if this is the right person for you, the infatuation will morph into lifetime love."

"Thanks for allowing me to ask these questions. The answers are not for me, only 'think-abouts' for you. My concern is for a lifetime of happiness for you and for your children. I will love whoever loves you and makes you happy."

That last statement is especially important in helping to avoid any defensiveness and only conveying loving concern. These are seed planting questions and statements, but not for just one conversation. Don't expect agreement, or even a response. Some of these questions will be most effective if inserted into conversations over a period of time. If they make the young person uncomfortable, back-off and save some for future seed planting opportunities. As parents of adult children or grandchildren, our job is not to approve or disapprove, but with some clever diplomacy, we can facilitate a bit of analytical thinking to enhance choices and give information for exploration. The essential task is to plant the seeds, facilitate a good outcome, but not to make the decision. Still, if we want our heirs to have the benefit of a stable home life, one of the most important issues we can carefully address is that of shared values. That's why, in Chapter 4, we stress the importance of developing values beginning in early childhood, and later, helping teens to clarify them.

The seeds that we've planted will grow beyond our days. Our children and grandchildren will become terrific parents and will build strong family bonds, remembering all that we've taught them. And if we've been successful with our introduction to faith in God, our great-grandchildren will grow-up in a Godly home.

No Ending

It's admirable to strive to live a "no regrets" life. Yet, it can take only a nano second for us to begin enumerating some of our own regrets. Mine begin with worrying too much about the small happenings that seemed so colossal at the time, but were really "warts on an elephant." My major regrets are not being able to provide a home life with two loving parents for my daughter's high school years, followed by not being a better manager of time during her childhood. The redeeming factor is that I have no regrets about the focus on my grandson, the amount of time I invested in my grandson, or the money spent on his Legos, toys, and trips. Maybe, instead of regrets, it's better if we focus on what we can learn from our earlier errors. As *Grandpa Berenstain Bear* taught us, it's never too late to correct our mistakes. As we coached our grandchildren on goal setting, to "begin with the end in mind," we can avoid regrets with a bit of thinking ahead about what will be important to us and to the grandchildren's future.

At some point, the reality of the end of life is upon us. If we've been blessed with good health, and been good stewards of our opportunities, perhaps we will be able to hug our great-grandchildren in a contagion free world and pass-on our legacy to the another generation. Leaving our children and grandchildren happy and successful is the accomplishment for which we work and strive. How can we ask more from this life.

One of the fears that children may encounter happens when they realize that grandparents are not immortal. If the death of another friend or family member occurs, the young child may begin to worry about the grandparents' longevity. The child may even decide that the way to avoid sadness and loss is to create a present distance so that the future loss won't be devastating. When such occurs, it's usually short lived. We grandparents understand and continue our loving relationship, ignoring the child's temporary emotional distance. We may need to encourage young children to talk about their fears as we reassure them of our love and that no matter what happens, even when we aren't with them, they will always have our love.

On one of our Saturday visits with Great-Grandpa in November after Great-Granny had died shortly before, I found my grandson pacing back and forth rubbing his fingers along the edge of the dining room table. Then he said quietly, "We can't have Thanksgiving this year because Granny isn't here to cook it." That's when I had to explain that Thanksgiving is about being grateful for the country and even though Granny was no longer with us, we would still be grateful for our freedom and our country. I added that even though someone else would cook the dinner, we would always remember Granny's love and thankfulness, as well as her cooking festive dinners. I smiled and said that we would miss Granny, but that we would always have her love and our memories of her. Then, after an insightful, articulate, and consoling response to her great-grandson, I went into the bathroom, closed the door, and sobbed at the loss of my dear 91-year-old mother whose love and memories I treasure.

When they're very young, the grandchildren will feel the love that we give them on a daily basis. As they mature, they will realize that we may die, *but the love they feel will not die* because they will remember our relationship. They will recall the fun times, the learning, the culture that we experienced together and the memories will not die. Perhaps it won't be the same without us. (I secretly hope that my absence will be noticed and that someone will send a gift to my beloved Saint Nicholas School on my birthday.) Nevertheless, what we want most is that the grandchildren will remember our love, what they learned from us, and that it will become part of their character, culture, and their legacy. We want our love to make a positive, significant difference in their entire lives. We want our love to be sustaining and for all they've learned from us to be the quiet voice in their heads that guides their actions and success throughout their lives.

Summary

In researching and writing this discussion for us, I've come to one strong conclusion. The world cannot have too many caring grandparents! Even if not tied by a family relationship, children benefit from adults who can nurture, guide, and care. From the music teacher who encouraged young Lana, to the old lady who taught the future neurosurgeon mindfulness and how to focus, caring adults of good character can enhance a child's life. In an era in which parents are occupied with so many responsibilities, and geographical distance separates many of us from our beloved grandchildren, there may be children nearby who need us. Perhaps we can adopt the grandchildren of friends who have died or live far away. There are always schools, libraries, and after school programs that can use a kind person who will listen to the children read, help with on-line learning assignments, or just listen to their problems. Perchance, we can find children and teens who will benefit from our experiences, the knowledge that we've gained, and the care and concern that we have to give, even if we must give it with social distance or via technology.

At a time in our society when parental addiction and unfortunate circumstances force many grandparents into the parenting role, some grandparents must provide, not only the love, but also the discipline, routines, and structure that children should receive in a home with two loving parents. Sometimes, we must be more than anticipated and provide everything in the child's life.

Regardless of grandparenting circumstances, if we can only accomplish a few things for them, we can make a profound difference in the quality of the young people's lives and the likelihood of their lifetime success. First, we consistently communicate the unconditional love that supports their self-confidence. Then, we nurture the development of character, self-discipline, good brain chemicals, and their love of learning. We give them pleasant memories and extensive knowledge that can guide their development. We do everything possible to prevent excessive stress in their growing-up years and addiction in their teens.

With our desires to maintain pleasant family relationships through both the parents' and grand-children's busy lives, we may be tempted to wait for them to initiate visits, activities, or interactions. Yet, as we assess our essential role in their lives, and in influencing their future, we recognize that we have a responsibility to initiate and be pro-active. By keeping invitations open, but not obnoxious or conditional, we keep the communications open. Recently, I found a message that I had saved from my daughter. It was when my grandson was eight-years-old saying, "Mom! He's asked three times today if he'll get to see Gran on Saturday." I smiled as I realized how quickly circumstances change, how complicated it is today to insert a dinner with me into my grandson's complex college schedule. We must never regard their busy days as rejection for us. Rather, it just requires a different approach from when we were asked to baby-sit. It's another opportunity for us to invoke *Rule #1.*

It's not about me. It's about focusing on the grandchildren with unconditional love and making memories that they, and we, will cherish.

And we must not forget *Rule #2.*

***It's not about just being right,
it's about being effective.***

Every day is an opportunity for learning. Every day is a chance for us to help grandchildren turn their dreams into noble actions. Every day is an opportunity for making memories and being influential in our grandchildren's entire lives—from the nursery to college and beyond.

All this we ask in the name of your child,
our savior, Jesus Christ, Amen.

References

Adler, A. *Understanding human nature.* (1923, 1998). London: Hazelden.

American Society of Addiction Medicine. (April 12, 2011). https://www.asam.org/resources/definition-of-addiction

Baumgardner, J. (2017). JulieBTV. https://www.juliebtv.com/

Bennis, W. (2009). *On Becoming a Leader*. Philadelphia, PA: Peresus Books.

Berne, E. (1961, 2015). *Transactional analysis in psychotherapy.* NY: Grove.

Berenstain, S. & J. *The Berenstain Bears* series. NY: Random House.

Bernstein, F. (2018, January 22). A rare look inside the private homes of one of America's most innovative architects. *Architectural Digest.* https://www.architecturaldigest.com/story/john-c-portman-jr-entelechy-homes

Burns,K. (Producer). (2014). *The Roosevelts - An intimate history.* Ep 1, Get Action. [Documentary]. U.S.: WETA, Florentine Films.

Candler, S. (2017). *Please, let us talk about politics.* Atlanta, GA: https://www.cathedralatl.org/Sermons/please-let-us-talk-about-politics/

Centers for Disease Control. *Adverse Childhood Experience.* https://www.cdc.gov/violenceprevention/acestudy/about_ace.html

Connelly, J & Mosher, B. (1957- 1963) Television series, *Leave it to Beaver.* Gomalco Productions, CA: Los Angeles.

Doty, J. (2016). *Into the magic shop: A neurosurgeon's quest to discover the mysteries of the brain and the secrets of the heart.* NY: Random House.

Fox, C. (June 4, 2016). Generation snowflake: How we train our kids to be censorious cry-babies. *The Spectator.* https://www.spectator.co.uk/2016/06/generation-snowflake-how-we-train-our-kids-to-be-censorious-cry-babies/

Frankl, V. (1946, 1992). *Man's search for meaning*. Boston: Beacon, p. x.

Franklin, B. (April 17, 1787) letter to the Abbes Chalet and Arnaud. Retrieved from https://www.fi.edu/benjamin-franklin/famous-quotes

Gottman, J. (2019) *Eight dates; Essential conversations for a lifetime of love.* NYC: Workman Publishing.

Greeley, H. (1868, 2006). *Recollections of a busy life.* Eugene, OR: Pacific University Press.

Iaacson, W. (2014). *Innovators. NY: Simon & Schuster.*

Jung, C.G. (1921, 1990). *Psychological types.* NJ: Princeton University Press.

Jung, C.G. (1961). *Memories, dreams reflections.* NY: Random House.

Kahn, S. (2013). *One world schoolhouse: Education reimagined.* NY: Twelve Publishing.

Kroeger, O. & Thuesen, J.M. (1995). *Basic three.* [Video]. Fairfax, VA: Otto Kroeger Associates.

Lansford, Z. (2007). Chapter 13 in Thompson, C. *Counseling children.* Belmont, CA: Brooks Cole, pp. 389-412.

Lencioni, P. (2016). *The ideal team player: How to recognize and cultivate the three essential virtues.* San Francisco, CA: Jossey Bass.

Lewinsky, M. (2015). The price of shame. TED Talk. https://www.ted.com/talks monica_lewinsky_the_price_of_shame

Mayer,J.; Salovey, P.; Caruso, D. (2008). Emotional intelligence: New Ability or Eclectic Traits? *American Psychologist,* Vol. 63, No, 6, pp. 503-517.

Minnesota Multiphasic Personality Inventory-2 (2008), Pearson Assessments. www.pearsonassessments.com

Mitchell, M. (July 3, 1936). Interview. *Atlanta Journal.*

Montessori, M. (1914, 1995). *The absorbent mind.* NY: Holt.

Myers, I & Myers, P. (1995). *Gifts differing*. Mountain View, CA: CPP, pp. xi, xiv.

Myers, I. (2016). *Manual: Guide to the development and use of the Myers-Briggs Type Indicator*. Mountain View (4th ed.). CA: The Myers-Briggs Co.

National Institutes of Health. (November 2, 2018). Brain research through advancing innovative neurotechnologies (BRAIN) initiative. https://www.nih.gov/news-events/news-releases/nih-greatly-expands-investment-brain-initiative.

Rogers, E. (1962, 2003). *Diffusion of innovation*. NY: Simon & Schuster.

Saint Nicholas School, 7525 MinTom Road, Chattanooga, TN 37421. https://www.stns.org

Stahl, L. (2017) *Becoming grandma, the joys and science of the new grandparenting*. NY: Blue Rider Press.

Thompson, C. & Henderson, D. (2007). *Counseling children* (7th Ed.) Belmont, CA: Brooks Cole, pp. 275-276.

Twenge, J.M. (2017). *iGen: Why today's super-connected kids are growing up less rebellious, more tolerant, less happy—and completely unprepared for adulthood*. NY: Atria.

University of Pennsylvania. (April, 2012). https:/ executiveeducation.wharton.upenn.edu/thought-leadership/ wharton-at-work/2012/04/after-action-reviews

U.S. Department of Health and Human Services, (Jan. 2018). *National Vital Statistics Report,* "Births: final data for 2018." Vol 68, No. 13, Retrieved from https://www.cdc.gov/nchs/ data/nvsr/nvsr68/nvsr68_13-508.pdf

U.S. Department of Justice. (2017, Nov. 22). Office of Public Affairs "Tobacco companies to begin issuing court-ordered statements in tobacco racketeering suit," 17-1331. https:/ www.tobaccofreekids.org/assets/content/what_we_do/ industry_watch/doj/corrective_statements/2017

Vance, J.D. (2016). *Hillbilly elegy: A memoir of a family and culture in crisis*. NY: HarperCollins, p. 228.

Appendix A

Making Grandparents' Home Safe

Since falls, burns, poisons, and water pose the biggest threats to children, grandparents must be alert to anything that can injure or threaten the child's safety. The following are checklists to help prepare for visits from grandchildren.

To prevent falls

Secure gates at bottom and top of all stairs
Secure loose rugs
Remove objects that could be trip-ups
Pad and cover sharp furniture corners
Secure or remove accessible electrical cords
Secure any furniture that will attract climbing
Attach furniture to walls to avoid tipping over
Keep exit doors locked
Lock basement, garage, or danger area doors

To prevent burns

Stove controls out-of-reach
Irons and cords secured
Curling/straightening irons stored
Avoid leaving a small child alone in kitchen or near a grill

To prevent drowning

Lock access to swimming pool, spa, and fish pond
Install a surface alarm on pools and any body of water that might pose a hazard
Assemble everything needed for bath before water is drawn
Never leave a child under age four alone in tub or bathroom

To maintain safety of caregivers, observe the airline protocol of "place your own oxygen mask before helping others."

Focus on the child and don't allow yourself to be distracted.
Maintain your own sleep and nutrition in order to be alert and energized with the child.
Keep the cell phone in a pocket or very nearby.
Always buckle your seatbelt when driving.
When emergencies or circumstances demand your attention elsewhere, call a friend or place the child in a restricted area where the child is seen, but cannot be harmed.
Remember, grandparent safety is essential to child safety.

Essential equipment

Locked gun cabinets
All plastic bags removed
Secured storage of all poisons
Weight appropriate car seats
Smoke & carbon monoxide alarms
Secured household cleaners
Electrical outlet/switch covers
Secured medicine storage

Appendix B

Ideas for Fun in Grandparents' Kitchen

Experiences in the kitchen can be delightful or disastrous, depending on grandparent supervision. The younger the child, the more we must anticipate problems and prevent them by adequate planning and a watchful eye. For example, holiday cookie making can be introduced with store bought or already baked and cooled cookies. They can be decorated with homemade icing in fancy tubes, or store bought icing from a can. When the child and the grandparent are ready, the process can begin with using a good recipe that yields dough easy enough for the child to handle with plastic cookie cutters. It can be great fun for the child to roll the dough when it's placed between two sheets of parchment paper or PVC/BPA free plastic wrap. Then, when there's no danger of the child's being burned, the whole baking process can be introduced, but it's essential that little fingers are not harmed by the food mixer or other utensils. With foods, materials, and utensils that the child can handle easily, many kitchen activities can be fun.

Measuring and mixing anything—water, dough, cake batter
Making sandwiches, spreading, slicing with a plastic knife.
Breaking asparagus tips and removing husks from corn
Peeling bananas, oranges, or other fruits easily manipulated
Washing and "floating" cranberries
Pulling caps from strawberries
Packing a picnic

Use imagination. Any grown-up activity can be made into a fun time. Often, the key to making a successful kitchen adventure is to plan and have some or all of the ingredients and utensils ready for the child's participation. Without such preparation, time in the kitchen can too quickly become a constant, "No! Don't touch that! Be careful! Oops!" Constant cautions might not create pleasant memories. Instead, anticipation and focused attention can make these times wonderful adventures.

Homemade Play Dough

1 cup of baking soda, 1/2 cup of corn starch, 3/4 cup water

This dough can be rolled flat, cut with plastic cookie cutters, and baked in a 200° oven to create holiday or other objects. Food coloring may be added or they may be painted. Required baking time depends on thickness of the object. Another similar dough is made from soda, salt, and warm water. There are many online sources for additional ideas and recipes. The uncooked doughs are grainier and drier but may be better for younger children. The cooked dough recipes may be saved until the child is older.

Appendix C

Special Books

Baby's first books should be of photographs of familiar objects and animals with no words. These books can be introduced as soon as baby is able to sit up and focus. When baby looks at the photos, we say one word to identify the object. The same technique can be used for pointing to real objects. The Night Before Christmas can be introduced at baby's first Christmas, even if it's only for annual photographs.

Excellent first books for beginning bedtime stories are *Good Night Moon, Pat the Bunny,* and similar types of books with pictures, a few words, or activities for little fingers. Toddler book choices should include whatever colorful board books appeal and that the little ones can handle. When they hold the child's interest, the following can be introduced:

Go Dog Go
Big Dog, Little Dog
Inside, Outside, Upside Down
Where the Wild Things Are
The *Bright and Early Series*

Many children enjoy such traditional stories as:

Mother Goose rhymes, The Three Bears, The Ginger Bread Man, Little Red Hen, Peter Rabbit, Benjamin Bunny, and the *Beatrix Potter* Series

Examples of stories that provide wonderful grandparent reading opportunities are:

Bedtime for Francis, Bread and Jam for Francis, and others from the Hoban series
The Berenstain Bears Series, especially *Trouble at School*
Tailor of Gloucester
The Dr. Seuss Series
The *How Do Dinosaurs* Series
You Read to Me, I'll Read to You series

Schools may provide reading lists for older children, but gifts of such books as the following could be considered:

Oh, the Places You'll Go by Dr. Seuss
Nancy Drew Mysteries
Number the Stars
Red Badge of Courage
Wrinkle in Time
Chronicles of Narnia
Six Most Important Decisions You'll Ever Make

Perhaps the best way to choose books is to take the child to the library or book store. A discerning grandparent will soon see the reading material that will sustain the child's interests. Sometimes, what captivates us is of little attraction for the child; however, we can coax their curiosity about our selections while still providing what they like.

Appendix D
*Resources**

To learn more about adults' preferences, the *Myers Briggs Type Indicator®* is the instrument of choice. Although other options can be found online, the *MBTI®* is worth the cost and additional effort. The instrument with required feedback is usually available at college counseling centers, private counseling resources, and online at:

https://www.mbtionline.com/TaketheMBTI

The online version is convenient, but there is an advantage in the self-scored edition, *Form M,* that may be available from an in-person counselor. The pen/paper edition allows the pages to be replaced together to see how the responses resulted in the score. This simple element makes it easier for us to understand our results as we can readily see how they were acquired from our selected responses.

For grandparents who have benefitted from the *MBTI®* earlier in their careers, the *MBTI® Step II* is available through counseling centers and from *MBTI®* certified professionals.

There are numerous books and resources available, but a good place to begin is with:

Introduction to Myers Briggs Type
Introduction to Type and Communication

The instrument designed for children must be administered by a certified professional. Additional information about the *MMTIC®* can be found at:

https://www.peoplestripes.org/assessment-mmtic/children-assessment-personality.htm

*Because much of Jung's original observations are no longer protected by copyright, his ideas have been adapted and sometimes misused. It is highly recommended that only materials available from *The Myers-Briggs Company* and *Center for Applications of Psychological Type (CAPT)* be considered.